GALILEO GALILEI

The Essential Galileo

GALILEO GALILEI

The Essential Galileo

Edited and Translated by
Maurice A. Finocchiaro

Hackett Publishing Company, Inc.
Indianapolis/Cambridge

Copyright © 2008 by Hackett Publishing Company, Inc.

14 13 12 11   2 3 4 5 6 7

For further information, please address
  Hackett Publishing Company, Inc.
  P.O. Box 44937
  Indianapolis, Indiana 46244-0937

  www.hackettpublishing.com

Cover design by Brian Rak and Abigail Coyle
Interior design by Elizabeth L. Wilson
Composition by Professional Book Compositors, Inc.
Printed at Edwards Brothers, Inc.

Library of Congress Cataloging-in-Publication Data

Galilei, Galileo, 1564–1642.
  [Selections. English. 2008]
  The essential Galileo / Galileo Galilei ; edited and translated by
Maurice A. Finocchiaro.
      p.   cm.
  Includes bibliographical references and index.
   ISBN 978-0-87220-937-4 (pbk.) — ISBN 978-0-87220-938-1 (cloth)
  1. Science—Early works to 1800. 2. Astronomy—Early works to 1800.
3. Science—History. 4. Galilei, Galileo, 1564–1642. 5. Scientists—
Italy. I. Finocchiaro, Maurice A., 1942– II. Title.
  Q155.G27 2008
  500—dc22   2008018659

Contents

Preface and Acknowledgments   vii

Introduction: Galileo's Legacy, Life, and Works   1

Chronology of Galileo's Career and Aftermath   17

Glossary of Terms and Names   26

Annotated Bibliography and Cited Works   37

Chapter 1: *The Sidereal Messenger* (1610)   45

Chapter 2: From *Discourse on Bodies in Water* (1612)   85
    §2.1 Shape vs. Density in Floating and Sinking   85

Chapter 3:
From *History and Demonstrations Concerning Sunspots* (1613)   97
    §3.1 Solar Rotation and Indifferent Motion   97
    §3.2 Heavenly Changes and Aristotelian Empiricism   99
    §3.3 Knowing Properties vs. Knowing Essences   101

Chapter 4:
Letters on Copernicanism and Scripture (1613–15)   103
    §4.1 Letter to Castelli (1613)   103
    §4.2 *Letter to the Grand Duchess Christina* (1615)   109

Chapter 5: Reply to Cardinal Bellarmine (1615)   146
    §5.1 Cardinal Bellarmine's Letter to Foscarini   146
    §5.2 Galileo's Considerations on the Copernican Opinion,
      Part I   148
    §5.3 Galileo's Considerations on the Copernican Opinion,
      Part II   160
    §5.4 Galileo's Considerations on the Copernican Opinion,
      Part III   163

Chapter 6: From the Earlier Trial-Documents (1615–16)   168
    §6.1 Lorini's Complaint (7 February 1615)   168
    §6.2 Caccini's Deposition (20 March 1615)   170
    §6.3 Special Injunction (26 February 1616)   175
    §6.4 Decree of the Index (5 March 1616)   176
    §6.5 Cardinal Bellarmine's Certificate (26 May 1616)   178

Chapter 7: From *The Assayer* (1623) 179

§7.1 Comets, Tycho, and the Book of Nature in
Mathematical Language 179

§7.2 Heat, Atoms, and Primary vs. Secondary Qualities 185

Chapter 8: From *Dialogue on the Two Chief World Systems* (1632) 190

§8.1 Preface: To the Discerning Reader 190

§8.2 Day II: Independent-mindedness and Aristotle's Authority 193

§8.3 Day II: Diurnal Rotation, Simplicity, and Probability 201

§8.4 Day II: The Case against Terrestrial Rotation, and the
Value of Critical Reasoning 213

§8.5 Day II: Vertical Fall, Conservation of Motion, and the
Role of Experiments 222

§8.6 Day III: Heliocentrism and the Role of the Telescope 233

§8.7 Day IV: The Cause of the Tides and the Inescapability
of Error 250

§8.8 Day IV: Ending 267

Chapter 9: From the Later Trial-Documents (1632–33) 272

§9.1 Special Commission's Report on the *Dialogue*
(September 1632) 272

§9.2 Galileo's First Deposition (12 April 1633) 276

§9.3 Galileo's Second Deposition (30 April 1633) 282

§9.4 Galileo's Third Deposition (10 May 1633) 284

§9.5 Galileo's Defense (10 May 1633) 285

§9.6 Galileo's Fourth Deposition (21 June 1633) 287

§9.7 Inquisition's Sentence (22 June 1633) 288

§9.8 Galileo's Abjuration (22 June 1633) 293

Chapter 10: From *Two New Sciences* (1638) 295

§10.1 Day I: The Problem of Scaling 295

§10.2 Day I: Critique of Aristotle's Law of Fall 300

§10.3 Day I: The Pendulum 306

§10.4 Day II: The Mathematics of Strength, Size, and Weight 315

§10.5 Day III: A New Science of Motion 334

§10.6 Day III: Definition of Uniform Acceleration 335

§10.7 Day III: Laws of Falling Bodies 342

§10.8 Day IV: The Parabolic Path of Projectiles 356

Index 368

Preface and Acknowledgments

This is a collection of Galileo's most important writings, covering his entire career. Here the relevant concept of importance centers on their historical impact, and the history in question includes not only Galileo's life and the 17th century, but also the historical aftermath up to our own day. Moreover, the relevant historical impact is interdisciplinary in the sense that it affects the history of science (especially physics and astronomy), the philosophy of science (especially epistemology and scientific methodology), and general culture (especially the relationship between science and the Catholic Church, or more broadly science and religion).

In making the selections by applying such a criterion of importance, I consulted a number of scholars who provided valuable suggestions that reflected this and additional noteworthy criteria. Their names will be acknowledged below, and I hope they will easily see that I adopted many of their suggestions. I could not adopt literally all of their good suggestions, simply for lack of space. In fact, an important guiding principle has been that the resulting volume should be relatively small and inexpensive, in accordance with a time-tested formula provided by the publisher.

The translations are based on the text found in the National Edition of Galileo's collected works (Galilei 1890–1909). To facilitate references, the page numbers of that edition are reproduced here by placing the corresponding numerals in square brackets in the text. Similarly, I have added section numbers preceded by the section sign (§), in order to keep track of the various selections, to provide a more convenient means of cross-referencing, and to give to the text some structure that may serve as a guide for discussion. Additionally, section titles have been added, except within the two works that are included in their entirety (*The Sidereal Messenger* and the *Letter to the Grand Duchess Christina*), in which only section numbers are provided. Such section numbers and titles are bracketed when referring to passages from longer Galilean works, but they are not when referring to letters, trial documents, and self-contained essays.

For some of the translations I have revised works that are in the public domain. Others are taken from my own previously published translations. And a few have been newly made for this volume.

In particular, for *The Sidereal Messenger* (Chapter 1), I have revised the translation published by Edward Stafford Carlos in 1880. For the selection from *Discourse on Bodies in Water* (Chapter 2), I have revised the translation first published by Thomas Salusbury in 1665, and reprinted without revision by Stillman Drake (1960). For the selections from *Two New Sciences* (Chapter 10), I have revised the translation first published by Henry Crew and Alfonso De Salvio in 1914. With rare exceptions indicated in the notes, my revisions are usually made without comment. In this I was guided by the desire to improve accuracy and readability. For these Galilean works, it would have been ideal to reprint (with or without revisions) the excellent translations published, respectively, by Albert Van Helden (1989) and by Drake (1981) and (1974). However, copyright considerations made this ideal unfeasible. On the other hand, a beneficial byproduct of this practical necessity has been that the translations in this volume have greater linguistic and stylistic uniformity than they would otherwise have.

For the selections from *Dialogue on the Two Chief World Systems, Ptolemaic and Copernican* (Chapter 8), I have reprinted parts of the translation found in my *Galileo on the World Systems* (1997). Similarly, I have reprinted parts of my *Galileo Affair* (1989) for the following translations: the "Letters on Copernicanism and Scripture" (Chapter 4), the "Reply to Cardinal Bellarmine" (Chapter 5), the selections "From the Earlier Trial-Documents" (Chapter 6), and the selections "From the Later Trial-Documents" (Chapter 9). Such reprintings are almost completely verbatim, but they do contain a few corrections, which have been indicated in the notes.

The new translations are the selections from the *History and Demonstrations Concerning Sunspots* (Chapter 3) and from *The Assayer* (Chapter 7).

Needless to say, in all these cases, I have consulted and benefited from the translations already available in multiple languages, especially the following: for *The Sidereal Messenger,* the translations by Van Helden (1989), Lanzillotta (in Galilei 1953), Drake (1983), Pantin (1992), and Maria Timpanaro Cardini (in Galilei 1993); for the *Discourse on Bodies in Water,* the translation by Drake (1981); for the *History and Demonstrations Concerning Sunspots,* the translations by Drake (1957) and Reeves and Van Helden (forthcoming); for

Chapters 4, 5, 6, 8, and 9, which come from my previously published books, the translations acknowledged in the prefaces to those works; for *The Assayer,* the translations by Arthur Danto (in Galilei 1954) and Drake and O'Malley (1960); and for the *Two New Sciences,* the translations by Drake (1974) and Adriano Carugo and Ludovico Geymonat (in Galilei 1958).

The notes, with very few exceptions, have been compiled especially for this volume, even when I was revising or reprinting previous translations. The reason is that some of those sources have too few annotations and some too many, and that in any case the notes had to be adopted for the present purpose. Thus, for example, since almost all terms and names requiring explanation occur in more than one selection, they are not explained in the notes but in the Glossary. A term or name is deemed as not requiring explanation when it is sufficiently explained or identified in the context of its occurrence (e.g., Lorini's name), or when it is commonly known or easily found in a small desk-dictionary (e.g., Archimedes, Aristotle, Copernicus, Euclid, Plato, Ptolemy, etc.). The few terms and names that occur only once (and that require explanation) are explained in notes at those places.

Finally, I would like to express thanks and acknowledgments to a number of people and institutions that helped in the creation of this book. Many scholars provided suggestions and encouragement: Mario Biagioli, Michele Camerota, Albert DiCanzio, Matthias Dorn, Paula Findlen, Owen Gingerich, Franco Giudice, André Goddu, W. Roy Laird, Ernan McMullin, David Miller, Ron Naylor, Margaret Osler, Paolo Palmieri, Michael Segre, Michael Shank, Robert Westman, and K. Brad Wray. The University of California Press granted me permission to reprint parts of my *Galileo Affair* and *Galileo on the World Systems.* The University of Nevada, Las Vegas, its Department of Philosophy, and my departmental colleagues have continued to provide institutional and moral support. And I thank Brian Rak, Editor at Hackett Publishing Company, for his initial and constant encouragement and for his continued patience.

Introduction
Galileo's Legacy, Life, and Works

Galileo's Legacy

[§0.1] Galileo Galilei was one of the founders of modern science. That is, science as we know it today emerged in the 16th and 17th centuries thanks to the discoveries, inventions, ideas, and activities of a group of people like Galileo that also included Nicolaus Copernicus, Johannes Kepler, René Descartes, Christiaan Huygens, and Isaac Newton. Frequently Galileo is singled out as the most pivotal of these founders and called the Father of Modern Science. Although many people have repeated or elaborated such a characterization, it is important that it originates in the judgment of practicing scientists themselves, such as Albert Einstein and Stephen Hawking.[1] Thus, scientists and other educated persons ought to know something about Galileo's scientific achievements. One of the aims of this book is to make available in a single volume those Galilean writings that contain his most important contributions to physics and astronomy, for example: the law of inertia, and the laws of falling bodies, of the pendulum, and of projectile motion; the telescope; the mountains on the moon, the satellites of Jupiter, the phases of Venus, and sunspots; and the confirmation of the Copernican theory of the earth's motion.

Galileo is also a cultural icon and symbol because he was tried and condemned as a suspected heretic by the Catholic Church through its institution of the Inquisition. This tragedy, which some have labeled the greatest scandal in Christendom, continues to have repercussions after four centuries. For example, in the period 1979–92, Pope John Paul II undertook a highly-publicized rehabilitation of Galileo, which however turned out to be partial and to add more fuel to the controversy known as the Galileo affair. The point is that the trial of Galileo continues to fascinate scientists, churchmen, scholars, and laypersons alike, and everybody seems to find in it something to learn regarding

---

1. Einstein 1954, 271; Hawking 1988, 179; 1992, xvii.

the relationship between science and religion, between individual freedom and institutional authority, between scientific research and political power or social responsibility, and so on. Thus, once again, all educated persons ought to have some accurate and reliable information about the trial and condemnation of Galileo. And a second purpose of this book is to make easily available the most important of the relevant documents, which happen to have survived through an almost miraculous set of circumstances, that is, documents such as the charges and complaints against Galileo, the various depositions recorded during the proceedings, the Inquisition's official sentence that announced the verdict and condemnation, and the abjuration which he was required to recite.

Thirdly, the historical circumstances of Galileo's time and his own personal inclinations made Galileo into a kind of philosopher. Of course, he was not a systematic metaphysician who speculated about the eternal problems of being and nothingness. Instead he was a concrete-oriented and practical-oriented critical thinker like Socrates, with the difference that whereas Socrates dealt with moral or ethical questions of good and evil and the meaning of life, Galileo dealt with epistemological and methodological questions about the nature of truth and knowledge and the truth and knowledge of nature.[2] His contributions to scientific knowledge were so radical that he constantly had to discuss with his opponents (scientific as well as ecclesiastic) not only what the facts were and what their best theoretical interpretation was, but also what the proper rules for establishing the facts and for interpreting them were. With scientific opponents he had to discuss questions like these: whether artificial instruments like the telescope have a legitimate role in learning new truths about reality; whether authorities such as Aristotle should be relied upon to the exclusion of one's own independence of mind; whether mathematics has an important, and perhaps essential, role to play in the study of natural phenomena. With ecclesiastic opponents, Galileo had to discuss whether Scripture should be treated as a source of scientific information about physical reality; whether scientific theories that contradict the literal meaning of Scripture should be treated as mere hypotheses; whether hypotheses are potentially true descriptions of reality or merely convenient instruments of calculation and prediction; and so on. Thus, a third aim of this book is to collect the most

---

2. Here I am adapting Gingerich's (1982) eloquent formulation.

important of these methodological and epistemological discussions, either from essays that contain relatively sustained arguments, or from passages that discuss primarily scientific issues but also offer the occasion for important philosophical clarifications.

Thus, Galileo's legacy clearly has a three-fold character, relating to science, philosophy, and culture.[3] However, this distinction ought not to be regarded as a separation. That is, this three-fold distinction reflects the various points of view which 21st-century readers can adopt toward Galileo and his writings and which can guide our assimilation of his legacy. The distinction does not reflect Galileo's own point of view and so is not something that guided his own thinking and activities. If we examine the latter, we find that the three aspects of his legacy were interwoven in various ways. The following sketch of Galileo's life and works gives us a glimpse at such interweaving, as well as a historical background to the selected writings collected here.

Galileo's Life and Works

[§0.2] Galileo was born in Pisa in 1564. His father Vincenzio was a musical practitioner and theorist who made a significant contribution to the theory of music, stressing the need to test the empirical accuracy of rules of harmony; he thus influenced Galileo's own empirical approach. In 1581 Galileo enrolled at the University of Pisa to study medicine but soon switched to mathematics, which he also studied privately outside the university. In 1585 he left the university without a degree and began several years of private teaching and independent research. In 1589 he was appointed professor of mathematics at the University of Pisa, and then from 1592 to 1610 at the University of Padua.

During this period, his research dealt primarily with the nature of motion in general and falling bodies in particular. His orientation was critical of Aristotelian physics and was fundamentally Archimedean; that is, he followed Archimedes' mathematical approach, accepted his physical principles of statics, and tried to build upon them for the

---

3. Here, I overlook a fourth aspect, which cannot be appreciated in translation. That is, Galileo also happened to be one of the greatest writers in the (800-year) history of the Italian language, and his writings can be appreciated from the literary and aesthetic point of view.

analysis of how bodies move. In his study of falling bodies, Galileo became an ingenious, skillful, and indefatigable experimenter who pioneered the method of experimentation as a procedure involving the combination of empirical observation with both quantitative mathematization and conceptual theorizing. By this procedure he formulated, justified, and to some extent systematized such mechanical principles as the following: an approximation to the law of inertia; the composition of motion into component elements; the laws that in free fall the distance fallen increases as the square of the time elapsed and that the velocity acquired is directly proportional to the time; and the parabolic path of projectiles. However, he did not publish any of these individual results during that earlier period of his career; and indeed he did not publish a systematic account of them until 30 years later, in the *Two New Sciences* (Leiden, 1638).

[§0.3] A main reason for this delay was that beginning in 1609 Galileo became actively involved in astronomy. To be sure, he had been previously acquainted with the new theory of a moving earth published by Nicolaus Copernicus in 1543. He had been appreciative of the fact that Copernicus had advanced a novel argument supporting that ancient idea, namely, a detailed mathematical demonstration that the known facts about the motion of the heavenly bodies could be explained more systematically and coherently (not just more simply) if we attribute to the earth a daily axial rotation and an annual heliocentric revolution. Galileo had also acquired the general impression that this geokinetic theory was more consistent with the new physics he was researching than was the geostatic theory. In particular, he had also been attracted to Copernicanism because he thought that the earth's motion could best explain why the tides occur. But he had not articulated, let alone published, this general impression and this particular feeling.

On the other hand, Galileo had been acutely aware of the considerable evidence against Copernicanism. The earth's motion seemed epistemologically absurd because it contradicted direct sense experience. It seemed astronomically false because it had consequences that could not be observed, such as the similarity between terrestrial and heavenly bodies, Venus' phases, and annual stellar parallax. It seemed mechanically impossible because the available laws of motion implied that bodies on a rotating earth would, for example, follow a slanted rather than vertical path in free fall, and would be thrown off by centrifugal force. And it seemed theologically heretical because it contradicted the literal meaning and the traditional interpretation of some passages in the Bible. Until 1609 Galileo apparently judged that the anti-Copernican arguments far outweighed the pro-Copernican ones. Thus we find him teaching geostatic astronomy in his courses and reacting in a lukewarm and evasive manner when an enthusiastic Copernican like Johannes Kepler tried to engage him.

[§0.4] However, the telescopic discoveries that began in 1609 led Galileo to a major reassessment of Copernicanism, and so for the next seven years he was seriously and explicitly involved in astronomical research and discussions. In 1609 he perfected the telescope to such an extent as to make it an astronomically useful instrument that could not be duplicated by others for some time. By its means he made several startling discoveries, which he immediately published in *The Sidereal Messenger* (Venice, 1610): that the moon's surface is full of mountains and valleys; that innumerable other stars exist besides those visible with the naked eye; that the Milky Way and the nebulas are dense collections of large numbers of individual stars; and that the planet Jupiter has four moons revolving around it at different distances and with different periods. As a result, Galileo became a celebrity, re-signed his professorship at Padua, was appointed Philosopher and Chief Mathematician to the grand duke of Tuscany, and moved to Florence the same year. Soon thereafter, he also discovered sunspots and the phases of Venus.

Although most of these discoveries were also made independently by other observers, no one understood their significance as well as Galileo. Their importance was threefold. Methodologically, the telescope implied a revolution in astronomy insofar at it was a new instrument that enabled the gathering of a new kind of data tran-scending the previous reliance on naked-eye observation. Substan-tively, those particular discoveries significantly strengthened the case in favor of the physical truth of Copernicanism by refuting almost all empirical astronomical objections and providing some new support-ing observational evidence. Finally, this enhancement of the eviden-tiary solidity of Copernicanism was not equivalent to a settling of the issue or a conclusive establishment of its truth, for several reasons: there was still some astronomical counterevidence (e.g., the lack of annual stellar parallax); the criticism of the mechanical objections and the physics of a moving earth had not yet been articulated (although, as stated above, Galileo had been working on both projects); and the theological objections had not yet been dealt with. Thus, Galileo began to conceive of a work on the system of the world in which all these aspects of the question would be discussed. This synthesis of Galileo's astronomy, physics, and methodology was not to be published for another twenty years, until his *Dialogue on the Two Chief World Systems, Ptolemaic and Copernican* (Florence, 1632).

This particular delay happened because Galileo got involved in several controversies over floating bodies, sunspots, the astronomical authority of Scripture, and comets. These discussions turned out to be fateful developments that had a drastic and permanent effect on the evolution of his life and career.

[§0.5] In July 1611, Galileo became involved in a controversy with some Tuscan Aristotelian philosophers over the behavior of solid bodies in water.[4] The occasion was provided by a casual remark Galileo made to the effect that ice is rarified water, since it floats in water, and hence it is lighter (in specific weight) than water. This was in accordance with the hydrostatic principles of Archimedes. But it contradicted the Aristotelian claim that ice is condensed water, and that it floats because its shape prevents it from overcoming the resistance of the water. The discussion soon turned to the cause of floating, sinking, and motion in water, and the relative role of shape and density. At one point, the Aristotelians introduced the allegedly crucial experiment that ebony wood sinks when shaped into a ball, but floats when shaped into a large thin flat plate; they regarded this experiment as a conclusive demonstration that shape, not specific weight, determines whether a body floats or sinks.

On more than one occasion, this discussion acquired the character of a formal debate. One of these debates took place at the house of Filippo Salviati, Galileo's Florentine friend whom he later immortalized as one the speakers in the *Dialogue* and *Two New Sciences*. Another debate occurred at the court of Grand Duke Cosimo II, in the presence of cardinals Ferdinando Gonzaga and Maffeo Barberini (1568–1644); the latter, who would become Pope Urban VIII in 1623, sided with Galileo. This sort of debate soon convinced Galileo that the philosophical discussion was degenerating into a competitive sport,[5] and so he decided to write down his thoughts. The result was the *Discourse on Bodies in Water,* which was published in the spring of

---

4. For more details on this controversy, see Drake 1978, 169–79, and 1981; Biagioli 1993, 159–209; Camerota 2004, 227–38.
5. Galilei 1890–1909, 4: 35; cf. Camerota 2004, 230.

1612. However, rather than ending the controversy, this publication merely moved it into the print medium. In fact, within about a year four books against Galileo's *Bodies in Water* were published by various Aristotelians, including one by Lodovico delle Colombe, who was also criticizing Galileo's ideas on the motion of the earth. Finally, a lengthy reply to these critics was written jointly by Galileo and his disciple Benedetto Castelli, and published only under Castelli's name in the spring of 1615.

[§0.6] At about the same time that Galileo was studying and disputing about bodies in water, he was also studying and disputing about sunspots.[6] It is uncertain when Galileo first observed sunspots with the telescope, but it is certain that while in Rome in the spring of 1611 he showed them to a number of people. It is also clear that he did not publish or write anything on the topic until stimulated by German Jesuit Christoph Scheiner (1573–1650).

In November and December 1611, Scheiner wrote three letters about sunspots to Marc Welser, an official of the German city of Augsburg. These were published under the pseudonym of Apelles in January 1612 in a small book entitled *Three Letters on Sunspots*. Welser immediately sent Galileo a copy, requesting his opinion. In May, Galileo replied with a long letter to Welser, criticizing Scheiner's views and observations and advancing his own. A second Galilean letter to Welser followed in August. In the meantime, after reading Galileo's first letter, Scheiner wrote another essay, which he published in September under the same pseudonym and with the title *A More Accurate Inquiry on Sunspots*. Galileo again received a copy from Welser and then in December wrote him a third long letter. Finally, in March 1613 the Lincean Academy published in Rome a volume containing Galileo's three letters and an appendix with Scheiner's two booklets. Such was the origin of Galileo's *History and Demonstrations Concerning Sunspots*.

Part of the dispute between Scheiner and Galileo involved priority of discovery. In 1612–13, this aspect of the controversy was relatively subdued, and the most sensible thing to say is that the phenomenon was discovered independently by both. Later, the priority dispute became bitter and nasty, as it came to encompass other aspects

---

6. For more details on the sunspots controversy, see Drake 1978, 179–213; Camerota 2004, 238–59; Biagioli 2006, 135–217; Reeves and van Helden forthcoming.

of the phenomenon (such as the inclination of the solar axis of rotation) and other more general issues (such as the Copernican controversy). However, the most significant intellectual aspect of the
controversy between Galileo and Scheiner concerned the interpretation of the sunspots and their implications for the Copernican theory.
Echoes of, and new twists on, the sunspot controversy can be found
in almost all of Scheiner's and Galileo's subsequent writings.

In the 1612–13 discussions, Scheiner held that sunspots were
swarms of small planets orbiting the sun at small distances. Individually they were invisible; but when several simultaneously reached the
line of sight (of an observer from earth), then they appeared as dark
spots projected onto the sun. Scheiner's interpretation saved an essential part of the Aristotelian worldview, namely, the earth-heaven
dichotomy; according to this doctrine heavenly bodies and terrestrial
bodies were very different, insofar as only the latter were subject to
physical changes, such as generation and destruction. For Scheiner the
only novelty required by sunspots was the existence of some previously unknown planets.

On the other hand, Galileo's interpretation was that sunspots were
phenomena occurring on the body of the sun, individually subject to
sporadic production and dissolution, but collectively undergoing regular eastward motion. This implied that the sun rotates on its axis
(with a period of about one month), and that it undergoes physical
changes similar to those on earth (sunspots being analogous to terrestrial clouds). And this in turn undermined a key tenet of the Aristotelian worldview—the earth-heaven dichotomy.

[§0.7] As it became known that Galileo was convinced that the
new telescopic evidence rendered the Copernican theory of the
earth's motion a serious contender for real physical truth, he came increasingly under attack from conservative philosophers and clergymen
in Florence. They started arguing that Galileo was a heretic because
he believed in the earth's motion and the earth's motion contradicted
the Bible. Underlying this personal attack was the biblical argument
against Copernicanism: the earth cannot move, because many biblical
passages state or imply that it stands still, and the Bible cannot err. The
most frequently mentioned biblical passage was Joshua 10:12–13
(King James Version): "Then spake Joshua to the Lord in the day
when the Lord delivered up the Amorites before the children of Israel, and he said in the sight of Israel, 'Sun, stand thou still upon
Gibeon; and thou, Moon, in the valley of Ajalon.' And the sun stood

still, and the moon staid, until the people had avenged themselves upon their enemies. Is not this written in the book of Jasher? So the sun stood still in the midst of heaven, and hasteth not to go down about a whole day."

Although Galileo was aware of the potentially explosive nature of this particular issue, he felt he could not remain silent, but decided to refute the argument. Because of the circumstances of the attacks and to avoid scandalous publicity, he wrote his criticism in the form of long private letters, in December 1613 to his former student Benedetto Castelli, a Benedictine monk and professor of mathematics at Pisa, and in spring 1615 to the grand duchess dowager Christina.

Galileo's critique may be summarized as follows. The biblical argument attempts to prove a conclusion (the earth's rest) on the basis of a premise (the Bible's commitment to the geostatic system) that can only be ascertained with a knowledge of that conclusion in the first place. In fact, the interpretation of the Bible is a serious business, and normally the proper meaning of its statements about natural phenomena can be determined only after we know what is true in nature; thus, the business of biblical interpretation is dependent on physical investigation, and to base a controversial physical conclusion on the Bible is to put the cart before the horse. Second, the biblical objection is a non sequitur, since the Bible is an authority only in matters of faith and morals, not in scientific ones; thus, its saying something about a natural phenomenon does not make it so, and therefore its statements do not constitute valid reasons for drawing corresponding scientific conclusions. Finally, it is questionable whether the earth's motion really contradicts the Bible, as one can show by an analysis of the passage (Joshua 10:12–13) where God stopped the sun to prolong daylight and give Joshua enough time to win a battle before nighttime; according to Galileo, a careful analysis shows that this passage cannot be easily interpreted in accordance with the geostatic theory, but that it accords better with the geokinetic view, especially as improved by Galileo's own discovery of solar axial rotation. The biblical objection is therefore groundless, aside from its other flaws.

Galileo's letter to Castelli was widely circulated, and the conservatives got increasingly upset. The situation was exacerbated in January 1615 when Galileo received the unexpected but welcome support of a Carmelite friar named Paolo Antonio Foscarini, who published a book entitled *Letter on the Opinion, Held by Pythagoreans and by Copernicus, of the Earth's Motion and Sun's Stability and of the New Pythagorean*

World System. Although this was written in the form of a letter to the head of the Carmelite order, the book was a public document. Moreover, although Foscarini's arguments overlapped with Galileo's, they had a distinct flavor and original emphasis: that the earth's motion was probably true and compatible with Scripture.

The publication of Foscarini's *Letter* did not go unnoticed. The Inquisition ordered an evaluation of the book, and a consultant wrote a very critical opinion. But before any formal proceedings started, Foscarini learned about the censure and informally contacted Cardinal Robert Bellarmine, the most authoritative theologian of that time and a member of the Congregation of the Inquisition as well as of the Index. Foscarini sent Bellarmine a copy of his book together with a long letter defending it from the type of criticism contained in the Inquisition consultant's report. Bellarmine replied courteously in a famous letter directed to Galileo as well as to Foscarini and discussing epistemological as well as scriptural issues. Galileo soon received a copy of Bellarmine's letter to Foscarini and immediately started writing a reply now known as "Considerations on the Copernican Opinion," in three parts. This reply was, however, never published, delivered, or even completely finished because other, more formal Inquisition proceedings soon became the center of attention.

In February 1615, a Dominican friar named Niccolò Lorini, from Florence, filed a written complaint against Galileo with the Inquisition in Rome, enclosing his "Letter to Castelli" as incriminating evidence. Then in March, another Dominican, Tommaso Caccini, made a personal deposition against Galileo with the Roman Inquisition. An investigation was launched that lasted about a year. As part of this inquiry, a committee of Inquisition consultants reported that the earth's motion is absurd and false as a matter of natural philosophy and heretical, or at least erroneous, as a matter of religion and theology. This judgment reflects the weight of the traditional objections to the earth's motion; the failure to know or appreciate the new arguments in its favor; and the unwillingness to question the biblical fundamentalism according to which the Bible is an authority on physical questions, as well as on questions of faith and morals. The Inquisition also interrogated other witnesses. Galileo himself was not summoned or interrogated partly because the key witnesses exonerated him and partly because Galileo's letters had not been published, whereas his published writings did not contain either a categorical assertion of Copernicanism or a denial of the scientific authority of the Bible.

However, in December 1615 Galileo went to Rome of his own accord to defend his views. He was able to talk to many influential Church officials and was received in a friendly and courteous manner; and he may be given some credit for having prevented the worst, insofar as the Inquisition did not issue a formal condemnation of Copernicanism as a heresy, in accordance with the consultants' report. Instead two milder consequences followed. In February 1616, Galileo himself was given a private warning by Cardinal Bellarmine (in the name of the Inquisition) to the effect that he was forbidden to hold or defend the truth of the earth's motion; Galileo agreed to comply. And in March, the Congregation of the Index published a decree which, without mentioning Galileo at all, declared that the earth's motion was physically false and contradicted the Bible; that Foscarini's *Letter on the Earth's Motion* was to be condemned and permanently banned; and that Copernicus' book *On the Revolutions of the Heavenly Spheres* (1543) was temporarily banned until appropriately corrected. These corrections were not specified until 1620 when the Congregation of the Index issued another decree explaining how a dozen passages in Copernicus' book were to be deleted or reworded in order to eliminate from it any suggestions that the earth's motion was or could be physically true and compatible with the Bible; the revisions were also meant to make it clear that the book was treating the earth's motion merely as a hypothesis, which in that context meant a mere instrument of astronomical calculation and prediction.

The events of 1616 marked a turning point in Galileo's career. He was no longer free to research the earth's motion, since he was not supposed to hold or defend it but was to limit himself to discussing it hypothetically or instrumentalistically. He might have taken this opportunity to abandon the Copernican research program and go back to the earlier studies of falling bodies, which he had set aside in 1609. But apparently he felt the Copernican possibility was too important to be set aside completely. At any rate, the import of the new restrictions was not clear; perhaps he could do some useful work while operating under them. This turned out to be the case on the occasion of the controversy over comets that led to *The Assayer*.[7]

---

7. For more details on the comets controversy, see Drake and O'Malley 1960; Drake 1978, 263–88; Biagioli 1993, 267–312; Camerota 2004, 363–98.

[§0.8] In 1618 three comets appeared in succession, the third being especially bright and long-lasting. As usual, the appearance of such phenomena produced considerable discussion. Sometime between mid–December 1618 and mid–January 1619, they were the subject of a lecture at the Jesuit Roman College. The lecture was published the following month with the title *Astronomical Disputation on the Three Comets of the Year 1618*. The author was anonymous, but the pamphlet indicated that he was a professor at the Roman College. He was soon identified as Orazio Grassi (1590–1654).

Due to ill health, Galileo was unable to make any observations of those comets. However, many people were soliciting his opinion. Thus, he decided to collaborate with a friend and disciple named Mario Guiducci (1585–1646) in writing a short work on the subject entitled *Discourse on the Comets*. This book was published in Florence in June 1619, but only under Guiducci's name. Since the *Discourse* was critical of the views advanced in the *Astronomical Disputation,* Grassi immediately wrote a lengthy reply, publishing it under the pseudonym of Lotario Sarsi, who was allegedly one of his students. Grassi's reply appeared in Perugia in October of the same year with the title *Astronomical and Philosophical Balance,* to convey the idea that Galileo's and Guiducci's ideas were being carefully weighed.

By then the discussion had become so heated that Galileo was being urged to publish under his own name a reply to Grassi's *Balance.* This pressure was coming especially from the other members of the Lincean Academy, who had come to dislike not only Grassi's view of comets but also the Jesuits' claims of leadership in mathematics, astronomy, and natural philosophy. Galileo worked on his reply for about two years, and then it took another two years for the manuscript to be revised, to be issued the imprimatur, and to be printed. Entitled *The Assayer,* the book was published in Rome in October 1623, under the sponsorship of the Lincean Academy. Moreover, it so happened that Cardinal Maffeo Barberini, who was an admirer of Galileo and a friend of the Lincean Academy, was elected Pope Urban VIII in the summer of 1623; so the new book was dedicated to the new pope, who appreciated the gesture very much.

The Assayer is written in the form of a letter to Virginio Cesarini (1595–1624), chamberlain to Pope Urban VIII, member of the Lincean Academy, poet, and friend of Galileo's. Additionally, it is structured as a series of long quotations from the *Balance,* each followed by a lengthy critical analysis. The controversy with Grassi did not end then, for in 1626 the latter published in Paris an even more voluminous work entitled *Comparison of the Weights of the Assayer and the Balance*. However, Galileo felt no need for a further reply.

There were several astronomical and philosophical issues underlying this controversy. One was whether comets were located in the earth's atmosphere (as Aristotle had claimed) or in the heavens (as Tycho Brahe had argued based on his study of the comet of 1577). A related question was whether or not the heavenly location of comets implied the existence of heavenly changes and so further undermined the earth-heaven dichotomy. Another issue was whether the precise trajectory followed by the third comet of 1618 could be explained in a geostatic geocentric theory, or whether the explanation had to include the Copernican hypothesis that the earth possesses an annual heliocentric motion. There was also the question whether the Tychonic system of the world was correct; this was the arrangement according to which the planets do revolve around the sun, but the sun (together with the planetary system) revolves both diurnally and annually around the motionless central earth. And there were more general issues: whether natural science should try to reduce secondary qualities, e.g., colors and sounds, to primary qualities, e.g., position and motion (as the corpuscular or atomistic worldview claimed); and what is the relative role of authority and independent-mindedness in scientific inquiry. Galileo and Grassi disagreed on almost all these questions. Even when they happened to agree (e.g., on the heavenly location of comets), they disagreed about the manner of arriving at the conclusion.

Galileo's *The Assayer* is thus not only an explicit discussion of comets and scientific method and an explicit critique of the Tychonic system, but also an implicit defense of the banned Copernican system.

[§0.9] The election of Barberini as Pope Urban VIII, and his enthusiasm for *The Assayer,* encouraged Galileo to pursue the Copernican research program. So Galileo went to work to write the book on the system of the world which he had conceived earlier and to adapt its form to the new restrictions.

Thus, he wrote the book in the form of a dialogue among three characters who discuss all the cosmological, astronomical, physical, and epistemological arguments on both sides of the questions; but no biblical or theological arguments are critically examined. This *Dialogue* was published in 1632 in Florence, and its key thesis is best stated as follows: the arguments and evidence in favor of the geokinetic theory are much stronger that those in favor of the geostatic view, and in that sense the earth's motion is much more probable than geostaticism. When so stated, the thesis is successfully established. In the process, Galileo managed to incorporate into the discussion the new telescopic discoveries, his conclusions about the physics of moving bodies, a geokinetic explanation of the tides, and various methodological reflections. From the viewpoint of the ecclesiastic restrictions, Galileo must have felt that the book did not "hold" the theory of the earth's motion because it was not claiming that the geokinetic arguments were conclusive; that it was not "defending" the geokinetic theory because it was merely a critical examination of the arguments on both sides; and that it was a hypothetical discussion because the earth's motion was being presented as a hypothesis that happened to be better than the alternative.

However, Galileo's enemies raised all kinds of charges against the book. One was that the book did not treat the earth's motion as a hypothesis, because it did not regard it merely as a convenient instrument of calculation and prediction, but also as a real possibility; that is, the proposition that the earth moves was regarded as a description of physical reality that could be true or false, even if one could not yet be sure as to which was the case. Another charge was that the book defended the earth's motion because the arguments against it were criticized but the arguments for it were favorably presented. Both of these points involved an alleged violation of the decree of the Index and of Bellarmine's warning. But there was a third charge: that the book violated a special injunction which Galileo had been given in 1616 and which prohibited him from discussing the earth's motion in any way whatsoever; a document reporting on this special injunction had been found in the file of the earlier Inquisition proceedings of 1615–16. Thus Galileo was summoned to Rome to stand trial.

After various delays, Galileo finally arrived in Rome in February 1633, although the proceedings did not begin until April. At the first hearing, Galileo was asked about the *Dialogue* and the events of 1616. He admitted receiving from Bellarmine the warning that the earth's motion could not be held or defended, but only discussed hypothetically. He denied receiving a special injunction not to discuss the topic "in any way whatever," and in his defense he introduced a certificate he had obtained from Bellarmine in 1616, which only mentioned the prohibition to hold or defend. Galileo also claimed that the book did not defend the earth's motion, but rather suggested that the favorable arguments were inconclusive, and so did not violate Bellarmine's warning.

The special injunction must have surprised Galileo as much as Bellarmine's certificate did the inquisitors. In fact, it took three weeks before they decided on the next step. The inquisitors opted for some out-of-court plea bargaining: they would not press the most serious but most questionable charge (violation of the special injunction), but Galileo would have to plead guilty to a lesser but more provable charge (transgression of the warning not to defend Copernicanism). He requested a few days to devise a dignified way of pleading guilty to the lesser charge. Thus, at later hearings, he stated that the first deposition had prompted him to reread his book; he was surprised to find that it gave readers the impression that the author was defending the earth's motion, even though this had not been his intention. He attributed his error to wanting to appear clever by making the weaker side look stronger. He was sorry and ready to make amends.

Although the authorities accepted this confession of guilt, they were unsure about Galileo's denial of a malicious intention. Thus, in accordance with standard practice, they decided to subject him to an interrogation under the verbal threat of torture. This occurred on June 21, and the transcript indicates that Galileo was threatened with torture but was not actually tortured, and that he was willing to be tortured rather than admit his transgression to have been intentional (thus vindicating the purity of his intention).

The trial ended on 22 June 1633 with a harsher sentence than Galileo had been led to believe he would receive. The verdict found him guilty of a category of heresy intermediate between the most and the least serious, called "vehement suspicion of heresy"; the objectionable beliefs were the cosmological thesis that the earth moves and the methodological principle that the Bible is not a scientific authority. Thus he was forced to recite a humiliating "abjuration." And the *Dialogue* was banned.

The sentence also states that he was to be held in prison indefinitely. However, this particular penalty was immediately commuted to house arrest. Accordingly, for about one week he was confined to the Villa Medici, a sumptuous palace in Rome belonging to the Tuscan grand duke. Then for about five months he was sent to the residence of Siena's archbishop, who was a good friend of Galileo's. Finally, in December 1633 he was allowed to live in seclusion at his own villa in Arcetri, near Florence.

One of the ironic results of this condemnation was that, to keep his sanity, Galileo went back to his earlier research on motion, organized his notes, and five years later published his most important contribution to physics, the *Two New Sciences* (1638). Without the tragedy of the trial, he might have never done it. This book was written in the form of a dialogue among the same characters (Salviati, Sagredo, and Simplicio) who appeared in the earlier *Dialogue,* with the addition that at various points in the discussion Salviati reads from the manuscript of a treatise on motion written by a so-called Academician; this is a reference to Galileo himself, who was proud of being a member of the Lincean Academy.

Galileo died in Arcetri in 1642, assisted and surrounded by his son Vincenzio and his disciples Vincenzio Vivani and Evangelista Torricelli.

Chronology of Galileo's Career and Aftermath

1543   Polish astronomer Nicolaus Copernicus publishes his book *On the Revolutions of the Heavenly Spheres;* he dies the same year.

1545   The Catholic Church convenes the Council of Trent to deal with the Protestant Reformation, and the Catholic Counter-Reformation begins; the Council will not conclude its work until 1563.

1564   *15 February:* Galileo is born in Pisa, which is part of the Grand Duchy of Tuscany ruled by the House of Medici.

1574   Galileo's family moves to Florence, the capital of the Grand Duchy.

1581   Galileo enrolls at the University of Pisa in medicine and studies mathematics privately. In 1585, he leaves without a degree.

1589   Galileo becomes professor of mathematics at the University of Pisa, where he teaches for the next three years. While there, he writes a work *On Motion* but does not publish it.

1592   Galileo leaves Pisa and becomes professor of mathematics at the University of Padua, which is part of the Republic of Venice.

1593   Galileo writes a *Treatise on Fortifications* for the use of his students, but does not publish it.

1594   Galileo finishes writing a treatise on practical *Mechanics* begun the previous year; again, it is for student use and is not published.

1597   Galileo writes, again for student use and without publishing it, a traditionally oriented *Treatise on the Sphere, or Cosmography.*

1600   Apostate Dominican friar Giordano Bruno is convicted of heresy and burned at the stake by the Inquisition in Rome. Galileo and his common-law wife, Marina Gamba, have a daughter named Virginia.

1601   Danish astronomer Tycho Brahe dies. A second daughter, Livia, is born to Galileo and Marina.

1604   Galileo is convinced of the truth of two laws of falling bodies and is attempting to derive them from some more fundamental principle: the law of squares, according to which the distance traversed by a freely falling body is proportional to the square of the time elapsed; and the law of odd numbers, according to which in free fall, the distances covered in successive equal times increase as the odd numbers from unity.

1605   During the summer vacation, Galileo tutors the fifteen-year-old prince Cosimo II de' Medici.

1606   Galileo publishes in Padua a booklet entitled *Operations of the Geometric and Military Compass,* containing instructions on using an instrument of his own invention that makes rapid calculations to solve engineering and military problems. A son named Vincenzio is born to Galileo and Marina.

1609   German astronomer Johannes Kepler publishes his *New Astronomy,* containing the first two of his famous three laws of elliptical planetary motion.
        February: Cosimo II becomes grand duke of Tuscany, after the death of his father Ferdinando I.
        June: Galileo claims to have arrived at several correct theoretical principles underlying the laws of falling bodies.
        Summer: Galileo builds his first telescope.
        Fall: He begins to observe the heavens with the telescope and to make various discoveries.

1610   *13 March:* Galileo's *Sidereal Messenger* is published in Venice, describing his discovery of mountains on the moon, satellites of Jupiter, new fixed stars, and the stellar composition of the Milky Way and nebulas.
        19 April: Kepler sends his *Conversation with the Sidereal Messenger* to Galileo, supporting the new discoveries.
        10 July: Cosimo II de' Medici appoints Galileo "Philosopher and Chief Mathematician" to the grand duke of Tuscany.
        Summer: Galileo observes Saturn as "three-bodied," a puzzle that was only solved after his death when better observations showed Saturn to have rings.
        September: Galileo leaves Padua and moves permanently to Florence.
        Fall: Galileo observes the phases of Venus.

1611   Kepler publishes in Frankfurt an account of his observations of Jupiter's satellites, further supporting Galileo.

25 April: Galileo is made a member of the Lincean Academy. *13 May:* The Jesuit Roman College holds a special meeting at which, in the presence of Galileo, Father Odo van Maelcote delivers a lecture praising *The Sidereal Messenger.*

1612 Galileo publishes in Florence his *Discourse on Bodies in Water,* attempting to resolve a controversy with Aristotelian philosophers.

1613 *22 March:* Galileo's *History and Demonstrations Concerning Sunspots* is published in Rome, sponsored by the Lincean Academy; it contains a collection of letters exchanged with German Jesuit astronomer Christoph Scheiner.

21 December: After his former pupil Benedetto Castelli reports that Galileo's views have been criticized at the ducal court on scriptural grounds, Galileo writes a refutation of the argument that Copernicanism is wrong because it contradicts Scripture; the refutation is in the form of a private letter to Castelli.

1614 *21 December:* At the church of Santa Maria Novella in Florence, Dominican friar Tommaso Caccini preaches a sermon against mathematicians in general and Galileo in particular, on the grounds that they hold beliefs contrary to Scripture and so are heretics.

1615 *January:* Carmelite friar Paolo Antonio Foscarini publishes in Naples a book entitled *Letter on the Opinion, Held by Pythagoreans and by Copernicus, of the Earth's Motion and Sun's Stability and of the New Pythagorean World System;* it argues that Copernicanism is compatible with Scripture and probably true.

6 February: Christoph Scheiner sends to Galileo, together with a courteous letter, a copy of a book (*Mathematical Investigations on Astronomical Novelties and Controversies*) written by one of his disciples (Johannes Locher); in it the proponents of the earth's motion are violently attacked. Galileo will include some harsh criticism of this book in his *Dialogue* (1632).

February: Dominican friar Niccolò Lorini sends a formal complaint against Galileo to Cardinal Paolo Sfondrati (member of the Inquisition and prefect of the Index), enclosing Galileo's "Letter to Castelli" as incriminating evidence.

March: Caccini gives a deposition to the Inquisition in Rome, charging Galileo with suspicion of heresy, based on the content of his "Letter to Castelli" and his book on *Sunspots*.

April: Cardinal Robert Bellarmine, influential theologian and member of the Congregations of the Inquisition and of the Index, replies to Foscarini's private request for an opinion on his *Letter on the Earth's Motion;* Bellarmine's letter explicitly states that his remarks apply to Galileo as well as to Foscarini.

Spring and summer: Galileo expands his "Letter to Castelli" into the *Letter to the Grand Duchess Christina* and writes his "Considerations on the Copernican Opinion" in response to Bellarmine's letter to Foscarini.

December: After a long delay due to illness, Galileo goes to Rome to defend himself and the Copernican doctrine from the charge of heresy.

1616   *8 January:* At the request of Cardinal Alessandro Orsini, Galileo writes his "Discourse on the Tides," containing a physical argument for the earth's motion based on its ability to explain the existence of tides; this argument will later be expanded and included in the *Dialogue*.

24 February: A committee of eleven consultants reports to the Roman Inquisition their unanimous opinion that the heliocentric and heliostatic thesis is philosophically absurd and formally heretical; and that the geokinetic thesis is philosophically absurd and theologically erroneous.

25 February: At an Inquisition meeting, Pope Paul V orders Cardinal Robert Bellarmine to warn Galileo to abandon his Copernican views.

26 February: Bellarmine calls Galileo to his house and gives him the warning.

3 March: Bellarmine reports to the Inquisition that Galileo has acquiesced.

5 March: The Congregation of the Index publishes a decree declaring the earth's motion physically false and contrary to Scripture, prohibiting and condemning Foscarini's book, suspending until corrected Copernicus' book, and ordering analogous censures for analogous works; Galileo is not mentioned at all.

26 May: Bellarmine writes a certificate for Galileo, denying rumors that he has been tried and condemned, and clarifying that he has been warned not to hold or defend the earth's motion.

June: Galileo returns to Florence.

1619 *June:* Mario Guiducci, a disciple of Galileo, publishes a booklet entitled *Discourse on the Comets;* it contains two lectures he (Guiducci) had given about the three comets that had appeared the previous year and had sparked wide discussion; although Galileo collaborated in its writing, the book is published under Guiducci's name.

October: Using a pseudonym, Orazio Grassi, a Jesuit professor of mathematics at the Roman College, publishes a book (*Astronomical and Philosophical Balance*) highly critical of Galileo's (and Guiducci's) view of comets; Grassi argues, among other things, that their view of comets is committed to Copernicanism and thus violates the anti-Copernican decree.

1620 *May:* The Congregation of the Index issues a decree containing the corrections of Copernicus' book *On the Revolutions,* promised in the Decree of 5 March 1616.

August: Florentine Cardinal Maffeo Barberini sends Galileo a Latin poem entitled *Dangerous Adulation,* which he has written in praise of Galileo.

1621 *January:* Pope Paul V dies; Alessandro Ludovisi is then elected Pope Gregory XV.

February: Grand Duke Cosimo II dies prematurely and is succeeded by his son Ferdinando II; but due to the latter's young age (10 years), Tuscany is governed by a regency council until 1627.

September: Cardinal Bellarmine dies.

1623 *July:* Pope Gregory XV dies.

August: Cardinal Maffeo Barberini is elected Pope Urban VIII.

October: Galileo's *The Assayer* is published in Rome, sponsored by the Lincean Academy and dedicated to the new pope; it contains a discussion of comets and is highly critical of Grassi's views.

1624 *Spring:* Galileo visits Rome to pay homage to his old patron, now Pope Urban VIII; he stays for six weeks, receiving weekly audiences from the pope and warm treatment from other Church officials.

Fall. Galileo begins working on a book that discusses the system of the world and ties together all his discoveries and ideas on the subject (except for questions of biblical interpretation).

1625   Sometime in 1625, or perhaps in 1624, a complaint is sent to a Church official, charging that the atomistic theory of matter in Galileo's *The Assayer* conflicts with the Catholic doctrine of the Eucharist; but the identities of the writer and the recipient are unknown, nor is it known whether the Inquisition conducted an investigation.

April: After investigating another complaint, that Galileo's *The Assayer* contains too much praise for Copernicanism, the Inquisition concludes the case with a clear and strong exoneration.

1626   Grassi, again using a pseudonym, publishes in Paris a book (*Comparison of the Weights of the Assayer and the Balance*) against Galileo's *The Assayer;* it argues that Galileo's physics implies a denial of the Catholic doctrine of the Eucharist, and more generally the other alleged impieties of the atomists. Galileo feels no need to reply.

1630   *Spring:* Galileo completes work on the book he had been writing since 1624; he goes to Rome to obtain the imprimatur from Church authorities, and to arrange for its publication by the Lincean Academy.

June: Scheiner publishes a massive book on sunspots, filled with valuable observations and interesting speculations; it also has a long beginning section that violently attacks Galileo, especially his claim of priority in the discovery of sunspots. Galileo will include a brief reply and criticism in the *Dialogue.*

August: Prince Federico Cesi, founder and head of the Lincean Academy, dies

1632   *February:* Printing is completed in Florence for Galileo's *Dialogue on the Two Chief World Systems, Ptolemaic and Copernican.*

Summer: The *Dialogue* is received with great enthusiasm and praise in many quarters; but a number of questions, rumors, complaints, and criticisms emerge in Rome concerning its content, form, and manner of publication; these lead the pope to prohibit the sale of the book and to appoint a special commission to investigate the matter.

September: At a meeting of the Inquisition presided by the pope, the special commission's report is discussed and the pope decides to forward the case to the Inquisition and to summon Galileo to Rome to stand trial.

1633   *13 February:* Galileo arrives in Rome and is lodged at the Tuscan embassy (Palazzo Firenze).

Spring: The Inquisition trial proceedings begin, go through several stages, and are concluded.

22 June: Galileo is convicted of "vehement suspicion of heresy"; the punishments include a formal abjuration, the prohibition of the *Dialogue,* imprisonment at the pleasure of the Inquisition, and some religious penances; he recites the abjuration at the convent of Santa Maria sopra Minerva.

23 June: Galileo's prison sentence is commuted to house arrest at Villa Medici, a sumptuous palace in Rome owned by the grand duke of Tuscany.

30 June: His prison sentence is again commuted to house arrest in Siena, at the residence of the archbishop, who was a good friend of Galileo's.

July–November: In Siena, Galileo starts writing a book on topics he had researched earlier, the strength of materials and the motion of falling bodies.

1 December: Galileo's prison sentence is commuted once again, now to house arrest at his villa in Arcetri near Florence.

1634   In Paris, Marin Mersenne publishes a French translation of Galileo's unpublished manuscript on *Mechanics.*

1635   A Latin translation of Galileo's *Dialogue* is published in Strasbourg, with the title *Systema cosmicum* and under the editorship of a friend of Galileo's, a French lawyer named Elia Diodati; it includes an appendix with a Latin translation of Foscarini's *Letter on the Earth's Motion* (banned and condemned by the Index's decree of 1616).

1636   Again in Strasbourg and under the editorship of Diodati, Galileo's *Letter to the Grand Duchess Christina* is published for the first time, in an edition that contains the original Italian text and a Latin translation. It is revealingly entitled: *New and Old Doctrine of the Most Holy Fathers and Esteemed Theologians on Preventing the Reckless Use of the Testimony of the Sacred Scripture in Purely Natural Conclusions That Can Be Established by Sense Experience and Necessary Demonstrations.*

1637   Galileo becomes completely blind.

1638   *July:* Galileo's *Two New Sciences* is published in Leiden, Holland; in the preface he speaks as if the book had been published without his knowledge (which was not the case).

1639   Mersenne publishes in Paris a French translation of Galileo's latest book, under the title *The New Thoughts of Galileo, Mathematician and Engineer to the Duke of Florence.* Vincenzio Viviani begins studying with Galileo and assisting him in his correspondence; for this he receives a modest salary from the grand duke.

1640   With his approval, Galileo's *Operations of the Geometric and Military Compass* is reprinted in Padua.

1641   The Latin translation of Galileo's *Dialogue* is reprinted in Lyons. Evangelista Torricelli begins living at Galileo's house and serving as his research assistant.

1642   *8 January:* Galileo dies at Arcetri.
        9 January: Galileo is quietly buried at the Church of Santa Croce in Florence, in an unmarked grave located in an out-of-the-way room behind the sacristy and under the bell tower.

1687   Isaac Newton publishes his *Mathematical Principles of Natural Philosophy,* providing a compelling indirect proof of the earth's motion based on a systematization of the general laws of motion and the formulation of the law of universal gravitation.

1729   English astronomer James Bradley discovers the aberration of starlight, providing direct observational evidence that the earth has translational motion.

1737   Galileo's body is exhumed from the original grave in Santa Croce and moved to a mausoleum in the church's main aisle, across from Michelangelo's tomb.

1744   With Church approval, a four-volume collection of Galileo's works is published in Padua; the fourth volume contains the *Dialogue,* preceded by the Inquisition's sentence and Galileo's abjuration of 1633.

1758   The new edition of the Catholic *Index of Prohibited Books* no longer lists the entry "all books teaching the earth's motion and the sun's immobility"; but it continues to include the three previously prohibited books by Copernicus, Foscarini, and Galileo.

1789   Italian priest and astronomer Giambattista Guglielmini begins to provide direct confirmation of terrestrial rotation by means of experiments detecting an easterly deviation of falling bodies.

1835   The new edition of the *Index* for the first time omits from the list Galileo's *Dialogue*, as well as the books by Copernicus and Foscarini.

1838   German astronomer and mathematician Friedrich Bessel observes that fixed stars exhibit an annual shift in apparent position, called annual stellar parallax; this provides direct evidence that the earth revolves annually around the sun.

1851   Léon Foucault in Paris invents a pendulum that demonstrates the earth's rotation; the experiment is repeated in many other places.

1893   In the encyclical letter *Providentissimus Deus*, Pope Leo XIII puts forth a view of the relationship between biblical interpretation and scientific investigation that corresponds to the one advanced by Galileo in the *Letter to the Grand Duchess Christina;* but Galileo is not even mentioned.

1942   The tercentennial of Galileo's death provides the occasion for a first partial and informal rehabilitation. In 1941–46, this was done by several clergymen who held the top positions at the Pontifical Academy of Sciences, the Catholic University of Milan, the Pontifical Lateran University in Rome, and the Vatican Radio. They publish accounts of Galileo as a Catholic hero who upheld the harmony between science and religion; who had the courage to advocate the truth even against the Catholic authorities of his time; and who had the piety to retract his views outwardly when the 1633 trial proceedings made his obedience necessary.

1979   Pope John Paul II begins a further informal rehabilitation of Galileo that was not concluded until 1992. In two speeches to the Pontifical Academy of Sciences, and in other statements and actions, the pope admits that Galileo's trial was not merely an error but also an injustice; that Galileo was theologically right about scriptural interpretation, as against his ecclesiastical opponents; that even pastorally speaking, his desire to disseminate novelties was as reasonable as his opponents' inclination to resist them; and that he provides an instructive example of the harmony between science and religion.

Glossary of Terms and Names

This glossary includes terms and names which appear in more than one section, and whose meaning is relatively peculiar, unusual, or obscure; such words are not explained in the notes. When such a word occurs in only one section, it is usually explained in a note and not here. Words whose meanings are generally known or commonly included in small desk-top dictionaries are not included here or in the notes.

Academician. A term referring to Galileo, used by him in some of his books written in dialogue form. It is meant to remind readers that he was a member of the Lincean Academy.

ad hominem. In the 17th century, this expression referred to an argument designed to examine the correctness of a controversial view by showing that it implies consequences not acceptable to those who hold that view. This Galilean meaning should not be confused with the most common modern meaning, referring to the fallacy of criticizing a controversial view by questioning the motives, character, or circumstances of those who hold that view, instead of criticizing the reasons and evidence they offer.

annual motion. In the geostatic worldview, this was the orbital revolution of the sun around the central motionless earth, in an eastward direction relative to the fixed stars and taking one year to complete. In the Copernican system, the annual motion is simply the earth's orbital revolution around the sun, also in an eastward direction and lasting one year.

apogee. In the orbit of a heavenly body, this is the point farthest from the earth.

Aristarchus of Samos (c. 310–250 B.C.). Greek astronomer who elaborated the theory that the earth moves around the sun.

Bellarmine, Robert (1542–1621). Jesuit theologian, perhaps the most influential Catholic churchman of his time, and now a saint. Besides being a cardinal, he also served as a professor at the Roman

College (the Jesuit university in Rome), an archbishop, the pope's theologian, a consultant to the Inquisition, and a member of both the Congregation of the Inquisition and the Congregation of the Index.

Brahe, Tycho. See *Tycho Brahe.*

Caccini, Tommaso (1574–1648). A Dominican friar from Florence who held various administrative positions in his order and earned various academic degrees and positions in theology. He accused Galileo of heresy in a sermon in 1614 and testified against him with the Inquisition in 1615.

Castelli, Benedetto (1578–1643). Benedictine monk, student of Galileo at the University of Padua, his successor at the University of Pisa, and friend and collaborator; also an important figure in his own right, mainly for his contributions to the science of hydraulics, and as the teacher of many outstanding Italian scientists of the period.

comet. A large heavenly body appearing as a luminous mass to which is attached a long tail, and visible for only brief periods ranging from a few days to several months. Though comets had been observed since antiquity, in Galileo's time their nature and origin remained controversial; the main issue was whether they were heavenly bodies or atmospheric phenomena. Nowadays, comets are known to be bodies of great volume but very small mass, to consist mostly of ice, and to follow definite (elliptical or parabolic) orbits around the sun; furthermore, the periodic recurrence of some of them can be predicted with great accuracy; but many more details remain controversial or unknown.

conjunction. A configuration in the apparent position of two heavenly bodies when they appear to be on the same side of the earth, namely, close to each other or separated by only a few degrees on the celestial sphere. For example, a new or thinly crescent moon occurs when it and the sun are in conjunction.

cubit. An ancient unit of distance corresponding to the length of a forearm, and thus approximately one and one-half to two feet. This is the term used to translate Galileo's term *braccio.*

declination. The angular distance of a star from the celestial equator as seen from the earth. The analogue for the celestial sphere of what latitude is for the earth's surface.

direct motion. Apparent motion which planets exhibit most of the time in their journeys against the background of the fixed stars; its direction is eastward, namely it follows the order of the constellations of the zodiac. Used primarily in contexts where one wants to contrast direct motion to retrograde motion, whose direction is opposite (namely, westward).

diurnal motion. At the level of observation, diurnal motion is the apparent motion of all heavenly bodies around the earth, occurring every day in a *westward* direction. In the geostatic worldview, such apparent motion corresponds to reality. In the Copernican system, the diurnal motion is simply the earth's daily rotation around its own axis, in an *eastward* direction.

eccentric. An eccentric is a circular orbit of one heavenly body around another such that the second body is not located at the geometrical center of the orbit but off that center. This device enables the distance between the two bodies to vary.

eclipse. An eclipse occurs when the sun or moon becomes partially or completely invisible due to their relative position vis-à-vis the earth. In a lunar eclipse, the moon is eclipsed; that is, the earth is directly between the sun and the moon, and the moon is in the earth's cone-shaped shadow. In a solar eclipse, the sun is eclipsed; that is, the moon is directly between the sun and the earth, and the earth is in the moon's cone-shaped shadow.

ecliptic. A term used to denote the annual orbit of the sun around the earth (in the geostatic system) or of the earth around the sun (in the Copernican system). The term also denotes both the plane on which the annual orbit lies and the circle resulting from projecting the annual orbit onto the celestial sphere.

element. One of the four basic substances out of which all terrestrial bodies were thought to be composed: earth, water, air, and fire.

elemental. Pertaining to the four terrestrial elements (earth, water, air, and fire).

epicycle. A circle whose center lies on and moves along the circumference of a larger circle, called *deferent*. The postulation of epicycles enabled astronomers to analyze the motion of heavenly bodies as a combination of circular motions, so that there would be variations in the distance from the heavenly body to the center of the deferent, as well as in the body's direction of motion as seen from that center.

equidistance of ratios. If $a, b, c, d, \ldots, l$ is one set of magnitudes, and $A, B, C, D, \ldots, L$ is another, such that $a{:}b = A{:}B$, $b{:}c = B{:}C$, $\ldots$, and $k{:}l = K{:}L$, then it follows by *equidistance of ratios* that $a{:}l = A{:}L$.

fixed star. A heavenly body that is visible normally only at night and appears to revolve daily around the earth without changing its position relative to other stars; thus all fixed stars appear to move in unison as if they were fixed on a celestial sphere, whose daily rotation carries them all along. A fixed star corresponds to what is nowadays called simply *star*, but in Galileo's time *star* meant simply *heavenly body* and stars were divided into fixed and wandering.

force. In modern physics, a force is defined by means of Newton's second law of motion, and so it is a cause of *changes* of speed or direction of motion. In Aristotelian physics, a force was a cause of motion and could be internal or external; internal forces caused natural motions, external forces caused violent motions. In Galileo's work, force had a less clear and less precise meaning that overlaps with both the Aristotelian and the Newtonian concepts, as well as with the concept of energy; although he was groping toward the Newtonian concept, he did not really possess it; Galileo's notion was also interwoven in confusing ways with his talk of *power* and *moment*.

Foscarini, Paolo Antonio (1580–1616). Head of the order of Carmelites in the province of Calabria and professor of theology at the University of Messina. He published in early 1615 a book that attempted to show the compatibility between the Bible and the earth's motion. This book was condemned and totally banned by the Index's Decree of 1616.

fourth proportional. Given three quantities *A, B, C,* the fourth proportional to them is a quantity *X* such that $A:B = C:X$.

geokinetic. Pertaining to the earth's motion or claiming that the earth moves. The geokinetic worldview claims that the earth rotates daily on its axis from west to east and revolves yearly around the sun in the same direction. This term is contrasted with *geostatic* and may be taken to correspond to *Copernican*.

gravity. A term used interchangeably with *weight* and *heaviness*. In the Aristotelian worldview, gravity is the property of the elements earth and water whereby they tend to move toward the center of the universe; it manifests itself either as weight or free fall; and it is contrasted with a property called *levity* (or *lightness*), which is attributed to the elements air and fire, which consists of the tendency to move away from the center of the universe, and which manifests itself as buoyancy or spontaneous upward motion; bodies with gravity are called *heavy bodies,* and those with levity are called *light bodies;* it follows that light bodies go up because of their intrinsic property of levity, and not because they weigh less than the surrounding medium; in short, bodies with levity are thought to have no weight. Galileo abandoned the dichotomy between gravity and levity and held that all bodies have weight, thus explaining buoyancy and spontaneous upward motion in terms of the relative weight or specific gravity of the bodies involved; for him gravity was a property belonging to all bodies in the universe (heavenly as well as terrestrial), but consisted of the tendency to go toward the center of the whole of which one was a part, so that a rock on the moon would tend to move toward the center of the moon. Thus for both Aristotle and Galileo gravity could be labeled a universal property, but in different senses; for Aristotle it was universal in the sense that it was defined in terms of the center of the universe, a unique point yielding an absolute frame of reference; for Galileo it was universal in the sense that it characterized all material bodies in the universe; but even Galileo did not conceive of gravity as universal in the sense of Newton's *gravitation,* namely, in terms of mutual attraction among all bodies in the universe, and thus as acting between the earth and the moon.

great circle. On a spherical surface, a circle whose center coincides with the center of the sphere. For example, on the earth the equator and the meridians are great circles, but the parallels are not.

Heraclides of Pontus. Ancient Greek who lived in the fourth century B.C.

Hicetas of Syracuse. Ancient Greek who lived about 400 B.C.

impetus. In late medieval physics, the impetus of a projectile was the power to move that had been transferred to it by the projector and that would be gradually lost. Galileo uses the term to refer to the power that a body has due to either the quantity of motion it embodies or the tendency it has to move in a particular way. Thus, the Galilean meaning is inexact and corresponds partly to the late medieval meaning and partly to what modern physics would call either momentum, kinetic energy, or even potential energy.

Index. Short for the Congregation of the Index, the department of the Catholic Church in charge of book censorship. Officially created in 1572 by Pope Gregory XIII, it was meant to formalize the periodic publication of the *Index of Prohibited Books,* whose first edition had already appeared in 1564 as a result of the Council of Trent. The Congregation was formally abolished by Pope Benedict XV in 1917, when the task of book censorship was taken over by the Inquisition. Then in 1966 the Inquisition relinquished this task by decreeing that within the Church book regulation is a moral and not a legal issue.

Inquisition. The common name for the Congregation of the Holy Office, the department of the Catholic Church whose purpose was to defend and uphold faith and morals. It was officially instituted in 1542 by Pope Paul III and was meant to take over the suppression of heresies and heretics begun by the medieval Inquisition. By the time of Galileo, the notion of heresy had been given a legal definition, and inquisitorial procedures had been codified. Nowadays this department is called the Congregation for the Doctrine of the Faith.

Jupiter. A planet whose orbit is bigger than the annual orbit and whose period of revolution is about twelve years. In the geostatic system, it is the sixth planet from the earth; in the Copernican system, it is the fifth planet from the sun.

Lincean Academy. Also called Academy of the Linceans (in Italian *Accademia dei Lincei,* which means literally "academy of those who have lynx eyes"), this was the first modern international scientific academy, founded in 1603 by Prince Federico Cesi (1585–1630), although it fell apart soon after his death. Galileo was made a member in 1611, became a friend of Cesi, and received support from the Academy for the publication of many of his works.

mean proportional. Given two quantities, A and B, their mean proportional is a quantity X such that $A:X = X:B$.

Medicean Planets or Stars. A term used by Galileo to refer to Jupiter's satellites, which he discovered. He named the new bodies in honor of Cosimo II de' Medici, who ruled Florence and the Grand Duchy of Tuscany.

meridian. A circle on the surface of a sphere passing through both poles and cutting the equator at right angles.

Milky Way. Wide band of faint light in the night sky stretching all the way around the celestial sphere. Corresponds to the galaxy of stars in which our solar system is located.

moment. Aside from the obvious connotation of an instant of time, this word is used by Galileo with several other meanings. One is an approximation to the *momentum* of modern physics. Another is synonymous with the terms *magnitude* or *intensity* or *degree*, as in the phrase "the moment of the speed a body possesses."

momentum. In classical (Newtonian) physics, momentum is defined as the product of a body's mass and its velocity, taking velocity as a vector quantity (which has both a numerical magnitude and a spatial direction). The law of conservation of momentum states that in a closed system the total amount of momentum neither increases nor decreases but remains constant. Galileo's counterpart of this law is his principle of conservation of motion; but the correspondence is inexact because he had no conception that momentum is a vector and because he did not clearly distinguish between momentum and kinetic energy.

natural motion. In Aristotelian natural philosophy, natural motion is the motion which a body has by nature; that is, motion which the body has because of its nature; namely, motion caused by the moving body's inherent nature; or again, motion caused by a force internal or inherent to the moving body. Thus, the natural motion of a terrestrial body is the motion it spontaneously tends to undergo in order to reach its natural place of rest, if it is not already there; for example, the natural motion of the elements earth and water is straight toward the center of the universe, and the natural motion of the elements air and fire is straight away from the center of the universe. Natural motion is contrasted with *violent motion*. Galileo partly accepted and partly modified this notion. He continued to speak of spontaneous (or internally caused) motion as one kind of natural motion, but dissociated it from the doctrine of natural places; so, for him the oscillation of a pendulum on the earth or the free fall of a rock on the moon would be as natural as the free fall of a rock on the earth. He sometimes added another meaning to the concept of natural motion, namely, motion that can last forever. And he contrasted natural motion with violent motion but also spoke of a third kind which is neither natural nor violent and which he labeled *indifferent* or *neutral* motion; an example of the latter would be horizontal motion on a frictionless surface.

opposition. A configuration in the apparent position of two heavenly bodies when they appear to be on opposite sides from the observer on earth, namely, 180 degrees apart on the celestial sphere. For example, a full moon occurs when it and the sun are in opposition.

orb. A term that is partly synonymous with the term *orbit,* namely, the path followed by one heavenly body around another. The term also refers to the region of the heavens where a given orbital path is located. For example, the *lunar orb* could refer either to the path of the moon around the earth, or to the region of space surrounding the earth at a distance equal to that between the earth and the moon.

orbit. The path followed by a heavenly body as it moves among the other bodies, usually around some particular body or point that is regarded as the center or focus of the orbit.

palm. A term used in this book to translate literally Galileo's word *palmo*. This was an ancient inexact unit of length corresponding to either the width of the palm of a hand, the length of a hand, or the distance from the tip of the thumb to the tip of the little finger when extended.

parabola. In mathematics, a plane curve defined as the set of all points equidistant from a fixed straight line (called the *directrix*) and a fixed point (called the *focus*). The shape generated is that of the intersection of a cone and a plane parallel to its side.

parallel. This term has two relevant meanings, as an adjective and as a noun. Two lines lying in the same plane are said to be parallel to each other when they never meet regardless of how far they are extended; similarly, two planes are parallel to each other when they never meet regardless of how far they are extended. Used as a noun, a parallel is a circle on the surface of a sphere (such as the earth or the celestial sphere) that is parallel to the equator; these parallels become smaller and smaller as one moves on the sphere's surface from the equator to the poles.

perigee. In the orbit of a heavenly body, this is the point closest to the earth.

Peripatetic. A Greek word meaning literally a person who walks around. A nickname given to Aristotelians in Galileo's time. Peripatetics acquired this nickname because in the school founded by Aristotle the teachers had the habit of walking around while lecturing.

perturbed equidistance of ratios. Given two sets of three magnitudes *a, b, c,* and *A, B, C,* such that $a:b = B:C$ and $b:c = A:B$, it follows by *perturbed equidistance of ratios* that $a:c = A:C$.

phases. The phases of a nearby heavenly body (such as the moon and Venus) are the periodic changes in its apparent shape from round disk to semicircle to crescent and back to semicircle and round disk. They are caused by changes in the relative position between the sun, the earth, and the other body: a crescent is seen when the body is in the region between the earth and the sun; a semicircle is seen when the line connecting the three bodies forms an angle close to a right angle; and a full disk is seen when the body's entire surface illuminated by the sun can be seen from the earth, either because the earth is between the sun and the body (as in the case of the moon) or because the sun is between the earth and the body (as in the case of Venus).

Philolaus of Croton (c. 470–c. 385 B.C.). Greek philosopher from southern Italy who accepted some of Pythagoras' ideas. He elaborated the view that the earth, together with the other planets (including the sun), moves around the center of the universe, where a central fire is located.

planet. A term originating from Greek and meaning a wandering star. In the geostatic worldview, a planet is a heavenly body that appears to move both around the earth and in relation to other heavenly bodies; that is, a heavenly body that simultaneously performs two

motions around the earth, the diurnal motion from east to west every
day and another revolution from west to east in a definite period of
time varying from one planet to another. There were seven planets,
and their arrangement in the order of increasing orbit and period was
as follows: moon, one month; Mercury, Venus, and sun, one year;
Mars, two years; Jupiter, twelve years; and Saturn, twenty-nine years.
In the Copernican view, a planet is a heavenly body that revolves
around the sun, again in a definite period of time that varies from one
planet to another: Mercury, three months; Venus, seven and a half
months; earth, one year; Mars, two years; Jupiter, twelve years; and
Saturn, twenty-nine years. In Galileo's time, the planets Uranus, Neptune, and Pluto had not yet been discovered.

Prime Mobile. A term meant to convey the idea of the "first
body in motion." In Aristotelian natural philosophy, the Prime Mobile was a sphere lying outside the celestial sphere and acted upon by
the First Unmoved Mover; by rotating daily, the Prime Mobile carried along all the other heavenly bodies (excluding the earth). The
Prime Mobile was needed by those Aristotelians for whom the celestial sphere could not be a source of the diurnal motion; in fact, there
was evidence that it had another slower movement in the opposite direction (the precession of the equinoxes), and the idea was to have a
distinct sphere for each distinct movement.

Pseudo-Aristotle. The unknown author of a book entitled *Questions of Mechanics,* wrongly attributed to Aristotle according to a tra-
dition that lasted past Galileo's time. The book was probably written
a generation after Aristotle's death, by one of his followers.

retrograde motion. Westward motion against the background of
the fixed stars which a planet appears to have periodically for a brief
period, thus reversing its usually eastward motion (called *direct motion*).
In the geostatic system, it was explained by means of epicycles. In the
Copernican system, it is explained in terms of the relative motion between the earth and the planet in question.

Sagredo, Giovanfrancesco (1571–1620). Venetian aristocrat and
diplomat who became Galileo's best friend when Galileo taught at
the University of Padua. Sagredo has been immortalized as one of the
three speakers in the *Dialogue* and the *Two New Sciences.*

Salviati, Filippo (1582–1614). Wealthy Florentine nobleman
whose interest in science and philosophy earned him membership in
the Lincean Academy in 1612. One of Galileo's closest friends in Florence, Salviati has been immortalized as one of the three characters in
the *Dialogue* and the *Two New Sciences.*

save the appearances (or the phenomena). To explain observed natural phenomena by means of assumptions that are taken not to describe real physical processes, but rather to be merely convenient instruments for making calculations and predictions.

Seleucus. A Babylonian who lived around 150 B.C. and who was a follower of Aristarchus' geokinetic theory.

Simplicio. One of the three characters in the *Dialogue* and the *Two New Sciences*. In Italian, *Simplicio* denotes both a simpleton and the philosopher Simplicius.

Simplicius. Greek philosopher who lived in the sixth century A.D., famous as one of the greatest commentators of Aristotle.

specific gravity. A term used by Galileo to mean weight per unit volume (the weighing being done presumably in air). This is analogous to the modern concept of density (which means *mass* per unit volume), except that Galileo did not have a clear concept of mass as distinct from weight. His point is that he wants a concept enabling him to compare the weights of equal volumes of different substances, so as to say, for example, that wax is "specifically" heavier than cork but lighter than lead.

spyglass. Term used by Galileo to refer to the telescope during the first two years that he used the instrument (*perspicillum* in Latin, *occhiale* in Italian). In 1611 the term *telescopium* was coined, and he adopted the new term.

telescope. Optical instrument consisting of an arrangement of lenses, mirrors, or both, that magnifies the image of distant objects so that they appear larger or nearer, thus rendering our vision more powerful and enabling us to see things that cannot be seen by the naked eye. Invented in Holland in 1608, it was significantly improved by Galileo the following year and turned into an effective scientific instrument for acquiring new knowledge about the world. The word (*telescopium* in Latin) was not coined until 1611, and before 1611 Galileo called the instrument a *spyglass*.

third proportional. Given two quantities *A* and *B*, their third proportional is a quantity *X* such that $A:B = B:X$.

Tycho Brahe (1546–1601). Danish astronomer, best known as an excellent observer and collector of data and as the promoter of the so-called Tychonic system. In the Tychonic system, the earth is motionless at the center of the universe; the planets revolve around the sun; but the sun (together with all the planets) moves around the earth, daily in a westward direction and annually in an eastward direction. Kepler worked with him and inherited his data.

Venus. A planet that revolves in its orbit in such a way that it always appears close to the sun. In the Copernican system, Venus is the second planet from the sun and completes its orbit in seven and a half months. In the geostatic system, opinions differed about whether it was the second, third, or fourth planet from the earth; but it was most commonly regarded as the third (between Mercury and the sun). With the telescope, Galileo discovered the phases of Venus, which are changes in its apparent shape similar to those which the moon exhibits each month; this proved conclusively that Venus revolves around the sun. However, this confirmed the system of Tycho Brahe as well as that of Copernicus, and so the choice between these two systems required other evidence for a conclusive demonstration.

violent motion. In Aristotelian natural philosophy, violent motion is motion that occurs because of the influence of some external force; examples are the motion of a cart pulled by a horse, the motion of a rowboat pushed by rowing, and the lifting of a weight with a pulley. Violent motion was contrasted with *natural motion*. Galileo partly accepted and partly modified this doctrine of violent motion.

wandering star. Heavenly body that appears not only to revolve daily around the earth, but also to change its position relative to other heavenly bodies; that is, in contrast to a *fixed star*, each wandering star moves around in the heavens according to a period that characterizes it. A wandering star is hence equivalent to a *planet*, a Greek word whose literal meaning is *wandering star*.

zodiac. Narrow belt on the celestial sphere along which the planets, sun, and moon appear to move. The zodiac is subdivided into twelve equal parts of thirty degrees, each part being the location of a group of stars arranged into a distinct pattern. These twelve patterns are the constellations of the zodiac: Aries, Taurus, Gemini, Cancer, Leo, Virgo, Libra, Scorpio, Sagittarius, Capricorn, Aquarius, and Pisces. The sun, moon, and planets are always seen somewhere in one of these constellations, moving from one constellation to the next in the order listed. This order corresponds to an eastward direction (from the viewpoint of terrestrial observation), and so the order of the signs of the zodiac is a direction of motion opposite to that of apparent diurnal rotation.

Zúñiga, Diego de (c. 1536–98). Augustinian friar from Salamanca (Spain) and author of a commentary on the book of Job that was published in the sixteenth century, favored the earth's motion, and was banned by the Index's Decree of 1616.

Annotated Bibliography
and Cited Works

This bibliography lists only works cited in the notes or deserving annotation here. Annotated entries are meant to provide an elementary guide for further reading and are marked with an asterisk.

Battistini, Andrea, ed. 1993. *Sidereus nuncius.* [Same as Galilei 1993.]

Beltrán Marí, Antonio. 2006. *Talento y poder: Historia de las relaciones entre Galileo y la Iglesia católica.* Pamplona: Laetoli.

*Biagioli, Mario. 1993. *Galileo Courtier.* Chicago: University of Chicago Press. [Focuses on questions of social institutions, psychological motivation, and political power, especially patronage.]

———. 2006. *Galileo's Instruments of Credit.* Chicago: University of Chicago Press.

Brahe, Tycho. 1596. *Epistolae astronomicae.* Uraniborg.

———. 1602. *Astronomiae instauratae progymnasmata.* Uraniborg.

Camerota, Michele. 2004. *Galileo Galilei e la cultura scientifica nell'età della Controriforma.* Rome: Salerno Editrice.

*Clavelin, Maurice. 1974. *The Natural Philosophy of Galileo.* Trans. A. J. Pomerans. Cambridge, MA: MIT Press. [The most comprehensive available account of Galileo's physics, astronomy, and methodology, focusing on published sources.]

Copernicus, Nicolaus. 1976. *On the Revolutions of the Heavenly Spheres.* Trans. A. M. Duncan. Newton Abbot: Davis & Charles.

———. 1992. *On the Revolutions.* Trans. and ed. Edward Rosen. Baltimore: Johns Hopkins University Press.

Crew, Henry, and Alfonso De Salvio, trans. and eds. 1914. *Dialogues Concerning Two New Sciences.* New York: Macmillan. [Same as Galilei 1914.]

Drake, Stillman. 1957. *Discoveries and Opinions of Galileo.* Garden City, NY: Doubleday & Company.

———, trans. and ed. 1967. *Dialogue Concerning the Two Chief World Systems.* [Same as Galilei 1967.]

————. 1970. *Galileo Studies*. Ann Arbor: University of Michigan Press.

————. 1973. "Galileo Gleanings XXII: Velocity and Eudoxian Proportion Theory." *Physis* 15: 49–64.

*————, trans. and ed. 1974. *Two New Sciences*. [Same as Galilei 1974. An excellent translation of the entire text, including useful commentary and notes.]

*————. 1978. *Galileo at Work*. Chicago: University of Chicago Press. [The most reliable, detailed, and up-to-date scientific biography in English.]

*————. 1981. *Cause, Experiment, and Science*. Chicago: University of Chicago Press. [A discussion of the topics mentioned in the title, written in dialogue form; interspersed in the discussion is a translation of the full text of Galileo's *Discourse on Bodies in Water*.]

*————. 1983. *Telescopes, Tides, and Tactics*. Chicago: University of Chicago Press. [A discussion of the topics mentioned in the title, written in dialogue form; interspersed in the discussion is a translation of the full text of Galileo's *Sidereal Messenger*.]

*Drake, Stillman, and C. D. O'Malley, trans. and eds. 1960. *The Controversy on the Comets of 1618*. Philadelphia: University of Pennsylvania Press. [A translation of all the works relating to this controversy, including the full text of Galileo's *The Assayer*.]

Einstein, Albert. 1954. *Ideas and Opinions*. Trans. Sonja Bargmann. New York: Crown Publishers.

*Fantoli, Annibale. 2003. *Galileo: For Copernicanism and for the Church*. 3rd edn. Trans. G. V. Coyne. Vatican City: Vatican Observatory Publications. [The most accurate, balanced, and comprehensive historical account of Galileo's trial in English.]

Favaro, Antonio, ed. 1890–1909. *Le Opere di Galileo Galilei*. [Same as Galilei 1890–1909.]

Finocchiaro, Maurice A. 1972. "Vires Acquirit Eundo: The Passage Where Galileo Renounces Space-Acceleration and Causal Investigation." *Physis* 14: 125–45.

————. 1973. "Galileo's Space-Proportionality Argument: A Role for Logic in Historiography." *Physis* 15: 65–72.

*————. 1980. *Galileo and the Art of Reasoning*. Boston: Reidel. [A detailed analysis of the scientific, methodological, logical, and rhetorical aspects of Galileo's *Dialogue*.]

*————, trans. and ed. 1989. *The Galileo Affair: A Documentary History*. Berkeley: University of California Press. [A collection of the

trial documents from 1613 to 1633, arranged, introduced, and annotated in such a way as to make them understandable to non-experts and useful to experts. It includes, in particular, the full text of the following essays by Galileo: "Letter to Castelli" (1613); "Considerations on the Copernican Opinion" (1615); *Letter to the Grand Duchess Christina* (1615); "Discourse on the Tides" (1616); and "Reply to Ingoli" (1624).]

★————, trans. and ed. 1997. *Galileo on the World Systems: A New Abridged Translation and Guide.* Berkeley: University of California Press. [An abridged translation and guide to the critical reading of Galileo's *Dialogue,* for specialists and nonspecialists alike.]

★————. 2005. *Retrying Galileo, 1633–1992.* Berkeley: University of California Press. [An introductory but comprehensive survey of the sources, facts, and issues of the controversy *about* the 1633 condemnation of Galileo.]

Flora, Ferdinando, ed. 1953. *Opere.* [Same as Galilei 1953.]

★Frova, Andrea, and Mariapiera Marenzana. 2006. *Thus Spoke Galileo.* Oxford: Oxford University Press. [A good introduction to Galileo, primarily for practicing scientists and science students, and useful for all interested readers; about evenly divided between Galilean texts and interpretive commentary.]

★Galilei, Galileo. 1636. *Nov-antiqua sanctissimorum Patrum, & probatorum theologorum doctrina de Sacrae Scripturae testimoniis, in conclusionibus mere naturalibus, quae sensata experientia et necessariis demonstrationibus evinci possunt . . . .* Ed. Matthias Bernegger. Trans. Elia Diodati. Strasbourg. [First edition of the Italian text of the *Letter to the Grand Duchess Christina,* together with a Latin translation.]

————. 1880. *The Sidereal Messenger of Galileo Galilei and a Part of the Preface to Kepler's* Dioptrics. Trans. and ed. Edward Stafford Carlos. London: Rivingtons. Rpt., London: Dawsons of Pall Mall, 1960.

★————. 1890–1909. *Opere.* 20 vols. National Edition by A. Favaro. Florence: Barbèra. Reprinted in 1929–39 and 1968. [The standard critical edition of Galileo's collected works and correspondence, including directly related works and correspondence by others.]

————. 1891. *Dialog über die beiden hauptsachlichsten Weltsysteme.* Trans. and ed. Emil Strauss. Leipzig: Teubner.

————. 1914. *Dialogues Concerning Two New Sciences.* Trans. Henry Crew and Alfonso De Salvio. New York: Macmillan. Rpt. Evanston, IL: Northwestern University Press, 1939, 1946, 1950 and New York: Dover, 1951.

————. 1953. *Opere.* Ed. Ferdinando Flora. Milan: Riccardo Ricciardi.

★————. 1954. "Two Kinds of Properties." Trans. Arthur Danto. In *Introduction to Contemporary Civilization in the West,* ed. Columbia University, 1: 719–24. 2nd edn. New York: Columbia University Press. [A good and useful translation of the passage on primary and secondary qualities in *The Assayer.*]

★————. 1958. *Discorsi e dimostrazioni matematiche intorno a due nuove scienze.* Ed. Adriano Carugo e Ludovico Geymonat. Turin: Boringhieri. [The most extensively annotated edition of *Two New Sciences;* also contains Italian translations of original Latin passages.]

★————. 1960. *Discourse on Bodies in Water.* Trans. Thomas Salusbury. With Introduction and Notes by Stillman Drake. Urbana: University of Illinois Press. [A translation of the complete text, first published in 1665, but left unrevised; thus the archaic English is hard to follow.]

————. 1964. *Opere.* 5 vols. Ed. Pietro Pagnini. Florence: Salani.

————. 1967. *Dialogue Concerning the Two Chief World Systems.* 2nd revised edn. Trans. and ed. Stillman Drake. Berkeley: University of California Press.

————. 1970. *Dialogo sopra i due massimi sistemi.* Ed. Libero Sosio. Turin: Einaudi.

————. 1974. *Two New Sciences.* Trans. and ed. Stillman Drake. Madison: University of Wisconsin Press.

————. 1989. *Sidereus nuncius, or the Sidereal Messenger.* Trans. and ed. Albert Van Helden. Chicago: University of Chicago Press.

————. 1992. *Sidereus nuncius/Le messager céleste.* Trans. and ed. Isabelle Pantin. Paris: Les Belles Lettres.

————. 1993. *Sidereus nuncius.* Ed. Andrea Battistini. Trans. Maria Timpanaro Cardini. Venice: Marsilio.

★————. 1998. *Dialogo sopra i due massimi sistemi.* 2 vols. Critical edition with commentary by Ottavio Besomi and Mario Helbing. Padua: Antenore. [Extremely valuable for specialists.]

★————. 2001. *Dialogue Concerning the Two Chief World Systems.* Trans. Stillman Drake. Ed. John L. Heilbron. New York: Modern Library. [A translation of the entire text, reprinted in a more user-friendly volume from the second (1967) edition published by the University of California Press.]

★————. 2002. *Dialogues Concerning Two New Sciences.* Edited with commentary by Stephen Hawking. Philadelphia: Running Press. [A translation of the full text, reprinted without alterations from the Crew-De Salvio translation, with two introductory essays by the great physicist Hawking, as part of the series "On the Shoulders of Giants" that also includes works by Copernicus, Kepler, Newton, and Einstein.]

Garin, Eugenio. 1971. "A proposito del Copernico." *Rivista critica di storia della filosofia* 26: 83–87.

———. 1975. "Alle origini della polemica anticopernicana." In *Colloquia Copernicana,* vol. 2 (Studia Copernicana, vol. 6), pp. 31–42. Wroclaw: Ossolineum.

Gingerich, Owen. 1982. "The Galileo Affair." *Scientific American,* August, pp. 132–43.

Granada, Miguel A. 1997. "Giovanni Maria Tolosani e la prima reazione romana di fronte al 'De revolutionibus.'" In *La diffusione del copernicanesimo in Italia, 1543–1610,* ed. Massimo Bucciantini and Maurizio Torrini, pp. 11–35. Florence: Olschki.

Hawking, Stephen W. 1988. *A Brief History of Time.* New York: Bantam Books.

———. 1992. "Galileo Galilei (1564–1642): His Life and Work." In Galilei 2002, pp. xi–xvii.

Julian, John, ed. 1892. *A Dictionary of Hymnology.* New York: Charles Scribner's Sons.

Koyré, Alexandre. 1943. "Traduttore-Traditore: A Propos de Copernic et Galilée." *Isis* 34: 209–10.

★———. 1978. *Galileo Studies.* Trans. J. Mepham. Hassocks, Sussex: Harvester Press, 1978. [A widely discussed and influential work by a leading Galilean scholar, first published in French in 1939.]

Langford, Jerome J. 1966. *Galileo, Science and the Church.* Ann Arbor: University of Michigan Press.

Mayaud, Pierre-Noël. 1997. *La condamnation des livres coperniciens et sa révocation à la lumière de documents inédits des Congrégations de l'Index et de l'Inquisition.* Rome: Editrice Pontificia Università Gregoriana.

McMullin, Ernan, ed. 2005a. *The Church and Galileo.* Notre Dame: University of Notre Dame Press.

———. 2005b. "Galileo's Theological Venture." In McMullin 2005a, pp. 88–116.

★Motta, Franco, ed. 2000. *Lettera a Cristina di Lorena: Sull'uso della Bibbia nelle argomentazioni scientifiche.* Genoa: Marietti. [Reprint of the Italian text of the original edition (Galilei 1636), with the addition of useful notes by the editor and a lengthy introduction by Mauro Pesce.]

Mourant, John A., ed. 1964. *Introduction to the Philosophy of Saint Augustine: Selected Readings and Commentary.* University Park: Pennsylvania State University Press.

Newton, Isaac. 1999. *The Principia: Mathematical Principles of Natural Philosophy.* Trans. and ed. I. Bernard Cohen and Anne Whitman. Berkeley: University of California Press.

*Pagnini, Pietro, ed. 1964. *Opere di Galileo Galilei.* [Same as Galilei 1964. Contains extremely useful notes and commentary.]

*Pantin, Isabelle, trans. and ed. 1992. *Sidereus nuncius/Le messager céleste.* [Same as Galilei 1992. Critical edition in Latin and French translation, with extremely useful notes and commentary.]

Pesce, Mauro. 1992. "Le redazioni originali della Lettera 'copernicana' di G. Galilei a B. Castelli." *Filologia e critica* 17: 394–417.

Redondi, Pietro. 1987. *Galileo Heretic.* Trans. R. Rosenthal. Princeton: Princeton University Press.

*Reeves, Eileen, and Albert Van Helden. Forthcoming. *Galileo and Scheiner on Sunspots.* Chicago: University of Chicago Press. [A translation, with notes and commentary, of the writings by Galileo and Christoph Scheiner published in 1612–13, including the full text of Galileo's *History and Demonstrations Concerning Sunspots.*]

Rosen, Edward. 1947. *The Naming of the Telescope.* New York: Schuman.

———. 1958. "Galileo's Misstatements about Copernicus." *Isis* 49: 319–30.

———. 1975. "Was Copernicus's *Revolutions* Approved by the Pope?" *Journal of the History of Ideas* 36: 531–42.

Russo, François. 1968. "Lettre de Galilée à Christine de Lorraine, Grande-Duchesse de Toscane (1615)." In *Galilée: Aspects de sa vie et de son oeuvre,* pp. 324–59. Paris: Presses Universitaires de France.

Salusbury, Thomas, trans. and ed. 1661–65. *Mathematical Collections and Translations.* 2 vols. London: Leybourne.

Santillana, Giorgio de, ed. 1953. *Dialogue on the Great World Systems.* Salusbury's translation revised by G. de Santillana. Chicago: University of Chicago Press.

———. 1955. *The Crime of Galileo.* Chicago: University of Chicago Press.

Schaff, Philip, and Henry Wace, eds. 1893. *A Select Library of Nicene and Post-Nicene Fathers.* 2nd series, vol. 6: *St. Jerome: Letters and Select Works.* New York: The Christian Literature Company.

Sosio, Libero, ed. 1970. *Dialogo sopra i due massimi sistemi.* [Same as Galilei 1970.]

Stafford Carlos, Edward, trans. and ed. 1880. *The Sidereal Messenger of Galileo Galilei and a Part of the Preface to Kepler's Dioptrics.* [Same as Galilei 1880.]

*Strauss, Emil, trans. and ed. 1891. *Dialog über die beiden hauptsachlichsten Weltsysteme.* [Same as Galilei 1891. Contains very useful notes.]

Tertullian, Quintus S. F. 1972. *Adversus Marcionem.* Trans. and ed. Ernest Evans. Oxford: Clarendon Press.

*Van Helden, Albert, trans. and ed. 1989. *Sidereus nuncius, or the Sidereal Messenger.* [Same as Galilei 1989. An excellent translation of the entire text, including very useful commentary and notes.]

*Wallace, William A. 1984. *Galileo and His Sources.* Princeton: Princeton University Press. [An excellent historical account of the connection between Galileo's work and that of his immediate Aristotelian predecessors.]

Westman, Robert S. 1986. "The Copernicans and the Churches." In *God and Nature,* ed. David C. Lindberg and Ronald L. Numbers, pp. 76–113. Berkeley: University of California Press.

CHAPTER 1

The Sidereal Messenger (1610)[1]

[55] To the Most Serene Cosimo II de' Medici, Fourth Grand Duke of Tuscany

[§1.1] There is certainly something very noble and humane in the intention of those who have endeavored to protect from envy the noble achievements of distinguished men, and to rescue their names, worthy of immortality, from oblivion and decay. This desire has given us the images of famous men, sculptured in marble, or fashioned in bronze, as a memorial of them to future ages; to the same feeling we owe the erection of statues, both ordinary and equestrian; hence, as the poet[2] says, has originated expenditure, mounting to the stars, upon columns and pyramids; with this desire, lastly, cities have been built, and distinguished by the names of those men, whom the gratitude of posterity thought worthy of being handed down to all ages. For the state of the human mind is such that, unless it be continually stirred by the likenesses of things obtruding themselves upon it from without, all recollection of them easily passes away from it.

Others, however, having regard for more stable and more lasting monuments, secured the eternity of the fame of great men by placing it under the protection, not of marble or bronze, but of the Muses' guardianship and the imperishable monuments of literature. But why do I mention these things? As if human wit, content with these regions, did not dare to advance further; whereas, since it well understood that all human monuments do perish at last by violence, by weather, or by age, it took a wider view and invented more imperishable signs, over which destroying Time and envious Age could

---

1. Cf. Galilei 1890–1909, 3: 53–96; translated by Edward Stafford Carlos (1880) from Galileo Galilei, *Sidereus nuncius* (Venice, 1610); revised by Finocchiaro for this volume. For the historical background, see the Introduction, especially §0.3 and §0.4.
2. Sextus Propertius (c. 50 B.C.–c. 16 B.C.), *Elegies*, iii, 2, 17–22.

claim no rights; so, betaking itself to the sky, it inscribed on the well-known orbs of the brightest stars—those everlasting orbs—the names of those who, for eminent and god-like deeds, were accounted worthy to enjoy an eternity in company with the stars. Wherefore the fame of Jupiter, Mars, Mercury, Hercules, and the rest of the heroes by whose names the stars are called, will not fade until the extinction of the splendor of the constellations themselves.

But this invention of human shrewdness, so particularly noble and admirable, [56] has gone out of date ages ago, inasmuch as primeval heroes are in possession of those bright abodes and keep them by a sort of right. Into such company the affection of Augustus in vain attempted to introduce Julius Caesar; for when he wished that the name Julian should be given to a star that appeared in his time (one of those which the Greeks and the Latins alike name, from their hair-like tails, comets), it vanished in a short time and mocked his too-eager hope. But we are able to prophesize far truer and happier things for your highness, Most Serene Prince, for scarcely have the immortal graces of your mind begun to shine on earth, when bright stars present themselves in the heavens, like tongues to tell and celebrate your most eminent virtues to all time. Behold then, reserved for your famous name four stars, belonging not to the ordinary and less-distinguished multitude of the fixed stars, but to the illustrious order of the planets; like genuine children of Jupiter, they accomplish their orbital revolutions around this most noble star with mutually unequal motions and with marvelous speed, and at the same time all together in common accord they also complete every twelve years great revolutions around the center of the world, certainly around the sun itself.

But the Maker of the Stars himself seemed to direct me by clear reasons to assign these new planets to the famous name of Your Highness in preference to all others. For just as these stars, like children worthy of their sire, never leave the side of Jupiter by any appreciable distance, so who does not know that clemency, kindness of heart, gentleness of manners, splendor of royal blood, nobility in public functions, wide extent of influence and power over others (all of which have fixed their common abode and seat in Your Highness),—who, I say, does not know that all these qualities, according to the providence of God, from whom all good things do come, emanate from the benign star of Jupiter? Jupiter, I maintain, at the instant of the birth of Your Highness having at length emerged from the turbid mists of the horizon, and occupying the middle quarter of the heavens, and illuminating the eastern angle from his own royal house, from that exalted throne Jupiter looked out upon your most happy birth and poured forth into a most pure air all the brightness of his majesty, in order that your tender body and your mind (already adorned by God with still more splendid graces) might imbibe with your first breath the whole of that influence and power. But why should I use only probable arguments when I can demonstrate my conclusion with an almost necessary reason? It was the will of Almighty God that I should be judged by your most serene parents not unworthy to be employed in teaching mathematics to Your Highness, which duty I discharged, during the four years just passed, at that time of the year when it is customary to relax from more severe studies. Wherefore, since it fell to my lot, evidently by God's will, to serve Your Highness [57] and so to receive the rays of your incredible clemency and beneficence in a position near your person, what wonder is it if you have so warmed my heart that it thinks about scarcely anything else day and night, but how I, who am under your dominion not only by inclination but also by my very birth and nature, may be known to be most anxious for your glory and most grateful to you? And so, inasmuch as under your auspices, Most Serene Cosimo, I have discovered these stars, which were unknown to all astronomers before me, I have, with very good right, determined to designate them with the most august name of your family. And as I was the first to investigate them, who can rightly blame me if I give them a name and call them the *Medicean Stars,* hoping that as much consideration may accrue to these stars from this title as other stars have brought to other heroes? For, not to speak of your most serene ancestors, to whose everlasting glory the monuments of all history bear witness, your virtue alone, most mighty hero, can confer on those stars an immortal name. Similarly, who can doubt that you will not only maintain and preserve the expectations, high though they be, about yourself which you have aroused by the very happy beginning of your government, but that you will also far surpass them, so that when you have conquered your peers, you may still vie with yourself and become day by day greater than yourself and your greatness?

Accept, then, Most Clement Prince, this addition to the glory of your family, reserved by the stars for you. And may you enjoy for many years those good blessings, which are sent to you not so much from the stars as from God, the Maker and Governor of the stars.

Your Highness's most devoted servant, Galileo Galilei. Padua, 12 March 1610.

[59] Astronomical Message Containing and Explaining Observations Lately Made with the Aid of a New Spyglass regarding the Moon's Surface, the Milky Way, Nebulous Stars, an Innumerable Multitude of Fixed Stars, and Also regarding Four Planets Never Before Seen, Which Have Been Named Medicean Stars

[§1.2] In the present small treatise I set forth some matters of great interest for all observers of natural phenomena to look at and consider. They are of great interest, I think, first, because of their intrinsic excellence; secondly, because of their absolute novelty; and lastly, also because of the instrument by the aid of which they have been presented to our senses.

The number of the fixed stars which observers have been able to see without artificial powers of sight up to this day can be counted. It is therefore decidedly a great feat to add to their number, and to set distinctly before the eyes other stars in myriads, which have never been seen before, and which surpass the old, previously known, stars in number more than ten times.

Again, it is a most beautiful and delightful sight to behold the body of the moon, which is distant from us nearly sixty radii[3] of the earth, as near as if it were at a distance of only two of the same measures. So the diameter of this same moon appears about 30 times larger, its surface about 900 times, and its solid mass nearly 27,000 times larger than when it is viewed only with the naked eye. And consequently anyone may know with the certainty that is due to the use of our senses that the moon certainly does not possess a smooth and polished surface, but [60] one rough and uneven, and, just like the face of the earth itself, it is everywhere full of vast protuberances, deep chasms, and sinuosities.

---

3. The original Latin text speaks of *diameters*. In correcting it to *radii*, I follow Stafford Carlos (1880, 8), but modernize his archaic *semi-diameters*. Favaro (1890–1909, 3: 59.18) also makes the correction. For more information, see Van Helden 1989, 35 n. 19; Pantin 1992, 56–57 n. 5; Battistini 1993, 187 n. 59.

Then to have got rid of disputes about the galaxy or Milky Way, and to have made its essence clear to the senses, as well as to the intellect, seems by no means a matter that ought to be considered of slight importance. In addition to this, to point out, as with one's finger, the substance of those stars which every one of the astronomers up to this time has called nebulous and to demonstrate that it is very different from what has hitherto been believed, will be pleasant and very beautiful.

But that which will excite the greatest astonishment by far, and which indeed especially moved me to call it to the attention of all astronomers and philosophers, is this: I have discovered four wandering stars, neither known nor observed by any one of the astronomers before my time; they have their orbits around a certain important star of those previously known and are sometimes in front of it, sometimes behind it, though they never depart from it beyond certain limits, like Venus and Mercury around the sun.

All these facts were discovered and observed a short time ago with the help of a spyglass[4] devised[5] by me, through God's grace first enlightening my mind. Perchance other discoveries still more excellent will be made from time to time by me and by other observers with the assistance of a similar instrument. So I will first briefly record its shape and preparation, as well as the occasion of its being devised, and then I will give an account of the observations made by me.

[§1.3] About ten months ago a report reached my ears that a Dutchman had constructed a spyglass, by the aid of which visible objects, although at a great distance from the eye of the observer, were seen distinctly as if near; and some demonstrations of its wonderful performances were reported, which some gave credence to, but others contradicted. A few days later I received confirmation of the report

---

4. Here and in the rest of *The Sidereal Messenger* I have changed Stafford Carlos' translation of *perspicillum* as *telescope* because the latter word was not coined until 1611. For more information, see Rosen 1947; Van Helden 1989, 112; Pantin 1992, 50 n. 5; Battistini 1993, 190 n. 72.

5. Here I retain Stafford Carlos' (1880, 9) translation of the original Latin *excogitati*. This rendition was also adopted by Drake (1983, 18). Other correct translations are *contrived* (Van Helden 1989, 36) and *conceived,* or *conçue* in French (Pantin 1992, 7). The more important point is to note that Galileo is *not* claiming to have been the *first* to *invent* the instrument, and his account in the next paragraph makes this disclaimer explicit.

in a letter written from Paris by a noble Frenchman, Jacques Badovere. This finally determined me to give myself up first to inquire into
the principle of the spyglass, and then to consider the means by which
I might arrive at the invention of a similar instrument. After a little
while I succeeded, through deep study of the theory of refraction. I
prepared a tube, at first of lead, in the ends of which I fitted two glass
lenses, both plane on one side, but on the other side one spherically
convex, and the other concave. Then bringing my eye to the concave
lens [61] I saw objects satisfactorily large and near, for they appeared
one-third of the distance and nine times larger than when they are
seen with the natural eye alone. Shortly afterwards I constructed another more precise spyglass, which magnified objects more than 60
times. Finally, by sparing neither labor nor expense, I succeeded in
constructing for myself an instrument so superior that objects seen
through it appear magnified nearly 1,000 times, and more than 30
times nearer than if viewed by the natural powers of sight alone.

It would be altogether a waste of time to enumerate the number
and importance of the benefits which this instrument may be expected to confer when used by land or sea. But without paying attention to its use for terrestrial objects, I betook myself to observations
of the heavenly bodies. First of all, I viewed the moon as near as if it
were scarcely two radii of the earth distant. After the moon, I frequently observed other heavenly bodies, both fixed stars and planets,
with incredible delight; and, when I saw their very great number, I
began to consider about a method by which I might be able to measure their distances apart, and finally I found one.

Here it is fitting that all who intend to turn their attention to observations of this kind should receive certain cautions. In the first
place, it is absolutely necessary for them to prepare a most perfect spyglass, one that will show very bright objects distinct and free from any
mistiness and will magnify them at least 400 times and show them as
if only one-twentieth of their distance. Unless the instrument be of
such power, it will be in vain to attempt to view all the things that
have been seen by me in the heavens, and that will be enumerated
below. Then in order that one may be a little more certain about the
magnifying power of the instrument, one shall fashion two circles or
two square pieces of paper, one of which is 400 times greater than the
other; this will happen when the diameter of the greater is twenty
times the length of the diameter of the other. Then one shall view
from a distance simultaneously both surfaces, fixed on the same wall,

the smaller with one eye applied to the spyglass, and the larger with
the other eye unassisted; for that may be done without inconvenience
at one and the same instant with both eyes open. Then both figures
will appear of the same size, if the instrument magnifies objects in the
desired proportion.

After such an instrument has been prepared, the method of measuring distances remains for inquiry, and this shall be accomplished by
the following contrivance. For the sake of being more easily understood, let *ABCD* be the tube and E the eye of the observer. When
there are no lenses in the tube, rays from the eye to the object *FG*
would be drawn in the straight lines *ECF* and *EDG;* [62] but when
the lenses have been inserted, the rays go in the bent lines *ECH* and
EDI and are brought closer together, and those that originally (when
unaffected by the lenses) were directed to the object *FG* will include

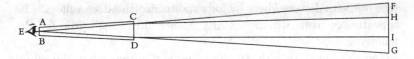

only the part *HI*. Then, the ratio of the distance *EH* to the line *HI*
being known, we shall be able to find, by means of a table of sines,
the magnitude of the angle subtended at the eye by the object *HI,*
which we shall find to contain only some minutes. Now, if we fit on
the lens *CD* thin plates pierced some with larger and others with
smaller apertures, by putting on over the lens sometimes one plate and
sometimes another, as may be necessary, we shall construct at our
pleasure different subtending angles of more or fewer minutes; by
their help we shall be able to measure conveniently the intervals between stars separated by an angular distance of some minutes, within
an error of one or two minutes. But let it suffice for the present to
have thus slightly touched, and as it were just put our lips to these
matters, for on some other opportunity I will publish the complete
theory of this instrument.

Now let me review the observations I made during the past two
months, again calling the attention of all who are eager for true philosophy to the beginnings of great contemplations.

[§1.4] Let me speak first of the surface of the moon that is turned toward us. For the sake of being understood more easily, I distinguish
two parts in it, which I call respectively the brighter and the darker.

The brighter part seems to surround and pervade the whole hemi-sphere; but the darker part, like a sort of cloud, stains the moon's sur-face and makes it appear covered with spots. Now these spots, as they are somewhat dark and of considerable size, are plain to everyone, and every age has seen them. Thus I shall call them *great* or *ancient* spots, to distinguish them from other spots, smaller in size, but so thickly scattered that they sprinkle the whole surface of the moon, es-pecially the brighter portions of it. The latter spots have never been observed by anyone before me. From my observation of them, often repeated, I have been led to the opinion which I have expressed; that is, I feel sure that the surface of the moon is not perfectly smooth, free from inequalities and exactly spherical (as a large school of philoso-phers holds with regard to the moon and the other heavenly bodies), but that on the contrary it is full of inequalities, uneven, [63] full of hollows and protuberances, just like the surface of the earth itself, which is varied everywhere by lofty mountains and deep valleys. The appearances from which we may gather this conclusion are the following.

On the fourth or fifth day after the new moon, when the moon presents itself to us with bright horns, the boundary that divides the dark part from the bright part does not extend smoothly in an ellipse,

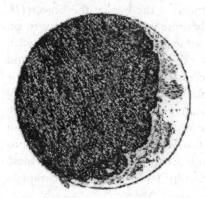

as would happen in the case of a perfectly spherical body, but it is marked out in an irregular, un-even, and very wavy line, as rep-resented in the figure given. Several bright excrescences, as they may be called, extend be-yond the boundary of light and shadow into the dark part, and on the other hand pieces of shadow encroach upon the bright.

Furthermore, a great quantity of small blackish spots, altogether separated from the dark part, sprinkle everywhere almost the whole space that is at the time flooded with the sun's light, with the excep-tion of that part alone which is occupied by the great and ancient spots. I have noticed that the small spots just mentioned have this common characteristic always and in every case: that they have the dark part towards the sun's position, and on the side away from the sun they have brighter boundaries, as if they were crowned with shining summits. Now we have an appearance quite similar on the earth at sunrise, when we behold the valleys, not yet flooded with light, but the mountains surrounding them on the side opposite to the sun always ablaze with the splendor of its beams; [64] and just as the shadows in the hollows of the earth diminish in size as the sun rises higher, so also these spots on the moon lose their blackness as the illuminated part grows larger and larger.

However, not only are the boundaries of light and shadow in the moon seen to be uneven and sinuous, but—and this produces still greater astonishment—there appear very many bright points within the darkened portion of the moon, altogether divided and broken off from the illuminated area, and separated from it by no inconsiderable interval; they gradually increase in size and brightness, and after an hour or two they become joined on to the rest of the bright portion, now become somewhat larger. But in the meantime others, one here and another there, shooting up as if growing, are lighted up within the shaded portion, increase in size, and at last are linked on to the same luminous surface, now still more extended. An example of this is given in the same figure. Now, is it not the case on the earth before sunrise that while the level plain is still in shadow, the peaks of the most lofty mountains are illuminated by the sun's rays? After a little while, does not the light spread further while the middle and larger parts of those mountains are becoming illuminated; and finally, when the sun has risen, do not the illuminated parts of the plains and hills join together? The magnitude, however, of such prominences and depressions in the moon seems to surpass the ruggedness of the earth's surface, as I shall hereafter show.

And here I cannot refrain from mentioning what a remarkable spectacle I observed while the moon was rapidly approaching her first quarter, a representation of which is given in the same illustration given above. A protuberance of the shadow, of great size, indented the illuminated part in the neighborhood of the lower cusp. When I had observed this indentation a while, and had seen that it was dark throughout, finally, after about two hours, a bright peak began to arise a little below the middle of the depression. This gradually increased, and presented a triangular shape, but was as yet quite detached and separated from the illuminated surface. Soon around it three other small points began to shine. Then when the moon was just about to set, that triangular figure, having now extended and widened, began to be connected with the rest of the illuminated part, and, still girt with the three bright peaks already mentioned, suddenly burst into the indentation of shadow like a vast promontory of light.

Moreover, at the ends of the upper [65] and lower cusps certain bright points, quite away from the rest of the bright part, began to rise out of the shadow, as is seen in the same illustration. In both horns also, but especially in the lower one, there was a great quantity of dark spots, of which those that are nearer the boundary of light and shadow appear larger and darker, but those that are more remote less dark and more indistinct. In all cases, however, as I have already mentioned before, the dark portion of the spot faces the direction of the sun's illumination, and a brighter edge surrounds the darkened spot on the side away from the sun and towards the region of the moon in shadow. This part of the surface of the moon, where it is marked with spots like a peacock's tail with its azure eyes, looks like those glass vases that, through being plunged while still hot from the kiln into cold water, acquire a crackled and wavy surface, from which circumstance they are commonly called frosted glasses.

Now, the great spots of the moon observed at the same time are not seen to be at all similarly broken, or full of depressions and prominences, but rather to be even and uniform; for only here and there some spaces, rather brighter than the rest, crop up. Thus, if anyone wishes to revive the old opinion of the Pythagoreans, that the moon is another earth, so to speak, the brighter portions may very fitly represent the surface of the land, and the darker the expanse of water; indeed, I have never doubted that if the sphere of the earth were seen from a distance, when flooded with the sun's rays, the part of the surface which is land would present itself to view as brighter, and that which is water as darker in comparison. Moreover, the great spots in the moon are seen to be more depressed than the brighter areas; for in the moon, both when crescent and when waning, on the boundary between the light and the shadow that is seen in some places around the great spots, the adjacent regions are always brighter, as I have indicated in drawing my illustrations; and the edges of the said spots are not only more depressed than the brighter parts, but are more even, and are not broken by ridges or ruggedness. But the brighter part stands out most near the spots so that both before the first quarter and near the third quarter also, around a certain spot in the upper part of the figure, that is, occupying the northern region of the moon, some vast prominences on the upper and lower sides of it rise to an enormous elevation, as the following illustrations show.

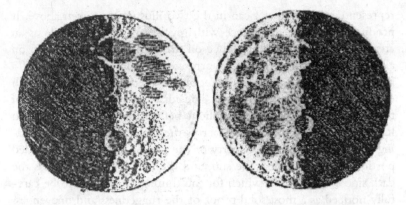

This same spot before the third quarter is seen to be walled around with boundaries of a deeper shade, which, just like very lofty [66] mountain summits, appear darker on the side away from the sun, and brighter on the side where they face the sun. But in the case of cavities the opposite happens, for the part of them away from the sun appears brilliant, and the part that lies nearer to the sun dark and in shadow. After a time, when the bright portion of the moon's surface has diminished in size, as soon as the whole or nearly so of the spot already mentioned is covered with shadow, [67] the brighter ridges of the mountains rise high above the shade. These two appearances are shown in the following illustrations.

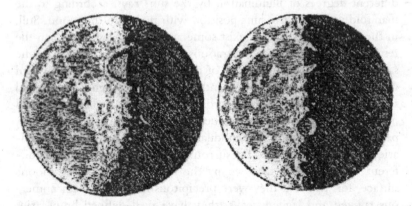

There is one other point which I must on no account forget, and which I have noticed and rather wondered at. [68] It is this. The middle of the moon, as it seems, is occupied by a certain cavity larger than all the rest, and in shape perfectly round. I have looked at this depression near both the first and third quarters, and I have represented it as well as I can in the two illustrations given above. It produces the same appearance with regard to light and shade as an area like Bohemia would produce on the earth, if it were shut in on all sides by very lofty mountains arranged on the circumference of a perfect circle; for this area in the moon is walled in with peaks of such enormous height that the furthest side adjacent to the dark portion of the moon is seen bathed in sunlight before the boundary between light and shade reaches halfway across the circular space. But according to the characteristic property of the rest of the spots, the shaded portion of this too faces the sun, and the bright part is towards the dark side of the moon, which for the third time I advise to be carefully noticed as a most solid proof of the ruggedness and unevenness spread over the whole of the bright region of the moon. Of these spots, moreover, the darkest are always those that are near to the boundary line between the light and the shadow, but those further off appear both smaller in size and less decidedly dark; so that finally, when the moon at opposition becomes full, the darkness of the cavities differs from the brightness of the prominences by a modest and very slight difference.

These phenomena which we have reviewed are observed in the bright areas of the moon. In the great spots, we do not see such differences of depressions and prominences as we are compelled to recognize in the brighter parts owing to the change of their shape under different degrees of illumination by the sun's rays, according to the manifold variety of the sun's position with regard to the moon. Still, in the great spots there do exist some areas rather less dark than the rest, as I have noted in the illustrations; but these areas always have the same appearance, and the depth of their shadow is neither intensified nor diminished; they do appear indeed sometimes slightly darker and sometimes slightly brighter, according as the sun's rays fall upon them more or less obliquely; and besides, they are joined to the adjacent parts of the spots with a very gradual connection, so that their boundaries mingle and melt into the surrounding region. But it is quite different with the spots that occupy the brighter parts of the moon's surface, for, just as if they were precipitous mountains with numerous rugged and jagged peaks, they have well-defined boundaries through the sharp contrast of light and shade. [69] Moreover, inside those great spots, certain other areas are seen brighter than the surrounding region, and some of them very bright indeed; but the appearance of these, as well as of the darker areas, is always the same;

there is not change of shape or brightness or depth of shadow; so it becomes a matter of certainty and beyond doubt that their appearance is due to the real dissimilarity of parts, and not to unevenness only in their configuration, changing in different ways the shadows of the same parts according to the variations of their illumination by the sun; this really happens in the case of the other smaller spots occupying the brighter portion of the moon, for day by day they change, increase, decrease, or disappear, inasmuch as they derive their origin only from the shadows of prominences.

But here I feel that some people may be troubled with grave doubt, and perhaps seized with a difficulty so serious as to compel them to feel uncertain about the conclusion just explained and supported by so many phenomena. For if that part of the moon's surface which reflects the sun's rays most brightly is full of innumerable sinuosities, protuberances, and cavities, why does the outer edge looking toward the west when the moon is waxing, and the other half-circumference looking toward the east when the moon is waning, and the whole circle at full moon appear not uneven, rugged, and irregular, but perfectly round and circular, as sharply defined as if marked out with a compass, and without the indentation of any protuberances or cavities? And most remarkably so, because the whole unbroken edge belongs to the brighter part of the moon's surface, which I have said to be full of protuberances and cavities; for not one of the great spots extends quite to the circumference, but all of them are seen to be together away from the edge. Of this phenomenon, which provides a handle for such serious doubts, I produce two causes, and so two solutions of the difficulty.

The first solution I offer is this. If the protuberances and cavities in the body of the moon existed only on the edge of the circle that bounds the hemisphere which we see, then the moon might, or rather would have to, show itself to us with the appearance of a toothed wheel, being bounded with an irregular and uneven circumference. But if instead of a single set of prominences arranged along the actual circumference only, there are many ranges of mountains with their cavities and ruggedness set one behind the other along the extreme edge of the moon (and that too not only in the hemisphere which we see but also in that which is turned away from us, but still near the boundary of the hemisphere), then the eye, viewing them from afar, will not at all be able to detect the differences of prominences and cavities; [70] for the intervals between the mountains situated in the same circle, or in the same chain, are hidden by the jutting forward of other prominences situated in other ranges, especially if the eye of the observer is placed in the same line with the tops of the prominences mentioned. Similarly, on the earth the summits of a number of mountains close together appear situated in one plane, if the spectator is a long way off and standing at the same elevation; and when the sea is rough, the tops of the waves seem to form one plane, although between the billows there is many a gulf and chasm, so deep that not only the hulls, but even the bulwarks, masts, and sails of stately ships are hidden among them. Therefore, within the moon as well as around her circumference, there is a manifold arrangement of prominences and cavities, and the eye, viewing them from a great distance, is placed in nearly the same plane with their summits, and so no one need think it strange that they present themselves to the visual ray which just grazes them as an unbroken line quite free from unevenness.

To this explanation may be added another, namely, that there is around the body of the moon, just as around the earth, an envelope of some substance denser than the rest of the aether, which is sufficient to receive and reflect the sun's rays, although it does not possess so much opaqueness as to be able to prevent our seeing through it— especially when it is not illuminated. That envelope, when illuminated by the sun's rays, renders the body of the moon apparently larger than it really is, and would be able to stop our sight from penetrating to the solid body of the moon, if its thickness were greater. Now, it is of greater thickness around the periphery of the moon— greater, I mean, not in actual thickness, but with reference to our sight-rays, which cut it obliquely. And so it may stop our vision, especially when it is in a state of brightness, and it may conceal the true circumference of the moon on the side towards the sun. This may be understood more clearly from the following figure:

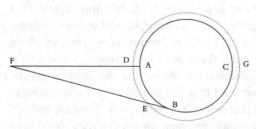

[71] Here, the body of the moon, *ABC,* is surrounded by an enveloping atmosphere, *DEG.* An eye at *F* penetrates to the middle parts of the moon, as at *A,* through a thickness, *DA,* of the atmosphere; but towards the extreme parts a mass of atmosphere of greater depth, *EB,* shuts out its boundary from our sight. An

argument in favor of this is that the illuminated portion of the moon appears of larger circumference than the rest of the globe that is in shadow. Perhaps some will also think that this same cause provides a very reasonable explanation why the greater spots on the moon are not seen to reach the edge of the circumference on any side, although it might be expected that some would be found near the edge as well as elsewhere; it seems credible that there are spots there, but that they cannot be seen because they are hidden by a mass of atmosphere too thick and too bright for the sight to penetrate.

I think it has been sufficiently made clear, from the description of the phenomena given above, that the brighter part of the moon's surface is dotted everywhere with protuberances and cavities. It only remains for me to speak about their size, and to show that the disparities of the earth's surface are far smaller than those of the moon's— smaller, I mean, absolutely, so to speak, and not only smaller in proportion to the size of the globes on which they are. And this is plainly shown thus.

I often observed in various positions of the moon with reference to the sun that some summits within the portion of the moon in shadow appeared illuminated, although at some distance from the boundary of the light. Then by comparing their distance with the complete diameter of the moon, I learned that it sometimes exceeded one-twentieth of the diameter. Suppose the distance to be exactly one-twentieth of the diameter, and let the following diagram represent the moon's globe:

Here, *CAF* is a great circle, *E* its center, and *CF* a diameter, which consequently bears to the diameter of the earth the ratio 2:7; and since the diameter of the earth, according to the most exact observations, contains 7,000 Italian miles, *CF* will be 2,000, *CE* 1,000, and one-twentieth of the whole *CF* will be 100 miles. Also let *CF* be a diameter of the great circle that divides the bright part of the moon from the dark part, [72] for owing to the very great distance of the sun from the moon this circle does not differ sensibly from a great

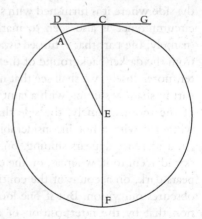

one; let the distance of *A* from point *C* be one-twentieth of that diameter; let the radius *EA* be drawn, and let it be extended to cut the tangent line *GCD* (which represents a light ray) at point *D*. Then the arc *CA*, or the straight line *CD*, will be 100 of such units, and *CE* is 1,000. But the sum of the squares of *CD* and *CE* is 1,010,000, and the square of *ED* is equal to this; thus, the whole *ED* will be more than 1,004, and *AD* will be more than four of such units since *CE* was 1,000. Therefore, the height of *AD* on the moon, which represents a summit reaching up to the sun's ray *GCD* and separated from the extremity *C* by the distance *CD*, is more than four Italian miles. But on the earth there are no mountains that reach to the perpendicular height of even one mile. We are therefore left to conclude that it is clear that the prominences on the moon are loftier than those on the earth.

I wish in this place to assign the cause of another lunar phenomenon well worthy of notice. This phenomenon was observed by me not lately, but many years ago, and it has been pointed out to some of my intimate friends and pupils, explained, and assigned to its true cause. Yet since the observation of it is rendered easier and more vivid by the help of a spyglass, I have considered that it would not be unsuitably introduced in this place. I wish to introduce it chiefly in order that the connection and resemblance between the moon and the earth may appear more plainly.

When the moon, both before and after conjunction, is found not far from the sun, not only does its globe show itself to our sight on the side where it is furnished with shining horns, but a slight and faint circumference is also seen to mark out the circle of the dark part (namely, the part that is turned away from the sun), and to separate it from the darker background of the sky. Now, if we examine the matter more closely, we shall see that not only is the extreme edge of the part in shadow shining with a faint brightness, but that the entire face of the moon (namely, the side that does not feel the sun's glare) is whitened with a not-inconsiderable light. At first glance only a fine circumference appears shining, on account of the darker part of the sky adjacent to it; whereas, on the contrary, the rest of the surface appears dark, on account of the contiguity of the shining horns, which obscures our vision. But if one looks at the moon from such a position that by the interposition of a distant roof, chimney, or some other object the shining horns are hidden and the rest of the lunar globe is left exposed to one's view, [73] then one will find that this part of the moon (although deprived of sunlight) also gleams with considerable light, and particularly so if the gloom of the night has already deepened from the absence of the sun; for with a darker background the same light appears brighter. Moreover, it is found that this secondary brightness of the moon, as I may call it, is greater in proportion as the moon is less distant from the sun, and that it abates more and more in proportion to the moon's distance from that body; thus, after the first quarter and before the end of the second it is found to be weak and very faint, even if it is observed in a darker sky; whereas, at an angular distance of sixty degrees or less, even during twilight, it is wonderfully bright, so bright indeed that, with the help of a good spyglass, the great spots may be distinguished in it.

This strange brightness has presented no small perplexity to philosophical minds; and some have mentioned one thing, some another, as the cause to be alleged for it. Some have said that it is the inherent and natural glow of the moon; some that it is imparted to that body by the planet Venus, or, as others maintain, by all the stars; while some have said that it comes from the sun, whose rays find a way through the solid mass of the moon. But statements of this kind are disproved without much difficulty and convincingly demonstrated to be false.

In fact, if this kind of light were the moon's own, or were contributed by the stars, the moon would retain it, particularly in eclipses, and would show it then, when she is in an unusually dark sky. But this is contrary to experience since the brightness that is seen on the moon in eclipses is far less intense, being somewhat reddish and almost copper-colored, whereas this is brighter and whiter. Moreover, the brightness seen during an eclipse is changeable and shifting, for it wanders over the face of the moon in such a way that the part near the circumference of the circle of shadow cast by the earth is bright, but the rest of the moon is always seen to be dark. From this circumstance we understand without hesitation that this brightness is due to the proximity of the sun's rays coming into contact with some denser region that surrounds the moon as an envelope; owing to this contact a sort of dawn-light is diffused over the neighboring regions of the moon, just as twilight spreads in the morning and evening on the earth. But I will treat more fully of this matter in my book *On the System of the World*.

On the other hand, to assert that this sort of light is imparted to the moon by the planet Venus is so childish as to be undeserving of an answer. For who is so ignorant as not to understand that at conjunction and within an angular distance of sixty degrees it is quite impossible for the part of the moon turned away from the sun to be seen by the planet Venus?

However, that this light is derived from the sun penetrating with its light the solid mass of the moon, and rendering it luminous, is equally untenable. For then this light would never lessen, since a hemisphere of the moon is always illuminated by the sun, except at the moment of a lunar eclipse; but in reality it quickly decreases while the moon [74] is drawing near to the end of her first quarter, and when she has passed her first quarter it becomes quite dull.

Now, since this kind of secondary brightness is not inherent in and characteristic of the moon, nor borrowed from the sun or any other heavenly body, and since there now remains in the whole universe no other body whatever except the earth, what, pray, must we think? What must we propose? Shall we propose that the body of the moon, or some other dark and opaque body, receives light from the earth? What is so strange about that? Look: the earth, with fair and grateful exchange, pays back to the moon an illumination like that which it receives from the moon nearly the whole time during the darkest gloom of night. Let me explain the matter more clearly.

At conjunction, when the moon occupies a position between the sun and the earth, the moon is illuminated by the sun's rays on her half towards the sun and turned away from the earth, and the other half facing the earth is covered with darkness and so does not illuminate the earth's surface in any way. When the moon has separated slightly from the sun, straightaway she is partly illuminated on the half directed towards us; she turns towards us a slender silvery crescent and illuminates the earth slightly. The sun's illumination increases upon the moon as she approaches her first quarter, and the reflection of that light increases on the earth. Next, the brightness of the moon extends beyond the semicircle, and our nights grow brighter. Then the entire face of the moon looking towards the earth is irradiated with the most intense brightness by the sun, which happens when the sun and moon are on opposite sides of the earth; then far and wide the surface of the earth shines with the flood of moonlight. After this the moon, now waning, sends out less powerful beams, and the earth is illuminated less powerfully. Finally, the moon draws near her first position of conjunction with the sun, and forthwith black night invades the earth. In such a cycle the moonlight gives us each month alternations of brighter and fainter illumination. But the benefit of her light to the earth is balanced and repaid by the benefit of the light of the earth to her; for while the moon is found near the sun about the time of conjunction, she has in front of her the entire surface of that hemisphere of the earth which is exposed to the sun and is vividly illuminated with his beams, and so she receives light reflected from the earth. Owing to such reflection, the hemisphere of the moon nearer to us, though deprived of sunlight, appears of considerable brightness. Again, when removed from the sun by a quadrant, the moon sees only one-half of the earth's illuminated hemisphere (namely the western half), for the other (the eastern) is covered with the shades of night; the moon is then less brightly illuminated by the earth, and accordingly that secondary light appears fainter to us. But if you imagine the moon to be set on the opposite side of the earth to the sun, she will see the hemisphere of the earth, now between the moon and the sun, quite dark, and steeped in the gloom of night; if, therefore, an eclipse should accompany such a position of the moon, [75] she will receive no light at all, being deprived of the illumination of the sun and earth together. In any other position with regard to the earth and the sun, the moon receives more or less light by reflection from the earth, according as she sees a greater or smaller portion of the hemisphere of the earth illuminated by the sun; for such a law is observed between these two globes, that at whatever times the earth is most highly illuminated by the moon, at those times, on the contrary, the moon is least illuminated by the earth; and vice versa.

Let these few words on this subject suffice in this place. I will consider it more fully in my *System of the World*. There, by very many arguments and experiments, it is shown that there is a very strong reflection of the sun's light from the earth, for the benefit of those who urge that the earth must be excluded from the dance of the stars, chiefly for the reason that it has neither motion nor light. For I will prove that the earth has motion, and surpasses the moon in brightness, and is not the place where the dull refuse of the universe has settled down; and I will support these conclusions by countless arguments taken from natural phenomena.

[§1.5] Hitherto I have spoken of the observations which I have made concerning the moon's body. Now I will briefly announce the phenomena that have been, as yet, seen by me with reference to the fixed stars. And first of all the following fact is worthy of consideration.

The stars, fixed as well as wandering, when seen with a spyglass, by
no means appear to be increased in magnitude in the same proportion
as other objects, and the moon herself, gain increase of size. In the
case of the stars such increase appears much less, so that you may consider that a spyglass which (for the sake of illustration) is powerful
enough to magnify other objects one hundred times will scarcely render the stars magnified four or five times. The reason for this is as follows. When stars are viewed with our natural eyesight, they do not
present themselves to us in their bare, real size, but beaming with a
certain vividness, and fringed with sparkling rays, especially when the
night is far advanced; and from this circumstance they appear much
larger than they would if they were stripped of those adventitious
fringes, for the angle which they subtend at the eye is determined not
by the primary disc of the star, but by the brightness that so widely
surrounds it. Perhaps you will understand this most clearly from the
well known circumstance that when stars rise at sunset, in the beginning of twilight they appear very small, although they may be stars of
the first magnitude; and even the planet Venus itself, on any occasion
when it may present itself to view in broad daylight, is so small to see
that it scarcely seems equal to a star of the last magnitude. It is different in the case of other objects, and even of the moon, which,
whether viewed in the light of midday or in the depth of night, always appears of the same size. We conclude, therefore, that [76] the
stars are seen at midnight in uncurtailed glory, but their fringes are of
such a nature that the daylight can cut them off, and not only daylight, but any slight cloud that may be interposed between a star and
the eye of the observer. A dark veil or colored glass has the same effect, for upon placing it between the eye and the stars, all the blaze
that surrounds them leaves them at once. A spyglass also accomplishes
the same result, for it removes from the stars their adventitious and accidental splendors before it enlarges their true globes (if indeed they
are of that shape), and so they seem less magnified than other objects;
for example, a star of the fifth or sixth magnitude seen through a spyglass is shown as of the first magnitude.

The difference between the appearance of the planets and of the
fixed stars seems also deserving of notice. The planets present their
bodies perfectly delineated and round, and appear as so many little
moons, completely illuminated and of a globular shape. However, the
fixed stars do not look to the naked eye bounded by a circular periphery, but rather like blazes of light, shooting out beams on all sides and

very sparkling; and with a spyglass they appear of the same shape as
when they are viewed by simply looking at them, but so much larger
that a star of the fifth or sixth magnitude seems to equal the Dog Star,
the largest of all the fixed stars.

Beyond the stars of the sixth magnitude, you will behold through
the spyglass a host of other stars that escape the unassisted eye, so numerous as to be almost beyond belief. You may see more than six
other magnitudes, and the largest of these (which one could call stars
of the seventh magnitude, or of the first magnitude of invisible stars)
appear with the aid of the spyglass larger and brighter than stars of the
second magnitude seen with the unassisted sight. In order that you
may see one or two proofs of the inconceivable manner in which they
are crowded together, I have wanted to give you drawings of two star
clusters, so that from them as specimen you may decide about the rest.

As my first example, I had determined to depict the entire constellation of Orion, but I was overwhelmed by the vast quantity of stars
and by want of
time, and so I have
deferred attempting
this to another oc-
casion; for there are
adjacent to, or scat-
tered among, the
old stars more than
five hundred new
stars within the lim-
its of one or two
degrees. For this
reason I have se-
lected the three stars
in Orion's Belt and
the six in his Sword,
which have long
been well known
groups, and I have
added eighty other
stars recently dis-
covered in their
vicinity, and I have
preserved as exactly

[77] Constellation of Orion's Belt and Sword

as possible the intervals between them. The well-known or old stars, for the sake of distinction, I have depicted of larger size, and I have outlined them with a double line; the others, invisible to the naked eye, I have marked smaller and with one line only. I have also preserved the differences in magnitude as much as I could.

[78] As a second example, I have depicted the six stars of the constellation Taurus, called the Pleiades (I say *six* intentionally, since the seventh is scarcely ever visible). This is a group of stars that appear in the heavens within very narrow limits. Near these there lie more than forty others invisible to the naked eye, no one of which is much more than half a degree off any of the aforesaid six. In my diagram, I have marked only thirty-six stars; I have preserved their intervals, magnitudes, and the distinction between the old and the new stars, just as in the case of the constellation Orion.

Constellation of the Pleiades

The third thing which I have observed is the essence or substance of the Milky Way. By the aid of a spyglass anyone may behold this in a manner which so distinctly appeals to the senses that all the disputes which have tormented philosophers through so many ages are exploded at once by the indubitable evidence of our eyes, and we are freed from wordy disputes upon this subject. In fact, the galaxy is nothing but a mass of innumerable stars planted together in clusters. For upon whatever part of it you direct the spyglass, straightaway a vast crowd of stars presents itself to view; many of them are tolerably large and extremely bright, but the number of small ones is quite beyond determination.

That milky brightness, like the brightness of a white cloud, is seen not only in the Milky Way, but also in several spots of a similar color that shine here and there in the heavens. If you turn the spyglass upon any of them, you will find a cluster of stars packed close together. [79] Furthermore—and you will be more surprised at this—the stars that

have been called by every one of the astronomers up to this day
nebulous are groups of small stars set thick together in a wonderful
way. Although each star escapes our sight on account of its smallness,
or of its immense distance from us, from the commingling of their
rays there arises that brightness which has hitherto been believed to
be the denser part of the heavens, able to reflect the rays of the stars
or the sun.

I have observed some of these, and I wish to reproduce the star clusters of two of these nebulas. First you have a diagram of the nebula
called Orion's Head, in which I have counted twenty-one stars. The
second cluster contains the nebula called Praesepe, which is not a single star but a mass of more than forty small stars; besides the two Aselli,
I have marked thirty-six stars, arranged as in the following diagram.

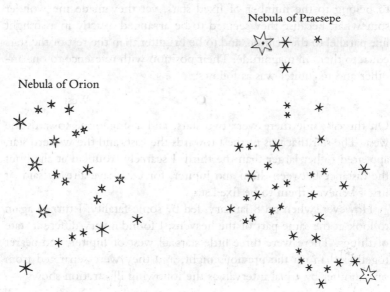

Nebula of Praesepe

Nebula of Orion

[§1.6] I have now finished my brief account of the observations
which I have thus far made with regard to the moon, the fixed stars,
and the galaxy. There remains the matter that seems to me to deserve
to be considered the most important in this work. That is, I should
disclose and publish to the world the occasion of discovering and observing four planets never seen from the beginning of the world up to
our own times, their positions, and the observations made during [80]
the last two months about their movements and their changes of

magnitude. And I summon all astronomers to apply themselves to examine and determine their periodic times, which it has not been permitted me to achieve up to this day owing to the restriction of my time. However, I give them warning again that they will need a very accurate spyglass, such as I have described at the beginning of this account, so that they may not approach such an inquiry to no purpose.

On the seventh day of January of the present year, 1610, at the first hour of the following night, when I was viewing the constellations of the heavens through a spyglass, the planet Jupiter presented itself to my view. As I had prepared for myself a very excellent instrument, I noticed a circumstance which I had never been able to notice before, owing to want of power in my other spyglass. That is, three little stars, small but very bright, were near the planet. Although I believed them to belong to the number of fixed stars, yet they made me wonder somewhat, because they seemed to be arranged exactly in a straight line parallel to the ecliptic, and to be brighter than the rest of the stars equal to them in magnitude. Their position with reference to one another and to Jupiter was as follows:

East   *   *   **O**   *   West

On the east side there were two stars, and a single one towards the west. The star that was furthest towards the east, and the western star, appeared rather larger than the third. I scarcely troubled at all about the distance between them and Jupiter, for, as I have already said, at first I believed them to be fixed stars.

However, when on 8 January, led by some fatality, I turned again to look at the same part of the heavens, I found a very different state of things. There were three little stars all west of Jupiter, and nearer together than on the previous night; and they were separated from one another by equal intervals as the following illustration shows:

East   **O**   *   *   *   West

At this point, although I gave no thought at all to the fact that the stars appeared closer to one another, yet I began to wonder how Jupiter could one day be found to the east of all the aforesaid fixed stars when the day before it had been west of two of them. And forthwith I wondered whether the planet might have been moving with direct motion, contrary to the calculation of astronomers, and so might have passed those stars by its own proper motion. I therefore waited for the next night with the most intense longing, but I was disappointed in my hope, for the sky was covered with clouds in every direction.

[81] But on 10 January the stars appeared in the following position with regard to Jupiter:

East　　★　★　O　　　　West

There were only two, and both on the east side of Jupiter, the third, as I thought, being hidden by the planet. They were situated, just as before, exactly in the same straight line with Jupiter, and along the zodiac. After seeing this, I understood that the corresponding changes of position could not by any means belong to Jupiter. Moreover, I knew that the stars I saw had always been the same, for there were no others either in front or behind, within a great distance along the zodiac. Finally, changing from perplexity to amazement, I became certain that the observed interchange of position was due not to Jupiter but to the said stars. Thus, I thought that henceforth they ought to be observed with more attention and precision.

Accordingly, on 11 January I saw an arrangement of the following kind:

East　★　★　　　O　　　　West

That is, there were only two stars to the east of Jupiter, the nearer of which was three times as far from it as from the star further to the east; and the star furthest to the east was nearly twice as large as the other one. But on the previous night they had appeared nearly of equal magnitude. I therefore concluded, and decided unhesitatingly, that there were three stars in the heavens moving around Jupiter, like Venus and Mercury around the sun. This was finally established as clear as daylight by numerous other subsequent observations. These observations also established that there are not only three, but four, wandering sidereal bodies performing their revolutions around Jupiter. The following account will report on the observations of these changes of position made with more exactness on succeeding nights. I have also measured the intervals between them with the spyglass, in the manner already explained. Besides this, I have given the times of observation, especially when several were made in the same night, for the revolutions of these planets are so swift that an observer may generally get differences of position every hour.

On 12 January at the first hour of the next night, I saw these heavenly bodies arranged in this manner:

East　　★　★O　★　　　West

The star furthest to the east was greater than the one furthest to the west, but both were very conspicuous and bright. The distance of each one from Jupiter was two minutes. [82] A third star, certainly not in view before, began to appear at the third hour; it nearly touched Jupiter on the east side and was exceedingly small. They were all arranged in the same straight line, along the ecliptic.

On 13 January, for the first time, four stars were in view in the following position with regard to Jupiter:

East   ⋆   **O**   ⋆   ⋆   ⋆   West

There were three to the west, and one to the east. They made almost a straight line, but the middle star of those to the west deviated a little from the straight line towards the north. The star furthest to the east was at a distance of two minutes from Jupiter. There were intervals of only one minute between Jupiter and the nearest star, and between the stars themselves, west of Jupiter. All the stars appeared of the same size, and though small they were very brilliant and far outshone the fixed stars of the same magnitude.

On 14 January the weather was cloudy.

On 15 January at the third hour of the night, the four stars were in a state with reference to Jupiter depicted in the next diagram:

East   **O**   ⋆   ⋆   ⋆   ⋆   West

All were to the west and arranged almost in the same straight line; but the star that counted third from Jupiter was raised a little to the north. The nearest to Jupiter was the smallest of all; the rest appeared successively larger. The intervals between Jupiter and the three nearest stars were all successively equal and of the magnitude of two minutes each; but the star furthest to the west was four minutes distant from the star nearest to it. They were very brilliant, and not at all twinkling, and such they have always appeared both before and since. But at the seventh hour there were only three stars, presenting with Jupiter an appearance of the following kind:

East   **O**   ⋆   ⋆   ⋆   West

They were, that is to say, in the same straight line to a hair. The nearest to Jupiter was very small and distant from the planet three minutes; the distance of the second from this one was one minute; and of the third from the second four minutes and thirty seconds. But after another hour the two middle stars were still nearer, for they were only thirty seconds, or less, apart.

[83] On 16 January at the first hour of the night, I saw three stars arranged in this order:

East   ★ O ★   ★   West

Jupiter was between two of them that were at a distance of forty seconds from the planet on either side, and the third was west of Jupiter at a distance of eight minutes. The stars near to Jupiter appeared brighter than the star further off, but not larger.

On 17 January at thirty minutes after sunset, the configuration was of this kind:

East   ★   O   ★   West

There was only one star to the east, at a distance of three minutes from Jupiter; to the west likewise there was only one star, distant eleven minutes from Jupiter. The star on the east appeared twice as large as the star to the west; and there were no more than these two. But four hours later, that is, at almost the fifth hour, a third star began to emerge on the east side, which I think before its appearance had been joined with the former of the two other stars. The position was this:

East   ★ ★   O   ★   West

The middle star was very near indeed to the star on the east, namely only twenty seconds from it; and it was a little towards the south of the straight line drawn through the two outermost stars and Jupiter.

On 18 January at twenty minutes after sunset, the appearance was such as this:

East   ★   O   ★   West

The star to the east was larger than the western one, and it was at a distance from Jupiter of eight minutes, the western one being at a distance of ten minutes.

On 19 January at the second hour of the night, the relative position of the stars was such as this:

East   ★   O   ★   ★   West

That is, there were three stars exactly in a straight line with Jupiter, one to the east at a distance of six minutes from Jupiter. Between Jupiter and the first star to the west, there was an interval of five minutes. This star was four minutes off the other one more to the west. At that time I was doubtful whether or not there was a star between the star to the east and Jupiter, but so very close to Jupiter as almost to touch the planet. But at the fifth hour I saw this star distinctly, [84] by that time occupying exactly the middle position between Jupiter and the eastern star, so that the configuration was thus:

East   ★ ★ **O**   ★ ★   West

Moreover, the star that had just come into view was very small. But at the sixth hour it was nearly as large as the rest.

On 20 January at one hour and fifteen minutes, the arrangement was like this:

East   ★ **O** ★ ★   West

There were three stars, so small as scarcely to be visible. Their distances from Jupiter, and from one another, were not more than one minute. I was doubtful whether on the western side there were two stars or three. At about the sixth hour, they were grouped in this way:

East   ★   **O**   ★ ★   West

The eastern star was twice as far away from Jupiter as before, that is two minutes. On the western side, the star in the middle was distant from Jupiter forty seconds, and from the star still further to the west twenty seconds. Finally, at the seventh hour, three stars were seen on the western side:

East   ★   **O** ★   ★ ★   West

The star nearest to Jupiter was distant from the planet twenty seconds. Between this one and the star furthest to the west there was an interval of forty seconds. But between these another star was in view slightly southward of them, and not more than ten seconds off the most westerly star.

On 21 January at thirty minutes, there were three stars on the east side; they and Jupiter were at equal distances apart:

East   ★ ★ ★ **O**   ★   West

The intervals were estimated to be fifty seconds each. There was also one star on the west, distant four minutes from Jupiter. The star on the east side nearest to Jupiter was the smallest of all.

On January 22 at the second hour, the arrangement of the stars was this:

East   ★   **O** ★★   ★   West

There was an interval of five minutes from the star on the east to Jupiter, [85] and from Jupiter to the star furthest to the west seven minutes. The two interior stars on the western side were forty seconds apart, and the star nearer to Jupiter was one minute from the planet. The inner stars were smaller than the outer ones, but they were situated all in the same straight line, along the zodiac, except that the middle of the three western stars was slightly to the south of it. However, at the sixth hour of the night, they appeared in this position:

East   ★   **O**   ★   ★   West

The star on the east was very small, at a distance from Jupiter of five minutes, as before. But the three stars on the west were separated by equal distances from Jupiter and from each other; and the intervals were nearly one minute and twenty seconds each. The star nearest Jupiter appeared smaller than the other two on the same side, but they all appeared arranged exactly in the same straight line.

On 23 January at forty minutes after sunset, the configuration of the stars was nearly after this fashion:

East   ★   ★ **O**   ★   West

There were three stars with Jupiter in a straight line along the zodiac, as they have always been. Two were on the east of the planet, one on the west. The star furthest to the east was seven minutes from the next one; this star was two minutes forty seconds from Jupiter; and the star on the west was three minutes twenty seconds from Jupiter. They were all of nearly the same size. But at the fifth hour the two stars that had been previously near Jupiter were no longer visible, being, I suppose, hidden behind Jupiter; and the appearance was this:

East   ★   **O**   West

On 24 January three stars, all on the east side, were visible and almost, but not quite, in the same straight line with Jupiter, for the star in the middle was slightly to the south of it:

East   ★   ★ ★ **O**   West

The star nearest to Jupiter was two minutes from it; the next was thirty seconds from that star; and the third was nine minutes further still. They were all very bright. But at the sixth hour only two stars presented themselves, in this position:

East   ★   ★   **O**   West

namely, in the same straight line with Jupiter exactly. [86] The distance of the nearest to it had lengthened to three minutes, and the next was eight minutes further off. Unless I am mistaken, the two stars previously observed in the middle had come together and appeared as one.

On 25 January at one hour and forty minutes, the stars were grouped thus:

East   ★   ★   O   West

There were only two stars on the east side, and they were rather large. The star furthest to the east was 5 minutes from the star in the middle, and it was six minutes from Jupiter.

On 26 January at forty minutes, the relative positions of the stars were thus:

East   ★   ★   O   ★   West

Three stars were in view, of which two were east and the third west of Jupiter. This third star was three minutes from the planet; on the east side, the star in the middle was at a distance of five minutes and twenty seconds, and the further star was six minutes beyond. They were arranged in a straight line and were of the same size. At the fifth hour the arrangement was nearly the same, with this difference only, that the fourth star was emerging on the east side near Jupiter. It was smaller than the rest and was then at a distance of thirty seconds from Jupiter; but it was raised a little above the straight line towards the north, as the following figure shows:

East   ★   ★   ˙O   ★   West

On 27 January at one hour after sunset, a single star was in view, on the east side of Jupiter, in this position:

East   ★   O   West

It was very small and at a distance of seven minutes from Jupiter.

On 28 and 29 January, owing to the interference of clouds, I could make no observation.

On 30 January at the first hour of the night, the stars were in view, arranged in the following way:

East   ★   O   ★ ★   West

There was one star on the east side, at a distance of two minutes and thirty seconds from Jupiter; and there were two stars on the west, of which the one nearer to Jupiter was three minutes off the planet, and the other star one minute further. The outer stars and Jupiter were in the same straight line; but the star in the middle was a little above it to the north. The star furthest to the west was smaller than the rest.

[87] On the last day of the month, at the second hour, two stars on the east side were visible, and one on the west:

East   ★ ★   O   ★   West

Of the stars east of the planet, the one in the middle was two minutes and twenty seconds from Jupiter, and the star further to the east was thirty seconds from the middle star; the star on the west was ten minutes from Jupiter. They were in the same straight line nearly, except that the star on the east nearest to Jupiter was raised a little towards the north. At the fourth hour, the two stars on the east were even closer together, for they were only twenty seconds apart, thus:

East   ★★   O   ★   West

In these two observations, the western star appeared rather small.

On 1 February at the second hour of the night, the arrangement was the following;

East   ★   ★ O   ★   West

The star furthest to the east was six minutes from Jupiter, and the western star eight minutes. On the east side, there was a very small star at a distance of twenty seconds from Jupiter. They made a perfectly straight line.

On 2 February the stars were seen arranged thus:

East   ★   O   ★   ★   West

There was only one on the east, at a distance of six minutes from Jupiter, which was four minutes from the nearest star on the west; and between this star and the one further to the west there was an interval of eight minutes. They were in the same straight line exactly and were nearly of the same magnitude. But at the seventh hour there were four stars, two on each side of Jupiter:

East   ★   ★ O   ★   ★   West

Of these stars, the most easterly was four minutes from the next; this star was one minute forty seconds from Jupiter, which was six minutes from the nearest star on the west; and this one was eight minutes from the star further to the west. And they were all again in the same straight line, drawn along the zodiac.

On 3 February at the seventh hour, the stars were arranged in the following way:

East   ★ O ★   ★ West

The star on the east was one minute and thirty seconds from Jupiter; the nearest star on the west, two minutes; [88] and there was a long distance, ten minutes, from this star to the star further to the west. They were exactly in the same straight line and of equal magnitude.

On 4 February at the second hour, four stars attended Jupiter, two on the east and two on the west, arranged in one perfectly straight line, as in the following figure:

East   ★ ★O   ★   ★ West

The star furthest to the east was three minutes from the next; this one was forty seconds from Jupiter, which was four minutes from the nearest star on the west; and this one was six minutes from the star further on the west. In magnitude they were almost equal, but the star nearest to Jupiter was rather smaller in appearance than the rest. Then at the seventh hour, the eastern stars were only thirty seconds apart:

East   ★★ O   ★   ★ West

Jupiter was two minutes from the nearest star on the east and four minutes from the next star on the west; and this one was three minutes from the star further to the west. They were all equal in magnitude and arranged in a straight line drawn along the ecliptic.

On 5 February the sky was cloudy.

On 6 February only two stars appeared, with Jupiter between them, as is seen in the following figure:

East   ★ O ★   West

The star on the east was two minutes from Jupiter, and the one on the west three minutes. They were in the same straight line with Jupiter and equal in magnitude.

On 7 February there were two stars by the side of Jupiter, both of them on the east of the planet, arranged in this manner:

East   ★ ★ O   West

The intervals between the stars and from Jupiter were equal, namely, one minute; and a straight line would go through them and the center of Jupiter.

On 8 February at the first hour, there were three stars, all on the east side of Jupiter, as in this diagram:

East   * *   *   **O**   West

The nearest to Jupiter, a rather small one, was one minute and twenty seconds from the planet; the middle one was four minutes from this star and was rather large; the star furthest to the east, a very small one, was twenty seconds from the second star. It was doubtful whether the one nearest to Jupiter [89] was a single star or two starlets, for sometimes it seemed that there was another star next to it further east, extraordinarily small and only ten seconds from it. They were all situated on a straight line drawn along the zodiac. At the third hour, the star nearest to Jupiter was almost touching the planet, for it was only ten seconds from it; but the others had gone further off, for the middle one was six minutes from Jupiter. Finally, at the fourth hour, the star that was previously the nearest to Jupiter joined with the planet and disappeared.

On 9 February at thirty minutes, there were two stars on the east side of Jupiter and one on the west, in an arrangement like this:

East   *   *   **O**   *   West

The star furthest to the east, which was a rather small one, was four minutes from the next star. The star in the middle was larger and seven minutes from Jupiter. And Jupiter was four minutes from the western star, which was a small one.

On 10 February at one hour and thirty minutes, a pair of stars, very small, and both on the east side of the planet, were visible, in the following configuration:

East   *   *   **O**   West

The further star was ten minutes from Jupiter; the nearer, twenty seconds; and they were in the same straight line. But at the fourth hour the star nearest to Jupiter no longer appeared, and the other seemed so diminished that it could scarcely be kept in sight, although the atmosphere was quite clear; it was further from Jupiter than before, since its distance was now twelve minutes.

On 11 February at the first hour, there were two stars on the east and one on the west:

East *   *   O   *   West

The western star was four minutes from Jupiter; the star on the east nearest to the planet was likewise four minutes from Jupiter; and the star further to the east was eight minutes from this one. They were fairly clear to view and in the same straight line. But at the third hour, the fourth star was visible near to Jupiter on the east, less in magnitude than the rest, separated from Jupiter by a distance of thirty seconds, and slightly to the north out of the straight line drawn through the rest:

East   * * *O   *   West

They were all very bright and extremely distinct. At the fifth hour and a half, the star on the east nearest to Jupiter had moved further away from the planet, [90] and was occupying a position midway between the planet and the neighboring star further to the east. They were all in the same straight line exactly, and of the same magnitude, as may be seen in the following diagram:

East   * * O   *   West

On 12 February at forty minutes, a pair of stars on the east and likewise a pair on the west were near the planet:

East   *   * O *   *   West

The star on the east further removed from Jupiter was at a distance of ten minutes, and the further of the stars on the west was eight minutes off. They were both fairly distinct. The other two were very near to Jupiter and very small, especially the star to the east, which was forty seconds from Jupiter; the distance of the western star was one minute. But at the fourth hour, the star that was nearest to Jupiter on the east was no longer visible.

On 13 February at thirty minutes, two stars were visible in the east and two also in the west:

East   *   * O   * *   West

The star on the east near Jupiter was fairly distinct; its distance from the planet was two minutes. The star further to the east was less noticeable; it was four minutes from the other. Of the stars on the west, the one furthest from Jupiter, which was very distinct, was parted from the planet by four minutes. Between this star and Jupiter intervened a small star close to the most westerly star, being not more than thirty seconds off. They were all in the same straight line, corresponding exactly to the direction of the ecliptic.

On 15 February (for on the 14th the sky was covered with clouds) at the first hour, the position of the stars was thus:

East　　　★　★★　O　　　　　West

That is, there were three stars on the east, but none were visible on the west. The star on the east nearest to Jupiter was fifty seconds from the planet; the next was twenty seconds from this star; and the furthest to the east was two minutes from the second star. The third star was larger than the others, and those nearer to Jupiter were very small. Then about the fifth hour, only one of the stars that had been near to Jupiter was to be seen; its distance from Jupiter was thirty seconds. The distance of the star furthest to the east from Jupiter had increased, for it was then four minutes:

East　　★　　★ O　　　　West

But at the sixth hour, besides the two [91] situated as just described on the east, one star was visible towards the west, very small, at a distance of two minutes from Jupiter:

East　　★　　★ O　　★　　　West

On February 16, at the sixth hour, their places were arranged as follows:

East　★　　　O　★　★　　　West

That is, the star on the east was seven minutes from Jupiter, which was five minutes from the next star on the west, and this was three minutes from the remaining star still further to the west. They were all approximately of the same magnitude, rather bright, and in the same straight line, corresponding accurately to the direction of the zodiac.

On 17 February at the first hour, two stars were in view, one on the east, three minutes from Jupiter; the other on the west, ten minutes distant:

East　　　★　O　　　　★　West

The latter was somewhat smaller than the star on the east. But at the sixth hour, the eastern star was nearer to Jupiter, being at a distance of

fifty seconds, and the western star was further off, namely twelve minutes. At both observations, they were in the same straight line with
Jupiter, and were both rather small, especially the eastern star in the
second observation.

On 18 February at the first hour, three stars were in view, of
which two were on the west and one on the east:

East   ⋆   **O**   ⋆   ⋆   West

The distance of the eastern star from Jupiter was three minutes, and of
the nearest star on the west two minutes; the remaining star, still further to the west, was eight minutes from the middle star. They were
all in the same straight line exactly, and of about the same magnitude.
Then at the second hour, the stars nearest to the planet were at equal
distances from Jupiter, for the western star was now also three minutes
from the planet. At the sixth hour, the fourth star was visible between
the star on the east and Jupiter, in the following configuration:

East   ⋆   ⋆   **O**   ⋆   ⋆   West

The star furthest to the east was three minutes from the next; this one
was one minute and fifty seconds from Jupiter, which was three minutes from the next star on the west; and the latter was seven minutes
from the star still further to the west. They were about equal in magnitude, except that the star on the east nearest to Jupiter was a little
smaller than the rest. And they were all in the same straight line parallel to the ecliptic.

[92] On 19 February at forty minutes, only two stars were in view,
west of Jupiter, rather large, and arranged in the same straight line
with Jupiter, in the direction of the ecliptic:

East   **O**   ⋆   ⋆   West

The nearer star was seven minutes from Jupiter and six minutes from
the star further to the west.

On 20 February the sky was cloudy.

On 21 February at one hour and thirty minutes, three stars, rather
small, were in view, placed thus:

East   ⋆   **O**   ⋆   ⋆   West

The star to the east was two minutes from Jupiter, which was three
minutes from the next on the west; and this one was seven minutes
from the star further on the west. They were exactly in the same
straight line parallel to the ecliptic.

On 25 February at one hour and thirty minutes (for on the three previous nights the sky was overcast), three stars appeared:

East   ★ ★ O ★   West

Two were on the east, four minutes apart, the same as the distance of the nearer star from Jupiter; on the west there was one star at a distance of two minutes from Jupiter. They were exactly in the same straight line in the direction of the ecliptic.

On 26 February at thirty minutes, only a pair of stars was present:

East   ★   O   ★   West

One was on the east, ten minutes from Jupiter; the other was on the west, at a distance of six minutes. The eastern star was slightly smaller than the western. But at the fifth hour, three stars were visible:

East   ★   O ★   ★   West

Besides the two already mentioned, a third star was in view, on the west, near Jupiter, very small; it had previously been hidden behind Jupiter, and it was now one minute from the planet. The star on the east was seen to be further off than before, being at a distance of eleven minutes from Jupiter. On this night, for the first time, I decided to observe the progression of Jupiter and its adjacent planets along the zodiac, by reference to some fixed star; for there was a fixed star in view, [93] eastwards of Jupiter, at a distance of eleven minutes from the eastern planet, and a little to the south, in the following manner:

East ★   O ★   ★   West

★ fixed star

On 27 February at one hour and four minutes, the stars appeared in the following configuration:

East ★   ★ O   ★   ˌ★   West

★ fixed star

The star furthest to the east was ten minutes from Jupiter; the next was near Jupiter, being at a distance of thirty seconds from the planet; the next star was on the western side, at a distance of two minutes and thirty seconds from Jupiter; and the star further to the west was one minute from this. The two stars near to Jupiter appeared small, especially the one on the east; the outer stars were very bright, particularly the one on the west. They made a straight line in the direction of the ecliptic exactly. The progression of these planets towards the east was plainly seen by reference to the aforesaid fixed star, for Jupiter and its attendant planets were nearer to it, as may be seen in the fig ure. At the fifth hour, the star on the east near to Jupiter was one minute from the planet.

On 28 February at the first hour, only two stars were visible, one on the east at a distance of nine minutes from Jupiter, and another on the west at a distance of two minutes. They were both rather bright, and in the same straight line with Jupiter. Moreover, a straight line drawn from the fixed star perpendicular to this straight line fell upon the planet on the east, as in this figure:

East   ★   O   ★   West

★ fixed star

But at the fifth hour a third star was seen at a distance of two minutes from Jupiter on the east, in the position shown in the figure:

East   ★   ★ O   ★   West

On 1 March at forty minutes, four stars, all on the east, were seen. The one nearest to Jupiter was two minutes from it; the next was one minute from this; the third was twenty seconds from the second, and was brighter than the others; [94] and the one still further to the east was four minutes from the third, and was smaller than the others. They formed a line that was almost straight; only the third from Jupiter was slightly above the line. The fixed star formed an equilat-eral triangle with Jupiter and the most easterly planet, as in the fol-lowing figure:

East   ★   ★ ★ ★   O   West

★ fixed star

On 2 March at forty minutes, three planets were in attendance, two on the east and one on the west, in the configuration shown in this diagram:

East ★ ★   O   ★   West

★ fixed star

The one furthest to the east was seven minutes from Jupiter and thirty seconds from the next; the one on the west was separated from Jupiter by an interval of two minutes. The outer ones were brighter and larger than the middle one, which appeared very small. The one furthest to the east seemed to be raised a little towards the north, out of the straight line drawn through the others and Jupiter. The fixed star already mentioned was at a distance of eight minutes from the western planet, along the perpendicular drawn from the same planet to the straight line passing through all the planets, as shown in the figure given.

I have wanted to report these comparisons of the position of Jupiter and its adjacent planets to a fixed star so that anyone may be able to understand from them that the movements of these planets both in longitude and in latitude agree exactly with the motions derived from tables.

These are my observations of the four Medicean Planets, recently discovered for the first time by me. Although I am not yet able to deduce by calculation from these observations the orbits of these bodies, I may be allowed to make some statements based upon them, well worthy of attention. In the first place, since they are sometimes behind and sometimes before Jupiter at like distances and deviate from this planet towards the east and towards the west only within very narrow limits of divergence, and since they accompany this planet when its motion is retrograde as well as when it is direct, no one can doubt that they perform their revolutions around this planet while at the same time they all together accomplish orbits of twelve years' duration around the center of the world. Moreover, they revolve in unequal circles, which is evidently the conclusion [95] from the fact that I never saw two planets in conjunction when their distance from Jupiter was great, whereas near Jupiter two, three, and sometimes all four have been found closely packed together. Furthermore, it may be deduced that the revolutions of the planets that describe smaller circles around Jupiter are more rapid, for the satellites nearer to Jupiter are often seen in the east when the day before they have appeared in the west, and vice versa; also the satellite moving in the greatest orbit seems to me, after carefully weighing the timing of its returning to positions previously noticed, to have a periodic time of half a month.

Additionally, we have a notable and splendid argument to remove the scruple of those who can tolerate the revolution of the planets around the sun in the Copernican system, but are so disturbed by the motion of one moon around the earth (while both accomplish an orbit of a year's length around the sun) that they think this constitution of the universe must be rejected as impossible. For now we have not just one planet revolving around another while both traverse a vast orbit around the sun, but four planets which our sense of sight presents to us circling around Jupiter (like the moon around the earth) while the whole system travels over a mighty orbit around the sun in the period of twelve years.

Lastly, I must not pass over the consideration of the reason why it happens that the Medicean Stars, in performing very small revolutions around Jupiter, seem sometimes more than twice as large as at other times. We can by no means look for an explanation in the mists of the earth's atmosphere, for they appear increased or diminished while the discs of Jupiter and the neighboring fixed stars are seen quite unaltered. It seems altogether untenable that they approach and recede from the earth at the points of their revolutions nearest to and furthest from the earth to such an extent as to account for such great changes, for a strict circular motion can by no means produce those phenomena; and an elliptical motion (which in this case would be almost rectilinear) seems to be both unthinkable and by no means in harmony with the observed phenomena. But I gladly offer the explanation that has occurred to me upon this subject, and I submit it to the judgment and criticism of all true philosophers. It is known that when atmospheric mists intervene, the sun and moon appear larger, but the fixed stars and planets smaller; hence the former luminaries, when near the horizon, are larger than at other times, but stars appear smaller and are frequently scarcely visible; and they are still more diminished if those mists are bathed in light; so stars appear very small by day and in the twilight, but the moon does not appear so, as I have previously remarked. Moreover, it is certain that not only the earth, but also the moon, has its own vaporous sphere enveloping it, [96] for the reasons which I have previously mentioned, and especially for those that shall be stated more fully in my *System;* and we may accordingly decide that the same is true with regard to the rest of the planets; so it seems to be by no means an untenable opinion to place also around Jupiter an atmosphere denser than the rest of the aether, around which, like the moon around the sphere of the elements, the Medicean Planets revolve; then by the interposition of this atmosphere, they appear smaller when they are at apogee; but when in perigee, through the absence or attenuation of that atmosphere, they appear larger. Lack of time prevents me from going further into these matters; my readers may expect further remarks upon these subjects in a short time.

CHAPTER 2

From *Discourse on Bodies in Water* (1612)[1]

[§2.1 Shape vs. Density in Floating and Sinking][2]

[87] Let us not then despise those hints, though very feeble, which after some contemplation reason offers to our intelligence. Let us agree to be taught by Archimedes that any solid body will sink to the bottom in water when its specific gravity is greater than that of water; that it will of necessity float if its specific gravity is less; and that it will rest indifferently in any place under water if its specific gravity is perfectly equal to that of water.

These things explained and proved, I come to consider what the diversity of shape of a given body has to do with its motion and rest. Again, I affirm the following.

The diversity of shapes given to this or that solid cannot in any way be the cause of its absolute sinking or floating.[3] Thus, for example, if a solid shaped into a spherical figure sinks or floats in water, I say that when shaped into any other figure the same solid shall sink or float in the same water; nor can its motion be prevented or taken away by the width or any other feature of the shape.

[88] The width of the shape may indeed retard its velocity of ascent or descent, and more and more according as the said shape is reduced to a greater width and thinness; but I hold it to be impossible that it may be reduced to such a form that the same material be wholly hindered from moving in the same water. In this I have met

---

1. For the historical background, see the Introduction, especially §0.5.
2. Galilei 1890–1909, 4: 87.21–99.12; translated by Thomas Salusbury (1661–65, 2: 426–36); revised by Finocchiaro for this volume.
3. Salusbury (1661–65, 2: 426) labels this proposition "theorem V," and he gives such sequentially numbered labels to other key propositions in this work. Such labeling was retained in Drake's reprint of that translation (Galilei 1960). But there is no such labeling in the original text (Galilei 1890–1909, 4: 63–140). So I follow Drake (1981) in doing without such labeling altogether.

with great opponents who produce some experiments, especially the following: they take a thin board of ebony and a ball of the same wood, and show that the ball in water descends to the bottom, and that if the board is placed lightly upon the water then it is not submerged but floats. They hold, and with the authority of Aristotle they confirm their opinion, that the cause of that floating is the width of the shape, unable by its small weight to pierce and penetrate the resistance of the coarseness of the water, which resistance is readily overcome by the other, spherical shape.

This is the principal point in the present controversy, in which I shall strive to make clear that I am on the right side.

Let us begin by trying to investigate, with the help of exquisite experiments, that the shape does not really alter one bit the descent or ascent of the same solid. We have already demonstrated that the greater or lesser gravity of the solid in relation to the gravity of the medium is the cause of descent or ascent. Whenever we want to test what effect the diversity of shape produces, it is necessary to make the experiment with materials whose gravities do not vary; for if we make use of materials that are different in their specific gravities and we meet with various effects of ascending and descending, we shall always be left uncertain whether in reality that diversity derives solely from the shape or else from the gravity as well. We may remedy this by using only one material that is malleable and easily reducible into every sort of shape. Moreover, it will be an excellent expedient to take a kind of material very similar to water in specific gravity; for such a material, as far as it pertains to the gravity, is indifferent to ascending or descending, and so we easily observe the least difference that derives from the diversity of shape.

Now, to do this, wax is most apt. Besides its incapacity to receiving any sensible alteration from its imbibing water, wax is pliant and [89] the same piece is easily reducible into all shapes. And since its specific gravity is less than that of water by a very inconsiderable amount, by mixing it with some lead filings it is reduced to a gravity exactly equal to that of water.

Let us prepare this material. For example, let us make a ball of wax as big as an orange, or bigger, and let us make it so heavy as to sink to the bottom, but so slightly that by taking out only one grain of lead it returns to the top and by adding one back it sinks to the bottom. Let the same wax afterwards be made into a very broad and thin flake or slab. Then, returning to make the same experiment, you shall see that when placed at the bottom with the grain of lead it shall rest there; that with the grain removed it shall ascend to the surface; and that when the lead is added again it shall dive to the bottom. This same effect shall happen always for all sorts of shapes, regular as well as irregular; nor shall you ever find any that will float without the removal of the grain of lead, or sink to the bottom unless it be added. In short, about the going or not going to the bottom, you shall discover no difference, although indeed you shall about its quickness or slowness; for the wider and more extended shapes move more slowly in diving to the bottom as well as in rising to the top, and the more contracted and compact shapes more speedily. Now I do not know what may be expected from the diversity of shapes, if the most different ones do not produce as much as does a very small grain of lead, when added or removed.

I think I hear some of my adversaries raise a doubt about the experiment I produced. First, they offer to my consideration that the shape, simply as shape and separate from matter, does not have any effect but requires to be conjoined with matter; and furthermore, not with every material, but only with that wherewith it may be able to execute the desired operation. For we see it verified by experience that the acute and sharp angle is more apt to cut than the obtuse, yet always provided that both the one and the other be joined with a material apt to cut, such as, for example, with steel. Therefore, a knife with a fine and sharp edge cuts bread or wood with much ease, which it will not do if the edge be blunt and thick; but he that will instead of steel take wax and mould it into a knife undoubtedly shall never know the effects of sharp and blunt edges, because neither of them [90] will cut, the wax being unable by reason of its flexibility to overcome the hardness of the wood and bread. Now, applying similar reasoning to our purpose, they say that the difference of shape will not show different effects regarding flotation and submersion when conjoined with any kind of matter, but only with those materials that by their gravity are apt to overcome the resistance of the viscosity of the water; thus, he that would choose cork or other light wood (unable through its lightness to overcome the resistance of the coarseness of the water) and from that material should form solids of various shapes, would in vain seek to find out what effect shape has in flotation and submersion; for all would float, and that not through any property of this or that shape, but through the weakness of the material, lacking sufficient gravity as is requisite to overcome and conquer the density and coarseness of the water. It is necessary, therefore, if we would see the effect produced by the diversity of shape, first to choose a material apt by its nature to penetrate the coarseness of the water. For this purpose, they have chosen a material that, being readily reduced into spherical shape, goes to the bottom; and it is ebony, of which they afterwards make a small board or splinter, as thin as a leaf, and show that, when placed upon the surface of the water, it rests there without descending to the bottom; on the other hand, having made a ball of the same wood no smaller than a hazelnut, they show that this does not float but descends. From this experiment they think they may frankly conclude that the width of the shape in the flat board is the cause of its not descending to the bottom, inasmuch as a ball of the same material, no different from the board in anything but in shape, sinks to the bottom in the same water. The reasoning and the experiment have really so much probability and likelihood that it would be no wonder if many should be persuaded by a certain initial appearance and yield credit to them; nevertheless, I think I can show that they are not free from fallacy.

Let us begin, therefore, to examine one by one all the particulars that have been produced. I say that shapes, as simple shapes, not only do not operate in natural things, but neither are they ever separated from corporeal substance. Nor have I ever alleged them to be stripped of sensible matter. Likewise, I also freely admit that in our endeavoring [91] to examine the diversity of effects dependent upon the variety of shapes, it is necessary to apply them to materials that do not obstruct the various operations of those various shapes. And I admit and grant that I should be wrong if I would experiment about the influence of acuteness of edge with a knife of wax, applying it to cut an oak, because there is no acuteness in wax able to cut that very hard wood. But yet such an experiment with this knife would not be besides the purpose to cut curdled milk, or other very yielding matter; indeed, with such materials, wax is more appropriate than steel for finding the diversity depending upon more or less acute angles because that milk is indifferently cut with a razor and with a knife that has a blunt edge. It is necessary, therefore, that regard be had not only to the hardness, solidity, or gravity of the bodies which under diverse shapes are to divide and penetrate some materials, but also to the resistance of the materials to be divided and penetrated. But in making the experiment concerning our controversy, I have chosen a material that penetrates the resistance of the water and in all shapes descends to the bottom, and so my adversaries can charge me with no defect; indeed, I have proposed a more excellent method than they have, inasmuch as I have removed all other causes of descending or not descending to the bottom and retained the sole and pure variety of shapes, demonstrating that the same shapes all descend with the addition of only one grain in weight and return to the surface and float with its removal. It is not true, therefore (returning to the example introduced by them), that I have gone about experimenting on the efficacy of acuteness in cutting with materials unable to cut; rather, I have done so with materials proportioned to our occasion, since they are subjected to no other variation than that alone which depends on the shape being more or less acute.

But let us proceed a little farther. Let us note how needlessly indeed they introduce the consideration that the material chosen ought to be proportionate for the making of our experiment; using the example of cutting, they declare that just as acuteness is insufficient to cut unless it exists in a material that is hard and apt to overcome the resistance of the wood or other material which we intend to cut, so the aptitude of descending or not descending in water can and should be recognized only in those [92] materials that are able to overcome the resistance and conquer the coarseness of the water. On this I say that it is indeed necessary to make a distinction and selection of this or that material on which to impress the shapes for cutting and penetrating this or that body based on whether the solidity or hardness of the said bodies shall be greater or less; but then I add that such distinction, selection, and caution would be superfluous and unprofitable if the body to be cut or penetrated should have no resistance or should not oppose at all the cutting or penetration; and if the knife were to be used in cutting mist or smoke, one of paper would be equally serviceable with one of Damascus steel. And so, because water does not have any resistance against penetration by any solid body, all choice of material is superfluous and needless; and the selection, which I said above to have been well made, of a material similar in gravity to water was made not because it was necessary for overcoming the coarseness of the water, but for overcoming its gravity with which only it resists the sinking of solid bodies; and for what concerns the resistance of the coarseness, if we carefully consider it, we shall find that all solid bodies (those that sink as well as those that float) are indifferently accommodated and apt to bring us to the knowledge of the truth in question. Nor will I be frightened off from believing these conclusions by the experiments that may be produced against me: that although many pieces of wood, cork, clay, and even thin plates of all sorts of stone and metal are ready by means of their natural gravity to move towards the center of the earth, nevertheless they are impotent (either because of their shape, as my adversaries think, or because of their lightness) to break and penetrate the continuity of the parts of the water and to disturb its union, and they continue to float without submerging in the least. Nor, on the other hand, shall I be moved by the authority of Aristotle, who in more than one place affirms the contrary of what experience shows me.

I return, therefore, to assert that there is no solid of such lightness, or of such shape, that being put upon the water does not divide and penetrate its coarseness. Indeed, if anyone with a more perspicacious eye shall return to observe more exactly the thin boards of wood, he shall see part of their thickness to be under water; their lower surface is not the only part that kisses the upper surface of the water, as those of necessity must have believed who have said that such [93] boards are not submerged, not being able to divide the tenacity of the parts of the water. Moreover, he shall see that when the very thin slivers of ebony, stone, or metal float, they not only have broken the continuity of the water, but also are under its surface with all their thickness, and more and more according as the materials are heavier; thus, a thin plate of lead shall be lower than the surface of the surrounding water by at least twelve times the thickness of the plate, and gold shall dive below the level of the water almost twenty times the thickness of the plate, as I shall show anon.

But let us proceed to evince that the water yields and allows itself to be penetrated by the lightest solid; and thereby demonstrate how, even from materials that are not submerged, we may come to know that shape accomplishes nothing about the going or not going to the bottom, given that the water allows itself to be penetrated equally by every shape.

Make a cone or pyramid of cypress, fir, or other wood of similar weight, or of pure wax, and let its height be very great, namely a palm or more; and put it into the water with the base downwards. First, you shall see that it will penetrate the water and will not be at all impeded by the width of the base; nor yet shall it sink all under water, but the part near the vertex shall lie above it. From this it is manifest that such a solid does not refrain from sinking out of an inability to divide the continuity of the water, having already divided it with its broad part, which in the opinion of my adversaries is less apt to make the division. The pyramid being thus positioned, note what part of it is submerged. Then, turn it with the vertex downwards. You shall see that it shall not penetrate the water more than before. Instead, if you observe how far it shall sink, every person expert in geometry may measure that those parts that remain out of the water are equal to a hair in the one as well as in the other experiment. Thus, one may manifestly conclude that the acute shape, which seemed most apt to part and penetrate the water, does not part or penetrate it any more than the large and spacious.

Now, whoever wants to make an easier experiment can take two cylinders of the same material, one long and thin, the other short but very broad; let him put them in water, not sideways but erect and endways. If he diligently measures the parts of the one and the other, he shall see that in each of them the part submerged retains exactly the same ratio to the part out of the water, and that no [94] greater part is submerged of the long and thin one than of the other more spacious and broad, although the latter rests upon a very large surface of water and the former upon a very small one. Therefore, the diversity of shape produces neither ease nor difficulty in parting and penetrating the continuity of water; consequently, it cannot be the cause of sinking or not sinking. One may likewise discover that the variation of shapes does not cause the rising from the bottom of the water towards the surface: take some wax and mix it with a large quantity of lead filings, so that it becomes considerably heavier than water; then make it into a ball and place it at the bottom of the water; then fasten to it as much cork, or other light material, as just suffices to raise it and draw it towards the surface; finally, changing the same wax into a thin plate, or into any other figure, that same cork shall raise it in the same manner to a hair.

This does not silence my antagonists. But they say that the whole argument hitherto made by me matters little to them; and that it serves their purpose to have demonstrated in only one particular case and for a material and a shape of their choice, namely, for a board and ball of ebony, that when placed in water the latter descends to the bottom and the former stays atop floating. The material being the same, and the two bodies differing in nothing but in shape, they affirm that they have with all perspicacity demonstrated and sensibly manifested what they undertook, and lastly, that they have attained their goal. Nevertheless, I believe and think I can demonstrate that the same experiment proves nothing against my conclusion.

First, it is false that the ball descends and the plate does not. For the plate shall also descend if you do to both shapes what the words of our controversy require: that is, if you place them both into the water.

The words were these: "My antagonists are of the opinion that shape would alter solid bodies in regard to the descending or not descending and the ascending or not ascending in the same medium; for example, in the same water, if a solid of spherical shape shall descend to the bottom, being reduced to some other shape it shall not descend. I hold the contrary and affirm that if a solid corporeal body shall go to the bottom when reduced into a spherical shape, or any other, it shall do the same under whatsoever other shape, etc."

But to be in the water means to be placed in the water; and by [95] Aristotle's own definition of place, to be placed implies to be surrounded by the surface of the ambient body; therefore, the two shapes shall be in the water when the surface of the water shall embrace and surround them. But when my adversaries show the board of ebony not descending to the bottom, they put it not into the water but upon the water; there, being held by a certain impediment (as by and by we will show), it is surrounded part by water and part by air. This is contrary to our agreement, which was that the bodies should be in the water, and not part in water and part in air.

This is again made manifest by the fact that the question being debated was about the things that go to the bottom as well as about those that rise from the bottom to float. And who does not see that things placed at the bottom must have water around them?

It is now to be noted that the plate of ebony and the ball, put *into* the water, both sink, but the ball more swiftly and the plate more slowly, and slower and slower according as it is broader and thinner; and the true cause of this slowness is the breadth of the shape. But these plates that descend slowly are the same that float when put lightly upon the water. Therefore, if what my adversaries affirm were true, the same identical shape in the same identical water would cause sometimes rest and other times slowness of motion. This is impossible, because every particular shape that descends to the bottom has of necessity its own determinate slowness, proper and natural unto it, according to which it moves, so that every other slowness (greater or lesser) is improper to its nature; for example, if a plate of one square palm descends naturally with six degrees of slowness, it is impossible that it should descend with ten or twenty unless some new impediment hinders it. Much less can it, by reason of the same shape, rest and wholly cease to move; but is it necessary that whenever it rests there be some greater impediment than the breadth of the shape. Therefore, it must be something else, and not the shape, that keeps the plate of ebony above water; the only effect of the shape is the retardation of the motion, according to which it descends more slowly than the ball. Let it be said, therefore, in accordance with the best reasoning, that the true and sole cause of the ebony's going to the bottom is the excess of its gravity over the gravity of [96] the water; and the cause of the greater or lesser slowness is the breadth of this shape or the smallness of that. But it can by no means be allowed that the quality of the shape is the cause of its rest; for by making the slowness greater according as the shape expands, there cannot be an expansion so immense that there may not be found a corresponding immense slowness not yet reduced to nullity of motion; besides, the shapes produced by my antagonists as causes of rest are the same that also go to the bottom.

I will not omit another reason also founded upon experience and, if I am not mistaken, manifestly showing that the introduction of the breadth of shape and the resistance of the water against penetration have nothing to do with the effect of descending, or ascending, or resting in the water. Take a piece of wood or other material a ball of which ascends from the bottom of the water to the surface more slowly than a ball of ebony of the same size descends to the bottom,[4] so that it is manifest that the ball of ebony more readily divides the water in descending than the other in ascending; for example, let the wood be walnut-tree. Then make a board of walnut-tree, similar and equal to the ebony board of my antagonists, that floats; and if it be true that this floats above water by reason of the shape being unable through its breadth to pierce the coarseness of the same, then unquestionably the other of walnut-tree when placed unto the bottom should stay there, being less apt through the same impediment of shape to divide the said resistance of the water. But if we should find and by experience see that not only the thin plate but every other

---

4. The last four words ("descends to the bottom") are omitted in Salusbury 1661–65, 2: 434, presumably due to a typographical error.

shape of the same walnut-tree will go up to float (as undoubtedly we do find and see), then I would ask my opponents to forbear to attribute the floating of the ebony to the shape of the board; for the resistance of the water is the same to the ascent as well as to the descent, and the force of the walnut's ascending is less than the force of the ebony's going to the bottom.

Indeed, I will say more. If we shall consider gold in comparison to water, we shall find that gold exceeds water almost twenty times in gravity; thus the force and impetus with which a ball of gold goes to the bottom is very great. On the contrary, there is no lack of materials, such as virgin wax and some woods, which are only about two percent lighter than water; thus, their ascent in water is very slow and a thousand times weaker in impetus than the descent of gold. Nevertheless, a thin [97] leaf of gold floats without descending to the bottom; and on the contrary, we cannot make a cake of wax or of the said wood which, when placed at the bottom of the water, shall rest there without ascending. Now, if the shape can obstruct the penetration and impede the descent of gold, which has such a great impetus, how can it not suffice to resist the same penetration of the other material in ascending, when it has scarcely a thousandth part of the impetus that the gold has in descending? It is necessary, therefore, that whatever suspends the gold leaf or thin board of ebony upon the water be something that is lacking to the other leaves and boards of materials less heavy than water, which rise up to the surface without any obstruction when placed at the bottom and left at liberty. But they do not lack flatness and breadth of shape. Therefore, the spaciousness of the shape is not what makes the gold and ebony float.

What, then, shall we say that it is?[5] For my part, I would say that it is the contrary of what causes the sinking; for sinking and floating are contrary effects, and the causes of contrary effects must be contrary. Now, when the flat plate of ebony and the thin leaf of gold go to the bottom, the cause of the sinking is unquestionably the excess of their gravity over the gravity of the water; therefore, of necessity, when they float, the cause of their staying above the water proceeds from their lightness. In this case, some circumstance perhaps not hitherto observed combines with the said plate, making it less heavy

---

5. This sentence and the next are missing from Salisbury 1661–65, 2: 434, presumably due to some typographical error; they correspond to four lines in Galilei 1890–1991, 4: 97.13–17.

than water rather than heavier, as it was earlier when it did sink. But such a new lightness cannot derive from the shape, both because shapes do not increase or decrease the weight, and because the plate undergoes no change of shape when it sinks as compared to when it floats.

Now, let us return to the thin leaf of gold or of silver, or the thin board of ebony; let us lay it lightly upon the water so that it stays there without sinking, and let us diligently observe the effect it produces. First, see how false the assertion of Aristotle and of our opponents is, to wit, that it stays above water through its inability to pierce and penetrate the resistance of the water's coarseness. For it will manifestly appear, not only that the said leaves have penetrated the water, but also that they are considerably lower than the surface of the same; this surface is elevated around the leaves and forms, as it were, an embankment at the bottom of which they remain floating. Now, [98] according as the said leaves shall be heavier than water two, four, ten, or twenty times, it is necessary that their surface stay below the general surface of the surrounding water an equal number of times more than the thickness of those leaves, as we shall more distinctly show anon. In the meantime, for the easier understanding of what I say, let us examine the following figure. Let us suppose the surface of the water to extend along the lines *FL* and *DB*. Now, if one shall put upon it a board of a material whose specific gravity is greater than that of water, 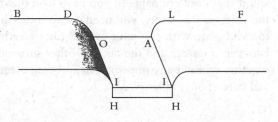 and one does this so lightly that the board does not submerge, it shall not rest above but enter with its whole thickness into the water. Moreover, it shall go down a little, as we see in the board *AIOI*; its thickness is wholly inside the water and is surrounded by the embankments *LA* and *DO* of the water, whose surface is notably higher than the surface of the board. See now whether it is true that the said board does not go to the bottom for having a shape that is inapt to penetrate the coarseness of the water.

But if it has already penetrated and overcome the continuity of the water and is of its own nature heavier than the said water, why does it not proceed in its sinking but stop and suspend itself within that little cavity which with its weight it has made in the water? I answer: because in going down until its surface is level with that of the water, it loses part of its weight; and it loses the rest as it descends beneath the surface of the water, which makes ramparts and embankments around it. It sustains this loss by drawing and carrying along with it the air that is above and adheres to it by contact; this air manages to fill the cavity that is surrounded by the embankments in the water. Thus, in this case what descends and is placed in the water is not only the slice or plate of ebony (or iron), but a mixture of ebony and air, whose result is a solid that is no longer heavier than water, as was the simple ebony or simple gold. Now, if we consider exactly what, and how large, is the solid that enters into the water in this experiment, it will be found to be everything that lies beneath the surface of the water; this is an aggregate and mixture of an [99] ebony plate and an almost equal quantity of air, or a bulk compounded of a lead plate and ten or twelve times as much air. But, Gentlemen, you who are my antagonists, in our controversy we require that the material be the same and only its shape be changed. Therefore, you must remove the air, which being conjoined with the plate makes it become another body lighter than water, and you must put only the ebony into the water; then you shall certainly see the plate descend to the bottom; and if that does not happen, you have won the day. Now, to separate the air from the ebony, you need do no more than wet the surface of the said plate with the same water; for water being thus interposed between the plate and the air, the other surrounding water shall run together without any impediment and shall receive into itself the sole and bare ebony, as required.

CHAPTER 3

From *History and Demonstrations Concerning Sunspots* (1613)[1]

[§3.1 Solar Rotation and Indifferent Motion][2]

[133] From the things said so far, it seems to me, if I am not mistaken, that we can draw several necessary conclusions. Sunspots are contiguous or extremely near to the body of the sun. They are not permanent or fixed, but variable with respect to shape and density. They also undergo to various degrees some small imprecise and irregular movements. Absolutely all of them are produced and dissipated, some in shorter and others in longer periods. Moreover, it is manifest and indubitable that they turn around the sun.

However, it remains somewhat doubtful whether their turning happens because the solar body rotates and turns around itself thus carrying them along, or whether while the solar body remains motionless there is a turning of the environment that contains them and carries them along; it could be either way. It seems to me much more probable that the motion belongs to the solar body than to the environment.

I am induced to believe this, first, by the certainty that such an environment is very tenuous, fluid, and flexible. My certainty comes from seeing the spots contained in it change shape, combine, and separate so easily, which could not happen in a solid and rigid material (a proposition that will seem very novel to the common philosophy). Now, it seems that for a constant and regular movement such as the one that is shared by all the spots, its root and primary foundation could not lie in a flexible substance made of parts that do not cohere together and are thus subject to the fluctuations and disturbances of many other accidental movements, but rather must lie in a solid and rigid body where the motion of the whole and the parts is necessarily a single one; and it is reasonable to believe that such is the solar

---

1. For the historical background, see the Introduction, especially §0.6.
2. Galilei 1890–1909, 5: 133.5–135.33; newly translated by Finocchiaro.

body, by contrast to its environment. Such a motion could carry the spots around either by being transmitted to the environment by contact and to the spots through the environment, or by being transferred directly to the spots, also by contact.

Additionally, if someone wanted to claim [134] that the turning of the spots around the sun derived from motion belonging to the environment and not to the sun, I would think that in any case it would be almost necessary that the same environment transmit the same motion also to the solar globe by contact. For I have observed that physical bodies have a natural inclination toward that motion which they undergo by an intrinsic principle, without the need of a particular external mover, whenever they are not impeded by some obstacle (as it happens to heavy bodies moving downwards). Physical bodies also have repugnance toward other motions, and so they never move in such ways unless compelled violently by an external mover (as it happens to heavy bodies with regard to upward motion). Finally, physical bodies are indifferent toward still other motions—for example, heavy bodies toward horizontal motion: these bodies have no inclination toward it because it is not toward the center of the earth, and they have no repugnance for it because it does not make them move away from the same center. Thus, if we remove all external impediments, a heavy body on a spherical surface concentric with the earth will be indifferent to rest and to motion toward any part of the horizon, and it will remain in that state in which it has been placed; that is, if it is placed in a state of rest, it will remain at rest, and if it is placed in motion (e.g., toward the west), it will remain in that motion. For example, if a ship [135] on a calm sea were to receive some impetus just once, it would move continuously around our globe without ever stopping; and if it were placed at rest, it would perpetually remain at rest; as long as in the first case all extrinsic impediments could be removed, and in the second case no external moving cause came about.[3]

_____

3. Galileo's principle of indifferent motion in this paragraph should be compared and contrasted to the law of inertia, or Isaac Newton's first law of motion: "Every body perseveres in its state of being at rest or of moving uniformly straight forward, except insofar as it is compelled to change its state by forces impressed" (Newton 1999, 416). As Drake (1957, 113 n. 8) notes, this paragraph contains an approximate formulation, as well as two applications "to the cases of (1) rotating bodies and (2) heavy bodies moving freely upon smooth spheres concentric with the earth." Cf. also the discussion in

If this is true, and indeed it is most true, what would a body of ambivalent nature do if it happened to be constantly surrounded by an environment that was moving with a motion to which that physical body was by nature indifferent? I do not think one can doubt that it would move with the motion of the environment. Now the sun, a spherical body suspended and balanced around its own center, cannot fail to follow the motion of its environment since it has neither an intrinsic repugnance nor an external impediment to such rotation. It cannot have an internal repugnance, given that by such rotation the whole is not removed from its location, and the parts are not permuted among themselves and do not change their natural constitution; thus, with regard to the relationship between the whole and the parts, it is as if such a motion did not exist. As regards the external impediments, it seems that no obstacle can hinder without contact (except perhaps the attraction of a loadstone); but in our case everything that touches the sun, that is to say, its environment, not only does not hinder the motion which we are trying to attribute to it, but also moves and transmits that motion as long as there is no resistance; this resistance cannot come from the sun, and hence there are no external impediments.

This can be confirmed even more strongly. For besides what I have already said, it does not seem that a movable body can have repugnance to a motion without having a natural propensity to the opposite (for there is no repugnance in indifference). So whoever wants to attribute to the sun an aversion to the circular motion of its environment would thereby attribute to it a natural propensity to circular motion in the opposite direction to that of the environment. This sounds wrong to any well-balanced intellect.

Therefore, since the apparent rotation of the spots must be attributed to the sun, it is better (for the first reason I gave) to regard solar rotation as natural rather than as acquired by participation.

[§3.2 Heavenly Changes and Aristotelian Empiricism][4]

[138] Now, to gather some fruit from the unexpected marvels that have remained hidden until our time, it will be good in the future to

---

Galileo's critique of the ship analogy argument, in Day II of the *Dialogue*, below in §8.5 (pp. 229–33).
4. Galilei 1890–1909, 5: 138.24–140.16; newly translated by Finocchiaro.

reconsider the wise philosophers who judged the heavenly substance differently from Aristotle, and from whom Aristotle himself would not have moved away if [139] he had been in possession of present-day sensory observations. For he not only allowed plain sense experience among the means capable of yielding conclusions about natural phenomena, but he also gave it first place.[5] Thus, since he argued for the immutability of the heavens from the fact that no alteration had ever been seen there in past times, it is very reasonable to believe that if the senses had shown to him what they have shown to us, he would have followed the contrary opinion, to which we are now led by such marvelous discoveries.

Indeed I shall go further. I think that by holding the heavenly material to be alterable (based on the truth of present-day observations), I am opposing Aristotle's doctrine much less than those who would still want to claim it to be inalterable. For I am sure that he never regarded the conclusion of inalterability as certain as the principle that plain sense experience must have priority over any human theory. Thus, one will philosophize better by giving assent to conclusions dependent on clear observations than by persisting in opinions that are repugnant to the senses and are confirmed only with probable or apparent reasons.

It is not difficult to understand the kind and the number of observed phenomena that lead us to more certain conclusions. Behold, to remove us from any ambiguity, a superior power [140] inspires someone to devise conclusive methods to understand that the generation of comets occurs in the heavenly region; but like a witness who quickly comes and goes, he is opposed by the majority of those who teach to others. Behold, we see new longer-lasting flames, looking like extremely bright stars, being produced and then dissipated in the farthest parts of the heavens; but this is not enough to convince those whose minds do not understand the necessity of geometrical demonstrations. Behold, finally, in the part of the heavens that deserves to be regarded as the purest and most genuine (that is, on the face of the sun itself), one discovers the constant production and quick dissipation of a countless multitude of dark, dense, and smoky spots. Here is a succession of things made and unmade that will not end any time soon; rather, lasting for all future ages, it will give human beings time

---

5. Cf. Aristotle, *On the Generation of Animals,* III, 10, 750b27 and 760b31.

to observe as much as they please and to learn doctrines that will make them certain about their place.

[§3.3 Knowing Properties vs. Knowing Essences][6]

[187] In my estimation, we should not totally refrain from the investigation of things, even if they are very far from us, unless we have first decided it best to postpone any speculative activity to all other occupations of ours. The reason is as follows.

Either we want, by theorizing, to try to penetrate the true and intrinsic essence of natural substances, or we want to limit ourselves to gain information about some of their properties. As for trying to penetrate the essence, I regard it as an undertaking and a job no less impossible and useless for the case of nearby elementary substances than for the case of heavenly and very remote substances. I feel equally ignorant about the substance of the earth and of the moon, of terrestrial clouds and of sunspots.

For understanding these nearby substances, I see no other advantage than the abundance of details; but these are equally not understood, and we keep searching through them with very little or no gain. If I ask what is the essence of clouds and am told that it is a humid vapor, next I will want to know what vapor is. Perhaps I will be told that it is water rarified by the action of heat and transformed accordingly. But equally unclear about what water is, I will ask for this, and finally I will hear that it is the fluid body which flows in rivers and which we constantly handle and deal with. But this information about water is merely more direct and dependent on more senses, but not more intrinsic than my earlier information about clouds. Similarly, I do not understand the true essence of earth or fire any more than that of the moon or the sun; this knowledge is reserved for our understanding when we reach the state of blessedness, [188] not before.

However, if we want to limit ourselves to knowledge of some properties, I do not think we should despair of being able to ascertain them in bodies that are extremely far from us as well as in those next to us; on the contrary, sometimes by chance we know more precisely

---

6. Galilei 1890–1909, 5: 187.8–188.19; newly translated by Finocchiaro.

a property of the former than one of the latter. Who does not know the periods of the motions of planets better than those of seawater? Who does not know that the spherical shape of the body of the moon was understood much earlier and more quickly than that of the earth? And is it not still controversial whether the earth remains motionless or goes wandering, whereas we are most certain about the motions of quite a few stars?

Thus, I want to conclude that although it would be fruitless to undertake the investigation of the essence of sunspots, it does not follow that we cannot know some of their properties, such as their location, motion, shape, size, opacity, mutability, production, and dissipation. These can then enable us to philosophize better about other more controversial questions regarding natural substances. Finally, lifting us to the final purpose of our efforts, namely, the love of the Divine Architect, they can sustain our hope of learning all other truths from Him, source of light and truth.

CHAPTER 4[1]

Letters on Copernicanism and Scripture (1613–15)[2]

§4.1 Letter to Castelli (1613)[3]

[281] Very Reverend Father and My Very Respectable Sir:

Yesterday Mr. Niccolò Arrighetti came to visit me and told me about you. Thus I took infinite pleasure in hearing about what I did not doubt at all, namely, about the great satisfaction you have been giving to the whole University, to its administrators as well as to the professors themselves and to the students from all countries. This approval has not increased the number of your rivals, as it usually happens in similar cases, but rather they have been reduced to very few; and these few too will have to acquiesce unless they want this competition (which is sometimes called a virtue) to degenerate and to change into a blameworthy and harmful feeling, harmful ultimately more to those who practice it than to anyone else. However, the seal of my pleasure was to hear him relate the arguments which, through the great kindness of their Most Serene Highnesses, you had the occasion of advancing at their table and then of continuing in the chambers of the Most Serene Ladyship, in the presence also of the Grand Duke and the Most Serene Archduchess, the Most Illustrious and Excellent Don Antonio and Don Paolo Giordano, and some of the very excellent philosophers there. What greater fortune can you wish than to see their Highnesses themselves enjoying discussing with you, putting forth doubts, listening to your solutions, and finally remaining satisfied with your answers?

1. Reprinted from: Maurice A. Finocchiaro, trans. and ed., *The Galileo Affair: A Documentary History*, © 1989 by the Regents of the University of California. Published by the University of California Press.
2. For the historical background, see the Introduction, especially §0.7.
3. Galilei 1890–1909, 5: 281–88; translated by Finocchiaro (1989, 49–54). For the historical background, see the Introduction, especially §0.7.

[282] After Mr. Arrighetti related the details you had mentioned, they gave me the occasion to go back to examine some general questions about the use of the Holy Scripture in disputes involving physical conclusions and some particular other ones about Joshua's passage,[4] which was presented in opposition to the earth's motion and sun's stability by the Grand Duchess Dowager with some support by the Most Serene Archduchess.

In regard to the first general point of the Most Serene Ladyship, it seems to me very prudent of her to propose and of you to concede and to agree that the Holy Scripture can never lie or err, and that its declarations are absolutely and inviolably true. I should have added only that, though Scripture cannot err, nevertheless some of its interpreters and expositors can sometimes err in various ways. One of these would be very serious and very frequent, namely, to want to limit oneself always to the literal meaning of the words; for there would thus emerge not only various contradictions but also serious heresies and blasphemies, and it would be necessary to attribute to God feet, hands, and eyes, as well as bodily and human feelings like anger, regret, hate, and sometimes even forgetfulness of things past and ignorance of future ones. Thus in Scripture one finds many propositions which look different from the truth if one goes by the literal meaning of the words but which are expressed in this manner to accommodate the incapacity of common people; likewise, for the few who deserve to be separated from the masses, it is necessary that wise interpreters produce their true meaning and indicate the particular reasons why they have been expressed by means of such words.

Thus, given that in many places Scripture is not only capable but necessarily in need of interpretations different from the apparent meaning of the words, it seems to me that in disputes about natural phenomena it should be reserved to the last place. For the Holy Scripture and nature both equally derive from the divine Word, the former as the dictation of the Holy Spirit, the latter as the most obedient executrix of God's commands; moreover, in order to adapt itself to the understanding of all people, it was appropriate for Scripture to say many things [283] which are different from absolute truth in appearance and in regard to the meaning of the words; on the other hand, nature is inexorable and immutable, and she does not care

---

4. Joshua 10:12–13; I quote this passage in the Introduction, §0.7.

at all whether or not her recondite reasons and modes of operations are revealed to human understanding, and so she never transgresses the terms of the laws imposed on her; therefore, whatever sensory experience places before our eyes or necessary demonstrations prove to us concerning natural effects should not in any way be called into question on account of scriptural passages whose words appear to have a different meaning, since not every statement of Scripture is bound to obligations as severely as each effect of nature. Indeed, because of the aim of adapting itself to the capacity of unrefined and undisciplined peoples, Scripture has not abstained from somewhat concealing its most basic dogmas, thus attributing to God himself properties contrary to and very far from his essence; so who will categorically maintain that, in speaking even incidentally of the earth or the sun or other creatures, it abandoned this aim and chose to restrict itself rigorously within the limited and narrow meanings of the words? This would have been especially problematic when saying about these creatures things which are very far from the primary function of the Holy Writ, indeed things which, if said and put forth in their naked and unadorned truth, would more likely harm its primary intention and make people more resistant to persuasion about the articles pertaining to salvation.

Given this, and moreover it being obvious that two truths can never contradict each other, the task of wise interpreters is to strive to find the true meanings of scriptural passages agreeing with those physical conclusions of which we are already certain and sure from clear sensory experience or from necessary demonstrations. Furthermore, as I already said, though Scripture was inspired by the Holy Spirit, because of the mentioned reasons many passages admit of interpretations far removed from the literal meaning, and also we cannot assert with certainty that all interpreters speak by divine inspiration; hence, I should believe that it would be prudent not to allow anyone to oblige [284] scriptural passages to have to maintain the truth of any physical conclusions whose contrary could ever be shown to us by the senses and demonstrative and necessary reasons. Who wants to fix a limit for the human mind? Who wants to assert that everything which is knowable in the world is already known? Because of this, it would be most advisable not to add anything beyond necessity to the articles concerning salvation and the definition of the Faith, which are firm enough that there is no danger of any valid and effective doctrine ever rising against them. If this is so, what greater disorder would result from adding them upon request by persons of whom we do not know whether they speak with celestial inspiration, and of whom also we see clearly that they are completely lacking in the intelligence needed to understand, let alone to criticize, the demonstrations by means of which the most exact sciences proceed in the confirmation of some of their conclusions?

I should believe that the authority of the Holy Writ has merely the aim of persuading men of those articles and propositions which are necessary for their salvation and surpass all human reason, and so could not become credible through some other science or any other means except the mouth of the Holy Spirit itself. However, I do not think it necessary to believe that the same God who has furnished us with senses, language, and intellect would want to bypass their use and give us by other means the information we can obtain with them. This applies especially to those sciences about which one can read only very small phrases and scattered conclusions in Scripture, as is particularly the case for astronomy, of which it contains such a small portion that one does not even find in it the names of all the planets; but if the first sacred writers had been thinking of persuading the people about the arrangement and the movements of the heavenly bodies, they would not have treated of them so sparsely, which is to say almost [285] nothing in comparison to the infinity of very lofty and admirable conclusions contained in such a science.

So you see, if I am not mistaken, how disorderly is the procedure of those who in disputes about natural phenomena that do not directly involve the Faith give first place to scriptural passages, which they quite often misunderstand anyway. However, if these people really believe to have grasped the true meaning of a particular scriptural passage, and if they consequently feel sure of possessing the absolute truth on the question they intend to dispute about, then let them sincerely tell me whether they think that in a natural dispute someone who happens to maintain the truth has a great advantage over another who happens to maintain the false.[5] I know they will answer yes, and that the one who supports the true side will be able to provide a thousand experiments and a thousand necessary demonstrations for his side, whereas the other person can have nothing but sophisms, paralogisms, and fallacies. But if they know they have such an advantage

5. In this sentence, the translation in Finocchiaro 1989, 52 has been corrected slightly.

over their opponents as long as the discussion is limited to physical questions and only philosophical weapons are used, why is it that when they come to the meeting they immediately introduce an irresistible and terrible weapon, the mere sight of which terrifies even the most skillful and expert champion? If I must tell the truth, I believe it is they who are the most terrified, and that they are trying to find a way of not letting the opponent approach because they feel unable to resist his assaults. However, consider that, as I just said, whoever has truth on his side has a great, indeed the greatest, advantage over the opponent, and that it is impossible for two truths to contradict each other; it follows therefore that we must not fear any assaults launched against us by anyone, as long as we are allowed to speak and to be heard by competent persons who are not excessively upset by their own emotions and interests.

To confirm this I now come to examining the specific passage of Joshua, concerning which you put forth three theses for their Most Serene Highnesses. I take the third one, which you advanced as mine (as indeed it is), but I add some other consideration that I do not believe I have ever told you.

Let us then assume and concede to the opponent that the words [286] of the sacred text should be taken precisely in their literal meaning, namely, that in answer to Joshua's prayers God made the sun stop and lengthened the day, so that as a result he achieved victory; but I request that the same rule should apply to both, so that the opponent should not pretend to tie me and to leave himself free to change or modify the meanings of the words. Given this, I say that this passage shows clearly the falsity and impossibility of the Aristotelian and Ptolemaic world system, and on the other hand agrees very well with the Copernican one.

I first ask the opponent whether he knows with how many motions the sun moves. If he knows, he must answer that it moves with two motions, namely, with the annual motion from west to east and with the diurnal motion in the opposite direction from east to west.

Then, secondly, I ask him whether these two motions, so different and almost contrary to each other, belong to the sun and are its own to an equal extent. The answer must be no, but that only one is specifically its own, namely, the annual motion, whereas the other is not but belongs to the highest heaven, I mean the Prime Mobile; the latter carries along with it the sun as well as the other planets and the stellar sphere, forcing them to make a revolution around the earth in twenty-four hours, with a motion, as I said, almost contrary to their own natural motion.

Coming to the third question, I ask him with which of these two motions the sun produces night and day, that is, whether with its own motion or else with that of the Prime Mobile. The answer must be that night and day are effects of the motion of the Prime Mobile, and that what depends on the sun's own motion is not night and day but the various seasons and the year itself.

Now, if the day derives not from the sun's motion but from that of the Prime Mobile, who does not see that to lengthen the day one must stop the Prime Mobile and not the sun? Indeed, is there anyone who understands these first elements of astronomy and does not know that, if God had stopped the sun's motion, He would have cut and shortened the day instead of lengthening it? For, the sun's motion being [287] contrary to the diurnal turning, the more the sun moves toward the east the more its progression toward the west is slowed down, whereas by its motion being diminished or annihilated the sun would set that much sooner; this phenomenon is observed in the moon, whose diurnal revolutions are slower than those of the sun inasmuch as its own motion is faster than that of the sun. It follows that it is absolutely impossible to stop the sun and lengthen the day in the system of Ptolemy and Aristotle, and therefore either the motions must not be arranged as Ptolemy says or we must modify the meaning of the words of Scripture; we would have to claim that, when it says that God stopped the sun, it meant to say that He stopped the Prime Mobile, and that it said the contrary of what it would have said if speaking to educated men in order to adapt itself to the capacity of those who are barely able to understand the rising and setting of the sun.

Add to this that it is not believable that God would stop only the sun, letting the other spheres proceed; for He would have unnecessarily altered and upset all the order, appearances, and arrangements of the other stars in relation to the sun, and would have greatly disturbed the whole system of nature. On the other hand, it is believable that He would stop the whole system of celestial spheres, which could then together return to their operations without any confusion or change after the period of intervening rest.

However, we have already agreed not to change the meaning of the words in the text; therefore it is necessary to resort to another arrangement of the parts of the world, and to see whether the literal meaning of the words flows directly and without obstacle from its point of view. This is in fact what we see happening.

For I have discovered and conclusively demonstrated that the [288] solar globe turns on itself, completing an entire rotation in about one lunar month, in exactly the same direction as all the other heavenly revolutions; moreover, it is very probable and reasonable that, as the chief instrument and minister of nature and almost the heart of the world, the sun gives not only light (as it obviously does) but also motion to all the planets that revolve around it; hence, if in conformity with Copernicus' position the diurnal motion is attributed to the earth, anyone can see that it suffices stopping the sun to stop the whole system, and thus to lengthen the period of the diurnal illumination without altering in any way the rest of the mutual relationships of the planets; and that is exactly how the words of the sacred text sound. Here then is the manner in which by stopping the sun one can lengthen the day on the earth, without introducing any confusion among the parts of the world and without altering the words of Scripture.

I have written much more than is appropriate in view of my slight illness. So I end by reminding you that I am at your service, and I kiss your hands and pray the Lord to give you happy holidays and all you desire.

Florence, 21 December 1613.

To Your Very Reverend Paternity.

Your Most Affectionate Servant,
Galileo Galilei.

§4.2 *Letter to the Grand Duchess Christina* (1615)[6]

[309] To the Most Serene Ladyship the Grand Duchess Dowager:[7]

[§4.2.1] As Your Most Serene Highness knows very well, a few years ago I discovered in the heavens many particulars which had been invisible until our time. Because of their novelty, and because of

---

6. Galilei 1890–1909, 5: 309–48; translated by Finocchiaro (1989, 87–118). For the historical background, see the Introduction, especially §0.7.
7. Christina of Lorraine (d. 1637), wife of Grand Duke Ferdinando I de' Medici and mother of Cosimo II.

some consequences deriving from them which contradict some physical propositions commonly accepted in philosophical schools, they roused against me no small number of such professors, as if I had placed these things in heaven with my hands in order to mess up nature and the sciences. These people seemed to forget that a multitude of truths contribute to inquiry and to the growth and strength of disciplines rather than to their diminution or destruction, and at the same time they showed greater affection for their own opinions than for the true ones; thus they proceeded to deny and to try to nullify those novelties, about which the senses themselves could have rendered them certain, if they had wanted to look at those novelties carefully. To this end they produced various matters, and they published some writings full of useless discussions and sprinkled with quotations from the Holy Scripture, taken from passages which they do not properly understand and which they inappropriately adduce. This was a very serious error, and they might not have fallen into it had they paid attention to St. Augustine's very useful advice [310] concerning how to proceed with care in reaching definite decisions about things which are obscure and difficult to understand by means of reason alone. For, speaking also about a particular physical conclusion pertaining to heavenly bodies, he writes this (*On the Literal Interpretation of Genesis*, book 2, at the end):[8] "Now then, always practicing a pious and serious moderation, we ought not to believe anything lightly about an obscure subject, lest we reject (out of love for our error) something which later may be truly shown not to be in any way contrary to the holy books of either the Old or New Testament."

Then it developed that the passage of time disclosed to everyone the truths I had first pointed out, and, along with the truth of the matter, the difference in attitude between those who sincerely and without envy did not accept these discoveries as true and those who added emotional agitation to disbelief. Thus, just as those who were most competent in astronomical and in physical science were convinced by my first announcement, so gradually there has been a calming down of all the others whose denials and doubts were not

---

8. Here and elsewhere in this essay, Galileo gives references for his Latin quotations by displaying the bibliographical information in the margin to his text, whereas I insert the references in parentheses in the text. Unless indicated otherwise in a note, I have translated the Latin passages from the wording as quoted by Galileo.

sustained by anything other than the unexpected novelty and the lack of opportunity to see them and to experience them with the senses. However, there are those who are rendered ill-disposed, not so much toward the things as much as toward the author, by the love of their first error and by some interest which they imagine having but which escapes me. Unable to deny them any longer, these people became silent about them; but, embittered more than before by what has mellowed and quieted the others, they divert their thinking to other fictions and try to harm me in other ways. These would not really worry me any more than I was disturbed by the other oppositions, which I always laughed off, certain of the result that the business would have; I should not worry if I did not see that the new calumnies and persecutions are not limited to matters of greater or less theoretical understanding, which are relatively unimportant, but that they go further and try to damage me with stains which I do abhor and must abhor more than death. Nor can I be satisfied that these charges be known as false only by those who know me and them; their falsity must be known to every other person. These people are aware that in my [311] astronomical and philosophical studies, on the question of the constitution of the world's parts, I hold that the sun is located at the center of the revolutions of the heavenly orbs and does not change place, and that the earth rotates on itself and moves around it. Moreover, they hear how I confirm this view not only by refuting Ptolemy's and Aristotle's arguments, but also by producing many for the other side, especially some pertaining to physical effects whose causes perhaps cannot be determined in any other way, and other astronomical ones dependent on many features of the new celestial discoveries; these discoveries clearly confute the Ptolemaic system, and they agree admirably with this other position and confirm it. Now, these people are perhaps confounded by the known truth of the other propositions different from the ordinary which I hold, and so they may lack confidence to defend themselves as long as they remain in the philosophical field. Therefore, since they persist in their original self-appointed task of beating down me and my findings by every imaginable means, they have decided to try to shield the fallacies of their arguments with the cloak of simulated religiousness and with the authority of the Holy Scriptures, unintelligently using the latter for the confutation of arguments they neither understand nor have heard.

At first, they tried on their own to spread among common people the idea that such propositions are against the Holy Scriptures, and consequently damnable and heretical. Then they realized how by and large human nature is more inclined to join those ventures which result in the oppression of other people (even if unjustly) than those which result in their just improvement, and so it was not difficult for them to find someone who with unusual confidence did preach even from the pulpit that it is damnable and heretical; and this was done with little compassion and with little consideration of the injury not only to this doctrine and its followers, but also to mathematics and all mathematicians. Thus, having acquired more confidence and with the vain hope that that seed which first took root in their insincere mind would grow into a tree and rise toward the sky, they are spreading among the people the rumor that it will shortly be declared heretical by the supreme authority. They also know that such a declaration not only would uproot these two conclusions, but also would render damnable all the other astronomical and physical observations and propositions [312] which correspond and are necessarily connected with them; hence, they alleviate their task as much as they can by making it look, at least among common people, as if this opinion were new and especially mine, pretending not to know that Nicolaus Copernicus was its author, or rather its reformer and confirmer. Now, Copernicus was not only a Catholic, but also a clergyman[9] and a canon, and he was so highly regarded that he was called to Rome from the remotest parts of Germany[10] when under Leo X the Lateran Council was discussing the reform of the ecclesiastical calendar; at that time this reform remained unfinished only because there was still no exact knowledge of the precise length of the year and of the lunar month. Thus he was charged by the Bishop of Fossombrone,[11] who was then supervising this undertaking, to try by repeated studies and

Do these errors make Galileo less trustworthy/convincing?

9. Here and in the rest of this paragraph, Galileo makes a number of misstatements about Copernicus. For example, although Copernicus was a canon and hence a type of cleric, he was not a clergyman in the sense of being a priest. Although he sent a written report to the Fifth Lateran Council, he did not go to Rome to attend it. Although the Copernican system played a role in the reform of the calendar, the new Gregorian calendar (which was implemented in 1582 during the papacy of Gregory XIII) was based on non-Copernican ideas. Although Copernicus' book was not officially condemned (before 1616), it was widely censured. See Rosen 1958; 1975.

10. Actually Poland.

11. Paul of Middelburg (1445–1533).

efforts to acquire more understanding and certainty about those celestial motions; and so he undertook this study, and, by truly Her-
culean labor and by his admirable mind, he made so much progress
in this science and acquired such an exact knowledge of the periods
of celestial motions that he earned the title of supreme astronomer;
then in accordance with his doctrine not only was the calendar regu-
larized, but tables of all planetary motions were constructed. Having
expounded this doctrine in six parts, he published it at the request of
the Cardinal of Capua[12] and of the Bishop of Kulm;[13] and since he
had undertaken this task and these labors on orders from the Supreme
Pontiff, he dedicated his book *On Heavenly Revolutions* to the successor of the latter, Paul III. Once printed this book was accepted by the
Holy Church, and it was read and studied all over the world, without
anyone ever having had the least scruple about its doctrine. Finally,
now that one is discovering how well-founded upon clear observations and necessary demonstrations this doctrine is, some persons
come along who, without having even seen the book, give its author
the reward of so much work by trying to have him declared a heretic;
this they do only in order to satisfy their special animosity, ground-
lessly conceived [313] against someone else who has no greater connection with Copernicus than the endorsement of his doctrine.

Now, in matters of religion and of reputation I have the greatest
regard for how common people judge and view me; so, because of
the false aspersions my enemies so unjustly try to cast upon me, I have
thought it necessary to justify myself by discussing the details of what
they produce to detest and to abolish this opinion, in short, to declare
it not just false but heretical. They always shield themselves with a
simulated religious zeal, and they also try to involve Holy Scripture
and to make it somehow subservient to their insincere objectives;
against the intention of Scripture and of the Holy Fathers (if I am not
mistaken), they want to extend, not to say abuse, its authority, so that
even for purely physical conclusions which are not matters of faith
one must totally abandon the senses and demonstrative arguments in
favor of any scriptural passage whose apparent words may contain a
different indication. Here I hope to demonstrate that I proceed with
much more pious and religious zeal than they when I propose not

---

12. Cardinal Nicolaus von Schoenberg (1472–1537), archbishop of Capua.
13. Tiedemann Giese (1480–1550), Polish friend of Copernicus.

that this book should not be condemned, but that it should not be condemned without understanding, examining, or even seeing it, as they would like. This is especially true since the author never treats of things pertaining to religion and faith, nor uses arguments dependent in any way on the authority of the Holy Scriptures, in which case he might have interpreted them incorrectly; instead, he always limits himself to physical conclusions pertaining to celestial motions, and he treats of them with astronomical and geometrical demonstrations based above all on sense experience and very accurate observations. He proceeded in this manner not because he did not pay any attention to the passages of the Holy Scripture, but because he understood very well that [314] if his doctrine was demonstrated it could not contradict the properly interpreted Scripture. Hence, at the end of the dedication, speaking to the Supreme Pontiff, he says: "There may be triflers who though wholly ignorant of mathematics nevertheless abrogate the right to make judgments about it because of some passage in Scripture wrongly twisted to their purpose, and will dare to criticize and censure this undertaking of mine. I waste no time on them, and indeed I despise their judgment as thoughtless. For it is known that Lactantius, a distinguished writer in other ways, but no mathematician, speaks very childishly about the shape of the Earth when he makes fun of those who reported that it has the shape of a globe. Mathematics is written for mathematicians, to whom this work of mine, if my judgment does not deceive me, will seem to be of value to the ecclesiastical Commonwealth over which Your Holiness now holds dominion."[14]

Of this sort are also those who try to argue that this author should be condemned, without examining him; and to show that this is not only legitimate but a good thing, they use the authority of Scripture, of experts in sacred theology, and of sacred Councils. I feel reverence for these authorities and hold them supreme, so that I should consider it most reckless to want to contradict them when they are used in accordance with the purpose of the Holy Church; similarly, I do not think it is wrong to speak out when it seems that someone, out of personal interest, wants to use them in a way different from the holiest intention of the Holy Church. Thus, while also believing that my sincerity will become self-evident, I declare not only that I intend to

---

14. Here quoted from Copernicus 1976, 26–27.

submit freely to the correction of any errors in matters pertaining to religion which I may have committed in this essay due to my ignorance, but I also declare that on these subjects I do not want to quarrel with anyone, even if the points are debatable. For my purpose is nothing but the following: if these reflections, which are far from my own profession, should contain (besides errors) anything that may lead someone to advance a useful caution for the Holy Church in her deliberations about the [315] Copernican system, then let it be accepted with whatever profit superiors will deem appropriate; if not, let my essay be torn up and burned, for I do not intend or pretend to gain from it any advantage that is not pious or Catholic. Moreover, although I have heard with my own ears many of the things which I mention, I freely grant to whoever said them that they did not say them, if they so wish, and I admit that I may have misunderstood them; thus what I answer should not apply to them, but to whoever holds that opinion.

So the reason they advance to condemn the opinion of the earth's mobility and sun's stability is this: since in many places in the Holy Scripture one reads that the sun moves and the earth stands still, and since Scripture can never lie or err, it follows as a necessary consequence that the opinion of those who want to assert the sun to be motionless and the earth moving is erroneous and damnable.

[§4.2.2] The first thing to note about this argument is the following. It is most pious to say and most prudent to take for granted that Holy Scripture can never lie, as long as its true meaning has been grasped; but I do not think one can deny that this is frequently recondite and very different from what appears to be the literal meaning of the words. From this it follows that, if in interpreting it someone were to limit himself always to the pure literal meaning, and if the latter were wrong, then he could make Scripture appear to be full not only of contradictions and false propositions, but also of serious heresies and blasphemies; for one would have to attribute to God feet, hands, eyes, and bodily sensations, as well as human feelings like anger, contrition, and hatred, and such conditions as the forgetfulness of things past and the ignorance of future ones. Since these propositions dictated by the Holy Spirit were expressed by the sacred writers in such a way as to accommodate the capacities of the very unrefined and undisciplined masses, therefore for those who deserve to rise above the common people it is necessary that wise interpreters [316] formulate the true meaning and indicate the specific reasons why it is expressed by such words. This doctrine is so commonplace and so definite among all theologians that it would be superfluous to present any testimony for it.

From this I think one can very reasonably deduce that, whenever the same Holy Scripture has seen fit to assert any physical conclusion (especially on things that are abstruse and difficult to understand), it has followed the same rule, in order not to sow confusion into the minds of the common people and make them more obstinate against dogmas involving higher mysteries. In fact, as I said and as one can clearly see, for the sole purpose of accommodating popular understanding, Scripture has not abstained from concealing the most important truths, attributing even to God characteristics that are contrary to or very far from His essence; given this, who will categorically maintain that in speaking incidentally of the earth, water, sun, or other created thing Scripture has set aside such regard and has chosen to limit itself rigorously to the literal and narrow meanings of the words? This would be especially implausible when mentioning features of these created things which are very remote from popular understanding, and which are not at all pertinent to the primary purpose of the Holy Writ, that is, to the worship of God and the salvation of souls.

Therefore, I think that in disputes about natural phenomena one must begin not with the authority of scriptural passages, but with sense experiences and necessary demonstrations. For the Holy Scripture and nature derive equally from the Godhead, the former as the dictation of the Holy Spirit and the latter as the most obedient executrix of God's orders; moreover, to accommodate the understanding of the common people it is appropriate for Scripture to say many things that are different (in appearance and in regard to the literal meaning of the words) from the absolute truth; on the other hand, nature is inexorable and immutable, never violates the terms of the laws imposed upon her, and does not care whether or not her recondite reasons and ways of operating are disclosed to human understanding; [317] but not every scriptural assertion is bound to obligations as severe as every natural phenomenon; finally, God reveals Himself to us no less excellently in the effects of nature than in the sacred words of Scripture, as Tertullian perhaps meant when he said, "We postulate that God ought first to be known by nature, and afterwards further known by doctrine—by nature through His works, by doctrine through official teaching" (*Against Marcion,* I.18);[15] and so it seems that a natural phenomenon which is placed before our eyes by sense experience or proved by necessary demonstrations should not be called into question, let alone condemned, on account of scriptural passages whose words appear to have a different meaning.

However, by this I do not wish to imply that one should not have the highest regard for passages of Holy Scripture; indeed, after becoming certain of some physical conclusions, we should use these as very appropriate aids to the correct interpretation of such Scriptures and to the investigation of the truths they must contain, for they are most true and agree with demonstrated truths. That is, I would say that the authority of Holy Scripture aims chiefly at persuading men about those articles and propositions which, surpassing all human reason, could not be discovered by scientific research or by any other means than through the mouth of the Holy Spirit himself. Moreover, even in regard to those propositions that are not articles of faith, the authority of the same Holy Writ should have priority over the authority of any human works composed not with the demonstrative method but with either pure narration or even probable reasons;[16] this principle should be considered appropriate and necessary inasmuch as divine wisdom surpasses all human judgment and speculation. However, I do not think one has to believe that the same God who has given us senses, language, and intellect would want to set aside the use of these and give us by other means the information we can acquire with them, so that we would deny our senses and reason even in the case of those physical conclusions which are placed before our eyes and intellect by our sense experiences or by necessary demonstrations. This is especially implausible for those sciences discussed in Scripture to a very minor extent and [318] with disconnected statements; such is precisely the case of astronomy, so little of which is contained therein that one does not find there even the

---

15. Tertullian 1972, 47; I have made some slight emendations to Evans' translation of this passage.

16. Here my translation of this sentence is a slight emendation of the one given in Finocchiaro 1989, 94. This improved translation results from my now taking into account the emendation in Galileo's own wording of this sentence in the first published edition of the *Letter to the Grand Duchess Christina* (Galilei 1636, 14; cf. Motta 2000, 97–98; Finocchiaro 2005, 379–80 n. 56), as well as the scholarly discussions found in Fantoli 2003, 437–38 n. 39, and McMullin 2005b, 109, 116.

names of the planets, except for the sun,[17] the moon, and only once or twice Venus, under the name of Morning Star. Thus, if the sacred authors had had in mind to teach people about the arrangement and motions of the heavenly bodies, and consequently to have us acquire this information from Holy Scripture, then, in my opinion, they would not have discussed so little of the topic—that is to say, almost nothing in comparison with the innumerable admirable conclusions which are contained and demonstrated in this science. Indeed, it is the opinion of the holiest and most learned Fathers that the writers of Holy Scripture not only did not pretend to teach us about the structure and the motions of the heavens and of the stars, and their shape, size, and distance, but that they deliberately refrained from doing it, even though they knew all these things very well. For example, one reads the following words in St. Augustine (*On the Literal Interpretation of Genesis,* book 2, chapter 9): "It is also customary to ask what one should believe about the shape and arrangement of heaven according to our Scriptures. In fact, many people argue a great deal about these things, which with greater prudence our authors omitted, which are of no use for eternal life to those who study them, and (what is worse) which take up a lot of time that ought to be spent on things pertaining to salvation. For what does it matter to me whether heaven, like a sphere, completely surrounds the earth, which is balanced at the center of the universe, or whether like a discus it covers the earth on one side from above? However, since the issue here is the authority of Scripture, let me repeat a point I have made more than once; that is, there is a danger that someone who does not understand the divine words may find in our books or infer from them something about these topics which seems to contradict received opinions, and then he might not believe at all the other useful things contained in its precepts, stories, and assertions; therefore, briefly, it should be said that our authors did know the truth about the shape of heaven, but that the Spirit of God, which was speaking through them, did not want to teach men these things which are of no use to salvation." (The same opinion is found in Peter Lombard's *Book of Sentences.*) The same contempt which the sacred writers had for the investigation of such properties of heavenly bodies is repeated by St. Augustine in the

---

17. The term *planet* originally meant "wandering star," namely, a heavenly body that appears to move relative to the fixed stars as well as to the earth, thus subsuming the sun and the moon.

following chapter 10, in regard to the question whether heaven should be thought to be in motion or standing still. He writes: "Some brethren have also advanced a question about the motion of heaven, [319] namely, whether heaven moves or stands still. For if it moves, they say, how is it a firmament? But if it stands still, how do the stars which are thought to be fixed in it revolve from east to west, the northern ones completing shorter circuits near the pole, so that heaven seems to rotate like a sphere (if there is at the other end another pole invisible to us) or like a discus (if instead there is no other pole)? To them I answer that these things should be examined with very subtle and demanding arguments, to determine truly whether or not it is so; but I do not have the time to undertake and to pursue these investigations, nor should such time be available to those whom we desire to instruct for their salvation and for the needs and benefit of the Holy Church."

Let us now come down from these things to our particular point. We have seen that the Holy Spirit did not want to teach us whether heaven moves or stands still, nor whether its shape is spherical or like a discus or extended along a plane, nor whether the earth is located at its center or on one side. So it follows as a necessary consequence that the Holy Spirit also did not intend to teach us about other questions of the same kind and connected to those just mentioned in such a way that without knowing the truth about the former one cannot decide the latter, such as the question of the motion or rest of the earth or sun. But, if the Holy Spirit deliberately avoided teaching us such propositions, inasmuch as they are of no relevance to His intention (that is, to our salvation), how can one now say that to hold this rather than that proposition on this topic is so important that one is a principle of faith and the other erroneous? Thus, can an opinion be both heretical and irrelevant to the salvation of souls? Or can one say that the Holy Spirit chose not to teach us something relevant to our salvation? Here I would say what I heard from an ecclesiastical person in a very eminent position (Cardinal Baronio[18]), namely, that the intention of the Holy Spirit is to teach us how one goes to heaven and not how heaven goes.

But let us go back and examine the importance of necessary demonstrations and of sense experiences in conclusions about natural phenomena, and how much weight has been assigned to them by

---

18. Cesare Baronio (1538–1607), appointed cardinal in 1596.

learned and holy theologians. Among hundreds of instances of such testimony we have the following. Near the beginning of his work *On Genesis* Pererius asserts: [320] "In treating of Moses' doctrine, one must take diligent care to completely avoid holding and saying positively and categorically anything which contradicts the decisive observations and reasons of philosophy or other disciplines; in fact, since all truths always agree with one another, the truth of Holy Scripture cannot be contrary to the true reasons and observations of human doctrines." And in St. Augustine (Letter to Marcellinus, section 7), one reads: "If, against the most manifest and reliable testimony of reason, anything be set up claiming to have the authority of the Holy Scriptures, he who does this does it through a misapprehension of what he has read and is setting up against the truth not the real meaning of Scripture, which he has failed to discover, but an opinion of his own; he alleges not what he has found in the Scriptures, but what he has found in himself as their interpreter."[19]

Because of this, and because (as we said above) two truths cannot contradict one another, the task of a wise interpreter is to strive to fathom the true meaning of the sacred texts; this will undoubtedly agree with those physical conclusions of which we are already certain and sure through clear observations or necessary demonstrations. Indeed, besides saying (as we have) that in many places Scripture is open to interpretations far removed from the literal meaning of the words, we should add that we cannot assert with certainty that all interpreters speak with divine inspiration, since if this were so then there would be no disagreement among them about the meaning of the same passages; therefore, I should think it would be very prudent not to allow anyone to commit and in a way oblige scriptural passages to have to maintain the truth of any physical conclusions whose contrary could ever be proved to us by the senses or demonstrative and necessary reasons. Indeed, who wants the human mind put to death? Who is going to claim that everything in the world which is observable and knowable has already been seen and discovered? Perhaps those who on other occasions admit, quite correctly, that the things we know are a very small part of the things we do not know? Indeed, we also have it from the mouth of the Holy Spirit that God "hath delivered the

---

19. Here quoted from Mourant 1964, 110. This letter is labeled number 143 in most editions of Augustine's works.

world to their consideration, so that man cannot find out the work which God hath made from the beginning to the end" (Ecclesiastes, chapter 3);[20] so one must not, in my opinion, contradict this statement and block the way of freedom of philosophizing about things [321] of the world and of nature, as if they had all already been discovered and disclosed with certainty. Nor should it be considered rash to be dissatisfied with opinions which are almost universally accepted; nor should people become indignant if in a dispute about natural phenomena someone disagrees with the opinion they favor, especially in regard to problems which have been controversial for thousands of years among very great philosophers, such as the sun's rest and earth's motion. This opinion has been held by Pythagoras and his whole school, by Heraclides of Pontus, by Philolaus (teacher of Plato), and by Plato himself (as Aristotle and Plutarch mention); the latter writes in the "Life of Numa" that when Plato was old he said it was very absurd to believe otherwise. The same opinion was accepted by Aristarchus of Samos (as Archimedes tells us), by the mathematician Seleucus, by the philosopher Hicetas (according to Cicero[21]), and by many others; finally, it was amplified and confirmed with many observations and demonstrations by Nicolaus Copernicus. Furthermore, in the book *On Comets,* the very distinguished philosopher Seneca tells us that one should attempt to ascertain with the greatest diligence whether the daily rotation belongs to the heavens or to the earth.

Therefore, it would perhaps be wise and useful advice not to add without necessity to the articles pertaining to salvation and to the definition of the faith, against the firmness of which there is no danger that any valid and effective doctrine could ever emerge. If this is so, it would really cause confusion to add them upon request from persons about whom not only do we not know whether they speak with heavenly inspiration, but we clearly see that they are deficient in the intelligence necessary first to understand and then to criticize the demonstrations by which the most acute sciences proceed in confirming similar conclusions. However, if I may be allowed to state my opinion, I should say further that it would be more appropriate to the dignity and majesty of Holy Writ to take steps to insure that not

---

20. Ecclesiastes 3:11 (Douay Version).
21. Flora (1953, 1019 n. 4) gives the following reference: Cicero, *Academia,* II, 39, 123.

every superficial and vulgar writer can lend credibility to his writings [322] (very often based on worthless fabrications) by sprinkling them with scriptural passages; these are often interpreted, or rather distorted, in ways which are as remote from the true intention of Scripture as they are ridiculously close to the aims of those who ostentatiously adorn their writings with them. Many examples of such an abuse could be adduced, but I shall limit myself to two which are not far from these astronomical subjects. One of them consists of the writings that were published against the Medicean Planets, which I recently discovered, and against the existence of which many passages of Holy Scripture were advanced; now that these planets can be seen by the whole world, I should very much like to hear in what new ways those same opponents interpret Scripture and excuse their blunder. The other example involves someone who has recently argued in print against astronomers and philosophers, to the effect that the moon does not receive its light from the sun but is itself luminous; ultimately he confirms, or rather convinces himself to be confirming, this fancy with various scriptural passages, which he thinks could not be accounted for if his opinion were not true and necessary. Nevertheless, it is as clear as sunlight that the moon is in itself dark.

It is thus obvious that, because these authors had not grasped the true meaning of Scripture, if they had commanded much authority they would have obliged it to compel others to hold as true conclusions repugnant to manifest reasons and to the senses. This is an abuse which I hope God will prevent from taking root or gaining influence, because it would in a short time require the prohibition of all ratiocinative sciences. In fact, the number of men ill-suited to understand adequately the Holy Scripture and the sciences is by nature much greater than the number of intelligent ones; thus the former, by superficially glancing through Scripture, would arrogate to themselves the authority of decreeing over all questions about nature in virtue of some word ill-understood by them and written by the sacred authors for some other purpose; nor could the small [323] number of the intelligent ones restrain the furious torrent of the others, who would find all the more followers, inasmuch as it is sweeter to be considered wise without study and labor than to wear oneself out unrelentingly in the pursuit of very arduous disciplines. However, we can render infinite thanks to the blessed God, whose benevolence frees us from this fear while it strips such persons of any authority. The deliberating, deciding, and decreeing about such important issues can be left to the excellent wisdom and goodness of very prudent Fathers and to the supreme authority of those who, guided by the Holy Spirit, can only behave in a holy manner and will not permit the irresponsibility of those others to gain influence. These sorts of men are, in my opinion, those toward whom serious and saintly writers become angry, not without reason. For instance, referring to the Holy Scripture, St. Jerome writes: "The chatty old woman, the doting old man, and the wordy sophist, one and all take in hand the Scriptures, rend them in pieces and teach them before they have learned them. Some with brows knit and bombastic words, balanced one against the other, philosophize concerning the sacred writings among weak women. Others—I blush to say it—learn of women what they are to teach men; and as if this were not enough, they boldly explain to others what they themselves by no means understand. I say nothing of persons who, like myself, have been familiar with secular literature before they have come to the study of the Holy Scriptures. Such men when they charm the popular ear by the finish of their style suppose every word they say to be a law of God. They do not deign to notice what prophets and apostles have intended but they adapt conflicting passages to suit their own meaning, as if it were a grand way of teaching—and not rather the faultiest of all—to misinterpret a writer's views and to force the Scriptures reluctantly to do their will" (Letter No. 53, to Paulinus).[22]

[§4.2.3] Among such lay writers should not be numbered some theologians whom I regard as men of profound learning and of the holiest lifestyle, and whom I therefore hold in high esteem and reverence. However, I cannot deny having some qualms, which I consequently wish could be removed; for in disputes about natural phenomena they seem to claim the right to force others by means of the authority of Scripture to follow the opinion which they think is most in accordance with its statements, and at the same time they believe they are not obliged to [324] answer observations and reasons to the contrary. As an explanation and a justification of this opinion of

---

22. Here quoted from Schaff and Wace 1893, 99. Galileo indicates the number of this letter as 103, but there is no doubt that his quotation is from what modern scholars and editors now designate as Letter No. 53. Further, I have slightly altered the punctuation and spelling in Schaff and Wace's translation for the sake of uniformity and easier comprehension.

theirs, they say that theology is the queen of all the sciences and hence must not in any way lower herself to accommodate the principles of other less dignified disciplines subordinate to her; rather, these others must submit to her as to a supreme empress and change and revise their conclusions in accordance with theological rules and decrees; moreover, they add that whenever in the subordinate science there is a conclusion which is certain on the strength of demonstrations and observations, and which is repugnant to some other conclusion found in Scripture, the practitioners of that science must themselves undo their own demonstrations and disclose the fallacies of their own observations, without help from theologians and scriptural experts; for, as stated, it is not proper to the dignity of theology to stoop to the investigation of the fallacies in the subordinate sciences, but it is sufficient for it to determine the truth of a conclusion with absolute authority and with the certainty that it cannot err. Then they say that the physical conclusions in regard to which we must rely on Scripture, without glossing or interpreting it in nonliteral ways, are those of which Scripture always speaks in the same way, and which all the Holy Fathers accept and interpret with the same meaning. Now, I happen to have some specific ideas on these claims, and I shall propose them in order to receive the proper advice from whoever is more competent than I in these subjects; I always defer to their judgment.

To begin with, I think one may fall into something of an equivocation if one does not distinguish the senses in which sacred theology is preeminent and worthy of the title of queen. For it could be such insofar as whatever is taught in all the other sciences is found explained and demonstrated in it by means of more excellent methods and of more sublime principles, in the way that, for example, the rules for measuring fields and for accounting are better contained in Euclid's geometry and arithmetic than they are [325] in the practices of surveyors and accountants; or else insofar as the topic on which theology focuses surpasses in dignity all the other topics which are the subject of the other sciences, and also insofar as its teaching proceeds in more sublime ways. I do not believe that theologians who are acquainted with the other sciences can assert that theology deserves the royal title and authority in the first sense; I think no one will say that geometry, astronomy, music, and medicine are treated more excellently and exactly in the sacred books than in Archimedes, Ptolemy, Boethius, and Galen. So it seems that the royal preeminence belongs to it in the second sense, namely, because of the eminence of the topic, and because of the admirable teaching of divine revelation in conclusions which could not be learned by men in any other way, and which concern chiefly the gaining of eternal bliss. So theology does deal with the loftiest divine contemplations, and for this it does occupy the royal throne and command the highest authority; and it does not come down to the lower and humbler speculations of the inferior sciences but rather (as stated above) it does not bother with them inasmuch as they are irrelevant to salvation. If all this is so, then officials and experts of theology should not arrogate to themselves the authority to issue decrees in the professions they neither exercise nor study; for this would be the same as if an absolute prince, knowing he had unlimited power to issue orders and to compel obedience, but being neither a physician nor an architect, wanted to direct medical treatment and the construction of buildings, resulting in serious danger to the life of the unfortunate sick and in the obvious collapse of structures.

Furthermore, to require astronomers to endeavor to protect themselves against their own observations and demonstrations, namely, to show that these are nothing but fallacies and sophisms, is to demand they do the impossible; for [326] that would be to require not only that they should not see what they see and not understand what they understand, but also that in their research they should find the contrary of what they find. That is, before they can do this, they should be shown how to manage having the lower faculties of the soul direct the higher ones, so that the imagination and the will could and would believe the contrary of what the intellect thinks (I am always speaking of purely physical propositions which are not matters of faith, rather than of supernatural propositions which are articles of faith). I should like to ask these very prudent Fathers to agree to examine very diligently the difference between debatable and demonstrative doctrines. Keeping firmly in mind the compelling power of necessary deductions, they should come to see more clearly that it is not within the power of the practitioners of demonstrative sciences to change opinion at will, choosing now this now that one; that there is a great difference between giving orders to a mathematician or a philosopher and giving them to a merchant or a lawyer; and that demonstrated conclusions about natural and celestial phenomena cannot be changed with the same ease as opinions about what is or is not legitimate in a contract, in a rental, or in commerce. This difference has been completely recognized by the Holy and very learned Fathers, as shown by their having made [327] a great effort to confute many philosophical arguments or, to be more exact, fallacies, and may be explicitly read in some of them. In particular, we read the following words in St. Augustine (*On the Literal Interpretation of Genesis,* book 1, chapter 21): "There should be no doubt about the following: whenever the experts of this world can truly demonstrate something about natural phenomena, we should show it not to be contrary to our Scriptures; but, whenever in their books they teach something contrary to the Holy Writ, we should without any doubt hold it to be most false, and also show this by any means we can; and in this way we should keep the faith of our Lord, in whom are hidden all the treasures of knowledge, in order not to be seduced by the verbosity of false philosophy or frightened by the superstition of fake religion."

These words imply, I think, the following doctrine: in the learned books of worldly authors are contained some propositions about nature which are truly demonstrated and others which are simply taught; in regard to the former, the task of wise theologians is to show that they are not contrary to Holy Scripture; as for the latter (which are taught but not demonstrated with necessity), if they contain anything contrary to the Holy Writ, then they must be considered indubitably false and must be demonstrated such by every possible means. So physical conclusions which have been truly demonstrated should not be given a lower place than scriptural passages, but rather one should clarify how such passages do not contradict those conclusions; therefore, before condemning a physical proposition, one must show that it is not conclusively demonstrated. Furthermore, it is much more reasonable and natural that this be done not by those who hold it to be true, but by those who regard it as false; for the fallacies of an argument can be found much more easily by those who regard it as false than by those who think it is true and conclusive, and indeed here it will happen that the more the followers of a given opinion thumb through books, examine the arguments, repeat the observations, and check the experiments, the more they will be testing [328] their belief. In fact, Your Highness knows what happened to the late mathematician of the University of Pisa:[23] in his old age he undertook an examination of Copernicus' doctrine with the hope of being able to refute it solidly, since he considered it false, even though he had never examined it; but it so happened that as soon as he understood

---

23. Antonio Santucci (d. 1613).

its foundations, procedures, and demonstrations he became convinced of it, and he turned from opponent to very strong supporter. I could also name other mathematicians (e.g., Clavius[24]) who, influenced by my recent discoveries, have admitted the necessity of changing the previous conception of the constitution of the world, since it can no longer stand up in any way.

It would be very easy to remove from the world the new opinion and doctrine if it were sufficient to shut the mouth of only one person; this is perhaps the belief of those who measure the judgments of others in terms of their own, and who thus think it is impossible that such an opinion can stand up and find followers. However, this business proceeds otherwise. For in order to accomplish that objective, it would be necessary not only to prohibit Copernicus' book and the writings of the other authors who follow the same doctrine, but also to ban all astronomical science completely; moreover, one would have to forbid men to look toward the heavens, so that they would not see that Mars and Venus are sometimes very close to and sometimes very far from the earth (the difference being that the latter sometimes appears forty times greater than at other times, and the former sixty times greater); nor should they be allowed to see the same Venus appear sometimes round and sometimes armed with very sharp horns[25] and many other observable phenomena which can in no way be adapted to the Ptolemaic system but provide very strong arguments for Copernicanism. At the moment, because of many new [329] observations and because of many scholars' contributions to its study, one is discovering daily that Copernicus' position is truer and truer and his doctrine firmer and firmer; so to prohibit Copernicus now, after being permitted for so many years when he was less widely followed and less well confirmed, would seem to me an encroachment on the truth and an attempt to step up its concealment and suppression in proportion to how much more it appears obvious and clear. Not to ban the whole book in its entirety, but to condemn as erroneous only this particular proposition, would cause greater harm to

---

24. Christoph Clavius (1538–1612), a Jesuit, professor at the Collegio Romano, one of the leading mathematicians and astronomers of his time, who was on friendly terms with Galileo.
25. Both the variation in the apparent magnitudes of Mars and Venus and the phases of Venus had been previously undetected, but they became observable with the telescope soon after the publication of *The Sidereal Messenger*.

souls, if I am not mistaken; for it would expose them to the possibility of seeing the proof of a proposition which it would then be sinful to believe. To prohibit the entire science would be no different than to reject hundreds of statements from the Holy Writ, which teach us how the glory and the greatness of the supreme God are marvelously seen in all of His works and by divine grace are read in the open book of the heavens. Nor should anyone think that the reading of the very lofty words written on those pages is completed by merely seeing the sun and the stars give off light, rise, and set, which is as far as the eyes of animals and of common people reach; on the contrary, those pages contain such profound mysteries and such sublime concepts that the vigils, labors, and studies of hundreds of the sharpest minds in uninterrupted investigations for thousands of years have not yet completely fathomed them. Even idiots realize that what their eyes see when they look at the external appearance of a human body is very insignificant in comparison to the admirable contrivances found in it by a competent and diligent philosopher-anatomist when he investigates how so many muscles, tendons, nerves, and bones are used; when he examines the function of the heart and of the other principal organs; when he searches for the seat of the vital faculties; when he observes the wonderful structures of the senses; and, with no end to his astonishment and curiosity, when he studies the location of the imagination, of memory, [330] and of reason. Likewise, what the unaided sense of sight shows is almost nothing in comparison to the sublime marvels which the mind of intelligent investigators reveals in the heavens through long and accurate observations. This is all I can think of in regard to this particular point.

[§4.2.4] Let us now examine their other argument: that physical propositions concerning which Scripture always says the same thing, and which all the Fathers unanimously accept in the same sense, should be understood in accordance with the literal meaning of the words, without glosses or interpretations, and should be accepted and held as most true; and that, since the sun's motion and earth's rest is a proposition of this sort, consequently it is an article of faith to hold it as true, and the contrary opinion is erroneous. Here it should be noticed, first, that some physical propositions are of a type such that by any human speculation and reasoning one can only attain a probable opinion and a verisimilar conjecture about them, rather than a certain and demonstrated science; an example is whether the stars are animate. Others are of a type such that either one has or one may firmly believe that it is possible to have, complete certainty on the basis of experiments, long observations, and necessary demonstrations; examples are whether or not the earth and the sun move, and whether or not the earth is spherical. As for the first type, I have no doubt at all that, where human reason cannot reach, and where consequently one cannot have a science, but only opinion and faith, it is appropriate piously to conform absolutely to the literal meaning of Scripture. In regard to the others, however, I should think, as stated above, that it would be proper to ascertain the facts first, so that they could guide us in finding the true meaning of Scripture; this would be found to agree absolutely with demonstrated facts, even though prima facie the words would sound otherwise, since two truths can never contradict each other. This doctrine seems to me very [331] correct and certain, inasmuch as I find it exactly written in St. Augustine. At one point he discusses the shape of heaven and what one should believe it to be, given that what astronomers affirm seems to be contrary to Scripture, since the former consider it round while the latter calls it stretched out like hide.[26] He decides one should not have the slightest worry that Scripture may contradict astronomers: one should accept its authority if what they say is false and based only on conjecture typical of human weakness; however, if what they say is proved with indubitable reasons, this Holy Father does not say that astronomers themselves be ordered to refute their demonstrations and declare their conclusion false, but he says one must show that what Scripture asserts about the hide is not contrary to those true demonstrations. Here are his words (*On the Literal Interpretation of Genesis*, book 2, chapter 9): "However, someone asks how what is written in our books, 'Who stretchest out the heavens like a hide,'[27] does not

---

26. This seems to refer to Psalm 103:2 (Douay), which reads in part "Who stretchest out the heaven like a pavilion," corresponding to Psalm 104:2 in the King James Version, which reads "who stretchest out the heavens like a curtain." Another relevant passage is Isaiah 40:22. Russo (1968, 346, nn. 1 and 2) comments that "neither St. Augustine nor Galileo seems to have understood that the hide concerned the hide of a tent," and that "the 'hide' in question is not a hide stretched out flat 'but the hide of a tent.'"
27. This presumably corresponds to Psalm 103:2 (Douay), Psalm 104:2 (King James), and Isaiah 40:22; however, I have translated the word *pellem* in this sentence as *hide* because this is how Galileo understands it here.

contradict those who attribute to heaven the shape of a sphere. Now, if what they say is false, let it contradict them by all means, for the truth lies in what is said by divine authority rather than what is conjectured by human weakness. But if, by chance, they can support it with such evidence that one cannot doubt it, then we have to demonstrate that what our books say about the hide is not contrary to those true reasons." Then he goes on to warn us that we must not be less careful in reconciling a scriptural passage with a demonstrated physical proposition than with another scriptural passage that may appear contrary. Indeed I think the caution of this saint deserves to be admired and emulated; for even in the case of obscure conclusions concerning which one cannot be sure whether they can be the subject of a science based on human demonstrations, he is very careful in declaring what one should believe. This can be seen from what he writes at the end of the second book of *On the Literal Interpretation of Genesis,* when discussing whether stars should be considered animate: "Although at present this cannot be easily known, nevertheless I think that in the course of examining Scripture one may find more appropriate passages whereby we would be entitled, if not to prove something for certain, at least to believe something on this topic based on the words of the sacred authority. Now then, always practicing a pious and serious moderation, we ought not to believe anything lightly about an obscure subject, lest [332] we reject (out of love for our error) something which later may be truly shown not to be in any way contrary to the holy books of either the Old or New Testament."

From this and other places it seems to me, if I am not mistaken, the intention of the Holy Fathers is that in questions about natural phenomena which do not involve articles of faith one must first consider whether they are demonstrated with certainty or known by sense experience, or whether it is possible to have such knowledge and demonstration. When one is in possession of this, since it too is a gift from God, one must apply it to the investigation of the true meanings of the Holy Writ at those places which apparently seem to read differently. These meanings will undoubtedly be grasped by wise theologians, along with the reasons why the Holy Spirit has sometimes wanted to hide them under words with a different literal meaning, whether in order to test us or for some other reason unknown to me.

Returning to the preceding argument, if we keep in mind the primary aim of the Holy Writ, I do not think that its always saying the same thing should make us disregard this rule; for if to accommodate popular understanding Scripture finds it necessary once to express a proposition with words whose meaning differs from the essence of the proposition, why should it not follow the same practice for the same reason every time it has to say the same thing? On the contrary, I think that to do otherwise would increase popular confusion and diminish the propensity to believe on the part of the people. Furthermore, in regard to the rest or motion of the sun and of the earth, experience clearly shows that to accommodate popular understanding it is indeed necessary to assert what the words of Scripture say; for even in our age when people are more refined, they are kept in the same opinion by reasons which, when carefully examined and pondered, will be found to be most frivolous and by observations which are either completely false or totally irrelevant; nor can one try to move them since they are not capable of understanding the contrary reasons, which are dependent on extremely delicate observations and on subtle demonstrations [333] supported by abstractions whose understanding requires a very vivid imagination. Therefore, even if the sun's rest and the earth's motion were more than certain and demonstrated among the experts, it would still be necessary to utter the contrary in order to maintain credibility with large numbers of people; for among a thousand laymen who might be asked about these details, perhaps not even one will be found who would not answer that he firmly believes that the sun moves and the earth stands still. However, no one should take this very common popular consensus as an argument for the truth of what is being asserted; for if we ask the same men about the reasons and motives why they believe that way, and if on the other hand we listen to the observations and demonstrations which induce those other few to believe the opposite, we shall find that the latter are convinced by very solid reasons and the former by the simplest appearances and by empty and ridiculous considerations.

It is therefore clear that it was necessary to attribute motion to the sun and rest to the earth in order not to confuse the meager understanding of the people, and not to make them obstinately reluctant to give assent to the principal dogmas which are absolutely articles of faith; but if it was necessary to do this, it is no wonder that this was most prudently done in divine Scripture. Indeed I shall say further that it was not only respect for popular inability, but also the current opinion of those times, that made the sacred writers accommodate themselves to received usage rather than to the essence of the matter in regard to subjects which are not necessary for eternal bliss. In fact,

speaking of this St. Jerome writes: "As if in the Holy Scriptures many
things were not said in accordance with the opinion of the time when
the facts are being reported, and not in accordance with the truth of
the matter" (Commentary on chapter 28 of Jeremiah). Elsewhere the
same saint says: "In Scripture it is customary for the historian to report many opinions as they were accepted by everyone at that time"
(Commentary on chapter 13 of Matthew). Finally, on the words in
chapter 27 of Job, "He stretched out the north [334] over the empty
space, and hangeth the earth upon nothing,"[28] St. Thomas notes that
Scripture calls empty and nothing the space which embraces and surrounds the earth, and which we know is not empty but full of air;
nevertheless, he says that Scripture calls it empty and nothing in order
to accommodate the belief of the people, who think there is nothing
in this space. Here are St. Thomas' words: "The upper hemisphere of
the heavens seems to us nothing but a space full of air, though common people consider it empty; thus it speaks in accordance with the
judgment of common people, as is the custom in Holy Scripture."
Now from this I think one can obviously argue that analogously the
Holy Scripture had a much greater reason to call the sun moving and
the earth motionless. For if we test the understanding of common
people, we shall find them much more incapable of becoming convinced of the sun's rest and earth's motion than of the fact that the
space surrounding us is full of air; therefore, if the sacred authors refrained from attempting to persuade the people about this point,
which was not that difficult for their understanding, it seems very reasonable to think that they followed the same style in regard to other
propositions which are much more recondite.

Indeed, Copernicus himself knew how much our imagination is
dominated by an old habit and by a way of conceiving things which
is already familiar to us since infancy, and so he did not want to increase the confusion and difficulty of his abstraction. Thus, after first
demonstrating that the motions which appear to us as belonging to
the sun or the firmament [335] really belong to the earth, then, in the
process of compiling their tables and applying them in practice, he
speaks of them as belonging to the sun and to the part of heaven
above the planets; for example, he speaks of the rising and setting of
the sun and of the stars, of changes in the obliquity of the zodiac and
in the equinoctial points, of the mean motion and the anomaly and

---

28. Job 26:7 (Douay).

the prosthaphaeresis[29] of the sun, and other similar things, which really belong to the earth. We call facts these things which appear to us as facts because, being attached to the earth, we are part of all its motions, and consequently we cannot directly detect these things in it but find it useful to consider it in relation to the heavenly bodies in which they appear to us. Therefore, note how appropriate it is to accommodate our usual manner of thinking.

Next consider the principle that the collective consensus of the Fathers, when they all accept in the same sense a physical proposition from Scripture, should authenticate it in such a way that it becomes an article of faith to hold it. I should think that at most this ought to apply only to those conclusions which the Fathers discussed and inspected with great diligence and debated on both sides of the issue and for which then they all agreed to reject one side and hold the other. However, the earth's motion and sun's rest are not of this sort, given that in those times this opinion was totally forgotten and far from academic dispute, and was not examined, let alone followed, by anyone; thus one may believe that the Fathers did not even think of discussing it, since the scriptural passages, their own opinion, and popular consensus were all in agreement, and no [336] contradiction by anyone was heard. Therefore, it is not enough to say that all the Fathers accept the earth's rest, etc., and so it is an article of faith to hold it; rather one would have to prove that they condemned the contrary opinion. For I can always say that their failure to reflect upon it and to discuss it made them leave it and allow it as the current opinion, but not as something resolved and established. I think I can say this with very good reason: for either the Fathers reflected upon this conclusion as if it were controversial or they did not; if not, then they could not have decided anything about it, even in their minds, nor should their failure oblige us to accept those principles which they did not, even in intention, impose; whereas if they examined it with care, then they would have condemned it had they judged it to be erroneous; but there is no record of their having done this. Indeed, after some theologians began to examine it, one sees that they did not deem it to be erroneous, as one can read in Diego de Zúñiga's *Commentaries on Job,* in regard to the words "Who shaketh the earth out of

---

29. In mathematical astronomy, prosthaphaeresis is "the correction necessary to find the 'true,' i.e., actual apparent, place of a planet, etc. from the mean place" (*Oxford English Dictionary*).

her place, etc." in chapter 9, verse 6; he discusses the Copernican position at length and concludes that the earth's motion is not against Scripture.

Furthermore, I would have doubts about the truth of this prescription, namely, whether it is true that the Church obliges one to hold as articles of faith such conclusions about natural phenomena, which are characterized only by the unanimous interpretation of all the Fathers. I believe it may be that those who think in this manner may want to amplify the decrees of the Councils in favor of their own opinion. For I do not see that in this regard they prohibit anything but tampering, in ways contrary to the interpretation of the Holy Church or of the collective consensus of the Fathers, with those propositions which are articles of faith, or which involve morals and pertain [337] to edification according to Christian doctrine; so speaks the Fourth Session of the Council of Trent. However, the motion or rest of the earth or the sun are not articles of faith and are not against morals; nor does anyone want to twist scriptural passages to contradict the Holy Church or the Fathers. Indeed, those who put forth this doctrine have never used scriptural passages, for it always remains the prerogative of serious and wise theologians to interpret the said passages in accordance with their true meaning. Moreover, it is very obvious that the decrees of the Councils agree with the Holy Fathers in regard to these details; for they are very far from wanting to accept as articles of faith similar physical conclusions or to reject as erroneous the contrary opinions, so much so that they prefer to pay attention to the primary intention of the Holy Church and consider it useless to spend time trying to ascertain those conclusions. Let me tell Your Most Serene Highness what St. Augustine (*On the Literal Interpretation of Genesis,* book 2, chapter 10) answers to those brethren who ask whether it is true that the heavens move or stand still: "To them I answer that these things should be examined with very subtle and demanding arguments, to determine truly whether or not it is so; but I do not have the time to undertake and to pursue these investigations, nor should such time be available to those whom we desire to instruct for their salvation and for the needs and benefit of the Holy Church."

However, suppose one were to decide that, even in the case of propositions about natural phenomena, they should be condemned or accepted on the basis of scriptural passages which are unanimously interpreted in the same way by all the Fathers; even then I do not see that this rule would apply in our case, given that one can read in the

Fathers different interpretations of the same passages. For example, Dionysius the Areopagite says that it was not the sun but the Prime Mobile which stopped;[30] St. Augustine thinks the same thing, namely, that all heavenly bodies stopped; and the bishop of Avila[31] is of the same opinion. Moreover, among the Jewish authors whom Josephus endorses, some thought that the sun did not really stop, but that it appeared so for the short time during which the Israelites defeated their enemies. Similarly, in the miracle at the time of Hezekiah, Paul of Burgos thinks that it did not take place in the sun but in the clock.[32] [338] At any rate, I shall demonstrate further below that, regardless of the world system one assumes, it is in fact necessary to gloss and to interpret the words of the text in Joshua.

[§4.2.5] Finally, let us grant these gentlemen more than they ask—namely, let us submit entirely to the opinion of wise theologians. Since this particular determination was not made by the ancient Fathers, it could be made by the wise ones of our age. The controversy concerns questions of natural phenomena and dilemmas whose answers are necessary and cannot be otherwise than in one of the two controversial ways; so they should first hear the experiments, observations, reasons, and demonstrations of philosophers and astronomers on both sides of the question, and then they would be able to determine with certainty whatever divine inspiration will communicate to them. No one should hope or fear that they would reach such an important decision without inspecting and discussing very minutely all the reasons for one side and for the other, and without ascertaining the facts: this cannot be hoped for by those who would pay no attention to risking the majesty and dignity of the Holy Writ to support their self-righteous creations; nor is this to be feared by those who seek nothing but the examination of the foundations of this doctrine

---

30. Dionysius the Areopagite was a disciple of St. Paul and bishop of Athens. Galileo is here referring to interpretations of the miracle described in Joshua 10:12–13, in which God stopped the sun in order to prolong daylight. This is discussed at great length a few pages below, where more precise references are also given.

31. Alfonso Tostado (1400–1455), professor of theology and philosophy at the University of Salamanca (Spain).

32. Paul of Burgos (d. 1435) was a Spanish Jew who converted to Christianity and became an influential scriptural theologian. The passage in question is Isaiah 38:8.

with the greatest care, and who do this only out of zeal for the truth and for the majesty, dignity, and authority of the Holy Writ, which every Christian must strive to uphold. No one can fail to see that this dignity is desired and upheld with much greater zeal by one group than by the other—by those who submit in every way to the Holy Church and who do not ask for the prohibition of this or that opinion, but only that they be allowed to present things whereby she could more reliably be sure of making the safest choice; and not by those who, blinded by their own interests or incited by malicious suggestions, preach that she immediately flash the sword since she has the power to do it, without considering that it is not always useful to do all that one can do. This opinion was not held by the holiest Fathers. Indeed, they knew how harmful and how contrary to the primary function of the Catholic Church it would be to want to use scriptural passages to establish conclusions about nature, when by means of observations and of necessary demonstrations one could at some point demonstrate the contrary of what [339] the words literally say; thus, not only were they very circumspect, but they left precepts for the edification of others. From St. Augustine, *On the Literal Interpretation of Genesis,* book 1, chapters 18 and 19,[33] we have the following: "In obscure subjects very far removed from our eyes, it may happen that even in the divine writings we read things that can be interpreted in different ways by different people, all consistent with the faith we have; in such a case, let us not rush into any one of these interpretations with such precipitous commitment that we are ruined if it is rightly undermined by a more diligent and truthful investigation; such recklessness would mean that we were struggling for our opinions and not for those of Scripture, and that we wanted to make scriptural opinion conform to ours, when we ought to want to make ours conform to that of Scripture." A little further, to teach us how no proposition can be against the faith unless it is first shown to be false, he adds: "It is not against the faith as long as it is not refuted by an unquestionable truth; if this happens, then it was not contained in the divine Scripture but originated from human ignorance." From this, one sees the falsehood of any meanings given to scriptural passages which do not agree with demonstrated truths; and so one must search for the correct meaning

---

33. Of the several quotations from Augustine in this paragraph and the next, the next is the only one that comes from chapter 18; the others six quotations all come from chapter 19.

of Scripture with the help of demonstrated truth, rather than taking the literal meaning of the words, which may seem to be the truth to our weak understanding, and trying somehow to force nature and to deny observations and necessary demonstrations.

Your Highness should also note with how much circumspection this very holy man proceeds before deciding to assert that some scriptural interpretation is so certain and sure that there is no fear of encountering disturbing difficulties; not satisfied with just any scriptural meaning which might agree with some demonstration, he adds: "But if this were proved to be true by an unquestionable argument, it would be still uncertain whether by these words the writer of the holy books meant this or something else no less true; for if the rest of the context of the passage showed that he did not intend this, then what he did intend would not thereby be falsified but would still be true and more beneficial to know." Now, what increases our amazement about the circumspection with which this author proceeds is the fact that he is still not completely sure upon seeing that demonstrative reasons, as well as the literal scriptural meaning and the preceding and subsequent text, [340] all point in the same direction, and so he adds the following words: "If the context of Scripture did not disprove that the writer meant this, one could still ask whether he might not have meant the other." Still he does not decide to accept this meaning or exclude that one, but rather he does not think he can ever be sufficiently cautious, and so he continues: "If we found that he could have meant the other, then it would be uncertain which of the two he intended; and if both interpretations were supported by solid documentation, it would not be implausible to believe that he meant both." Next, he seems to want to give the rationale for his procedure by showing to us the dangers to which certain people would expose themselves, Scripture, and the Church; these are people who, concerned more with the preservation of their own errors than with the dignity of Scripture, would want to extend its authority beyond the limits which it prescribes for itself. And so he adds the following words, which by themselves should suffice to repress and to temper the excessive license which some people arrogantly take: "In fact, it often happens that even a non Christian has views based on very conclusive reasons or observations about the earth, heaven, the other elements of this world, the motion and revolutions or the size and distances of the stars, the eclipses of the sun and moon, the cycles of years and epochs, the nature of animals, of plants, of rocks, and similar things. Now, it is very scandalous, as well as harmful and to be avoided at all costs, that any infidel should hear a Christian speak about these things as if he were doing so in accordance with the Christian Scriptures and should see him err so deliriously as to be forced into laughter. The distressing thing is not so much that an erring man should be laughed at, but that our authors should be thought by outsiders to believe such things, and should be criticized and rejected as ignorant, to the great detriment of those whose salvation we care about. For how can they believe our books in regard to the resurrection of the dead, the hope of eternal life, and the kingdom of heaven, when they catch a Christian committing an error about something they know very well, when they declare false his opinion taken from those books, and when they find these full of fallacies in regard to things they have already been able to observe or to establish by unquestionable argument?" Finally, we can see how offended are the truly wise and prudent Fathers by these people who, in order to support propositions they do not [341] understand, constrain scriptural passages in certain ways and then compound their first error by producing other passages which they understand even less than the former ones. This is explained by the same saint with the following words: "It is impossible to express sufficiently well how much harm and sorrow those who are reckless and presumptuous cause to prudent brethren. This happens when they begin to be rebuked and refuted for their distorted and false opinions by those who do not accept the authority of our books, and so they put forth those same books to prove and to defend what they had said with very superficial recklessness and very obvious falsity, and they even quote many of their passages from memory, considering them supporting testimony, but without understanding either what they say or what they are talking about."

To this type belong, I think, those who will not or cannot understand the demonstrations and the observations with which the originator and the followers of this position confirm it, and who thus are concerned with putting forth Scripture. They do not notice that the more scriptural passages they produce, and the more they persist in claiming that these are very clear and not susceptible to other meanings besides what they advance, the greater the harm resulting to the dignity of Scripture if later the truth were known to be clearly contrary and were to cause confusion (especially if these people's judgment had much authority in the first place). There would be harm

and confusion at least among those who are separated from the Holy
Church, toward whom she is nevertheless very zealous like a mother
who wants to be able to hold them on her lap. Your Highness can
therefore see how inappropriate is the procedure of those who, in
disputes about nature, as a first step advance arguments based on scriptural passages, especially when very often they do not adequately understand these.

However, if these people truly feel and fully believe they have the
true meaning of some particular scriptural passage, it would have to
follow necessarily that they are also sure of possessing the absolute
truth about the physical conclusion they intend to discuss and, at the
same time, that they know they have a very great advantage over the
opponent, who has to defend the false side; for whoever is supporting the truth can have many sense experiences and many necessary
demonstrations on his side, [342] whereas the opponent cannot use
anything but deceptive presentations, paralogisms, and fallacies. Now,
if they know that by staying within the limits of the physical subject
of discussion and using only philosophical weapons, they are in any
case so superior to the opponent, why is it that when they come to
the debate they immediately seize an irresistible and fearful weapon,
so that their opponent is frightened at its mere sight? To tell the truth,
I believe they are the ones who are frightened and are trying to find
a way of repelling the enemy because they are unable to resist his assaults. That is why they forbid him to use the reason which he received through the Divine Goodness and why they abuse the very
proper authority of the Holy Scripture, which (when adequately understood and used) can never conflict with clear observation and necessary demonstrations, as all theologians agree. However, the fact that
these people take refuge in Scripture, to cover up their inability to
understand and to answer the contrary arguments, should be of no
advantage to them, if I am not mistaken, since till now such an opinion has never been condemned by the Holy Church. Therefore, if
they wanted to proceed with sincerity, they could remain silent and
admit their inability to discuss similar subjects; or else they could first
reflect that it is not within their power, nor within that of anyone but
the Supreme Pontiff and the sacred Councils, to declare a proposition
erroneous, but that they are free to discuss whether it is false; then,
understanding that it is impossible for a proposition to be both true
and heretical, they should focus on the issue which more concerns
them, namely, on demonstrating its falsity; if they were to discover

this falsity, then either it would no longer be necessary to prohibit it because no one would follow it, or its prohibition would be safe and without the risk of any scandal.

Thus let these people apply themselves to refuting the arguments of Copernicus and of the others, and let them leave its condemnation as erroneous and heretical to the proper authorities; but let them not hope that the very cautious and very wise Fathers and the Infallible One with his absolute wisdom are about to make rash decisions like those into which they would be rushed by their special interests and feelings. [343] For in regard to these and other similar propositions which do not directly involve the faith, no one can doubt that the Supreme Pontiff always has the absolute power of permitting or condemning them; however, no creature has the power of making them be true or false, contrary to what they happen to be by nature and de facto. So it seems more advisable to first become sure about the necessary and immutable truth of the matter, over which no one has control, than to condemn one side when such certainty is lacking; this would imply a loss of freedom of decision and of choice insofar as it would give necessity to things which are presently indifferent, free, and dependent on the will of the supreme authority. In short, if it is inconceivable that a proposition should be declared heretical when one thinks that it may be true, it should be futile for someone to try to bring about the condemnation of the earth's motion and sun's rest unless he first shows it to be impossible and false.

[§4.2.6] There remains one last thing for us to examine: to what extent it is true that the Joshua passage[34] can be taken without altering the literal meaning of the words, and how it can be that, when the sun obeyed Joshua's order to stop, from this it followed that the day was prolonged by a large amount.

Given the heavenly motions in accordance with the Ptolemaic system, this is something which in no way can happen. For the sun's motion along the ecliptic takes place in the order of the signs of the zodiac, which is from west to east; this is contrary to the motion of the Prime Mobile from east to west, which is what causes day and night; therefore, it is clear that if the sun stops its own true motion, the day becomes shorter and not longer and that, on the contrary, the

---

34. Joshua 10:12–13; I quote this passage in the Introduction, §0.7.

way to prolong it would be to speed up the sun's motion; thus, to make the sun stay for some time at the same place above the horizon, without going down toward the west, [344] it would be necessary to accelerate its motion so as to equal the motion of the Prime Mobile, which would be to accelerate it to about three hundred and sixty times its usual motion. Hence, if Joshua had wanted his words taken in their literal and most proper meaning, he would have told the sun to accelerate its motion by an amount such that, when carried along by the Prime Mobile, it would not be made to set; but his words were being heard by people who perhaps had no other knowledge of heavenly motions except for the greatest and most common one from east to west; thus he adapted himself to their knowledge and spoke in accordance with their understanding, because he did not want to teach them about the structure of the spheres but to make them understand the greatness of the miracle of the prolongation of the day.

Perhaps it was this consideration that first led Dionysius the Areopagite (in the Letter to Polycarpus) to say that in this miracle the Prime Mobile stopped and, as a consequence of its stopping, all other celestial spheres stopped. The same opinion is held by St. Augustine himself (in book 2 of *On the Miracles of the Holy Scripture*), and the Bishop of Avila supports it at length (in questions 22 and 24 of his commentary on chapter 10 of Joshua). Indeed one sees that Joshua himself intended to stop the whole system of celestial spheres, from his giving the order also to the moon, even though it has nothing to do with the prolongation of the day; in the injunction given to the moon one must include the orbs of the other planets, which are not mentioned here, as they are not in the rest of the Holy Scripture, since its intention has never been to teach us the astronomical sciences.

I think therefore, if I am not mistaken, that one can clearly see that, given the Ptolemaic system, it is necessary to interpret the words in a way different from their literal meaning. Guided by St. Augustine's very useful prescriptions, I should say that the best nonliteral interpretation is not necessarily this, if anyone can find another which is perhaps better and more suitable. So now I want to examine whether the same miracle could be understood in a way more in accordance with what we read in Joshua, if to the Copernican system we add [345] another discovery which I recently made about the solar body. However, I continue to speak with the same reservations—to the effect that I am not so enamored with my own opinions as to want to place them ahead of those of others; nor do I believe it is impossible to put forth interpretations which are better and more in accordance with the Holy Writ.

Let us first assume, in accordance with the opinion of the abovementioned authors, that in the Joshua miracle the whole system of heavenly motions was stopped, so that the stopping of only one would not introduce unnecessarily universal confusion and great turmoil in the whole order of nature. Second, I think that although the solar body does not move from the same place, it turns on itself, completing an entire rotation in about one month, as I feel I have conclusively demonstrated in my *Sunspot Letters;* this motion is sensibly seen to be inclined southward in the upper part of the globe and thus to tilt northward in the lower part, precisely in the same manner as the revolutions of all planetary orbs. Third, the sun may be regarded as a noble body, and it is the source of light illuminating not only the moon and the earth but also all the other planets, which are in themselves equally dark; having conclusively demonstrated this, I do not think it would be far from correct philosophizing to say that, insofar as it is the greatest minister of nature and, in a way, the heart and soul of the world, it transmits to the surrounding bodies not only light, but also (by turning on itself) motion; thus, just as all motion of the limbs of an animal would cease if the motion of its heart were to cease, in the same way if the sun's rotation stopped then all planetary revolutions would also stop. Now, concerning the admirable power and strength of the sun I could quote the supporting statements of many serious writers, but I want to restrict myself to just one passage from the book *The Divine Names* by the Blessed Dionysius the Areopagite. He writes this about the sun: "Light also gathers and attracts to itself all things that are seen, that move, that are illuminated, that are heated, and, in a word, that are surrounded by its splendor. Thus the sun is called Helios because [346] it collects and gathers all things that are dispersed." And a little below that he again writes about the sun: "If in fact this sun, which we see and which (despite the multitude and dissimilarity of the essences and qualities of observed things) is nevertheless one, spreads its light equally and renews, nourishes, preserves, perfects, divides, joins, warms up, fertilizes, increases, changes, strengthens, produces, moves, and vitalizes all things; and if everything in this universe in accordance with its own power partakes of one and the same sun and contains within itself an equal anticipation of the causes of the many things which are shared; then certainly all the more reason, etc." Therefore, given that the sun is both the source of light and the origin of motion, and given that God wanted the whole world system to remain motionless for several hours as a result of Joshua's order, it was sufficient to stop the sun, and then its immobility stopped all the other turnings, so that the earth as well as the moon and the sun (and all the other planets) remained in the same arrangement; and during that whole time the night did not approach, and the day miraculously got longer. In this manner, by stopping the sun, and without changing or upsetting at all the way the other stars appear or their mutual arrangement, the day on the earth could have been lengthened in perfect accord with the literal meaning of the sacred text.

Furthermore, what deserves special appreciation, if I am not mistaken, is that with the Copernican system one can very clearly and very easily give a literal meaning to another detail which one reads about the same miracle; that is, that the sun stopped in the middle of heaven. Serious theologians have raised a difficulty about this passage: it seems very probable that, when Joshua asked for the prolongation of the day, the sun was close to setting and not at the meridian; for it was then about the time of the summer solstice, and consequently the days were very long, so that if the sun had been at the meridian then it does not seem likely that it would have been necessary to pray for a lengthening of the day in order to win a battle, since the still remaining time of seven hours or more could very well have been sufficient. Motivated by this argument, very serious theologians have held that the sun really was close to setting; [347] this is also what the words "Sun, stand thou still" seem to say, because if it had been at the meridian, then either there would have been no need to seek a miracle or it would have been sufficient to pray merely for some slowing down. This opinion is held by the Bishop of Gaeta,[35] and it is also accepted by Magalhaens,[36] who confirms it by saying that on the same day, before the order to the sun, Joshua had done so many other things that it was impossible to complete them in half a day; thus they really resort to interpreting the words "in the midst of heaven" somewhat implausibly, saying they mean the same as that the sun stopped while it was in our hemisphere, namely, above the horizon. We can remove this and every other implausibility, if I am not mistaken, by placing the sun, as the Copernican system does and as it is most

---

35. Thomas de Vio (1468–1534), author of a commentary on St. Thomas Aquinas' *Summa theologiae.*
36. Cosme Magalhaens (1553–1624), author of a commentary on Joshua published in 1612.

necessary to do, in the middle, namely, at the center of the heavenly orbs and of the planetary revolutions; for at any hour of the day, whether at noon or in the afternoon, the day would have been lengthened and all heavenly turnings stopped by the sun stopping in the middle of the heavens, namely, at the center of the heavens, where it is located. Furthermore, this interpretation agrees all the more with the literal meaning inasmuch as, if one wanted to claim that the sun's stopping occurred at the noon hour, then the proper expression to use would have been to say that it "stood still at the meridian point," or "at the meridian circle," and not "in the midst of heaven"; in fact, for a spherical body such as heaven, the middle is really and only the center.

As for other scriptural passages which seem to contradict this position, I have no doubt that, if it were known to be true and demonstrated, those same theologians who consider such passages incapable of being interpreted consistently with it (as long as they regard it as false) would find highly congenial interpretations for them; this would be especially true if they were to add some knowledge of the astronomical sciences to their expertise about Holy Writ. Just as now, when they consider it false, they think that whenever they read Scripture they only find statements repugnant to it, so if they thought otherwise they would perchance find an equal number of passages agreeing with it. Then perhaps they would judge [348] it very appropriate for the Holy Church to tell us that God placed the sun at the center of heaven and that therefore He brings about the ordered motions of the moon and the other wandering stars by making it turn around itself like a wheel, given that she sings:

> Most holy Lord and God of heaven,
> Who to the glowing sky hast given
> The fires that in the east are born
> With gradual splendors of the morn;
> Who, on the fourth day, didst reveal
> The sun's enkindled flaming wheel,
> Didst set the moon her ordered ways,
> And stars their ever-winding maze.[37]

---

37. Here quoted from *The English Hymnal with Tunes*, p. 89. These are the first two of five stanzas of the hymn whose first Latin line is "*Caeli Deus sanctissime*," deriving from the fourth or fifth century; cf. Julian 1892, 241.

They could also say that the word firmament is *literally* very appropriate for the stellar sphere and everything above the planetary orbs, which is totally still and motionless according to this arrangement. Similarly, if the earth were rotating, then, where one reads "He had not yet made the earth, nor the rivers, nor the poles of the terrestrial globe,"[38] one could understand its poles literally; for there would be no point in attributing these poles to the terrestrial globe if it did not have to turn around them.

Using a Biblical account to boost

---

38. Cf. Proverbs 8:26. I have translated Galileo's Latin quotation literally in order to appreciate his point, which would certainly be lost with the King James Version and might still be with the Douay Version.

CHAPTER 5[1]

Reply to Cardinal Bellarmine (1615)[2]

§5.1 Cardinal Bellarmine's Letter to Foscarini[3]

[171] To the Very Reverend Father Paolo Antonio Foscarini, Provincial of the Carmelites in the Province of Calabria:

My Very Reverend Father,

I have read with interest the letter in Italian and the essay in Latin which Your Paternity sent me; I thank you for the one and for the other and confess that they are all full of intelligence and erudition. You ask for my opinion, and so I shall give it to you, but very briefly, since now you have little time for reading and I for writing.

First, I say that it seems to me that Your Paternity and Mr. Galileo are proceeding prudently by limiting yourselves to speaking suppositionally and not absolutely, as I have always believed that Copernicus spoke. For there is no danger in saying that, by assuming the earth moves and the sun stands still, one saves all the appearances better than by postulating eccentrics and epicycles; and that is sufficient for the mathematician. However, it is different to want to affirm that in reality the sun is at the center of the world and only turns on itself without moving from east to west, and the earth is in the third heaven[4] and revolves with great speed around the sun; this is a very dangerous thing, likely not only to irritate all scholastic philosophers and theologians, but also to harm the Holy Faith by rendering Holy Scripture false. For Your Paternity has well shown many ways of interpreting Holy Scripture, but has not applied them to particular cases; without a doubt you would have encountered very great

---

1. Reprinted from: Maurice A. Finocchiaro, trans. and ed., *The Galileo Affair: A Documentary History,* © 1989 by the Regents of the University of California. Published by the University of California Press.
2. For the historical background, see the Introduction, especially §0.7.
3. Galilei 1890–1909, 12: 171–72; translated by Finocchiaro (1989, 67–69).
4. "In the third heaven" just means in the third orbit around the sun.

difficulties if you had wanted to interpret all those passages you yourself cited.

[172] Second, I say that, as you know, the Council[5] prohibits interpreting Scripture against the common consensus of the Holy Fathers; and if Your Paternity wants to read not only the Holy Fathers, but also the modern commentaries on Genesis, the Psalms, Ecclesiastes, and Joshua, you will find all agreeing in the literal interpretation that the sun is in heaven and turns around the earth with great speed, and that the earth is very far from heaven and sits motionless at the center of the world. Consider now, with your sense of prudence, whether the Church can tolerate giving Scripture a meaning contrary to the Holy Fathers and to all the Greek and Latin commentators. Nor can one answer that this is not a matter of faith, since if it is not a matter of faith "as regards the topic," it is a matter of faith "as regards the speaker"; and so it would be heretical to say that Abraham did not have two children and Jacob twelve, as well as to say that Christ was not born of a virgin, because both are said by the Holy Spirit through the mouth of the prophets and the apostles.

Third, I say that if there were a true demonstration that the sun is at the center of the world and the earth in the third heaven, and that the sun does not circle the earth but the earth circles the sun, then one would have to proceed with great care in explaining the Scriptures that appear contrary, and say rather that we do not understand them than that what is demonstrated is false. But I will not believe that there is such a demonstration, until it is shown me. Nor is it the same to demonstrate that by assuming the sun to be at the center and the earth in heaven one can save the appearances, and to demonstrate that in truth the sun is at the center and the earth in heaven; for I believe the first demonstration may be available, but I have very great doubts about the second, and in case of doubt one must not abandon the Holy Scripture as interpreted by the Holy Fathers. I add that the one who wrote, "The sun also ariseth, and the sun goeth down, and hasteth to his place where he arose,"[6] was Solomon, who not only spoke inspired by God, but was a man above all others wise and learned in the human sciences and in the knowledge of created things; he received all this wisdom from God; therefore it is not likely that he was affirming something that was contrary to truth already

5. The Council of Trent (1545–63).
6. Ecclesiastes 1:5 (King James Version).

demonstrated or capable of being demonstrated. Now, suppose you say that Solomon speaks in accordance with appearances, since it seems to us that the sun moves (while the earth does so), just as to someone who moves away from the seashore on a ship it looks like the shore is moving. I shall answer that when someone moves away from the shore, although it appears to him that the shore is moving away from him, nevertheless he knows that this is an error and corrects it, seeing clearly that the ship moves and not the shore; but in regard to the sun and the earth, no scientist has any need to correct the error, since he clearly experiences that the earth stands still and that the eye is not in error when it judges that the sun moves, as it also is not in error when it judges that the moon and the stars move. And this is enough for now.

With this I greet dearly Your Paternity, and I pray to God to grant you all your wishes.

At home, 12 April 1615.

To Your Reverend Paternity.

As a Brother,
Cardinal Bellarmine.

§5.2 Galileo's Considerations on the Copernican Opinion, Part I[7]

[351] In order to remove (as much as the blessed God allows me) the occasion to deviate from the most correct judgment about the resolution of the pending controversy, I shall try to do away with two ideas. These are notions which I believe some are attempting to impress on the minds of those persons who are charged with the deliberations, and, if I am not mistaken, they are concepts far from the truth.

The first is that no one has any reason to fear that the outcome might be scandalous; for the earth's stability and sun's motion are so well demonstrated in philosophy that we can be sure and indubitably certain about them; on the other hand, the contrary position is such an immense paradox and obvious foolishness that no one can doubt in any way that it cannot be demonstrated now or ever, or indeed that it can never find a place in the mind of sensible persons. The other

---

7. Galilei 1890–1909, 5: 351–63; translated by Finocchiaro (1989, 70–80).

idea which they try to spread is the following: although that contrary assumption has been used by Copernicus and other astronomers, they did this in a suppositional manner and insofar as it can account more conveniently for the appearances of celestial motions and facilitate astronomical calculations and computations, and it is not the case that the same persons who assumed it believed it to be true de facto and in nature; so the conclusion is that one can safely proceed to condemning it. However, if I am not mistaken, these ideas are fallacious and far from the truth, as I can show with the following considerations. These will only be general and suitable to be understood without much effort and labor even by someone who is not well versed in the natural and astronomical sciences. For if there were the opportunity to treat these [352] points with those who are very experienced in these studies, or at least who have the time to do the work required by the difficulty of the subject, then I should propose nothing but the reading of Copernicus' own book; from it and from the strength of his demonstrations one could clearly see how true or false are the two ideas we are discussing.

That it is not to be disparaged as ridiculous is, therefore, clearly shown by the quality of the men, both ancient and modern, who have held and do hold it. No one can regard it as ridiculous unless he considers ridiculous and foolish Pythagoras with all his school, Philolaus (teacher of Plato), Plato himself (as Aristotle testifies in his book *On the Heavens*), Heraclides of Pontus, Ecphantus,[8] Aristarchus of Samos, Hicetas, and Seleucus the mathematician. Seneca himself not only does not ridicule it, but he makes fun of those who do, writing in his book *On Comets:* "It is also important to study these questions in order to learn whether the universe goes around the motionless earth, or the earth rotates but the universe does not. For some have said that we are naturally unaware of motion, that sunrise and sunset are not due to the motion of the heavens, but that it is we ourselves who rise and set. The matter deserves consideration, so that we may know the conditions of our existence, whether we stand still or move very fast, whether God drives everything around us or drives us."[9] Regarding

---

8. Ecphantus was an ancient Greek who lived in Syracuse at the beginning of the fifth century B.C.

9. Galileo gives no exact reference for this passage, which he leaves in Latin; it is here translated directly from his quotation. Cf. Seneca, *Quaestiones naturales,* book vii, chapter 2.

the moderns, Nicolaus Copernicus first accepted it and amply confirmed it in his whole book. Then there were others: William Gilbert, a distinguished physician and philosopher, who treats it at length and confirms it in his book *On the Loadstone;*[10] Johannes Kepler, a living illustrious philosopher and mathematician in the service of the former and the current emperor, follows the same opinion; Origanus (David Tost) at the beginning of his *Ephemerides*[11] supports the earth's motion with a very long discussion; and there is no lack of other authors who have published their reasons on the matter. Furthermore, though they have not published anything, I could name very many followers of this doctrine living in Rome, Florence, Venice, Padua, Naples, Pisa, Parma, and other places. This doctrine is not, therefore, ridiculous, having been accepted by great men; and, though their number is small compared to the followers of the common position, this is an indication of its being difficult to understand, rather than of its absurdity.

Moreover, that it is grounded on very powerful and effective [353] reasons may be shown from the fact that all its followers were previously of the contrary opinion, and indeed that for a long time they laughed at it and considered it foolish. Copernicus and I, and all others who are alive, are witnesses to this. Now, who will not believe that an opinion which is considered silly and indeed foolish, which has hardly one out of a thousand philosophers following it, and which is disapproved by the Prince[12] of the prevailing philosophy, can become acceptable through anything but very firm demonstrations, very clear experiences, and very subtle observations? Certainly no one will be dissuaded of an opinion imbibed with mother's milk from his earliest training, accepted by almost the whole world, and supported by the authority of very serious writers, unless the contrary reasons are more than effective. If we reflect carefully, we find that there is more value in the authority of a single person who follows the Copernican

---

10. William Gilbert (1540–1603), *De Magnete magneticisque corporibus et de magno magnete Tellure physiologia nova* (London, 1600); the full title translates as: *New Physics of the Loadstone, of Magnetic Bodies, and of the Great Loadstone the Earth;* published as *On the Loadstone and Magnetic Bodies,* Mottelay translation (New York, 1893).

11. I.e., *Origani novae coelestium motuum ephemerides* (Frankfurt, 1609); *ephemerides* (plural of *ephemeris*) are astronomical tables showing in a systematic way the positions of heavenly bodies at various times.

12. This is probably a reference to Aristotle.

opinion than in that of one hundred others who hold the contrary, since those who are persuaded of the truth of the Copernican system were in the beginning all very opposed. So I argue as follows.

Either those who are to be persuaded are capable of understanding the reasons of Copernicus and others who follow him, or they are not; moreover, either these reasons are true and demonstrative, or they are fallacious. If those who are to be persuaded are incapable, then they will never be persuaded by the true or by the false reasons; those who are capable of understanding the strength of the demonstrations will likewise never be persuaded if these demonstrations are fallacious; so neither those who do nor those who do not understand will be persuaded by fallacious reasons. Therefore, given that absolutely no one can be dissuaded from the first idea by fallacious reasons, it follows as a necessary consequence that, if anyone is persuaded of the contrary of what he previously believed, the reasons are persuasive and true. But as a matter of fact there are [354] many who are already persuaded by Copernican reasons. Therefore, it is true both that these reasons are effective, and that the opinion does not deserve the label of ridiculous but the label of worthy of being very carefully considered and pondered.

Furthermore, how futile it is to argue for the plausibility of this or that opinion simply from the large number of followers may be easily inferred from this: no one follows this opinion who did not previously believe the contrary; but instead you will not find even a single person who, after holding this opinion, will pass to the other one, regardless of any discussion he hears; consequently, one may judge, even if he does not understand the reasons for one side or for the other, that probably the demonstrations for the earth's motion are much[13] stronger than those for the other side. But I shall say more, namely, that if the probability of the two positions were something to be won by ballot, I would be willing to concede defeat when the opposite side had one more vote than I out of one hundred; not only that, but I would be willing to agree that every individual vote of the opponents was worth ten of mine, as long as the decision was made by persons who had perfectly heard, intimately penetrated, and subtly examined all the reasons and evidence of the two sides; indeed it is

---

13. Here the translation in Finocchiaro 1989, 73, has been corrected by inserting "much."

reasonable to expect that such would be those who cast the votes. Hence this opinion is not ridiculous and contemptible, but somewhat shaky is the position of whoever wanted to capitalize on the common opinion of the many who have not accurately studied these authors. What then should we say of the noises and the idle chatter of someone who has not understood even the first and simplest principles of these doctrines, and who is not qualified to understand them ever? What importance should we give him?

Consider now those who persist in wanting to say that as an astronomer Copernicus considered the earth's motion and the sun's stability only a hypothesis which is more adequate to save celestial appearances and to calculate the motions of planets, but that he did not believe it to be true in reality and in nature. With all due respect, these people show that they have been too prone to believe the word of someone who speaks more out of whim than out of experience with Copernicus' book or with understanding the nature of this business. For this reason they talk about it in a way that is not altogether right.

[355] First, limiting ourselves to general considerations, let us see his preface to Pope Paul III, to whom he dedicates the work. We shall find, to begin with, as if to comply with what they call the astronomer's task, that he had done and completed the work in accordance with the hypothesis of the prevailing philosophy and of Ptolemy himself, so that there was in it nothing lacking. But then, taking off the clothes of a pure astronomer and putting on those of a contemplator of nature, he undertook to examine whether this astronomical assumption already introduced, which was completely satisfactory regarding the calculations and the appearances of the motions of all planets, could also truly happen in the world and in nature. He found that in no way could such an arrangement of parts exist: although each by itself was well-proportioned, when they were put together the result was a very monstrous chimera. And so he began to investigate what the system of the world could really be in nature, no longer for the sole convenience of the pure astronomer, whose calculations he had complied with, but in order to come to an understanding of such a noble physical problem; he was confident that, if one had been able to account for mere appearances by means of hypotheses which are not true, this could be done much better by means of the true and physical constitution of the world. Having at his disposal a very large number of physically true and real observations of

the motions of the stars (and without this knowledge it is wholly impossible to solve the problem), he worked tirelessly in search of such
a constitution. Encouraged by the authority of so many great men,
he examined the motion of the earth and the stability of the sun.
Without their encouragement and authority, by himself either he
would not have conceived the idea, or he would have considered it a
very great absurdity and paradox, as he confesses to have considered
it at first. But then, through long sense observations, favorable results,
and very firm demonstrations, he found it so consonant with the harmony of the world that he became completely certain of its truth.
Hence this position is not introduced to satisfy the pure astronomer,
but to satisfy the necessity of nature.

Furthermore, Copernicus knew and wrote in the same place that
publishing this opinion would have made him look insane to the
numberless followers of current philosophy, and especially to each and
every [356] layman. Nevertheless, urged by the requests of the Cardinal of Capua[14] and the Bishop of Kulm,[15] he published it. Now, would
he not have been really mad if, considering this opinion physically
false, he had published that he believed it to be true, with the certain
consequence that he would be regarded as a fool by the whole world?
And why would he not have declared that he was using it only as an
astronomer, but that he denied it as a philosopher, thus escaping the
universal label of foolishness, to the advantage of his common sense?

Moreover, Copernicus states in great detail the grounds and reasons why the ancients believed the earth to be motionless, and then,
examining the value of each in turn, he shows them to be ineffective.
Now, who ever saw a sensible author engaged in confuting the
demonstrations that confirm a proposition he considers true and real?
And what kind of judgment would it be to criticize and to condemn a
conclusion while in reality he wanted the reader to believe that he accepted it? This sort of incoherence cannot be attributed to such a man.

Furthermore, note carefully that, since we are dealing with the
motion or stability of the earth or of the sun, we are in a dilemma of
contradictory propositions (one of which has to be true), and we cannot in any way resort to saying that perhaps it is neither this way nor
that way. Now, if the earth's stability and sun's motion are de facto

---

14. Cardinal Nicolaus von Schoenberg (1472–1537), archbishop of Capua.
15. Tiedemann Giese (1480–1550), Polish friend of Copernicus.

physically true and the contrary position is absurd, how can one reasonably say that the false view agrees better than the true one with the phenomena clearly visible and sensed in the movements and arrangement of the stars? Who does not know that there is a most agreeable harmony among all truths of nature, and a most sharp dissonance between false positions and true effects? Will it happen, then, that the earth's motion and sun's stability agree in every way with the arrangement of all other bodies in the universe and with all the phenomena, a thousand of them, which we and our predecessors have observed in great detail, and that this position is false? And can the earth's stability and sun's motion be considered true and not agree in any way with the other truths? If one could say that neither this nor that position is true, it might happen that one would be more convenient than the other in accounting for the appearances. But, given two [357] positions, one of which must be true and the other false, to say that the false one agrees better with the effects of nature is really something that surpasses my imagination. I add: if Copernicus confesses to having fully satisfied astronomers by means of the hypothesis commonly accepted as true, how can one say that by means of the false and foolish one he could or would want to satisfy again the same astronomers?

However, I now go on to consider the nature of the business from an internal viewpoint, and to show with how much care one must discuss it.

Astronomers have so far made two sorts of suppositions: some are primary and pertain to the absolute truth of nature; others are secondary and are imagined in order to account for the appearances of stellar motions, which appearances seem not to agree with the primary and true assumptions. For example, before trying to account for the appearances, acting not as a pure astronomer but as a pure philosopher, Ptolemy supposes—indeed he takes from philosophers—that celestial movements are all circular and regular, namely, uniform; that heaven has a spherical shape; that the earth is at the center of the celestial sphere, is spherical, motionless, etc. Turning then to the inequalities we see in planetary movements and distances, which seem to clash with the primary physical suppositions already established, he goes on to another sort of supposition; these aim to identify the reasons why, without changing the primary ones, there is such a clear and sensible inequality in the movements of planets and in their approaching and their moving away from the earth. To do this he introduces some motions that are still circular, but around centers other

than the earth's, tracing eccentric and epicyclic circles. This secondary supposition is the one of which it could be said that the
astronomer supposes it to facilitate his computations, without committing himself to maintaining that it is true in reality and in nature.

Let us now see in what kind of hypothesis Copernicus places the
earth's motion and sun's stability. There is no doubt whatever, if we
reflect carefully, that he places it among the primary and necessary
suppositions about nature. For, as I have already stated, it seems that
he had already given satisfaction to astronomers by the other road,
and that he takes this one only to try to solve the greatest problem
[358] of nature. In fact, to say that he makes this supposition to facilitate astronomical calculations is so false that instead we can see him,
when he comes to these calculations, leaving this supposition and returning to the old one, the latter being more readily and easily understood and still very quick even in computations. This may be seen as
follows. Intrinsically, particular calculations can be made by taking
one position as well as the other, that is, by making the earth or the
heavens rotate; nevertheless, many geometers and astronomers in
many books have already demonstrated the properties of orthogonal
and oblique displacements of parts of the zodiac in relation to the
equator, the declinations of the parts of the ecliptic, the variety of angles between it and both meridians and oblique horizons, and a thousand other specific details necessary to complete astronomical science.
This ensures that, when he comes to examining these details of the
primary motions, Copernicus himself examines them in the old manner, namely, as occurring along circles traced in the heavens and
around the motionless earth, even though stillness and stability should
belong to the highest heaven, called the Prime Mobile, and motion
to the earth. Thus in the introduction to Book 2 he concludes: "People should not be surprised if we still use the ordinary terms for the
rising and setting of the Sun and stars and similar occurrences, but
should recognize that we are speaking in customary language, which
is acceptable to everyone, yet always bearing in mind that 'For us who
ride the Earth, the Sun and Moon are passing; patterns of stars return,
and then again recede.'"[16]

---

16. Here quoted from Copernicus 1976, 79; I have emended this text, as
translated by Duncan, by using quotation marks rather than displaying the last
two clauses.

We should therefore understand clearly that Copernicus takes the earth's motion and sun's stability for no other reason and in no other way than to establish it, in the manner of the natural philosopher, as a hypothesis of the primary sort; on the contrary, when he comes to astronomical computations, he goes back to the old hypothesis, which takes the circles of the basic motions with their details to be located in the highest heaven around the motionless earth, being easier for everyone to understand on account of ingrained habit. But what am I saying? Such is the strength of truth and the weakness of falsehood, that those who speak this way reveal themselves not completely capable of understanding these subjects and not well versed in them; this happens when they let themselves be persuaded that the secondary kind of hypothesis is considered chimerical and fictional by Ptolemy and by other serious astronomers, [359] and that they really regard them as physically false and introduced only for the sake of astronomical computations. The only support they give for this very fanciful opinion is a passage in Ptolemy where, unable to observe more than one simple anomaly in the sun, he wrote that to account for it one could take the hypothesis of a simple eccentric as well as that of an epicycle on a concentric, and he added he preferred the first for being simpler than the second; from these words some very superficially argue that Ptolemy did not consider necessary, but rather wholly fictional, both this and that supposition, since he said they are both equally convenient, while one and only one can be attributed to the sun's behavior. But what kind of superficiality is this? Who can do both of the following? First, to suppose as true the primary suppositions that planetary motions are circular and regular, and to admit (as the senses themselves necessarily force us) that in running through the zodiac all planets are now slow and now fast, indeed that most of them can be not only slow but also stationary and retrograde, and that we see them now very large and very near the earth and now very small and very far; and then, having understood these former points, to deny that eccentrics and epicycles can really exist in nature? This is wholly excusable for men who are not specialists in these sciences, but for others who would claim to be experts in them it would be an indication that they do not even understand the meaning of the terms *eccentric* and *epicycle*. One might just as well first admit that there are three letters, the first of which is G, the second O, and the third D, and then at the end deny that their combination yields GOD and claim that the result is SHADOW. But if rational arguments were not sufficient to make one understand the necessity of having to place eccentrics and epicycles really in nature, at least the senses themselves would have to persuade him: for we see the four Medicean Planets trace four small circles around Jupiter which are very far from enclosing the earth, in short, four epicycles; Venus, which is seen now full of light and now very thinly crescent, provides conclusive evidence that its revolution is around the sun and not around the earth, and consequently that its orbit is an epicycle; and the same may be argued for the case of Mercury. Moreover, the three outer planets are [360] very near the earth when they are in opposition to the sun, and very far when in conjunction; for example, Mars at its closest appears to the senses more than fifty times larger than at its farthest, so that some have occasionally feared that it had gotten lost or had vanished, being really invisible because of its great distance; now, what else can one conclude but that their revolution is made in eccentric circles, or in epicycles, or in a combination of the two, if we take the second anomaly into consideration? So, to deny eccentrics and epicycles in the motions of planets is like denying the light of the sun, or else it is to contradict oneself. Let us apply what I am saying more directly to our purpose: some say that modern astronomers introduce the earth's motion and sun's stability suppositionally in order to save the appearances[17] and to facilitate calculations, just as epicycles and eccentrics are assumed in the same manner, though the same astronomers consider them physically chimerical and repugnant; I answer that I shall gladly agree with all this talk, as long as they limit themselves to staying within their own conceptions, namely, that the earth's motion and sun's stability is as false or true in nature as epicycles and eccentrics. Let them, then, make every effort to do away with the true and real existence of these circles, for if they succeed in demonstrating their nonexistence in nature, I shall immediately surrender and admit the earth's motion to be a great absurdity. But if, on the contrary, they are forced to accept them, let them also accept the earth's motion, and let them admit to have been convinced by their own contradictions.

I could present many other things for this same purpose. However, since I think that whoever is not persuaded by what I have said would not be persuaded by many more reasons either, I want these to suffice. I shall only add something about what could have been the

---

17. Here the translation in Finocchiaro 1989, 78, has been made more literal by replacing "account for the phenomena" with "save the appearances."

motive why some have concluded with any plausibility that Copernicus himself did not really believe his own hypothesis.

There is on the reverse side of the title page of Copernicus' book a certain preface to the reader, which is not by the author since it mentions him in the third person and is without signature.[18] It clearly states that no one should believe in the least that Copernicus regarded his position as true, but only that he feigned [361] and introduced it for the calculation of celestial motions; it ends its discussion by concluding that to hold it as true and real would be foolish. This conclusion is so explicit that whoever reads no further, and believes it to have been placed at least with the author's consent, deserves to be somewhat excused for his error. But what weight to give to the opinion of those who would judge a book without reading anything but a brief preface by the printer or publisher, I let each one decide for himself. I say that this preface can only have originated from the publisher to facilitate the sale of a book which common people would have regarded as a fanciful chimera if a similar preface had not been added; for most of the time buyers are in the habit of reading such prefaces before buying the work. Not only was this preface not written by the author, but it was included without his consent, and also without his knowledge; this is shown by the errors it contains, which the author would have never committed.

This preface says no one can consider it verisimilar, unless he is completely ignorant of geometry and optics, that Venus has such a large epicycle enabling it now to precede and now to follow the sun by forty degrees or more; for it would have to happen that when it is highest its diameter should appear only one-fourth of what it appears when it is lowest, and that in the latter location its body should be seen as sixteen times bigger than in the former; but these things, he says, are repugnant to the observations made throughout the centuries. In these assertions we see, first, that the writer does not know that Venus departs on one side and on the other of the sun by about forty-eight degrees, and not forty as he says. Moreover, he asserts that

---

18. This preface was in fact written by Andreas Osiander (1498–1552), a Lutheran theologian who supervised the last phase of the printing of Copernicus' book at Nuremberg. The action was soon discovered by Copernicus' friends and followers, causing a controversy, but it did not become generally known for some time, perhaps not until Kepler announced it in his book on Mars of 1609.

its diameter should appear four times, and its body sixteen times, larger in one position than in the other. Here, first, due to a geometrical oversight he does not understand that when a globe has a diameter four times larger than another, its body is sixty-four times bigger, and not sixteen, as he stated. Hence, if he considered such an epicycle absurd and wanted to declare it to be physically impossible, if he had understood this subject, he could have made the absurdity much greater; for, according to the position he wants to refute (well known to astronomers), Venus digresses from the sun almost forty-eight degrees, and when farthest from the earth its distance [362] must be more than[19] six times greater than when closest, and consequently its apparent diameter in the latter position is more than six times larger than in the former (not four times), and its body more than two hundred and sixteen times greater (and not just sixteen). These errors are so gross that it is impossible to believe they were committed by Copernicus, or by anyone else but the most unqualified persons. Moreover, why label such a large epicycle most absurd, so that because of such an absurdity we would conclude that Copernicus did not regard his assumptions as true, and that neither should others so regard them? He should have remembered that in chapter 10 of the first book Copernicus is speaking ad hominem and is attacking other astronomers who allege that it is a great absurdity to give Venus such an epicycle, which is so large as to exceed the whole lunar orbit by more than two hundred times, and which does not contain anything inside; he then removes the absurdity when he shows that inside Venus' orbit is contained the orbit of Mercury and, placed at the center, the body of the sun itself. What frivolity is this, then, to want to show a position mistaken and false on account of a difficulty which that position not only does not introduce in nature but completely removes? Similarly it removes the immense epicycles which out of necessity other astronomers assumed in the other system. This only touches the writer of Copernicus' preface; so we may argue that if he had included something else professionally relevant, he would have committed other errors.

But finally, to remove any shadow of a doubt, if the failure to observe such great variations in the apparent sizes of the body of Venus

---

19. Here the translation in Finocchiaro 1989, 79, has been corrected by inserting "more than."

should cast doubt on its circular revolution around the sun (in conformity with[20] the Copernican system), then let us make careful observations with a suitable instrument, namely, with a good telescope, and we shall find all effects and experiences exactly agreeing; that is, we shall see Venus crescent when it is nearest to the earth, and with a diameter six times larger than when it is at its maximum distance, namely, above the sun, where it is seen round and very small. I have discussed elsewhere the reasons for not detecting these variations with our simple eyesight, but just as from this failure we could reasonably deny that supposition, so now, from seeing the very exact correspondence in this and every other detail, we should abandon any doubt and consider the supposition true and real. As for the rest of this admirable [363] system, whoever desires to ascertain the opinion of Copernicus himself should not read the fanciful preface of the printer, but the whole work of the author himself; without a doubt he will grasp first-hand that Copernicus held as very true the stability of the sun and the motion of the earth.

§5.3 Galileo's Considerations on the Copernican Opinion, Part II[21]

[364] The motion of the earth and stability of the sun could never be against Faith or Holy Scripture, if it were correctly proved to be physically true by philosophers, astronomers, and mathematicians, with the help of sense experiences, accurate observations, and necessary demonstrations. However, in this case, if some passages of Scripture were to sound contrary, we would have to say that this is due to the weakness of our mind, which is unable to grasp the true meaning of Scripture in this particular case. This is the common doctrine, and it is entirely right, since one truth cannot contradict another truth. On the other hand, whoever wants to condemn it judicially must first demonstrate it to be physically false by collecting the reasons against it.

Now, one wants to know where to begin in order to ascertain its falsity, that is, whether from the authority of Scripture or from the refutation of the demonstrations and observations of philosophers and

---

20. Here the translation in Finocchiaro 1989, 80, has been corrected by replacing "from the viewpoint of" with "in conformity with."
21. Galilei 1890–1909, 5: 364–66; translated by Finocchiaro (1989, 80–83).

astronomers. I answer that one must start from the place which is safest and least likely to bring about a scandal; this means beginning with physical and mathematical arguments. For if the reasons proving the earth's motion are found fallacious, and the contrary ones conclusive, then we have already become certain of the falsity of this proposition and of the truth of the opposite, which we now say corresponds to the meaning of Scripture; so one would be free to condemn the false proposition, and there would be no danger. But if those reasons are found true and necessary, this will not bring any harm to the authority of Scripture; instead we shall have been cautioned that due to our ignorance we had not grasped the true sense of Scripture, and that we can learn this meaning with the help of the newly acquired physical truth. Therefore, beginning with the arguments is safe in any case. On the other hand, if we were to fix only on what seemed to us the true and certain meaning of Scripture, and we were to go on to condemn such a proposition without examining the strength of the arguments, what a scandal would follow if sensible experiences and reasons were to show the opposite? And who would have brought confusion to [365] the Holy Church? Those who had suggested the greatest consideration of the arguments, or those who had disparaged them? One can see, then, which road is safer.

Moreover, we admit that a physical proposition which has been proved true by physical and mathematical demonstrations can never contradict Scripture, but that in such a case it is the weakness of our mind which prevents us from grasping its true meaning. On the other hand, whoever wants to use the authority of the same passages of Scripture to confute and prove false the same proposition would commit the error called "begging the question."[22] For, the true meaning of Scripture being in doubt in the light of the arguments, one cannot take it as clear and certain in order to refute the same proposition; instead one must cripple the arguments and find the fallacies with the help of other reasons and experiences and more certain observations. When the factual and physical truth has been found in this manner, then, and not before, can one be assured of the true meaning of

---

22. Begging the question is the fallacy of assuming, in the course of a dispute, the truth of what is being questioned; thus, for example, if part of the dispute is about what is the correct meaning of a particular scriptural passage, then to argue against the earth's motion on the basis of a given meaning of that passage would be to beg the question.

Scripture and safely use it. Thus the safe road is to begin with the arguments, confirming the true and refuting the fallacious ones.

If the earth de facto moves, we cannot change nature and arrange for it not to move. But we can rather easily remove the opposition of Scripture with the mere admission that we do not grasp its true meaning. Therefore, the way to be sure not to err is to begin with astronomical and physical investigations, and not with scriptural ones.

I am always told that, in interpreting the passages of Scripture relevant to this point, all Fathers agree to the meaning which is simplest and corresponds to the literal meaning; hence, presumably, it is improper to give them another meaning or to change the common interpretation, because this would amount to accusing the Fathers of carelessness or negligence. I answer by admitting that the Fathers indeed deserve reasonable and proper respect, but I add that we have an excuse for them very readily: it is that on this subject they never interpreted Scripture differently from the literal meaning, because at their time the opinion of the earth's motion was totally buried, and no one even talked about it, let alone wrote about it or maintained it. But there is no trace of negligence by the Fathers for not thinking about what was completely hidden. That they did not think about it is [366] clear from the fact that in their writings one cannot find even a word about this opinion. And if anyone were to say that they considered it, this would make its condemnation more dangerous; for after considering it, not only did they not condemn it, but they did not express any doubt about it.

Thus the defense of the Fathers is readily available and very easy. On the contrary, it would be very difficult or impossible to excuse or exonerate from a similar charge of carelessness the popes, Councils, and Congregations of the Index of the last eighty years, if this doctrine were erroneous and deserving of condemnation; for they have let this opinion circulate[23] in a book which was first written on orders from a pope and then printed on orders from a cardinal and a bishop, dedicated to another pope, and, most important, received by the Holy

---

23. This statement is literally correct, but Copernicus' book came close to being prohibited immediately after its publication. This did not happen then because of the death of the persons involved: Giovanni Maria Tolosani, a Florentine Dominican theologian and astronomer, and Bartolomeo Spina, the Master of the Sacred Palace, or chief censor, in Rome. See Garin (1971; 1975); Rosen 1975; Westman 1986; Granada 1997; Beltrán Marí 2006, 124–30.

Church, so that one cannot say that it had remained unknown. If, then, the inappropriateness of charging our highest authorities with negligence is to be taken into account, as it should, let us make sure that in trying to escape one absurdity we do not fall into a greater one.

But assume now that someone regards it as inappropriate to abandon the unanimous interpretation of the Fathers, even in the case of physical propositions not discussed by them and whose opposite they did not even consider; I then ask what one should do if necessary demonstrations showed the facts of nature to be the opposite. Which of the two decrees should be changed? The one which stipulates that no proposition can be both true and erroneous, or the other one which obliges us to regard as articles of faith physical propositions supported by the unanimous interpretation of the Fathers? It seems to me, if I am not mistaken, that it would be safer to modify this second decree than to be forced to hold as an article of faith a physical proposition which had been demonstrated with conclusive reasons to be factually false in nature. It also seems to me that one could say that the unanimous interpretation of the Fathers should have absolute authority in the case of propositions which they aired, and for which no contrary demonstrations exist and for which it is certain that none could ever exist. I do not bring in the fact that it is very clear that the Council[24] requires only that one agree with the unanimous interpretation of the Fathers "in matters of faith and morals, etc."

§5.4 Galileo's Considerations on the Copernican Opinion, Part III[25]

[367] 1. Copernicus uses eccentrics and epicycles, but these were not the reason for rejecting the Ptolemaic system, since they undoubtedly exist in the heavens; it was other difficulties.

2. In regard to philosophers, if they were true philosophers, namely, lovers of truth, they should not get irritated, but, learning that they were wrong, they should thank whoever shows them the truth; and if their opinion were to stand up, they would have reason to take pride in it, rather than being irritated. Theologians should not get irritated because, if this opinion were found false then they could

---

24. The Council of Trent (1545–63).
25. Galilei 1890–1909, 5: 367–70; translated by Finocchiaro (1989, 83–86).

freely prohibit it, and if it were discovered true then they should re-
joice that others have found the way to understand the true meaning
of Scripture and have restrained them from perpetrating a serious
scandal by condemning a true proposition.

In regard to falsifying Scripture, this is not and will never be the
intention of Catholic astronomers such as ourselves; rather our view
is that Scripture corresponds very well to truths demonstrated about
nature. Moreover, certain theologians who are not astronomers
should be careful about falsifying Scripture by wanting to interpret it
as opposed to propositions which may be true and demonstrable.

3. It might happen that we could have difficulties in interpreting
Scripture, but this would occur because of our ignorance, and not be-
cause there really are or can be insuperable difficulties in reconciling
Scripture with demonstrated truths.

4. The Council speaks "about matters of faith and morals, etc." So
there is an answer to saying that such a proposition is "an article of
faith by reason of the speaker," though not "by reason of the topic,"
and that therefore it is among those covered by the Council. The answer is that everything in Scripture is "an article of faith by reason of
the speaker," so that in this regard it should be included in the rule of
the Council; but this clearly has not been done because in that case
the Council would have said that "the interpretation of the Fathers is
to be followed for every word of Scripture, etc.," and not "for matters of faith and morals"; having thus said "for matters of faith," we
see that its intention was to mean "for matters of faith by reason of
the topic."

Then consider that [368] it is much more a matter of faith to hold
that Abraham had some children and that Tobias had a dog, because
Scripture says it, than it would be to hold that the earth moves, even
if this were found in the same Scripture, and further that to deny the
former is a heresy, but not to deny the latter. It seems to me that this
depends on the following reason. There have always been in the
world men who had two, four, six children, etc., or none, and similarly, people who have dogs and who do not, so that it is equally credible that some have children or dogs and others do not; hence there
appears to be no reason why in such propositions the Holy Spirit
should speak differently from the truth, the negative and the affirmative sides being equally credible to all men. But it is not so with the
motion of the earth and the stability of the sun; for these propositions
are very far removed from the understanding of the masses, and on

these matters not relevant to their eternal life the Holy Spirit chose to conform its pronouncements with their abilities, even when facts are otherwise from the point of view of the thing in itself.[26]

5. In regard to placing the sun in heaven and the earth outside it, as Scripture seems to affirm, etc., this truly seems to me to be a simple perception of ours and a manner of speaking only for our convenience. For in reality all that is surrounded by heaven is in heaven, just as all that is surrounded by the city walls is in the city; indeed, if one were to express a preference, what is in the middle is more in heaven and in the city, being, as it were, at the heart of the city and of heaven. That difference exists because one takes the elemental region surrounding the earth as being very different from the celestial region. But such a difference will always exist regardless of where these elements are placed; and it will always be true that from the viewpoint of our convenience the earth is below us and heaven above, since all the inhabitants of the earth have heaven above our heads, which is our upwards, and the center of the earth under our feet, which is our downwards; so, in relation to us the center of the earth and the surface of heaven are the farthest places, that is, the endpoints of our up and down, which are diametrically opposite points.

6. Not to believe that there is a demonstration of the earth's mobility until it is shown is very prudent, nor do we ask that anyone believe such a thing without a demonstration. On the contrary, we only seek that, for the advantage of the Holy Church, one examine with [369] the utmost severity what the followers of this doctrine know and can advance, and that nothing be granted them unless the strength of their arguments greatly exceeds that of the reasons for the opposite side. Now if they are not more than ninety percent right, they may be dismissed; but if all that is produced by philosophers and astronomers on the opposite side is shown to be mostly false and wholly inconsequential, then the other side should not be disparaged nor deemed paradoxical, so as to think that it could never be clearly proved. It is proper to make such a generous offer since it is clear that those who hold the false side cannot have in their favor any valid reason or experiment, whereas it is necessary that all things agree and correspond with the true side.

---

26. The translation of this sentence has been revised from the one in Finocchiaro 1989, 84.

7. It is true that it is not the same to show that one can save the appearances with the earth's motion and the sun's stability, and to demonstrate that these hypotheses are really true in nature. But it is equally true, or even more so, that one cannot account for such appearances with the other commonly accepted system. The latter system is undoubtedly false, while it is clear that the former hypotheses, which can account for the appearances, may be true. Nor can or should one seek any greater truth in a position than that it corresponds with all particular appearances.

8. One is not asking that in case of doubt the interpretation of the Fathers should be abandoned, but only that an attempt be made to gain certainty regarding what is in doubt, and that therefore no one disparage what attracts and has attracted very great philosophers and astronomers. Then, after all necessary care has been taken, the decision may be made.

9. We believe that Solomon, Moses, and all other sacred writers knew perfectly the constitution of the world, as they also knew that God has no hands, no feet, and no experience of anger, forgetfulness, or regret; nor will we ever doubt this. But we say what the Holy Fathers and in particular St. Augustine say about these matters, namely, that the Holy Spirit inspired them to write what they wrote for various reasons, etc.

10. The error of the apparent movement of the shore and stability of the ship is known by us after having many times observed the motion of boats from the shore, and many other times observed the shore from a boat; and so, if we could now stay on earth and now go to the sun [370] or other star, perhaps we would acquire sensible and certain knowledge of which one of them moves. To be sure, if we looked only at these two bodies, it would always seem to us that the one we were on was standing still, just as looking only at the water and the boat always gives the appearance that the water is flowing and the boat is standing still. Moreover, the two situations are very different: there is great disparity between a small boat, separable from its environment, and the immense shore, known by us through thousands of experiences to be motionless, that is, motionless in relation to the water and the boat; but the other comparison is between two bodies both of which are substantial and equally inclined toward motion and toward rest. Thus it would be more relevant to compare between themselves two boats, in which case it is absolutely certain that the one we were on would always appear to us as motionless, as long

as we could not consider any other relationship but that which holds between these two ships.

There is, therefore, a very great need to correct the error about observing whether the earth or else the sun moves, for it is clear that to someone on the moon or any other planet it would always appear that it was standing still and the other stars were moving. But these and many other more plausible reasons of the followers of the common opinion are the ones that must be untied very openly, before one can pretend even to be heard, let alone approved; unfortunately we have not done a very detailed examination of what is produced against us. Moreover, neither Copernicus nor his followers will ever use this phenomenon of the shore and the boat to prove that the earth is in motion and the sun at rest. They only adduce it as an example that serves to show, not the truth of their position, but the absence of contradiction between the appearance of a stable earth and moving sun to our simple sense experience, and the reality of the contrary. For, if this were one of Copernicus' demonstrations, or if his others did not argue more effectively, I really think that no one would agree with him.

CHAPTER 6[1]

From the Earlier Trial-Documents (1615–16)[2]

§6.1 Lorini's Complaint (7 February 1615)[3]

[297] Most Illustrious and Most Reverend Lord:[4]

Besides the common duty of every good Christian, there is a limitless obligation that binds all Dominican friars, since they were designated by the Holy Father the black and white hounds of the Holy Office. This applies in particular to all theologians and preachers, and hence to me, lowest of all and most devoted to Your Most Illustrious Lordship. I have come across a letter[5] that is passing through everybody's hands here, originating among those known as "Galileists," who, following the views of Copernicus, affirm that the earth moves and the heavens stand still. In the judgment of all our Fathers at this very religious convent of St. Mark, it contains many propositions which to us seem either suspect or rash: for example, that certain ways of speaking in the Holy Scripture are inappropriate; that in disputes about natural effects the same Scripture holds the last place; that its expositors are often wrong in their interpretations; that the same Scripture must not meddle with anything else but articles concerning faith; and that, in questions about natural phenomena, philosophical or astronomical argument has more force than the sacred and the divine one. Your Most Illustrious Lordship can see these propositions underlined by me in the above-mentioned letter, of which I send you

---

1. Reprinted from: Maurice A. Finocchiaro, trans. and ed., *The Galileo Affair: A Documentary History,* © 1989 by the Regents of the University of California. Published by the University of California Press.
2. For the historical background, see the Introduction, especially §0.7.
3. Galilei 1890–1909, 19: 297–98; translated by Finocchiaro (1989, 134–35).
4. Cardinal Paolo Sfondrati (1561–1618), who was a member of the Congregation of the Inquisition in Rome, as well as head of the Congregation of the Index.
5. Galileo's letter to Castelli of 21 December 1613 (see §4.1).

a faithful copy.[6] Finally, it claims that when Joshua ordered the sun to stop one must understand that the order was given to the Prime Mobile and not to the sun itself. Besides this letter passing through everybody's hands, without being stopped by any of the authorities, it seems to me that some want to expound Holy Scripture in their own way and against the common exposition of the Holy Fathers and to defend [298] an opinion apparently wholly contrary to Holy Scripture. Moreover, I hear that they speak disrespectfully of the ancient Holy Fathers and St. Thomas; that they trample underfoot all of Aristotle's philosophy, which is so useful to scholastic theology; and that to appear clever they utter and spread a thousand impertinences around our whole city, kept so Catholic by its own good nature and by the vigilance of our Most Serene Princes. For these reasons I resolved, as I said, to send it to Your Most Illustrious Lordship, who is filled with the most holy zeal and who, for the position that you occupy, is responsible, together with your most illustrious colleagues, for keeping your eyes open in such matters; thus if it seems to you that there is any need for correction, you may find those remedies that you judge necessary, in order that a small error at the beginning does not become great at the end. Though perhaps I could have sent you a copy of some notes on the said letter made at this convent, nevertheless, out of modesty I refrained since I was writing to you who know so much and to Rome where, as St. Bernard said, the holy faith has lynx eyes. I declare that I regard all those who are called Galileists as men of goodwill and good Christians, but a little conceited and fixed in their opinions; similarly, I state that in taking this action I am moved by nothing but zeal. I also beg Your Most Illustrious Lordship that this letter of mine (I am not referring to the other letter mentioned above) be kept secret by you, as I am sure you will, and that it be regarded not as a judicial deposition but only as a friendly notice

---

6. The copy of Galileo's letter to Castelli enclosed by Lorini differs somewhat from the one regarded as the most genuine copy by Antonio Favaro, the editor of the critical edition of Galileo's complete works (Galilei 1890–1909). The Favaro copy is the one translated in §4.1. Lorini's copy contains several variations in wording (cf. Finocchiaro 1989, 331 n. 16), all to Galileo's disadvantage, but it is regarded as a faithful copy by some scholars (Pesce 1992). In any case, there is clear evidence that in February 1615 Galileo became suspicious that his original letter had been inaccurately copied and started to circulate the accurate version (cf. Finocchiaro 1989, 55).

between you and me, like between a servant and a special patron. And I also inform you that the occasion of my writing was one or two public sermons given in our church of Santa Maria Novella by Father Tommaso Caccini, commenting on the book of Joshua and chapter 10 of the said book. So I close by asking for your holy blessing, kissing your garment, and asking for a particle of your holy prayers.

§6.2 Caccini's Deposition (20 March 1615)[7]

[307] Friday, 20 March 1615.

There appeared personally and of his own accord at Rome in the great hall of examinations in the palace of the Holy Office, in the presence of the Reverend Father Michelangelo Segizzi, O.P., Master of Sacred Theology and Commissary General of the Holy Roman and Universal Inquisition, etc., the Reverend Father Tommaso Caccini, son of the late Giovanni Caccini, Florentine, a professed priest of the Order of Preachers, Master and Bachelor from the convent of Santa Maria sopra Minerva in Rome, about thirty-nine years of age. Having been administered the oath to tell the truth, he declared as follows:

I had spoken with the Most Illustrious Lord Cardinal Aracoeli about some things taking place in Florence, and yesterday he sent for me and told me that I should come here and tell everything to you. Since I was told that a legal deposition is needed, I am here for this purpose. I say then that on the fourth Sunday of Advent of this past year I was preaching at the church of Santa Maria Novella in Florence, where I had been assigned by superiors this year as a reader of Holy Scripture, and I continued with the story of Joshua begun earlier. Precisely on this Sunday I happened to read the passage of the tenth chapter of that book where the sacred writer relates the great miracle which God made in answer to Joshua's prayers by stopping the sun, namely "Sun, stand thou still upon Gibeon,"[8] etc. After interpreting this passage first in a literal sense and then in accordance with its spiritual intention for the salvation of souls, I took the opportunity to criticize, with that modesty which befits the office I held, a certain view once proposed by Nicolaus Copernicus and nowadays

---

7. Galilei 1890–1909, 19: 307–11; translated by Finocchiaro (1989, 136–41).
8. Joshua 10:12.

held and taught by Mr. Galileo Galilei, mathematician, according to public opinion very widespread in the city of Florence. This is the view that the sun, being [308] for him the center of the world, is immovable as regards progressive local motion, that is, motion from one place to another. I said that such a view is regarded as discordant with Catholic faith by very serious writers since it contradicts many passages of the divine Scripture whose literal sense, as given unanimously by the Holy Fathers, sounds and means the opposite; for example, the passage of the eighteenth Psalm, of the first chapter of Ecclesiastes, of Isaiah 38, besides the Joshua passage cited. And in order to impress upon the audience that such a teaching of mine did not originate from my whim, I read them Nicolaus Serarius'[9] doctrine (fourteenth question on chapter 10 of Joshua): after saying that such a position of Copernicus is contrary to the common account of almost all philosophers, all scholastic theologians, and all the Holy Fathers, he added that he could not see how such an opinion is not almost heretical, due to the above-mentioned passages of Scripture. After this discussion I cautioned them that no one was allowed to interpret divine Scripture in a way contrary to the sense on which all the Holy Fathers agree, since this was prohibited both by the Lateran Council under Leo X and by the Council of Trent.

Although this charitable warning of mine greatly pleased many educated and devout gentlemen, it displeased certain disciples of the above-mentioned Galilei beyond measure; thus some of them approached the preacher at the cathedral so that he would preach on this topic against the doctrine I expounded. Having heard so many rumors, out of zeal for the truth, I reported to the very reverend Father Inquisitor of Florence what my conscience had led me to discuss concerning the Joshua passage; I also suggested to him that it would be good to restrain certain petulant minds, disciples of the said Galilei, of whom the reverend Father Fra Ferdinando Ximenes,[10] regent of Santa Maria Novella, had told me that from some of them he had heard these three propositions: "God is not otherwise a substance, but an accident"; "God is sensuous because there are in him divine

---

9. Nicolaus Serarius (1555–1609), Jesuit, author of several influential commentaries on the Bible.
10. Ferdinando Ximenes (c.1580–1630), a Dominican who, as a result of being mentioned here, will be called for a deposition to the Inquisition on 13 November 1615.

senses"; and, "in truth the miracles said to have been made by the saints are not real miracles."

After these events Father Master Fra Niccolò Lorini showed me a copy of a letter written by the above-mentioned Mr. Galileo Galilei to Father Benedetto Castelli, Benedictine monk and professor of mathematics at Pisa, in which it seemed to me are contained questionable doctrines in the domain of theology. Since a copy of it was sent to the Lord Cardinal of Santa Cecilia,[11] I have nothing else to add to that.

Thus I declare to this Holy Office that it is a widespread opinion that the above-mentioned Galilei holds these two propositions: the earth moves as a whole as well as with diurnal motion; the sun is motionless. These are propositions which, according to my [309] conscience and understanding, are repugnant to the divine Scriptures expounded by the Holy Fathers and consequently to the faith, which teaches that we must believe as true what is contained in Scripture. And for now I have nothing else to say.

He was asked: How he knows that Galileo teaches and holds the sun to be motionless and the earth to move, and whether he learned this expressly from others.

He answered: Aside from public notoriety, as I said before, I also heard from Monsignor Filippo de' Bardi, Bishop of Cortona, at the time I stayed there and then in Florence, that Galilei holds the above-mentioned propositions as true; he added that this seemed to him very strange, as not agreeing with Scripture. I also heard it from a certain Florentine gentleman[12] of the Attavanti family, a follower of the same Galilei, who said to me that Galilei interpreted Scripture in such a way as not to conflict with his opinion. I do not recall this gentleman's name, nor do I know where his house is in Florence; I am sure that he often comes to service at Santa Maria Novella in Florence, that he wears priest's clothes, and that he is twenty-eight or thirty years of age perhaps, of olive complexion, chestnut beard, average height, and sharply delineated face. He told it to me this past summer, about the month of August, in Father Ferdinando Ximenes' room,

---

11. This was the title of Cardinal Paolo Sfondrati, to whom Lorini's complaint was addressed.
12. Giannozzo Attavanti (c. 1582–1657), a minor cleric who had not yet been ordained priest and would be examined by the Inquisition on 14 November 1615.

the occasion being that Father Ximenes was telling me that I should not take too long discussing the miracle of the stopping of the sun when he (Ximenes) was around. I have also read this doctrine in a book printed in Rome, dealing with sunspots, published under the name of the said Galileo, and lent to me by the said Father Ximenes.

Q:[13] Who the preacher at the cathedral is, to whom Galileo's disciples went in order to have a public sermon against the doctrine taught equally publicly by the plaintiff himself, and who those disciples are who made such a request to the said preacher.

A: The preacher at the Florence cathedral whom Galileo's disciples approached about preaching against the doctrine I taught is a Jesuit Father from Naples, whose name I do not know. Nor have I learned these things from the said preacher, since I did not even speak with him. Rather they have been told me by Father Emanuele Ximenes,[14] a Jesuit, whom the said preacher had asked for advice, and who dissuaded him. Nor do I know who were the disciples of Galilei who contacted the preacher about the above-mentioned matters.

Q: Whether he has ever talked to the said Galileo.

A: I do not even know what he looks like.

Q: What the reputation of the said Galileo is in the city of Florence regarding matters of faith.

A: By many he is regarded as a good Catholic. By others he is regarded with suspicion in matters of faith because they say he is very close to Fra Paolo,[15] of the Servite order, so [310] famous in Venice for his impieties; and they say that letters are exchanged between them even now.

Q: Whether he remembers from which person or persons he learned about these matters.

---

13. Note that, here and in subsequent depositions, the letter Q is meant as an abbreviation for the sentence "He was asked," which yields, together with the expression that follows, an *indirect* rather than a direct question.

14. Emanuele Ximenes (b. 1542), at the time a consultant to the Inquisition in Florence, died soon after this incident in 1614. This Jesuit is not to be confused with either the earlier-named Dominican Ferdinando Ximenes, or with a third individual (Sebastiano Ximenes) by the same surname mentioned below.

15. Paolo Sarpi (1552–1623), Venetian lawyer, theologian, and historian, who also wrote on scientific subjects. Galileo and Sarpi were indeed friends, especially during the eighteen years that Galileo taught at the University of Padua, which is near Venice and was a public institution financially supported by the Republic of Venice.

A: I heard these things from Father Master Niccolò Lorini and from another Mr. Ximenes,[16] Prior of the Knights of Santo Stefano. They told me the above-mentioned things. That is, Father Niccolò Lorini has repeated to me several times and even written to me here in Rome that between Galileo and Master Paolo there is an exchange of letters and great friendship, and that the latter is a suspect in matters of faith. And Prior Ximenes did not tell me anything different about the closeness between Master Paolo and Galileo, but only that Galilei is a suspect and that, while being in Rome once, he learned how the Holy Office was trying to seize him, on account of which he ran away. This was told me in the room of the above-mentioned Father Ferdinando, his cousin, though I do not remember exactly if the said Father was present there.

Q: Whether he learned from the above-mentioned Father Lorini and the Knight Ximenes why they regarded the said Galileo to be suspect in matters of faith.

A: They did not say anything else to me, except that they regarded him as suspect on account of the propositions he held concerning the immobility of the sun and the motion of the earth, and because this man wants to interpret Holy Scripture against the common meaning of the Holy Fathers.

He added on his own: This man, together with others, belongs to an academy—I do not know whether they organized it themselves—which has the title of "Lincean." And they correspond with others in Germany, at least Galileo does, as one sees from that book of his on sunspots.

Q: Whether he had been told himself in detail by Father Ferdinando Ximenes the persons from whom he learned about those propositions: that God is not a substance but an accident, that God is sensuous, and that the miracles of the Saints are not true miracles.

A: I seem to remember that he gave the name of Attavanti, whom I have described as one of those who uttered the said propositions. I do not remember any others.

Q: Where, when, in the presence of whom, and on what occasion Father Ferdinando related that Galilei's disciples had mentioned to him the said propositions.

---

16. Sebastiano Ximenes, founder in 1593 of the order of the Knights of Santo Stefano.

A: It was on several occasions (sometimes in the cloister, sometimes in the dormitory, sometimes in his cell) that Father Ferdinando told me he had heard the said propositions from Galileo's disciples; he did this after I had preached that sermon, the occasion being that of telling me that he had defended me against these people. And I do not remember that there ever was anyone else present.

Q: About his hostility toward the said Galileo, toward the Attavanti character, and also toward other disciples of the said Galileo.

A: Not only do I not have any hostility toward the said Galileo, but I do not even know him. Similarly, I do not have any hostility or hatred toward Attavanti, or toward other disciples of Galileo. Rather I pray to God for them.

[311] Q: Whether the said Galileo teaches publicly in Florence, and what discipline; and whether his disciples are numerous.

A: I do not know whether Galileo lectures publicly, nor whether he has many disciples. I do know that in Florence he has many followers who are called Galileists. They are the ones who extol and praise his doctrine and opinions.

Q: What home town the said Galileo is from, what his profession is, and where he studied.

A: He regards himself as a Florentine, but I have heard that he is a Pisan. His profession is that of mathematician. As far as I have heard, he studied in Pisa and has lectured at Padua. He is past sixty years old.

With this he was dismissed, having been bound to silence by oath and his signature having been obtained.

I, Fra Tommaso Caccini, bear witness to the things said above.

§6.3 Special Injunction (26 February 1616)[17]

[321] Friday, the 26th of the same month.

At the palace of the usual residence of the said Most Illustrious Lord Cardinal Bellarmine and in the chambers of His Most Illustrious Lordship, [322] and fully in the presence of the Reverend Father Michelangelo Segizzi of Lodi, O.P., and Commissary General of the Holy Office, having summoned the above-mentioned Galileo before himself, the same Most Illustrious Lord Cardinal warned Galileo that

---

17. Galilei 1890–1909, 19: 321–22; translated by Finocchiaro (1989, 147–48).

the above-mentioned opinion was erroneous and that he should abandon it; and thereafter, indeed immediately, before me and witnesses,
the Most Illustrious Lord Cardinal himself being also present still, the
aforesaid Father Commissary, in the name of His Holiness the Pope
and of the whole Congregation of the Holy Office, ordered and en-
joined the said Galileo, who was himself still present, to abandon
completely the above-mentioned opinion that the sun stands still at
the center of the world and the earth moves, and henceforth not to
hold, teach, or defend it in any way whatever, either orally or in writing; otherwise the Holy Office would start proceedings against him.
The same Galileo acquiesced in this injunction and promised to obey.

Done in Rome at the place mentioned above, in the presence, as
witnesses, of the Reverend Badino Nores of Nicosia in the kingdom
of Cyprus, and of Agostino Mongardo from the Abbey of Rose in
the diocese of Montepulciano, both belonging to the household of
the said Most Illustrious Lord Cardinal.

§6.4 Decree of the Index (5 March 1616)[18]

[322] Decree of the Holy Congregation of the Most Illustrious Lord
Cardinals especially charged by His Holiness Pope Paul V and by the
Holy Apostolic See with the Index of books and their licensing, prohibition, correction, and printing in all of Christendom. To be published everywhere.

In regard to several books containing various heresies and errors,
to prevent the emergence of more serious harm throughout Christendom, the Holy Congregation of the Most Illustrious Lord Cardinals in charge of the Index has decided that they should be altogether
condemned and prohibited, as indeed with the present decree it condemns and prohibits them, wherever and in whatever language they
are printed or about to be printed. It orders that henceforth no one,
of whatever station or condition, should dare print them, or have
them printed, or read them, or have them in one's possession in any
way, under penalty specified in the Holy Council of Trent and in the
Index of prohibited books; and under the same penalty, whoever is

---

18. Galilei 1890–1909, 19: 322–23; translated by Finocchiaro (1989,
148–50).

now or will be in the future in possession of them is required to surrender them to ordinaries[19] or to inquisitors, immediately after learning of the present decree. The books are listed below:[20]

Calvinist Theology (in three parts) by Conradus Schlusserburgius.

Scotanus Redivivus, or Erotic Commentary in Three Parts, etc.

[323] Historical Explanation of the Most Serious Question in the Christian Churches Especially in the West, from the Time of the Apostles All the
Way to Our Age by Jacobus Usserius, professor of sacred theology at
the Dublin Academy in Ireland.

Inquiry Concerning the Preeminence among European Provinces, Conducted at the Illustrious College of Tübingen, in 1613 A.D., by Fridericus
Achilles, Duke of Wittenberg.

Donellus' Principles, or Commentaries on Civil Law, Abridged so as . . . , etc.

This Holy Congregation has also learned about the spreading and
acceptance by many of the false Pythagorean doctrine, altogether
contrary to the Holy Scripture, that the earth moves and the sun is
motionless, which is also taught by Nicolaus Copernicus' On the Revolution of the Heavenly Spheres and by Diego de Zúñiga's On Job. This
may be seen from a certain letter published by a certain Carmelite Father, whose title is Letter of the Reverend Father Paolo Antonio Foscarini,
on the Pythagorean and Copernican Opinion of the Earth's Motion and Sun's
Rest and on the New Pythagorean World System (Naples: Lazzaro Scorig-
gio, 1615), in which the said Father tries to show that the above-
mentioned doctrine of the sun's rest at the center of the world and of
the earth's motion is consonant with the truth and does not contradict Holy Scripture. Therefore, in order that this opinion may not advance any further to the prejudice of Catholic truth, the
Congregation has decided that the books by Nicolaus Copernicus
(On the Revolutions of Spheres) and by Diego de Zúñiga (On Job) be
suspended until corrected; but that the book of the Carmelite Father
Paolo Antonio Foscarini be completely prohibited and condemned;
and that all other books which teach the same be likewise prohibited,
according to whether with the present decree it prohibits, condemns,
and suspends them respectively. In witness thereof, this decree has
been signed by the hand and stamped with the seal of the Most

---

19. An "ordinary" would usually be a bishop.
20. For an attempt to precisely identify these works and authors, see Mayaud
1997, 40 n. 8, 301–7. Here I have limited myself to making a few minor
emendations to Finocchiaro 1989, 149.

Illustrious and Reverend Lord Cardinal of St. Cecilia, Bishop of Albano, on 5 March 1616.

P.,²¹ Bishop of Albano, Cardinal of St. Cecilia.

Fra Franciscus Magdalenus Capiferreus, O.P., Secretary.

Rome, Press of the Apostolic Palace, 1616.

§6.5 Cardinal Bellarmine's Certificate (26 May 1616)²²

[348] We, Robert Cardinal Bellarmine, have heard that Mr. Galileo Galilei is being slandered or alleged to have abjured in our hands and also to have been given salutary penances for this. Having been sought about the truth of the matter, we say that the above-mentioned Galileo has not abjured in our hands, or in the hands of others here in Rome, or anywhere else that we know, any opinion or doctrine of his; nor has he received any penances, salutary or otherwise. On the contrary, he has only been notified of the declaration made by the Holy Father and published by the Sacred Congregation of the Index, whose content is that the doctrine attributed to Copernicus (that the earth moves around the sun and the sun stands at the center of the world without moving from east to west) is contrary to Holy Scripture and therefore cannot be defended or held.²³ In witness whereof we have written and signed this with our own hands, on this 26th day of May 1616.

The same mentioned above,
Robert Cardinal Bellarmine.

---

21. Paolo Sfondrati, head of the Congregation of the Index.
22. Galilei 1890–1909, 19: 348; translated by Finocchiaro (1989, 153).
23. The content of this sentence should be compared and contrasted with that of the Decree of the Index (5 March 1616) [see §6.4] and with that of the Special Injunction (26 February 1616) [see §6.3]; many of the issues in the affair hinge on this.

CHAPTER 7

From *The Assayer* (1623)[1]

[§7.1 Comets, Tycho, and the Book of Nature in Mathematical Language][2]

[228] Read this, Your Most Illustrious Lordship:[3] "In order not to waste time with complaints, first I do not see by what right he accuses my teacher and blames him for appearing to have sworn by Tycho's words and to follow him in all his futile machinations. All this is plainly false because, except for the methods of investigating and proving the location of the comet, nothing else can be found in our *Disputation* that closely follows Tycho, as the express words testify. Certainly the Lincean astronomer even with his telescope could not look at the inner feelings inside the mind. At any rate, let it be granted that my teacher follows Tycho. What crime is there in that? Whom should he follow instead? Ptolemy, whose followers are at risk of having their throat cut by the sword of Mars, which has already come closer? Copernicus, when anyone who is pious will rather keep everybody away from him and will likewise condemn and reject his recently condemned hypothesis? Thus Tycho was the only one left whom we could take as a guide in the unknown paths of the stars. Why then should Galileo be angry with my teacher for not rejecting him? In vain does Galileo here appeal to Seneca; in vain does he here lament the calamity of our time for our not knowing the true and certain arrangement of the parts of the world; in vain does he deplore

---

1. For the historical background, see the Introduction, especially §0.8.
2. Galilei 1890–1909, 6: 228.31–233.23; newly translated by Finocchiaro.
3. Recall (from the Introduction) that *The Assayer* is written in the form of a letter to Virginio Cesarini; that it is structured as a series of criticisms of quotations from Orazio Grassi's *Astronomical and Philosophical Balance*, published under the pseudonym of Lotario Sarsi; that the *Balance* was a critique of Mario Guiducci's *Discourse on the Comets*; and that the *Discourse* was in turn a critique of Grassi's *Astronomical Disputation on the Three Comets of the Year 1618*.

the misfortune of this age if he has nothing to offer to improve it but rather regards it as miserable."

From what Sarsi writes in this passage, it seems to me that he has not read with due attention not only Mr. Mario's *Discourse,* but not even that of Fr. Grassi; for he attributes to the former as well as to the latter propositions that are not found in them. The truth is that in order to pave the way for being able to involve me in something or other [229] pertaining to Copernicus, he needed those propositions to have been written there; so, not having found them there, he decided to provide them on his own.

First, in Mr. Mario's essay one does not find tossed around and attributed to Fr. Grassi the fault of having sworn allegiance to Tycho and having followed to the letter his futile machinations. Here are the passages cited by Sarsi:[4] "later I shall come to the professor of mathematics at the Roman College, who in a recently published essay seems to subscribe to everything Tycho said, adding also some new reasons in confirmation of his opinions" (p. 18); "the mathematician of the Roman College has likewise accepted the same hypothesis about the last comet; and I am led to affirm this by the fact that the little he writes about it accords with Tycho's position and the rest of his essay agrees considerably with the other Tychonic ideas" (p. 38). Here Your Most Illustrious Lordship can see whether any fault or shortcoming is being charged. Moreover, it is very clear that since the whole work deals only with phenomena pertaining to the comets, to say that the mathematician of the College agrees with Tycho's other ideas refers only to views related to the comets; thus I do not see that this is the proper place to compare Tycho with Ptolemy and Copernicus, who never dealt with hypotheses about the comets.

Then when Sarsi says that in his teacher's essay there is nothing that follows Tycho except the demonstration to find the location of the comet, this is not true, if I may be allowed to say so; on the contrary, such a demonstration is impossible to find there. God forbid that Fr. Grassi should have followed Tycho in this and should not have noticed how lacking he is in elementary mathematical knowledge when he investigates the distance of the comet based on observations made

---

4. These passages were quoted in the *Balance* from the *Discourse;* the page numbers refer to the original edition.

at two different places on the earth.[5] So that Your Most Illustrious Lordship can see that I am not talking gratuitously, look at the demonstration that begins on p. 123 of his treatise on the comet of 1577, which is in the last part of his *Progymnasmata*. Here he wants to prove that the comet was not lower than the moon, by a comparison of the observations made by himself in [230] Uraniborg and by Thaddaeus Hagecius[6] in Prague. First, draw the chord AB for the arc of the terrestrial globe that spans the two said places. From point A look at the fixed star located at D, and assume that DAB is a right angle. This is very far from what is possible because line AB is the chord of an arc of less than six degrees (as Tycho himself asserts), and so in order for the said angle to be a right angle, star D must be less than three degrees from A's zenith; this is false insofar as its minimum distance is more than forty-eight degrees, for (as Tycho himself says) star D is Aquila (or, more precisely, Altair) and its declination is 7:52 degrees toward the north, and

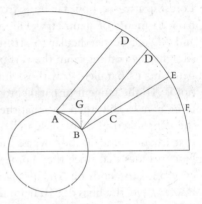

the latitude of Uraniborg is 55:54 degrees. Furthermore, he writes that from the two locations A and B the fixed star D is seen at the same place of the eighth sphere because the whole earth (not just the small part AB) is nothing in proportion to the immensity of the eighth sphere. But with apologies to Tycho, the large or small size of the earth is irrelevant in this case, because the fact that the star is seen in the same place from all parts of the earth derives from its being really on the eighth sphere and from nothing else. In the same manner, the characters on this page will never change apparent location in relation to the same page regardless of how much your eye moves when looking at them; but an object placed between the eye and the paper will indeed change its apparent location relative to the characters as

5. The following criticism of Tycho is unfair, since he was aware of the approximations involved. For some details, see Pagnini 1964, 1: 144–46 n. 1; Drake and O'Malley 1960, 339–40, 369 n. 8.
6. Thaddaeus Hagecius (1525–1600), professor of mathematics at the University of Prague and personal physician to several Holy Roman Emperors.

your head moves; and so the same character will be seen now to the right, now to the left, now higher, and now lower than the object. Similarly, when the planets are seen from different parts of the earth, they change apparent position on the stellar sphere because they are very far from it. In this case the effect of the smallness of the earth is that, while those that are nearer to us show greater changes of position and those that are farther show smaller changes, for a body that is extremely far away the size of the earth is insufficient to make such a change perceptible. Next, regarding what he claims to happen in accordance with the laws of arcs and chords, Your Most Illustrious Lordship can see how far he is from such laws and indeed from the basic elements of geometry. He says that the two straight lines AD and BD are perpendicular to AB; this is impossible because only the straight line coming from the vertex is perpendicular to the [231] tangent and its parallels, and those lines do not come from the vertex, nor is AB the tangent or parallel to it. Furthermore, he requires them to be parallel, but then says that they meet at the center; here, besides the contradiction of being parallel and convergent, there is the fact that when extended, they bypass the center at a great distance. Finally, he concludes that since they come from the center of the circumference onto the ends of AB, they are perpendicular; this is impossible insofar as, of the lines drawn from the center to all points of the chord AB, only the one that falls onto the midpoint is perpendicular to it, and those that fall onto the end points are more inclined and oblique than all the others. Thus Your Most Illustrious Lordship can see the kind and the number of errors which according to Sarsi, his teacher would be committing if what Sarsi wrote in this regard were true, namely, that in investigating the location of the comet his teacher followed Tycho's reasons and methods of demonstration.

Additionally, Sarsi himself can see how much better than he, I have penetrated the meaning of what he wrote, which is not to say the meaning inside his mind (since to detect this I have neither eyes nor ears); the meaning of what he wrote is so clear and manifest that one does not need to employ astronomy or the telescope; nor does one need lynx eyes, nicely interjected by Sarsi, I believe, to make fun of our Academy. Now since Your Most Illustrious Lordship, as well as other princes and great lords, are with me the target of this joke, I shall exploit what I learned from Sarsi and take refuge under their shadow, or better, I shall brighten up my shadow with their brilliance.

But let us return to the topic. See how he repeats that I faulted Fr.

Grassi for accepting Tycho's doctrine. He asks angrily: Whom should he follow? Ptolemy, whose doctrine is falsified by the new observations of Mars? Copernicus, from whom everyone must turn away on account of the recently condemned hypothesis? Here I note several things. First, I reply that it is most false that I have ever blamed anyone for following Tycho, although I could have done so, as even his followers can see on account of Chiaramonti's *Anti-Tycho*;[7] thus what Sarsi writes here is very far from being pertinent. The introduction of Ptolemy and Copernicus is even more irrelevant, for there is no evidence [232] that they ever wrote a word about the distances, sizes, and motions of comets and the corresponding theories, whereas the topic of discussion was comets and nothing else. One might as well have interjected Sophocles, Bartolo,[8] or Livy.

Furthermore, I seem to detect in Sarsi the firm belief that in philosophizing one must rely upon the opinions of some famous author, so that if our mind does not marry the thinking of someone else, it remains altogether sterile and fruitless. Perhaps he thinks that philosophy is the creation of a man, a book like the *Iliad* or *Orlando Furioso,*[9] in which the least important thing is whether what is written in them is true. Mr. Sarsi, that is not the way it is. Philosophy is written in this all-encompassing book that is constantly open before our eyes, that is the universe; but it cannot be understood unless one first learns to understand the language and knows the characters in which it is written. It is written in mathematical language, and its characters are triangles, circles, and other geometrical figures; without these it is humanly impossible to understand a word of it, and one wanders around pointlessly in a dark labyrinth.

But let us assume that, as Sarsi seems to think, our intellect should become a slave to the intellect of another man (and here I overlook the fact that by thus requiring everyone, including himself, to become

---

7. Scipione Chiaramonti (1565–1652) was at the time (1623) professor of mathematics at the University of Perugia and later (1627–36) professor of philosophy at the University of Pisa. His *Anti-Tycho* had been published in Venice in 1621. He is mentioned favorably in *The Assayer* in regard to the nature of comets, but he is frequently and sharply criticized in the *Dialogue* for his anti-Copernican views.
8. Bartolo da Sassoferrato (1313–55), a jurist who wrote a famous commentary on ancient Roman law.
9. *Orlando Furioso,* by Ludovico Ariosto (1474–1533), is one of the greatest epic poems of the Italian language and was especially liked by Galileo.

an imitator, he praises in himself what he blames in Mr. Mario); and let us assume that in the investigation of heavenly motions we should follow somebody. Then I do not see for what reason he chooses Tycho, preferring him over Ptolemy and Nicolaus Copernicus. From the last two we have systems of the world that are unified, constructed with the greatest sophistication, and brought to completion. But I do not see that Tycho did anything of the kind, unless Sarsi is satisfied with having rejected the other two, having promised another one, and then not having carried it out.

Nor would I want anyone to credit Tycho with having shown the falsity of the other two, for the following reasons. Regarding the Ptolemaic system, neither Tycho nor other astronomers, not even Copernicus himself, could directly falsify it, given that the principal argument (from the motions of Mars and Venus) always had sense experience against it. That is, the disk of Venus at its two conjunctions with the sun showed very little difference in apparent size, and the disk of Mars at perigee was hardly three or four times greater than at apogee; and so one could never hold that the former actually appeared forty times greater, and the latter sixty times greater, in their two respective positions; yet this had to happen [233] if their revolutions were around the sun, in accordance with the Copernican system. However, that this is true and observable by the senses has been demonstrated by me, and with a good telescope I have enabled anyone who wanted to see it to grasp it as if by hand. Regarding the Copernican hypothesis, if we Catholics had not had the benefit of being removed from error and having our blindness illuminated by a higher wisdom, I do not believe such favor and benefit could have been obtained from Tycho's reasons and observations.

Thus, the two systems being surely false, and that of Tycho null, Sarsi should not blame me if like Seneca I desire to know the true constitution of the universe. And although this is to ask a lot and I very much crave the answer, I do not thereby deplore with sorrow and tears the poverty and misfortune of our age, as Sarsi writes; nor is there the least trace of such laments in Mr. Mario's whole essay. However, Sarsi needed to elaborate and support some idea of his which he wanted to advance, and so he prepared the groundwork himself by launching at himself attacks which others did not initiate. And even if I were to deplore our misfortune, I do not see how appropriate it would be for Sarsi to say that my complaints are pointless because I have no means or power to do away with such poverty; for it seems to me that precisely for this reason I would be entitled to complain, whereas complaints would be pointless if I could take away the misfortune.

[§7.2 Heat, Atoms, and Primary vs. Secondary Qualities][10]

[347] In accordance with my earlier promise to Your Most Illustrious Lordship, there now remains for me to say what I think about the proposition "motion is the cause of heat," indicating in what sense I think it may be true. But first I must make a comment about what we call *heat*. I very much suspect that the conception which people generally form of it is very far from the truth inasmuch as it is believed to be a real attribute, property, and quality that truly inheres in the material by which we feel warmed.

Accordingly, I say that as soon as I conceive of a corporeal substance or material, I feel indeed drawn by the necessity of also conceiving that it is bounded and has this or that shape; that it is large or small in relation to other things; that it is in this or that location and exists at this or that time; that it moves or stands still; that it touches or does not touch another body; and that it is one, a few, or many. Nor can I, by any stretch of the imagination, separate it from these conditions. However, my mind does not feel forced to regard it as necessarily accompanied by such conditions as the following: that it is white or red, bitter or sweet, noisy or quiet, [348] and pleasantly or unpleasantly smelling; on the contrary, if we did not have the assistance of our senses, perhaps the intellect and the imagination by themselves would never conceive of them. Thus, from the point of view of the subject in which they seem to inhere, these tastes, odors, colors, etc., are nothing but empty names; rather they inhere only in the sensitive body, such that if one removes the animal, then all these qualities are taken away and annihilated. However, since we have given them particular names different from those of the primary and real attributes, we have a tendency to believe that these qualities are truly and really different from the primary ones.

I think I can explain my meaning more clearly with some examples. Suppose I move my hand first over a marble statue and then over

---

10. Galilei 1890–1909, 6: 347.22–352.14; newly translated by Finocchiaro.

a living man. Regarding the action coming from my hand, from the point of view of the hand the action over one subject is the same as that over the other; it consists of primary attributes, namely, motion and touch, and we do not use any other names. But the animate body that receives such an action feels various sensations depending on where it is touched. For example, if it is touched on the soles of the feet, on the knees, or on the armpits, besides touch it feels another sensation to which we have given a particular name, calling it *tickling*. This sensation is entirely ours and not at all in the hand; I think it would be a great error to want to say that, besides motion and touching, the hand has within itself another property different from these, namely, the power to tickle, such that tickling is an attribute inherent in it. Similarly, a piece of paper or a feather lightly brushed over any part of our body performs exactly the same operation with regard to itself, namely, moving and touching. But with regard to us, by touching between the eyes, or on the nose, or under the nostrils, it produces an almost intolerable titillation, whereas in other parts it is hardly felt. That titillation is entirely in us and not in the feather, and if the animate and sensitive body is removed, it is nothing but an empty name. Now, I believe that many qualities that are attributed to natural bodies (such as tastes, odors, colors, and others) may have a similar and not greater reality.

A solid and, so to speak, highly material body, when moved and applied to any part of my person, produces in me [349] a sensation which we call *touch*. Although this sensation covers the whole body, nevertheless it seems to reside chiefly in the palms of the hands, and especially in the fingertips, with which we feel extremely small differences of roughness, smoothness, softness, and hardness, whereas with other parts of the body we do not distinguish them as well. Some of these sensations are more pleasant, others less so, depending on the shapes of tangible bodies, whether they are smooth or rough, acute or obtuse, hard or soft. This sense, being more material than the others and deriving from the solidity of matter, seems to correspond to the element earth.

Now, some of these bodies are constantly being subdivided into tiny particles,[11] of which some are heavier than air and fall downwards and others are lighter and rise upwards. And perhaps here is how two

---

11. Here and in the rest of this selection, *tiny particle*, or simply *particle*, is my translation of Galileo's *particella minima*, or *corpicello minimo*, or simply *minimo*.

other senses are generated, when those particles go and strike two parts of our body that are much more sensitive than our skin, which does not feel the effect of materials that are so fine, delicate, and soft. The particles that go down are received by the upper part of the tongue, becoming mixed with its humidity and penetrating its substance; thus they produce taste, likable or disagreeable, depending on the kind of contact with the various shapes of the particles, on the greater or smaller number of particles, and on their velocity. The other particles, which go up, enter through the nostrils and strike some small nodules that are the instrument of our sense of smell; here likewise their touch and movements are recorded with pleasure or annoyance, depending on whether their shapes are these or those, their movements are slow or fast, and their number is small or large. And indeed we see that, with regard to their location, the tongue and the nasal passages are wisely arranged: the former is extended underneath in order to receive the descending signals; the latter are set up for the ascending ones. And perhaps there is an analogy between the production of tastes and the descent of fluids through air and between the production of odors and the ascent of fires.

There remains the question of the correspondence between the element air and sounds. These come to us equally from all parts (lower, higher, and lateral) since we are located in air, whose motion in its own region is propagated equally in all directions. And the placement of the ear is arranged as much as possible to respond to all positions. Sounds are produced in us and heard when, without any sonorous or sound-like qualities, a rapid vibration of the air in the form of extremely minute waves moves some cartilage in the tympanum that is [350] in our ear. The external means capable of producing this rippling in the air are extremely numerous, but perhaps they reduce mostly to the vibration of bodies that strike the air and thereby ripple it; the waves propagate through it at great velocity, with higher frequencies generating sharper sounds and lower frequencies deeper tones.

However, I do not believe that in order to stimulate in us tastes, odors, and sounds, external bodies require anything other than sizes, shapes, quantity, and slow or fast motions. I think that if one takes away ears, tongues, and noses, there indeed remain the shapes, numbers, and motions, but not the odors, tastes, or sounds; outside the living animal these are nothing but names, just as tickling and titillation are nothing but names if we remove the armpits and the skin around the nose. And just as the four elements correspond to the four senses considered so far, I believe that light corresponds to vision, the sense that is the most eminent of all; indeed its excellence is such that the comparison is like that of finite to infinite, time consuming to instantaneous, divisible to indivisible, and dark to light. I understand very little about this sense and related matters, and to explain the little I do understand, or better to adumbrate it on paper, I would need a long time; so I pass it over in silence.

But let us return to my primary purpose here. We have already seen that many properties, which are considered to be qualities inherent in external objects, do not really have any other existence except in us, and that outside of us they are nothing but names. Now I say that I am inclined to believe that heat is of this kind. The materials which produce heat in us and make us feel it, and which we call by the general name *fire,* are large collections of tiny corpuscles shaped in such and such a manner and moving with such and such a speed; when they meet our body they penetrate it because of their extremely small size. Their contact, which they make as they pass through our bodily substance and which we feel, is the property we call *heat,* which is pleasing or hurtful depending on the lesser or greater number and speed of the particles that are pricking and penetrating us. Such penetration is pleasing when it facilitates our unfelt but necessary perspiration, and hurtful when it causes too much division and separation of our bodily substance. In short, the action of [351] fire works exactly this way: because of its extreme flexibility, by moving it penetrates all bodies and so dissolves them sooner or later depending on the number and velocity of the igneous particles in it and on the density or rarity of the matter in those bodies; as they are being destroyed, the greater part of many bodies turns into tiny igneous particles, and the decomposition continues as long as there remains decomposable material.

However, I do not believe in the least that besides shape, quantity, motion, penetration, and touch, there is in fire another quality, and that this quality is heat. Rather, I think that heat is in us, so much so that if we remove the animate and sensitive body, heat remains nothing but a simple word. Furthermore, since this property is produced in us by the touch of the tiny igneous particles and their passing through our bodily substance, it is clear that if they were to stand still then their operation would remain null. Thus we see that the considerable amount of fire contained in the pores and cavities of a piece of quicklime does not warm us when we hold it in our hand, because the fire is standing still. But let us place the quicklime in water, where the fire has a greater propensity to move than it had in air because of the weight of the water, and where the cavities are opened more by the water as compared to the situation in air; then the tiny igneous particles escape and meet and penetrate our hand, and we feel the heat.

Since, then, the presence of the igneous particles is not sufficient to stimulate heat, but their motion is also needed, therefore it seems to me very reasonable to say that motion is the cause of heat.

This is the motion that burns arrows and the wood of catapults and liquefies the lead of gunshots and other metals:[12] moving at high speed, whether by their own power or by the strong blast of a bellows if that is insufficient, the tiny particles of fire penetrate all bodies; some of these are decomposed into flying igneous particles, others are decomposed into extremely minute dust, and still others are liquefied into fluids like water. But if this proposition is taken in its ordinary meaning (i.e., that moving a rock or a piece of iron or of wood heats them up), then I regard it as a solemn falsehood. Now, the friction and rubbing of two hard bodies does reduce them to motion, in the sense that either parts of them are decomposed into extremely fine flying particles, or the igneous particles contained in them are allowed to escape; as these moving particles meet our bodies, penetrate them, and pass through them, the sensitive soul feels their motion and touch and experiences the pleasing or hurtful sensation which we have [352] named *heat, burning,* or *scorching.* Perhaps while the rubbing and grinding are limited to producing particles that are tiny but still finite, their motion is temporal and their operation merely calorific. But then if one arrives at the ultimate and highest decomposition into really indivisible atoms, one creates light, whose motion (or rather, expansion or propagation) is instantaneous; and it is capable of filling immense spaces on account of its subtlety, rarefaction, and immateriality, although I do not know whether these words are correct or whether we should speak of some other property as yet unnamed and different from all these.

Your Most Illustrious Lordship, I do not want inadvertently to engulf myself in an infinite ocean such that I cannot get back to port. Nor do I want, while removing one doubt, to give rise to a hundred others, as I fear it may have happened as a result of my little departure from the shore. So I want to postpone further discussion to some other more appropriate occasion.

---

12. Cf. the discussion in section 44 of *The Assayer:* Galilei 1890–1909, 6: 336–39; Drake and O'Malley 1960, 297–300.

CHAPTER 8[1]

From *Dialogue on the Two Chief World Systems* (1632)[2]

[§8.1 Preface: To the Discerning Reader][3]

[29] Some years ago there was published in Rome a salutary edict[4] which, to prevent the dangerous scandals of the present age, imposed opportune silence upon the Pythagorean opinion of the earth's motion. There were some who rashly asserted that that decree was the offspring of extremely ill-informed passion and not of judicious examination; one also heard complaints that consultants who are totally ignorant of astronomical observations should not cut the wings of speculative intellects by means of an immediate prohibition. Upon noticing the audacity of such complaints, my zeal could not remain silent. Being fully informed about that most prudent decision, I thought it appropriate to appear publicly on the world scene as a sincere witness of the truth. For at that time I had been present in Rome; I had had not only audiences but also endorsements by the most eminent prelates of that court; nor did the publication of that decree follow without some prior knowledge on my part. Thus it is my intention in the present work to show to foreign nations that we in Italy, and especially in Rome, know as much about this subject as transalpine diligence can have ever imagined. Furthermore, by collecting together all my own speculations on the Copernican system, I intend to make it known that an awareness of them all preceded the

---

1. Reprinted from: Galileo Galilei, *Galileo on the World Systems: A New Abridged Translation and Guide*, trans. and ed. by Maurice A. Finocchiaro, © 1997 by the Regents of the University of California. Published by the University of California Press.
2. For the historical background, see the Introduction, especially §0.9.
3. Galilei 1890–1909, 7: 29–31; translated by Finocchiaro (1997, 77–82). This preface was compiled jointly by Galileo and the Master of the Sacred Palace, or chief censor in Rome, a Dominican named Niccolò Riccardi (1585–1639).
4. The anti-Copernican Decree of the Index (5 March 1616); cf. §6.5.

Roman censorship, and that from these parts emerge not only dogmas for the salvation of the soul, but also ingenious discoveries for the delight of the mind.

To this end I have in the discussion taken the Copernican point of view, proceeding in the manner of a pure mathematical hypothesis and striving in every contrived way [30] to present it as superior to the viewpoint of the earth being motionless, though not absolutely but relative to how this is defended by some who claim to be Peripatetics; however, they are Peripatetics only in name since they do not walk around but are satisfied with worshipping shadows, and they do not philosophize with their own judgment but only with the memory of a few ill-understood principles.

Three principal points will be treated. First, I shall attempt to show that all experiments feasible on the earth are insufficient to prove its mobility but can be adapted indifferently to a moving as well as to a motionless earth; and I hope that many observations unknown to antiquity will be disclosed here. Second, I shall examine celestial phenomena, strengthening the Copernican hypothesis as if it should emerge absolutely victorious and adding new speculations; these, however, are advanced for the sake of astronomical convenience and not for the purpose of imposing necessity on nature. Third, I shall propose an ingenious fancy. Many years ago I had occasion to say that the unsolved problem of the tides could receive some light if the earth's motion were granted. Flying from mouth to mouth, this assertion of mine has found charitable people who adopt it as a child of their own intellect. Now, so that no foreigner can ever appear who, strengthened by our own weapons, would blame us for our insufficient attention to such an important phenomenon, I decided to disclose those probable arguments which would render it plausible, given that the earth were in motion. I hope these considerations will show the world that if other nations have navigated more, we have not speculated less, and that to assert the earth's rest and take the contrary solely as a mathematical whim does not derive from ignorance of others' thinking but, among other things, from those reasons provided by piety, religion, acknowledgment of divine omnipotence, and awareness of the weakness of the human mind.

Furthermore, I thought it would be very appropriate to explain these ideas in dialogue form; for it is not restricted to the rigorous observation of mathematical laws, and so it also allows digressions which are sometimes no less interesting than the main topic.

Many years ago in the marvelous city of Venice I had several occasions to engage in conversation with Giovanfrancesco Sagredo, a man of most illustrious family and of sharpest mind. From Florence we were visited by [31] Filippo Salviati, whose least glory was purity of blood and magnificence of riches; his sublime intellect fed on no delight more avidly than on refined speculations. I often found myself discussing these subjects with these two men, and with the participation of a Peripatetic philosopher, who seemed to have no greater obstacle to the understanding of the truth than the fame he had acquired in Aristotelian interpretation.

Now, since Venice and Florence have been deprived of those two great lights by their very premature death at the brightest time of their life, I have decided to prolong their existence, as much as my meager abilities allow, by reviving them in these pages of mine and using them as interlocutors in the present controversy. There will also be a place for the good Peripatetic, to whom, because of his excessive fondness of Simplicius'[5] commentaries, it seemed right to give the name of his revered author, without mentioning his own. Those two great souls will always be revered in my heart; may they receive with favor this public monument of my undying friendship, and may they assist me, through my memory of their eloquence, to explain to posterity the aforementioned speculations.

These gentlemen had casually engaged in various sporadic discussions, and, as a result, in their minds their thirst for learning had been aroused rather than quenched. Thus they made the wise decision to spend a few days together during which, having put aside every other business, they would attend to reflecting more systematically about God's wonders in heaven and on earth. They met at the palace of the most illustrious Sagredo, and after the proper but short greetings, Salviati began as follows.

---

5. The Italian name of this philosopher is Simplicio, which is also a word with the connotation of *simpleton*. I have retained the name Simplicio in order to capture Galileo's double-entendre.

[§8.2 Day II: Independent-mindedness and Aristotle's Authority][6]

[132] SALV.   Yesterday's digressions from the direct path of our main discussions were many, and so I do not know whether I can get back and proceed further without your help.

SAGR.   I am not surprised that you are in a state of confusion, given that you have your mind full not only of what has been said but also of what remains; but I, who am a mere listener and know only the things I have heard, will perhaps be able to bring the argument back into line by briefly recalling them. As far as I can remember then, the gist of yesterday's discussions was the examination from its foundations of the question of which of the two following opinions is more probable and reasonable: the one holding that the substance of the heavenly bodies is ingenerable, indestructible, unchangeable, inert, in short, exempt from any but changes of place, and that therefore there is a fifth essence[7] very different from the familiar one of our elemental, generable, degradable, and changeable bodies; or else the other opinion which, taking this division of parts away from the world, holds that the earth enjoys the same perfections as the other constitutive bodies of the universe, and is in short a movable and moving globe no less than the moon, Jupiter, Venus, or other planets. Lastly we drew many particular parallels between the earth and the moon, concentrating on the latter perhaps because we have greater and more sensible knowledge of it on account of its lesser distance. Having concluded that this second opinion is more likely than the other, I think that the next step is to begin [133] to examine whether the earth must be considered immovable, as most people have so far believed, or else movable, as some ancient philosophers and others more recently have held; and if it is movable, we must ask what its motion may be.

SALV.   I understand already and recognize the direction of our path. However, before beginning to proceed further, I must say something about the last words you uttered—that we concluded that the opinion holding the earth to have the same properties as the

---

6. Galilei 1890–1909, 7: 132.1–39.35; translated by Finocchiaro (1997, 117–28).

7. That is, a fifth substance, besides the four terrestrial elements of earth, water, air, and fire; it was also called *quintessence* or *aether*.

heavenly bodies is more likely than the contrary one. For I have not
concluded this, just as I am not about to conclude any other controversial proposition; instead I have meant to produce, for one side as
well as for the other, those reasons and answers, questions and solutions which others have found so far, together with some that have
come to my mind after long reflection, leaving the decision to the
judgment of others.[8]

SAGR.   I let myself be carried away by my own feelings and made
universal a conclusion that should have been left individual, thinking
that others should feel what I felt within myself. Indeed I erred, especially since I do not know the opinion of Simplicio present here.

SIMP.   I confess to you that I thought about yesterday's discussions
the whole night, and I really find many beautiful, new, and forceful
considerations. Nevertheless, I feel drawn much more by the authority of so many great writers, and in particular . . .[9] You shake your
head and sneer, Sagredo, as if I were saying a great absurdity.

SAGR.   I merely sneer, but believe me that I am about to explode
by trying to contain greater laughter; for you reminded me of a beautiful incident that I witnessed many years ago together with some
other worthy friends of mine, whom I could still name.

SALV.   It will be good for you to tell us about it, so that perhaps
Simplicio does not continue to believe that it was he who moved you
to laughter.

SAGR.   I am happy to do that. One day I was at the house of a
highly respected physician in Venice; here various people met now
and then, some to study, others for curiosity, in order to see anatomical dissections performed by an anatomist who was really no less
learned than diligent and experienced. It happened that day that they
were looking for the origin and [134] source of the nerves, concerning which there is a famous controversy between Galenist[10] and

8. This disclaimer is only one of many similar ones interspersed throughout
the *Dialogue;* it is part of Galileo's attempt to have this book interpreted as a
legitimate hypothetical or critical discussion of the issues, rather than as an
assertion or defense of Copernicanism, which would have violated the ecclesiastic restrictions placed upon him. Of course, his attempt was not entirely
successful, as the trial of 1633 shows.
9. This ellipsis is in Galileo's text.
10. The Galenists were followers of Galen (c. 130–c. 200), Greek physician
to the Roman emperor Marcus Aurelius, and writer of many treatises that
made him the supreme authority on medicine until the 16th century. They

Peripatetic physicians. The anatomist showed how the great trunk of nerves started at the brain, passed through the nape of the neck, extended through the spine, and then branched out through the whole body, and how only a single strand as thin as a thread arrived at the heart. As he was doing this he turned to a gentleman, whom he knew was a Peripatetic philosopher and for whose sake he had made the demonstration; the physician asked the philosopher whether he was satisfied and sure that the origin of the nerves is in the brain and not in the heart, and the latter answered after some reflection: "You have made me see this thing so clearly and palpably that one would be forced to admit it as true, if Aristotle's texts were not opposed in saying plainly that the nerves originate in the heart."

SIMP.   Gentlemen, I want you to know that this dispute about the origin of the nerves is not as settled and decided as some believe.

SAGR.   Nor will it ever be decided as long as one has similar opponents. At any rate what you say does not diminish at all the absurdity of the answer of the Peripatetic, who against such a sensible experience did not produce other experiences or reasons of Aristotle, but mere authority and the simple ipse dixit.[11]

SIMP.   Aristotle has acquired such great authority only because of the strength of his arguments and the profundity of his discussions. However, you must understand him, and not only understand him, but also know his books so well that you have a complete picture of them and all his assertions always in mind. For he did not write for the common people, nor did he feel obliged to spin out his syllogisms by the well-known formal method; instead, using an informal procedure, he sometimes placed the proof of a proposition among passages that seem to deal with something else. Thus, you must have that whole picture and be able to combine this passage with that one and connect this text with another very far from it. There is no doubt that

---

held (correctly) that the nerves originate in the brain, whereas the Aristotelians held (incorrectly) that they originate in the heart; cf. Aristotle, *On the Generation of Animals,* V, 2, 781a20.

11. Galileo uses the Latin phrase *ipse dixit* in his Italian dialogue, since the phrase has been adopted by other languages, including English. It derives from the traditional Latin version of the Bible, which uses the phrase in Genesis to refer to God's acts of creation. It literally means "he himself said it," referring to someone who is regarded as an authority; it is a way of appealing to authority in the course of a discussion.

whoever has this skill will be able to draw from his books the demonstrations of all knowable things, since they contain everything.

SAGR.   So, my dear Simplicio, you are not bothered by things being scattered here and there, and you think that by collecting [135] and combining various parts you can squeeze their juice. But then, what you and other learned philosophers do with Aristotle's texts, I will do with the verses of Virgil or Ovid, by making patchworks of passages and explaining with them all the affairs of men and secrets of nature. But why even go to Virgil or other poets? I have a booklet much shorter than Aristotle or Ovid in which are contained all the sciences, and with very little study one can form a very complete picture of them: this is the alphabet. There is no doubt that whoever knows how to combine and order this and that vowel with this and that consonant will be able to get from them the truest answers to all questions and the teachings of all sciences and of all arts. In the same way a painter, given various simple colors placed separately on his palette, by combining a little of this with a little of that and that other, is able to draw men, plants, buildings, birds, fishes—in short, all visible objects—without having on his palette either eyes, or feathers, or scales, or leaves, or rocks; on the contrary, it is necessary that none of the things to be drawn nor any part of them be actually among the colors, which can serve to represent everything, for if there were, for example, feathers, they would not serve to depict anything but birds and bunches of feathers.

SALV.   There are still alive some gentlemen who were present when a professor teaching at a famous university, upon hearing descriptions of the telescope which he had not yet seen, said that the invention was taken from Aristotle. Having asked that a book be brought to him, he found a certain passage where Aristotle explains how it happens that from the bottom of a very deep well one can see the stars in heaven during the day,[12] and he said to the bystanders: "here is the well, which corresponds to the tube; here are the thick vapors, from which is taken the invention of lenses; and lastly here is the strengthening of vision as the rays pass through the denser and darker transparent medium."

SAGR.   This way of all knowledge being contained in a book is very similar to that by which a piece of marble contains within itself a very beautiful statue, or a thousand of them for that matter; but the

---

12. Cf. Aristotle, *On the Generation of Animals*, V, 1, 780b21.

point is to be able to discover them. We can say that it is also similar to Joachim's[13] prophecies or to the answers given by heathen oracles, which are understood only after the occurrence of prophesied events.

[136] SALV. And where do you leave the predictions of astrologers,[14] which after the event can be so clearly seen in the horoscope, or should we say in the configuration of the heavens?

SAGR. In the same vein alchemists,[15] driven by their melancholic humor, find that all the greatest minds in the world have never written about anything except the process of making gold, but that, in order to say this without revealing it to the common people, they have contrived in various ways to conceal it under various covers. It is very amusing to listen to their comments on ancient poets, as they reveal the very important mysteries lying hidden under those fables:[16] what is the meaning of the love affairs of the moon, of her coming down to earth for Endymion, and of her anger at Actaeon; when does Jupiter change himself into golden rain, and when into burning flames; and how many great secrets of the art are to be found in

---

13. Joachim of Floris (c. 1132–1202) was an Italian clergyman whose writings contain numerous vague and ambiguous prophecies, especially about the coming of a new age when the hierarchical structure of the Church and the separation between Christianity and other religions would no longer be needed.

14. Astrology is the pseudoscience that tries to predict human behavior and future events based on the positions and configurations of the heavenly bodies. It should not be confused with the science of astronomy. But until Galileo's time, astronomy and astrology were usually practiced by the same persons, and the two terms were often used interchangeably. Galileo's criticism reinforced a preexisting trend critical of astrology that eventually resulted in the separation of the two. The relationship between astrology and astronomy is analogous to that between alchemy and chemistry.

15. Alchemy was the ancient quest to turn base metals (such as iron) into precious ones (such as gold). Though this quest was impossible and alchemy was largely a pseudoscience, some aspects of it (such as its emphasis on experimental tinkering) made alchemy into a forerunner of the modern science of chemistry. As with astrology, Galileo's dismissal of alchemy was rare for his time and shows his remarkably modern outlook.

16. The rest of this speech refers to figures of classical Greek and Roman mythology, and not to heavenly bodies. The moon was a goddess; Endymion was a young shepherd with whom she fell in love; and Actaeon was the unfortunate hunter who watched her bathe, for which she turned him into a stag, whereupon he was killed by his own dogs. Jupiter was the supreme god, Mercury was the messenger of the gods, and Pluto was the god who ruled the afterlife.

Mercury the interpreter, in Pluto's kidnappings, and in those golden boughs.

SIMP.   I believe and to some extent know that the world is full of very extravagant brains, whose follies should not redound to the discredit of Aristotle. You seem sometimes to speak of him with too little respect, but the mere antiquity and the great name he has acquired in the minds of so many outstanding men should suffice to make him respectable among all educated men.

SALV.   That is not the way it is, Simplicio. It is some of his excessively cowardly followers who are responsible for making us think less of him, or to be more exact, who would be so responsible should we want to applaud their triflings. Tell me, if you do not mind, are you so simple minded that you do not understand that if Aristotle had been present to listen to the doctor who wanted to make him inventor of the telescope, he would have been more angry with him than with those who were laughing at the doctor and his interpretations? Do you have any doubt that if Aristotle were to see the new discoveries in the heavens, he would change his mind, revise his books, accept the more sensible doctrines, and cast away from himself those who are so weak minded as to be very cowardly induced to want to uphold every one of his sayings? Do they not realize that if Aristotle were as they imagine him, he would be an intractable brain, an obstinate mind, a barbarous soul, a tyrannical will, someone who, regarding everybody else as a silly sheep, would want his decrees to be preferred [137] over the senses, experience, and nature herself? It is his followers who have given authority to Aristotle, and not he who has usurped or taken it. Since it is easier to hide under someone else's shield than to show oneself openly, they are afraid and do not dare to go away by a single step; rather than putting any changes in the heavens of Aristotle, they insolently deny those which they see in the heavens of nature.

SAGR.   These people make me think of that sculptor who carved a large piece of marble into an image of Hercules or of a thundering Jupiter (I forget which); with admirable skill he gave it so much liveliness and fierceness that it terrified anyone who looked at it; then he himself began to be afraid even though these qualities were the work of his own hands; and his terror was such that he no longer dared to face him with his chisel and mallet.

SALV.   I have often wondered how it can be that those who rigidly maintain everything Aristotle said do not notice how much damage they do to his reputation, how much discredit they bring him, and how much they diminish his authority instead of increasing it. For I often see them stubbornly wanting to defend propositions that I find palpably and manifestly false, and wanting to persuade me that this is what a true philosopher is supposed to do and what Aristotle himself would do; their behavior greatly undermines my belief that he may have philosophized correctly in regard to other conclusions less well known to me; on the other hand, if I saw them yielding and changing their minds in regard to the obvious truths, I would be inclined to believe that when they persisted they might have sound demonstrations which I did not know or understand.

SAGR.   Still, if they felt they were risking too much of Aristotle's reputation or their own by admitting not knowing this or that conclusion discovered by others, would it not be better to find it in his texts by combining them in accordance with the practice mentioned by Simplicio? For, if all knowledge is contained there, one must be able to find it.

SALV.   Sagredo, do not make fun of this advice, which you seem to propose in jest. In fact, not long ago a philosopher of great renown wrote a book on the soul which discussed Aristotle's opinion on whether or not the soul is immortal by presenting many passages that suggested a pernicious answer (these were passages discovered by himself in little known places rather than the ones quoted by Alexander[17] [138] because in these Aristotle allegedly did not even discuss this subject, let alone establish anything pertaining to it); when he was warned that he would have encountered difficulties in getting the printing license, he wrote back to his friend not to let this stop the application process because, if there were no other obstacles, he would have had no difficulty changing Aristotle's doctrine and supporting the contrary opinion with other assertions and passages also corresponding to Aristotle's mind.

SAGR.   Oh, what a scholar! I am at his command; he does not want to be duped by Aristotle, but wants to lead him by the nose and make him speak as he himself commands! See how important it is to

---

17. Alexander of Aphrodisias, a Greek philosopher who lived around 200 A.D., best known for his commentaries on Aristotle, especially the one dealing with the book *On the Soul*. He interpreted Aristotle as implying that a person's soul is not immortal, and so was condemned at the Fifth Lateran Council in 1512 (Santillana 1953, 125 n. 8).

know how to seize an opportunity. One should not deal with Hercules when he is in a rage and overtaken by fury, but rather while he is playing with Lydian maids.[18] Oh, the unbelievable cowardice of slavish minds! To make oneself spontaneously a slave, to accept decrees as inviolable, to be obliged to call oneself persuaded and convinced by arguments so effective and clearly conclusive that its proponents cannot decide even whether they are written for that purpose and are meant to prove that conclusion! But let us mention the greatest folly: that they themselves are still uncertain whether the same author holds the affirmative or negative side. Is not this like regarding a wooden statue as their oracle, resorting to it for answers, fearing it, revering it, and worshipping it?

SIMP.   But, if one abandons Aristotle, who will be the guide in philosophy? Name some author.

SALV.   One needs a guide in an unknown and uncivilized country, but in a flat and open region only the blind need a guide; whoever is blind would do well to stay home, whereas anyone who has eyes in his head and in his mind should use them as a guide. Not that I am thereby saying that one should not listen to Aristotle; on the contrary, I applaud his being examined and diligently studied and only blame submitting to him in such a way that one blindly subscribes to all his assertions and accepts them as unquestionable dictates, without searching for other reasons for them. This abuse carries with it another extreme impropriety, namely, that no one makes an effort any longer to try to understand the strength of his demonstrations. Is there anything more shameful in a public discussion [139] dealing with demonstrable conclusions than to see someone slyly appear with a textual passage (often written for some different purpose) and use it to shut the mouth of an opponent? If you want to persist in this manner of studying, lay down the name of philosophers and call yourselves either historians or memory experts, for it is not right that those who never philosophize should usurp the honorable title of philosopher.

However, we should get back to shore in order not to enter an infinite ocean from which we could not get out all day. So, Simplicio,

---

18. According to classical Greek mythology, in one of his many exploits Hercules was condemned by the Delphic Oracle to be a servant to the queen of Lydia; she had him dress in women's clothes, live with her maids, spin wool like them, and make love to her.

come freely with reasons and demonstrations (yours or Aristotle's) and not with textual passages or mere authorities because our discussions are about the sensible world and not about a world on paper. In yesterday's discussions the earth was drawn out of darkness and brought to light in the open heavens, and we showed that to want to number it among those bodies called heavenly is not so doomed and prostrate a proposition as to be left devoid of any vital energy; and so today we should examine how much probability there is in holding it fixed and completely motionless (referring to the globe as a whole) and how much likelihood there is in making it move with any motion (and if so what type this is). I am undecided about this question, while Simplicio together with Aristotle is firmly on the side of immobility; because of this, he will present step-by-step the motives for their opinion, I will present the answers and arguments for the contrary side, and Sagredo will say what goes on in his mind and to which side he feels drawn.

SAGR.   I am happy with this arrangement, but on the condition that I am free to introduce whatever simple common sense may suggest to me.

SALV.   Indeed, I beg you to do exactly that; for I think the various authors have left out few of the easier and (so to speak) cruder considerations, so that only some of the more subtle and esoteric ones may be wanting and lacking; but to investigate these, what subtlety can be more appropriate than that of Sagredo's intellect, which is most acute and penetrating?

SAGR.   I may be all that Salviati says, but please, let us not start on another sort of ceremonial digression because right now I am a philosopher and have come to school and not to city hall.

[§8.3 Day II: Diurnal Rotation, Simplicity, and Probability][19]

SALV.   So let the beginning of our reflections be the following consideration: whatever motion is attributed to the earth, [140] it must remain completely imperceptible and seem nonexisting for us living there and sharing that motion, as long as we look only at terrestrial things; on the other hand, it is equally necessary that the same

---

19. Galilei 1890–1909, 7: 139.36–150.12; translated by Finocchiaro (1997, 128–42).

motion appear to us to be common to all other visible bodies and objects which are separated from the earth and so lack that motion.[20] Thus, the true method of investigating whether any motion may be attributed to the earth and, if so, what kind it may be is to consider and observe whether in the bodies separated from the earth one sees any appearance of motion belonging equally to all; for if a motion were seen, for example, only in the moon and had nothing to do with Venus or Jupiter or other stars, it could not belong to the earth in any way but only to the moon. Now, there is a motion which is very general and most important of all: it is the motion by which the sun, moon, other planets, and fixed stars (in short, the whole universe except only the earth) appear to us to move together from east to west in a period of twenty-four hours. In regard to this first phenomenon, this motion may belong either to the earth only or to the rest of the universe without the earth, for the same appearances would be seen in the one situation as in the other. Aristotle and Ptolemy grasped this consideration, and so when they try to prove the earth to be motionless, they argue only against this diurnal motion; but Aristotle mentions something or other against another motion attributed to it by an ancient author, of which we shall speak in due course.[21]

SAGR.   I understand very well the necessity of which you speak, but I have a difficulty which I do not know how to remove. Copernicus attributed to the earth another motion besides the diurnal one; so by the rule just stated, as regards the appearances, that other motion should remain imperceptible when we look at the earth but be visible in the whole rest of the universe; thus it seems one can necessarily conclude either that he clearly erred in attributing to the earth a motion which does not appear to be general in the heavens, or that if it is general then Ptolemy was equally wrong in not refuting it as he did the other.

[141] SALV.   Your difficulty is a very reasonable one; when we treat of the other motion you will see how much Copernicus' intellect surpassed Ptolemy's in cleverness and profundity, insofar as the former saw what the latter did not, namely, the wonderful accuracy

---

20. This sentence is the first of several statements in this selection of the principle of the relativity of motion, a basic principle of classical physics.
21. This other motion is the annual motion, which Galileo discusses in Day III, whereas Day II deals with the diurnal motion; the Aristotelian and Ptolemaic arguments are presented in §8.4.

with which this motion is reflected in all other heavenly bodies.[22] However, for now let us put off this aspect and return to the first point; in regard to this, I shall begin with the more general considerations and propose the reasons that seem to favor the earth's mobility, and then I shall listen to Simplicio for the opposite ones.

Firstly, let us consider the immense size of the stellar sphere in comparison to that of the terrestrial globe, which can fit inside the former many millions of times, and let us also think of the speed required for it to make one entire rotation in twenty-four hours; given these considerations, I cannot persuade myself that anyone can be found who would think it is more reasonable and credible for the celestial sphere to undergo rotation and the terrestrial globe to stand still.

SAGR.   Let us assume that all phenomena which may be naturally dependent on these motions are such that the same consequences follow, without a difference, from one supposition as well as the other one; if this were so, my initial and general impression would be that whoever thought it more reasonable to make the whole universe move to keep the earth motionless was more unreasonable than someone who went up to the top of your cathedral to look at the city and its surroundings and demanded that they turn around him so that he would not have to bother turning his head. To overcome this absurdity and revise my impression, thus rendering this supposition more credible than the other one, the advantages deriving from it rather than the other would have to be great and many. But Aristotle, Ptolemy, and Simplicio must think that there are advantages in it; now, if these exist we should be told what they are, or else let it be admitted that there are not or cannot be any.

SALV.   Despite my having thought about it for a long time, I have been unable to find any difference, and so my finding seems to be that there cannot be any difference; hence I feel it is useless to continue searching for one. Let me explain. Motion exists as motion and acts as motion [142] in relation to things that lack it, but in regard to things that share it equally, it has no effect and behaves as if it did not

---

22. Observationally speaking, at the time of Copernicus and Galileo, the earth's annual motion was "reflected" in the appearances of only the planets, not in those of the fixed stars. In fact, this lack of "reflection" constituted a key difficulty for Copernicanism; it was formalized in the objection from stellar parallax, which Galileo discussed in Day III but could not really refute because even his telescope did not reveal any stellar parallax.

exist. Thus, for example, the goods loaded on a ship move insofar as they leave Venice, go by Corfu, Crete, and Cyprus, and arrive in Aleppo, and insofar as these places (Venice, Corfu, Crete, etc.) stay still and do not move with the ship; but for the bales, boxes, and packages loaded and stowed on the ship, the motion from Venice to Syria is as nothing and in no way alters their relationship among themselves or to the ship itself; this is so because this motion is common to all and shared equally by all; on the other hand, if in this cargo a bale is displaced from a box by a mere inch, this alone is for it a greater motion (in relation to the box) than the journey of two thousand miles made by them together.

SIMP.   This doctrine is correct, sound, and entirely Peripatetic.

SALV.   I think it is even more ancient. Moreover, I suspect that, when Aristotle took it from some good school, he did not entirely grasp it, and that therefore he wrote it in altered form and so was the source of confusion with the help of those who want to support all his statements. I also suspect that, when he wrote that everything which moves, moves upon something unmoved, he engaged in an equivocation on the assertion that everything which moves, moves in relation to something unmoved; the latter proposition suffers no difficulties, the former many.[23]

SAGR.   Please, let us not break the thread, and let us proceed with the discussion we began.

SALV.   It is clear, then, that motion common to many movable things is idle and null in regard to their relationship among themselves (because nothing changes among them), and that it acts only in regard to the relationship between those movable things and others which lack that motion (for this is the relationship which changes). We have also divided the universe into two parts, for which it is necessary that one of them is mobile and the other immobile; in regard to whatever may depend on this motion, to make the earth alone move is equivalent to making the rest of the universe move because the action for this motion lies only in the relationship between the heavenly bodies and the earth, and this is the only relationship that changes. Again, let us assume that, in order to bring about the same effect in the finest detail, one can either have the earth alone moving with the whole rest of the universe stopped or have the earth alone still with the whole

---

23. Cf. Aristotle, *Physics,* VIII, 4–5, 254b7–258b9; and *On the Motion of Animals,* 2, 698b8ff.

universe [143] moving by the same motion; if this assumption holds, who will believe that nature has chosen to let an immense number of very large bodies move at immeasurable speed to bring about what could be accomplished with the moderate motion of a single body around its own center? Indeed, who will believe this, given that by common consent, nature does not do by means of many things what can be done by means of a few?[24]

SIMP.   I do not understand very well how this very great motion is null for the sun, the moon, the other planets, and the innumerable array of fixed stars. How can you say it is nothing for the sun to pass from one meridian to another, rise above this horizon, set below that one, and bring day and night in turn; and also for the moon, other planets, and fixed stars to go through similar variations?

SALV.   All these variations you mention are nothing except in relation to the earth. To see that this is true, imagine that the earth is taken away: there will no longer be in the world any rising or setting of the sun or moon, any horizons or meridians, any days or nights; nor would their motion ever produce any changes among the moon, the sun, or any other stars whatever (be they fixed or wandering). In other words, to say that all these changes relate to the earth means that the sun appears first in China, then in Persia, and afterwards in Egypt, Greece, France, Spain, America, etc., and that the moon and the other heavenly bodies do the same. This phenomenon occurs in exactly the same way if, without involving such a large part of the universe, the terrestrial globe is made to turn on itself.

However, let us double the difficulty with another very great one. That is, if this great motion is attributed to the heavens, it is necessary to make it contrary to the particular motion of all the planetary orbs; each of these unquestionably has its own characteristic motion from west to east, at a very leisurely and moderate speed; but then one has to let this very rapid diurnal motion carry them off violently in the contrary direction, namely, from east to west. On the other hand, by making the earth turn on itself, the contrariety of motions is removed, and motions from west to east alone accommodate all appearances and satisfy them all completely.

---

24. This is the first of many statements of the principle of simplicity (or economy), which is a premise in the geokinetic argument of this selection; this argument may thus be called the simplicity argument for the earth's diurnal motion.

SIMP.   As for the contrariety of the motions, it matters little because Aristotle demonstrates that circular motions are not contrary to
each other, and that theirs cannot be called true contrariety.

[144] SALV.   Does Aristotle demonstrate this, or does he merely
assert it because it fits his purpose? If, as he himself states, contrary motions are those that reciprocally destroy each other, I do not see how
two moving bodies that collide along a circular line would damage each
other any less than if they were colliding along a straight line.

SAGR.   Please, stop for a moment. Tell me, Simplicio, when two
knights meet jousting in an open field, or when two whole fleets or
armadas clash at sea breaking up and sinking each other, would you
call such encounters contrary to one another?

SIMP.   Let us call them contrary.

SAGR.   How is it then that there is no contrariety for circular motions? For these occur on the surface of the land or the ocean, which
(as you know) is spherical, and so they are circular after all. Do you
know, Simplicio, which circular motions are not contrary to one another? They are those of two circles tangent to each other and such that
the turning of one naturally makes the other one move in a different
direction; but, if one is inside the other, it is impossible that their motions in different directions should not contrast with each other.

SALV.   In any case, whether the motions are contrary or not,
these are verbal disputes. I know that in fact it is much simpler and
more natural to explain everything by means of a single motion
rather than by introducing two of them. If you do not want to call
them contrary, call them opposite. Moreover, I am not saying that
this introduction of opposite motions is impossible; nor am I claiming to be giving a necessary demonstration, but only inferring a
greater probability.

The unlikelihood is tripled by upsetting in a very disproportionate
manner the ordered pattern we unquestionably see existing among
those heavenly bodies whose revolution is not in doubt but most certain. The pattern is that when an orbit is larger, the revolution is completed in a longer period of time; and when smaller, in a shorter
period.[25] Thus Saturn, which traces a greater circle than any other

---

25. I call this generalization Galileo's law of revolution. It is reminiscent of,
and should be compared and contrasted with, Kepler's third law of planetary
motion. The latter states that the planets revolve around the sun in such a way
that the square of the period of revolution is proportional to the cube of the

planet, completes it in thirty years; Mars in two; the moon goes through its much smaller orbit in just a month; and, in regard to the Medicean Stars, we see no less sensibly that the one nearest Jupiter completes its revolution in a very short time (namely, about forty-two hours), the next one in three and one-half days, the third one in seven days, and the most remote one in sixteen. This very harmonious pattern is not changed in the least [145] as long as the motion of twenty-four hours is attributed to the terrestrial globe (rotating on itself). However, if one wants to keep the earth immobile, it is necessary first to go from the very short period of the moon to others correspondingly longer; that is, to that of Mars lasting two years, from there to the larger orbit of Jupiter requiring twelve years, and from this to the bigger one of Saturn with a period of thirty years; but then it is necessary to go to an incomparably greater orb and have an entire revolution completed in twenty-four hours.[26] This is the least disorder that would follow; for someone may first want to go from Saturn to the stellar sphere and make it larger than the orbit of Saturn in a proportion appropriate to its very slow motion with a period of many thousands of years;[27] but then one would have to make a much more disproportionate jump in going from the stellar sphere to an even larger one, and make the latter revolve in twenty-four hours. On the other hand, once we give motion to the earth, the order of the periods is very strictly followed, and from the very sluggish orb of Saturn we go to the fixed stars, which completely lack such motions.

The earth's rotation also enables one to escape a fourth difficulty, which must necessarily be admitted if the stellar sphere is made to move. The difficulty is the immense disparity among the motions of the stars: some would move at very great speed in very large circles, while others would move very slowly in very small circles, depending on whether they are respectively further away from or closer to the poles. This is problematic because we see those heavenly bodies whose motion is not in doubt all moving in great circles, as well as

mean distance from the sun (that is, the period varies as the three-halves power of the distance).

26. This refers to the celestial sphere or the orb of the Prime Mobile.

27. This period refers to the precession of the equinoxes, namely, the apparent westward movement of the equinoctial points on the celestial sphere. Since the time of Copernicus, it has been estimated to have a period of 26,000 years, but ancient astronomers gave the higher figure of 36,000 years.

because it does not seem to be good planning that bodies which are supposed to move in circles be placed at immense distances from the center and then be made to move in very small circles.

Aside from the fact that the pattern of the magnitude of the circles and the consequent speed of the motions of these stars would be very different from the pattern of circles and motions of the others, each of these same stars would be changing its circle and speed,[28] and this is a fifth disadvantage. For there are stars which two thousand years ago were positioned on the celestial equator, and consequently described great circles with their motion; but in our time they are located away from it by several degrees, and so one must attribute to them a slower motion and make them move in smaller circles; and it may even happen that the time will come when some star which in the past always moved will become motionless by being joined to the pole, and then again (after resting [146] for some time) it will get back in motion. On the other hand, as previously stated, all the other stars that are unquestionably in motion describe the greatest circle of their orb and keep themselves constantly in it.

The unlikelihood is increased by a sixth disadvantage. Anyone with sound common sense will be unable to conceive the degree of solidity of that very large sphere in whose thickness would be embedded so many stars so firmly that they do not change their relative positions in the least, and yet they are made to revolve together with such great disparity. On the other hand, it is more reasonable to believe that the heavens are fluid,[29] so that each star wanders about in space by itself; if this belief is true, what law would regulate their motions and to what end, while making sure that (when observed from the earth) they would appear as if they were produced by a single sphere? It seems to me that an easier and more manageable way of accomplishing this would be to make them motionless, rather than making them wandering, just as it is easier to keep track of the many stones cemented into the pavement of a marketplace than of the bands of children running over them.

---

28. Once again, this is a reference to the precession of the equinoxes.
29. One of the issues in the Copernican controversy was whether the heavens are solid or fluid; that is, whether or not there exist crystalline spheres made out of impenetrable aether in which the various planets and fixed stars are embedded and whose rotation makes these heavenly bodies revolve.

Finally, there is a seventh objection: if we attribute the diurnal turning to the highest heaven,[30] it must have so much force and power as to carry with it innumerably many fixed stars (all very huge bodies and much larger than the earth) and also all the planetary orbs, even though both the latter and the former by nature move in the contrary direction;[31] moreover, it is necessary to admit that even the element fire and most of the air would be carried along as well, and that only the tiny terrestrial globe would be stubborn and recalcitrant vis-à-vis so much power; this seems to me to be a very problematic thing, and I would be unable to explain how the earth (as a body suspended and balanced on its center, indifferent to motion and to rest, and placed in and surrounded by a fluid environment) would not yield and be carried along the rotation. However, we do not find such obstacles in giving motion to the earth; it is an insignificant and very small body compared to the universe, and thus unable to do any violence to it.

SAGR.   I feel some of these concepts whirling in my mind, and indeed I am very confused after the discussions we have just had; if I want to be able to concentrate on what remains to be said, I must try to put some order in my ideas and draw some useful lesson (if possible). Proceeding by questioning will perhaps help me to explain myself better. So I first ask Simplicio whether he believes that [147] different natural motions may belong to the same simple body, or else only one is appropriate as its own natural motion.

SIMP.   For a simple movable body, only one, and no more, can be the motion that naturally belongs to it; all other motions can belong to it only by accident or by participation.[32] For example, for someone walking on a ship, his own motion is that of walking, and by participation he has the motion bringing him to port; for he will never arrive there unless the ship's motion takes him there.

SAGR.   Tell me a second thing, in regard to the motion that by participation is transferred to some moving body while the latter moves on its own with some motion different from the shared one;

---

30. The orb of the Prime Mobile.
31. In the Ptolemaic system, the diurnal motion is actually (as well as apparently) westward, whereas the individual planetary revolutions are actually (as well as apparently) eastward.
32. Cf. Aristotle, *Physics*, II, 14, 296b31–32. This was a basic principle of Aristotelian physics. Here it is applied to derive the existence of the Prime Mobile.

must this transferred motion belong to some subject by itself, or can it exist in nature without other support?

SIMP.   Aristotle answers all these questions. He says that, just as to a given moving thing there corresponds one particular motion, to a given motion there corresponds one particular moving thing; consequently, no motion can exist or be imagined without it inhering in its subject.[33]

SAGR.   Thirdly, I should like you to tell me whether you believe that the moon and the other planets and heavenly bodies have their own proper motions and what these motions are.

SIMP.   They have them, and the motions are those whereby they run through the zodiac: the moon in one month, the sun in one year, Mars in two years, and the stellar sphere in so many thousands; these are their own proper and natural motions.

SAGR.   But in regard to the motion whereby I see the fixed stars and all the planets proceed together from east to west and return to the east in twenty-four hours, in which way does it belong to them?

SIMP.   They have it by participation.

SAGR.   Therefore, this motion does not reside in them; now, since it does not reside in them, and since there must be some subject in which it resides, it is necessary that it should be the proper and natural motion of some other sphere.

SIMP.   In this regard, astronomers and philosophers have found a very high sphere without stars to which the diurnal rotation naturally belongs; it is called the Prime Mobile and carries along with it all the lower spheres, thus transferring its motion to them and sharing it with them.

SAGR.   However, suppose everything fits and agrees with perfect harmony without the introduction of unknown and very huge spheres, [148] without additional shared motions and transfers, by giving each sphere only its own simple motion, without mingling contrary motions, but having them all go in the same direction (as they must when they all depend on a single principle); then, why reject this proposal and accept those very strange and problematic complications?

SIMP.   The point is to find an easy and handy way of accomplishing this.

---

33. Cf. Aristotle, *Physics,* VIII, 1, 251a10.

SAGR.   The way is promptly found, I think. Let the earth be the Prime Mobile, that is, let it rotate on itself every twenty-four hours in the same direction as all the other planets or stars; then they will all appear to rise and set in the usual way and exhibit all the other phenomena without that terrestrial motion being transferred to any of them.

SIMP.   The important point is to be able to move the earth without a thousand inconveniences.

SALV.   All the inconveniences will be removed as you propose them. The things said so far are only the initial and more general reasons why it seems not to be entirely improbable that the diurnal turning belongs to the earth rather than to the rest of the universe; I do not advance them as inviolable laws but as likely reasons. Now, I understand very well that a single contrary experience or conclusive demonstration suffices to shoot down these and a hundred thousand other probable arguments; thus, one must not stop here, but proceed and hear what Simplicio has to say and what better probabilities and stronger reasons he advances against them.

SIMP.   I will first say something in general about all these considerations taken together, and then I will come to particulars. It seems to me that in general you base yourself on the greater simplicity and facility of producing the same effects; you do this when you judge that, in regard to the fact of causing them, it is the same to move the earth alone as to move the rest of the universe without the earth, but in regard to the manner of operation, the former is much easier than the latter. To this I answer that it seems the same to me too as long as I consider my own strength, which is not only finite but very puny; but from the standpoint of the power of the Mover, which is infinite, it is no harder to move the universe than the earth or a straw. Now, if the power is infinite, why should He not exercise a greater [149] rather than a smaller part of it? Thus it seems to me that your account in general is not cogent.

SALV.   If I had ever said that the universe does not move due to insufficient power in the Mover, I would have made a mistake and your correction would be appropriate; for I admit that to an infinite power it is the same to move one hundred thousand things as to move one. What I said does not regard the Mover but only the bodies moved; that is, not only their resistance, which is undoubtedly less for the earth than for the universe, but also the other particulars mentioned above. Moreover, I want to respond to your saying that an infinite power is such that it is better to exercise a greater than a smaller part of it: a part of the infinite is never greater than another, if both are finite; nor can one say that one hundred thousand is a greater part of an infinite number than two, even though the former is fifty thousand times greater than the latter; if to move the universe one needs a finite power (although very great in comparison to what would suffice to move the earth alone), one would not thereby be using a greater part of the infinite, nor would the unused part be less than infinite; thus it makes no difference to use a little more or a little less power to bring about a particular effect. It should also be mentioned that the action of such a power does not aim at the diurnal motion alone, but that there are in the world many other motions known to us, and there may be many others unknown to us. So, from the standpoint of the things moved, there is no doubt that the shorter and quicker mode of operation is to move the earth rather than the universe; let us also keep in mind the many other conveniences and benefits it brings about; and let us remember the very true Aristotelian principle saying that it is useless to do with more means what can be done with fewer;[34] all these considerations render it more probable that the diurnal motion belongs only to the earth, rather than to the universe except the earth.

SIMP.   In mentioning this principle you left out a clause that is all important, especially in the present context; it is the phrase "equally well." Therefore, one must examine whether everything can be accommodated equally well with each of the two assumptions.

SALV.   Whether both positions satisfy equally well is something that will be understood from the particular examinations of the phenomena which must be accommodated; so far we have discussed, and we are now discussing, hypothetically, namely, by supposing that in regard to accommodating the phenomena, both [150] positions are equally satisfactory. Moreover, in regard to the phrase you say I have left out, I suspect that instead you have superfluously added it; for "equally well" is a relationship, which necessarily requires at least two terms, since a thing cannot have a relation with itself (for example, one cannot say that rest is equally good as rest); furthermore, when one says "it is useless to do with more means what can be done with fewer means," one understands that what is to be done must be the

---

34. Cf. Aristotle, *Physics,* I, 6, 189b17–29.

same thing and not two different things; now, since the same thing cannot be said to be equally well done as itself, adding the phrase "equally well" is superfluous and exemplifies a relation with only one term.

[§8.4 Day II: The Case against Terrestrial Rotation, and the Value of Critical Reasoning][35]

SAGR.   If we do not want the same thing happening as yesterday, let us please return to the subject; and let Simplicio begin to produce the difficulties which seem to him to contradict this new arrangement of the world.

SIMP.   The arrangement is not new but very old. That this is true may be seen from the fact that Aristotle refuted it. His refutations are the following:[36]

"First, if the earth were in motion (either around itself while located at the center, or in a circle while placed outside the center), this motion would have to be a violent one because it is not its own natural motion; if it were natural, it would also belong to every one of its particles, whereas each of them moves in a straight line toward the center. Being thus violent and preternatural, it could not be everlasting. But the world order is everlasting. Therefore, etc.

"Secondly, except for the Prime Mobile, all the other bodies moving with circular motion seem to fall behind and to move with more than one motion. Because of this, it would be necessary for the earth to move with two motions. If this were so, there would necessarily have to be variations in the fixed stars. But this is not seen; instead, the same stars always rise at the same places and always set at the same places, without any variations.

"Thirdly, the motion of the parts and of the whole is naturally toward the center of the universe; therefore, the whole stands still

---

35. Galilei 1890–1909, 7: 150.13–159.28; translated by Finocchiaro (1997, 142–55).
36. Cf. Aristotle, *On the Heavens,* II, 14, 296a24–297a8. Galileo places quotation marks around the text of the next five paragraphs, thus suggesting that he is quoting from an edition of Aristotle; but the language of these quotations is Italian rather than Latin, indicating that they are his own translations. My translation is from Galileo's Italian text. I have closed the quotation marks in the middle of the statement of the third argument because the subsequent text makes it clear that what follows is paraphrase or indirect quotation.

therein." He also asks whether the motion of the parts is to go naturally to the center of the universe or to the center of the earth; he concludes that their proper instinct is to go to the center of the universe, and that their accidental instinct is to go to the center of the earth. We discussed this question at length yesterday.

[151] Fourthly, he confirms the same conclusion with an argument based on our experience with heavy bodies. As these fall down from on high, they move perpendicularly to the earth's surface. Similarly, projectiles thrown perpendicularly upwards come back down perpendicularly by the same lines, even when they are thrown to an immense height. These experiences provide a necessarily conclusive argument that their motion is toward the center of the earth, which awaits and receives them without moving at all.

Lastly, he mentions that astronomers have produced other reasons to confirm the same conclusions, namely, that the earth is at the center of the universe and motionless. He gives only one of these; that is, all phenomena seen in regard to the motions of stars correspond to the position of the earth at the center, and there could not be such a correspondence unless it were true.

There are other arguments produced by Ptolemy and other astronomers.[37] I can bring them up now, if you so desire; or I can do it after you tell me what occurs to you in response to these Aristotelian ones.

SALV. The arguments produced in this matter are of two kinds: some regard terrestrial phenomena and have no relation to the stars; others are taken from the appearances and observations of heavenly bodies. Aristotle's arguments are mostly taken from things near us, and he leaves the others to astronomers; thus, it is appropriate, if you agree, to examine the ones taken from terrestrial experience first, and then we will come to the other kind. Moreover, Ptolemy, Tycho, and other astronomers and philosophers produced other such arguments besides accepting, confirming, and strengthening those of Aristotle; hence, these can all be considered together in order not to have to repeat twice the same or similar replies. So, Simplicio, whether you wish to relate them, or whether you want me to release you from this burden, I am here to please you.

---

37. Cf. Ptolemy, *Almagest,* I, 4–7; Brahe (1596, 167, 188–89; 1602, 662).

SIMP. It will be better for you to present them since you have studied them more, and so you will be able to present them more readily and in greater number.

SALV. As the strongest reason, everyone produces the one from heavy bodies, which when falling down from on high move in a straight line perpendicular to the earth's surface. This is regarded as an unanswerable argument that the earth is motionless. For, if it were in a state of diurnal rotation and a rock were dropped from the top of a tower, then during the [152] time taken by the rock in its fall, the tower (being carried by the earth's turning) would advance many hundreds of cubits toward the east and the rock should hit the ground that distance away from the tower's base. They confirm this effect with another experiment. That is, they drop a lead ball from the top of the mast of a ship which is standing still, and they note that the spot where it hits is near the foot of the mast; but if one drops the same ball from the same place when the ship is moving forward, it will strike at a spot as far away from the first as the ship has moved forward during the time the lead was falling. This happens only because the natural motion of the ball in free fall is in a straight line toward the center of the earth.

This argument is strengthened with the experiment of a projectile thrown upward to a very great height, such as a ball shot by a cannon aimed perpendicular to the horizon. The time required for it to go up and down is such that at our latitude we, together with the cannon, would be carried by the earth many miles toward the east; thus the ball could never fall back near the gun, but rather would fall as far to the west as the earth would have moved forward.

Moreover, they add a third and very effective experiment, which is the following: if one shoots a cannon aimed at a great elevation toward the east, and then another with the same charge and the same elevation toward the west, the westward shot would range much farther than the eastward one. For, since the ball goes westward and the cannon (carried by the earth) goes eastward, the ball would strike the ground at a distance from the cannon equal to the sum of the two journeys (the westward one made by itself and the eastward one of the cannon carried by the earth); by contrast, from the journey made by the ball shot toward the east, one would have to subtract the one made by the cannon while following it; for example, given that the ball's journey in itself is five miles and that at that particular latitude the earth moves forward three during the ball's flight, in the westward shot the ball would strike the ground eight miles from the cannon (namely, its own westward five plus the cannon's eastward three), whereas the eastward shot would range two miles (which is the difference between the five of the shot and the three of the cannon's motion in the same direction). However, experience shows that the ranges are equal. Therefore, [153] the cannon is motionless, and consequently so is the earth.

No less than this, shooting toward the south or toward the north also confirms the earth's stability. For one would never hit the mark aimed at, but instead the shots would always be off toward the west, due to the eastward motion of the target (carried by the earth) while the ball is in midair.

These shots along the meridians would not be the only ones that would hit off the mark. If one were shooting point-blank, the eastward shots would strike high and the westward ones low. For in such shooting, the ball's journey is made along the tangent, namely, along a line parallel to the horizon; moreover, if the diurnal motion should belong to the earth, the eastern horizon would always be falling and the western one rising (which is why the eastern stars appear to rise and the western ones to fall); therefore, the eastern target would drop below the shot and so the shot would strike high, while the rising of the western target would make the westward shot hit low. Thus, one could never shoot straight in any direction; but, because experience shows otherwise, one is forced to say that the earth stands still.

SIMP.   Oh, these arguments are beautiful, and it will be impossible to find answers to them.

SALV.   Do they perhaps strike you as novel?

SIMP.   Frankly, yes. Now I see how many beautiful observations nature has graciously provided to help us come to know the truth. Oh, how well one truth agrees with another, and all conspire to make themselves invulnerable!

SAGR.   What a pity that there were no cannons in Aristotle's time! With them he would have indeed conquered ignorance and spoken without hesitation of the things of the world.

SALV.   I am very glad you find these arguments novel, so that you will not remain of the opinion held by most Peripatetics; they believe that if anyone disagrees with Aristotle's doctrine, this happens because of not having heard or properly grasped his demonstrations. However, you will certainly hear other novelties, and you will hear the followers of the new system produce against themselves observations, experiments, and reasons much stronger than those produced by Aristotle, Ptolemy, and other opponents of the same [154] conclusions; you will thus establish for yourself that it is not through ignorance or lack of observation that they are induced to follow this opinion.

SAGR.   I must take this opportunity to relate to you some things which have happened to me since I began hearing about this opinion. When I was a young man and had just completed the study of philosophy (which I then abandoned to apply myself to other business), it happened that a man from Rostock beyond the Alps (whose name I believe was Christian Wursteisen)[38] came into these parts and gave two or three lectures on this subject at an academy; he was a follower of Copernicus and had a large audience, I believe more for the novelty of the subject than anything else. However, I did not go, having acquired the distinct impression that this opinion could be nothing but solemn madness. When I asked some who had attended, they all made fun of it, except one who told me that this business was not altogether ridiculous. Since I regarded him as a very intelligent and very prudent man, I regretted not having gone. From that time on, whenever I met someone who held the Copernican opinion, I began asking whether he had always held it; although I have asked many persons, I have not found a single one who failed to tell me that for a long time he believed the contrary opinion, but that he switched to this one due to the strength of the reasons supporting it; moreover, I examined each one of them to see how well he understood the reasons for the other side, and I found everyone had them at his fingertips; thus, I cannot say that they accepted this opinion out of ignorance or vanity or (as it were) to show off. On the other hand, out of curiosity I also asked many Peripatetics and Ptolemaics how well they had studied Copernicus' book, and I found very few who had seen it and none who (in my view) had understood it; I also tried to learn from the same followers of the Peripatetic doctrine whether any of them had ever held the other opinion, and similarly I found none who had. Now, let us consider these findings: that everyone who follows Copernicus' opinion had earlier held the contrary one and is very well informed about the reasons of Aristotle and Ptolemy; and that, on the contrary, no one who follows Aristotle and Ptolemy

---

38. Wursteisen (1544–88), a German-Swiss astronomer and one of the first to be favorably disposed toward Copernicanism.

has in the past held Copernicus' opinion [155] and abandoned it to accept Aristotle's. Having considered these findings, I began to believe that when someone abandons an opinion imbibed with mother's milk and accepted by infinitely many persons, and he does this in order to switch to another one accepted by very few and denied by all the schools (and such that it really does seem a very great paradox), he must be necessarily moved (not to say forced) by stronger reasons.[39] Therefore, I have become most curious to go, as it were, to the bottom of this business, and I regard myself very fortunate to have met the two of you; without any great effort I can hear from you all that has been said (and perhaps all that can be said) on this subject, and I am sure that by virtue of your arguments I will lose my doubts and acquire certainty.

SIMP.   But beware that your belief and hope will not be frustrated, and that you will not end up being more confused than before.

SAGR.   I think I am sure that this cannot happen in any way.

SIMP.   Why not? I myself am a good witness that the further we go, the more confused I become.

SAGR.   That is an indication that those reasons, which so far seemed conclusive to you and kept you certain of the truth of your opinion, are beginning to feel different in your mind and to gradually let you, if not switch, at least incline toward the contrary one. However, I, who am and have been so far undecided, am very confident to be able to reach a state of serenity and certainty; and you yourself will not deny it, if you want to listen to my reasons for this expectation.

SIMP.   I will be glad to listen, and no less glad if the same effect should be produced in me.

SAGR.   Please, then, answer my questions. Tell me, first, Simplicio, whether the conclusion whose correctness we are trying to determine is not one of the following: whether one must hold, with Aristotle and Ptolemy, that the earth stands still at the center of the universe and all the heavenly bodies move; or whether the stellar sphere stands still, the sun is placed at the center, and the earth is

---

39. Here (last four sentences) Galileo advances an important argument involving the greater open-mindedness of Copernicans vis-à-vis Ptolemaics. This argument was held against him and generated one of the charges that led to the 1633 trial; see §9.1.2.6.vii. Galileo had elaborated the argument even more fully in his reply to Bellarmine; see §5.2.

located off the center and has those motions which appear to belong to the sun and to the fixed stars.

SIMP.   These are the conclusions about which we are disputing.

SAGR.   Are these two conclusions such that it is necessary for one of them to be true and the other false?

[156] SIMP.   That is correct. We are facing a dilemma in which it is necessary that one alternative should be true and the other false. For rest and motion are contradictories, and there is no third alternative such that one might say: "The earth neither moves nor stands still, and the sun and stars neither move nor stand still."

SAGR.   Are the earth, sun, and stars insignificant or substantial bodies in nature?

SIMP.   These bodies are the most important, magnificent, huge, substantial, and integral parts of the universe.

SAGR.   What kind of phenomena are motion and rest in nature?

SIMP.   They are so pervasive and important that nature herself is defined in their terms.[40]

SAGR.   Thus, to be eternally in motion and to be completely immobile are two very significant conditions in nature, especially when attributed to the most important bodies of the universe; as a result of those conditions one can get only very dissimilar occurrences.

SIMP.   Certainly.

SAGR.   Now, respond to another point. Do you believe that in logic, rhetoric, physics, metaphysics, mathematics, and reasoning in general, there are good arguments proving false as well as true conclusions?

SIMP.   No, sir! Instead I firmly believe and am sure that for the proof of a true and necessary conclusion there are in nature not just one but many very powerful demonstrations, that one can discuss and approach it from thousands of points of view without ever encountering any contradiction, and that the more a sophist would want to taint it the clearer its certainty would become. On the contrary, to make a false proposition appear true and to persuade someone of it one can produce nothing but fallacies, sophisms, paralogisms, equivocations, and arguments that are pointless, incoherent, and full of inconsistencies and contradictions.

SAGR.   Now, if eternal motion and eternal rest are such important properties in nature and so different that their effects must be

---

40. Cf. Aristotle's *Physics*, 192b21–24.

very different, especially when attributed to such huge and noteworthy bodies in the universe as the earth and the sun; if it is impossible
that one of the two contradictory propositions [157] should not be
true and the other false; and if to prove a false proposition one can
only produce fallacies, whereas a true one is supportable by all kinds
of conclusive and demonstrative arguments; if all this is true, how can
it be that someone undertaking to support a true proposition would
not be able to persuade me? I would have to have a stupid understanding, a perverse judgment, a dull mind and intellect, and a dim-witted
common sense; and I would have to be unable to discern light from
darkness, gems from coals, and truth from falsehood.

SIMP.   As I have said other times, I tell you that the greatest master from whom to learn how to recognize sophisms, paralogisms, and
other fallacies is Aristotle; in this regard, he can never be deceived.

SAGR.   You again mention Aristotle, who cannot speak; and I tell
you that if Aristotle were here, he would be persuaded by us or he
would dissolve our reasons and persuade us with better ones. At any
rate, in hearing the gunshot experiments related, did you yourself not
admire them and recognize and admit them to be more conclusive
than those of Aristotle? Nevertheless, I do not see that Salviati (who
has produced them, has undoubtedly examined them, and has probed
them most fastidiously) is admitting being persuaded by them, or even
by the stronger ones which he indicates he is about to present. I do
not know why you would want to portray nature as having become
senile and having forgotten how to produce theoretical intellects, except those who make themselves servants of Aristotle in order to understand with his brain and perceive with his senses. However, let us
listen to the remaining reasons favorable to his opinion, and then go
on to test them by refining them in the assayer's crucible and weighing them in his balance.[41]

SALV.   Before proceeding further, I must tell Sagredo that in
these discussions I act as a Copernican and play his part with a mask,
as it were. However, in regard to the internal effect on me of the reasons I seem to advance in his favor, I do not want to be judged by

---

41. The exchange between Sagredo and Simplicio of the last several paragraphs is an elaboration and refinement of a point briefly made by Galileo in
his reply to Bellarmine; see §5.4.6. Galileo is making a plea for the value of
critical reasoning, namely the ability to distinguish good from bad arguments;
for more details, see Finocchiaro 1997, 142–55 nn. 57–89; 339–41.

what I say while we are involved in the [158] enactment of the play, but by what I say after I have put away the costume; for perhaps you will find me different from what you see when I am on stage. Now, let us go on.

Ptolemy and his followers advance another observation, similar to that of projectiles: it concerns things that are separate from the earth and remain at length in the air, such as clouds and birds in flight. Since clouds are not attached to the earth, they cannot be said to be carried by it, and so it does not seem possible that they could keep up with its speed; instead, they should all appear to us to be moving very fast toward the west. And, if we are carried by the earth and in twenty-four hours move along our parallel (which is at least sixteen thousand miles), how could birds keep up with so much drift? On the contrary, we see them fly toward the east as well as toward the west and toward any other direction, without any sensible difference.

Furthermore, when we run on horseback we feel the air strike very hard against our face, and so what a wind should we constantly feel blowing from the east if we are carried with such rapid motion against the air? Yet, no such effect is felt.

Here is another very ingenious argument, taken from the following observation; it is this: circular motion has the property of extruding, scattering, and throwing away from its center the parts of the moving body whenever the motion is not very slow or the parts are not attached together very firmly. For example, consider those huge treadmill wheels designed so that the walking of a few men on their inner surface causes them to move very great weights, such as the massive rollers of a calender press or loaded barges dragged overland to move them from one river to another; now, if we made one of these huge wheels turn very rapidly and its parts were not very firmly put together, they would all be scattered along with any rocks or other material substances however strongly tied to its external surface; nothing could resist the impetus which would throw them with great force in various directions away from the wheel, and consequently away from its center. If, then, the earth were rotating with a very much greater speed, what weight and what strength of mortar or cement would keep rocks, buildings, and entire cities from being hurled toward the sky by such a reckless turning? And think of people and animals, which are not attached to the earth at all; how would they resist so much impetus? On the contrary, we see them and other things with much less resistance (pebbles, sand, [159] leaves) rest very calmly on the earth and fall back to it even when their motion is very slow.

Here, Simplicio, are the very powerful reasons taken from terrestrial things, so to speak. We are left with the other kind, namely, those that relate to heavenly phenomena. Actually, those reasons tend to demonstrate instead that the earth is at the center of the universe and consequently lacks the annual motion around it, which Copernicus attributed to the earth; since they deal with a somewhat different subject, they can be produced after we have examined the strength of the ones presented so far.

SAGR.   What do you say, Simplicio? Does it seem that Salviati knows and can explain the Ptolemaic and Aristotelian reasons? Do you think that any Peripatetic is equally knowledgeable of the Copernican demonstrations?

SIMP.   If the discussions so far had not produced in me such a high opinion of Salviati's well-founded understanding and of Sagredo's sharp intelligence, I (with their permission) would be ready to leave without listening to anything else. For it seems to me impossible that one can contradict such palpable observations; moreover, I would like to keep my old opinion without having to hear anything else, because it seems to me that even if it were false, the fact that it is supported by such likely reasons would render it excusable. If these are fallacies, what true demonstrations were ever so beautiful?

SAGR.   Still, it will be good to hear Salviati's answers. If these should be true, they must be even more beautiful and infinitely more beautiful, and those others must be ugly, indeed very ugly; this would follow if there is truth in the metaphysical proposition that truth and beauty are the same thing, as falsehood and ugliness also are. However, Salviati, let us not lose any more time.

[§8.5 Day II: Vertical Fall, Conservation of Motion, and the Role of Experiments][42]

[164] SALV.   So we can now go on to the fourth argument, which should be discussed at great length since it is based on an observation from which most of the remaining arguments then derive their

---

42. Galilei 1890–1909, 7: 164.30–175.23; translated by Finocchiaro (1997, 155–70).

strength. Aristotle says[43] that a most certain argument for the earth's immobility is based on the fact that we see bodies which have been cast upwards return perpendicularly by the same line to the same place from which they were thrown, and that this happens even when the motion reaches a great height; this could not happen if the [165] earth were moving because, while the projectile moves up and down separated from the earth, the place of ejection would advance a long way toward the east due to the earth's turning, and in falling the projectile would strike the ground that much distance away from the said place. Here we may also include the argument from the cannon ball shot upwards, as well as another one used by Aristotle and Ptolemy, namely, that one sees bodies falling from great heights move in a straight line perpendicular to the earth's surface. Now, to begin to untie these knots, I ask Simplicio how Aristotle and Ptolemy would prove, if someone denied it, that bodies falling freely from on high move in a straight and perpendicular line, namely, in the direction of the center.

SIMP.   By means of the senses: they assure us that the tower is straight and perpendicular; they show us that the falling rock grazes it without inclining so much as a hairbreadth to one side or the other; and they show that the rock lands at the foot of the tower exactly under the place from which it was dropped.

SALV.   But if by chance the terrestrial globe were rotating and consequently were also carrying the tower along with it, and if the falling rock were still seen to graze the edge of the tower, what would its motion have to be?

SIMP.   In that case one would rather have to speak of "its motions"; for there would be one that would take it from above downwards, and it would have to have another in order to follow the course of the tower.

SALV.   Therefore, its motion would be a compound of two, namely, one with which it grazes the edge of the tower, and another one with which it follows the tower; the result of this compound would be that the rock would no longer describe a simple straight and perpendicular line, but rather an inclined, and perhaps not straight, one.[44]

---

43. Cf. Aristotle, *On the Heavens*, II, 14, 296b22–26.
44. The resulting compound path would not be straight if (as indeed is the case) the downward fall is accelerated while the horizontal motion is

SIMP.   I am not sure about its not being straight; but I understand well that it would have to be inclined and different from the straight perpendicular one it would describe on a motionless earth.

SALV.   Therefore, from just seeing the falling rock graze the tower, you cannot affirm with certainty that it describes a straight and perpendicular line unless you first assume the earth to be standing still.

SIMP.   That is correct; for if the earth were moving, the rock's motion would be inclined and not perpendicular.

[166] SALV.   Here, then, is the paralogism of Aristotle and Ptolemy made clear and evident, and discovered by yourself; the argument is assuming as known what it is trying to prove.

SIMP.   In what way? To me it seems to be a syllogism in proper form and not a fallacy of question begging.

SALV.   Here is how. Tell me: does not the demonstration regard the conclusion as unknown?

SIMP.   Yes, unknown, for otherwise it would be superfluous to demonstrate it.

SALV.   But, should not the middle term be known?

SIMP.   That is necessary, for otherwise it would be an attempt to prove the unknown by means of what is equally unknown.

SALV.   Is not the conclusion to be proved, and which is unknown, the proposition that the earth stands still?

SIMP.   It is.

SALV.   Is not the middle term, which must be already known, the straight and perpendicular fall of the rock?

SIMP.   That is the middle term.

SALV.   But, did we not just conclude that we can have no knowledge that this fall is straight and perpendicular unless we first know that the earth is standing still? Therefore, in your syllogism the certainty of the middle term is inferred from the uncertain conclusion. So you see the type and the seriousness of the paralogism.

SAGR.   On behalf of Simplicio, I should like to defend Aristotle, if possible, or at least to understand better the strength of your inference. You say: seeing the rock graze the tower is not enough to become certain that its motion is perpendicular (which is the middle term of the syllogism) unless one assumes that the earth stands still

---

uniform; thus, the actual path is parabolic, as Galileo proved in *Two New Sciences*. Cf. §10.8.

(which is the conclusion to be proved); for, if the tower were moving together with the earth and the rock grazed it, the rock's motion would be inclined and not perpendicular. However, I will answer that, if the tower were moving, it would be impossible for the falling rock to graze it; hence, from seeing the falling rock graze it one infers that the earth is motionless.

SIMP.   That is correct. For, if the falling rock should graze the tower while the latter was carried along by the earth, the rock would have to have two natural motions (namely, straight toward the center and circular around the center); and this is impossible.

SALV.   Therefore, Aristotle's defense consists in its being impossible, [167] or at least in his having regarded it as impossible, that the rock could move with a motion mixed of straight and circular; for, if he had not regarded it as impossible that the rock could move simultaneously toward the center and around the center, he would have understood that it could happen that the falling rock could graze the tower when it is moving as well as when it is standing still; consequently, he would have realized that from this grazing nothing could be inferred regarding the motion or the rest of the earth. However, this does not in any way excuse Aristotle, because he should have said so if he had had this thought in mind, it being such a key point in his argument; moreover, one cannot say either that this effect is impossible or that Aristotle regarded it as impossible. The first cannot be said, because I will soon show that it is not only possible but necessary. Nor can one say the second, for Aristotle himself grants[45] that fire goes naturally upward in a straight line and turns by participation with the diurnal motion, which is transferred by the heavens to all of the element fire and to most of the air; if, then, he did not regard it as impossible to mix straight upward motion with the circular one communicated to fire and air by the inside of the lunar orb, much less should he regard it as impossible to mix the rock's straight downward with the circular one that would be natural for the whole terrestrial globe of which the rock is a part.

SIMP.   It does not look that way to me; for, if the element fire turns together with the air, it is very easy and indeed necessary that a particle of fire rising from the earth and going through the rotating air should receive the same motion, since it is such a rarefied and light

---

45. Aristotle, *Meteorology,* I, 7, 344a11.

body and most ready to move; but it is completely incredible that a very heavy rock or cannon ball falling through the air should let itself be carried along by it or anything else. Furthermore, there is the very appropriate experiment of the rock dropped from the top of a ship's mast; that is, when the ship is standing still it falls at the foot of the mast, but when the ship is going forward it falls away from the same place at a distance equal to that traversed by the ship during the rock's fall (which amounts to many cubits when the ship's course is fast).

SALV.   There is a great disparity between the case of the ship and that of the earth, if the diurnal motion should belong to the terrestrial globe. For it is most evident that the ship's motion does not belong to it naturally, [168] just as it is an accidental property of all things in it; so it is not surprising that, when the rock is let go after being held at the top of the mast, it should fall without any obligation to follow the ship's motion. However, the diurnal rotation would be attributed to the terrestrial globe (and consequently to all its parts) as their own natural motion, and it would be regarded as indelibly impressed in them by nature; hence, a primary instinct of the rock at the top of the tower would be to go around the center of the whole of which it is a part every twenty-four hours, and it would eternally exercise this natural inclination regardless of the conditions in which it might be placed. To be persuaded of this, you have only to change an old impression and say to yourself: "Up to now, I have thought it is a property of the terrestrial globe to stay motionless at the center, and so I have never felt any difficulty or repugnance in understanding that every one of its particles is also naturally in the same state of rest; similarly, if the terrestrial globe had the natural instinct to rotate in twenty-four hours, then one would have to say that every one of its parts has the intrinsic and natural inclination to follow the same course and not to stand still." Thus, without encountering any inconvenience, one may conclude that when the rock is separated from the ship, it must regain its natural state and return to exercise its pure and simple natural instinct, for the motion transmitted from the power of the oars to the ship and from the ship to all the things it contains is not natural but foreign to them.

It should be added that it is necessary that the lower part of the air below the higher mountains would be captured and carried around by the roughness of the earth's surface, or that it would naturally follow the diurnal motion insofar as it is mixed with many earthly vapors and emanations; this does not happen to the air around the ship, which is propelled by the oars. Therefore, to argue from the case of the ship to the case of the earth has no inferential force. For the rock falling from the top of the mast enters a medium that does not share the ship's motion; but the one released from the top of the tower finds itself in a medium that shares the same motion as the terrestrial globe, and so it can follow the general course of the earth without being hindered by the air but rather being favored by its motion.

SIMP.   I do not understand how the air can impart its own motion to a very large rock or a large iron or lead ball, which, [169] for example, might exceed two hundred pounds. Perhaps it transmits its motion to feathers, snow, and other very light objects; but I see that a weight of that kind is not displaced by a single inch even when exposed to the fiercest wind. Now, think whether the air can carry it along.

SALV.   There is a great disparity between your experiment and our case. You have the wind come upon the rock lying at rest, whereas we expose to the already moving air a rock which is itself moving at the same speed; thus, the air does not have to impart to it some new motion, but rather must keep it in motion, or (to be more exact) not hinder the motion already acquired. You want to push the rock into a motion foreign to it and against its nature; we want to conserve it in its natural motion. If you want to present a more appropriate experiment, you could say that one should observe (with the mind's eye, if not with the real one) what would happen when an eagle carried by the wind releases a rock from its claws; because the rock is moving like the wind at the moment of separation from the claws, and thereafter it enters a medium which is moving at the same speed, I am strongly inclined to think that we would not see it fall perpendicularly, but that it would follow the course of the wind and add to this the motion due to its own gravity, and so it would move with an inclined motion.

SIMP.   One would have to be able to make such an experiment and then form a judgment depending on the result; however, so far the ship experiment seems to favor our opinion.

SALV.   Well said, "so far"; for perhaps before long, appearances may change. In order not to keep you in suspense any longer, tell me, Simplicio, do you think the ship experiment fits our purpose so well that it is reasonable to believe that what is seen to happen on the ship should likewise happen on the terrestrial globe?

SIMP.   Up to now I think so; although you have advanced some small differences, they do not seem to me to be of such import as to make me change my mind.

SALV.   On the contrary, I wish you to continue believing firmly that the result on the earth should correspond to the one on the ship, as long as you do not feel like changing your mind if this were discovered to be prejudicial to your cause.

You say: because when the ship [170] stands still the rock falls at the foot of the mast, and when the ship is in motion it falls away from the foot, therefore, inverting, from the rock falling at the foot one infers the ship to be standing still, and from its falling away one argues for the ship being in motion; but what happens to the ship must likewise happen to the terrestrial globe; hence, from the rock falling at the foot of the tower, one necessarily infers the immobility of the terrestrial globe. Is this not your reasoning?

SIMP.   Exactly. You have made it concise and very easy to understand.

SALV.   Now, tell me, if the rock released from the top of the mast were to strike the same spot on the ship when it is going forward at great speed as when it is standing still, what use would these experiments have for ascertaining whether the vessel is standing still or going forward?

SIMP.   Absolutely none. Similarly, for example, from a pulse beat we cannot learn whether someone is asleep or awake since the pulse beats in the same manner in people who are asleep and who are awake.

SALV.   Very well. Now, have you ever made the ship experiment?

SIMP.   I have never made it, but I really believe that those authors who put it forth have diligently made the observations. Furthermore, the cause of the disparity is so well known that there is no room for doubt.

SALV.   It is possible that those authors put it forth without having made it; you are a good witness to this yourself, for without having made it you present it as certain and in good faith rely on their assertion. At any rate, it is not only possible but necessary that they too relied on their predecessors, without ever arriving at someone who made it; for whoever performs the experiment will find it to show the complete opposite of what is written; that is, it will show that the rock always falls at the same spot on the ship, whether it is standing still or moving at any speed. Hence, since the same holds for the earth as for the ship, from the rock falling always perpendicularly to the foot of the tower nothing can be inferred about the earth's motion or rest.

SIMP.   If you were referring me to some means other than experiment, I really think our disagreements would not end very soon; for this seems to me an issue so remote from any human speculation that it leaves no room for considerations of credibility or probability.

[171] SALV.   And yet I think it does.

SIMP.   So, you did not make one hundred tests, or even one, and yet you claim the result to be certain and unequivocal? I am skeptical about this, and I go back to my certainty that the experiment has been made by the principal authors who use it, and that it shows what they claim.

SALV.   Without experiment I am certain the result will happen as I say because it is necessary that it should happen that way; I add that even you yourself know that it cannot happen otherwise, although you pretend (or try to pretend) not to know it. However, I am so good at picking people's brains that I will make you admit it by force. Sagredo is very quiet, but I thought I saw him gesturing to say something.

SAGR.   Truly I wanted to say something or other. But then I heard you threaten Simplicio with violence, to make him reveal the knowledge he wants to conceal from us; this made me so curious that I put away any other desire. So I beg you to make good your boast.

SALV.   As long as Simplicio is willing to answer my questions, I will not fail.

SIMP.   I will answer what I know and am certain I will have little difficulty; for knowledge is about truths and not about falsehoods, and thus I do not think I know anything about the things I regard as false.

SALV.   I do not want you to say or answer anything but what you are sure you know. So, tell me, suppose you had a plane surface very polished like a mirror and made of a hard material like steel; suppose it was not parallel to the horizon but somewhat inclined; and suppose that on it you placed a perfectly spherical ball made of a heavy and very hard material like bronze, for example; what do you think it would do when released? Do you not think (as I believe) that it would stand still?

SIMP.   If that surface were inclined?

SALV.   Yes, for this is the supposition.

SIMP.   I do not think it would stand still; rather I am sure it would spontaneously move downward along the incline.

SALV.   Be very careful about what you say, Simplicio; for I am sure it would stand still in any spot you had placed it.

SIMP.   Salviati, when you make this sort of [172] assumption, I begin to be less surprised that you should arrive at very false conclusions.

SALV.   Are you thus very sure that it would spontaneously move downwards along the incline?

SIMP.   What is there to doubt?

SALV.   And you firmly believe this not because I taught it to you (for I tried to persuade you of the opposite), but because you arrived at it on your own using your natural judgment.

SIMP.   Now I understand your trick; you said what you did in order to lead me on and (as the popular expression goes) to trap me, not because you really believed that.

SALV.   That is correct. Now, how long would the ball's motion last, and what speed would it have? Notice that I am referring to a perfectly round ball and a fastidiously polished plane, in order to remove all external and accidental impediments; similarly, I want you to disregard the impediment offered by the air through its resistance to being parted, and any other accidental obstacles there may be.

SIMP.   I understand everything very well. As for your question, I answer that the ball would continue to move ad infinitum, as far as the inclination of the plane extends; that it would move with continuously accelerated motion, for such is the nature of falling bodies, which "acquire strength as they keep going";[46] and that the greater the inclination, the greater would be the speed.

SALV.   However, if someone wanted to have the ball move upward along the same surface, do you think it would move that way?

SIMP.   Not spontaneously; but it would if dragged along or thrown by force.

SALV.   So, if it were propelled by some impetus forcibly impressed on it, what would its motion be and how long would it last?

SIMP.   Its motion would keep on being continuously reduced and retarded, due to its being against nature; and it would last more or less depending on the greater or smaller impulse and on the steeper or gentler inclination.

SALV.   Therefore, I think that up to now you have explained to me the following properties of a body moving along a plane in two different directions: when descending on an inclined plane, the heavy body is spontaneously and continuously accelerated, and it requires the use of force to keep it at rest; on the other hand, in an [173] ascending path a force is needed to make it move that way (as well as to

---

46. Cf. Virgil, *Aeneid*, IV, 175, which refers to rumors and how they spread.

keep it at rest), and the motion impressed on it is continuously diminishing, so that eventually it is annihilated. You also say that in both cases there is a difference stemming from the greater or smaller inclination of the plane; so that a greater inclination leads to a greater downward speed, but on an upward path the same body thrust by the same force moves a greater distance when the inclination is less. Now tell me what would happen to the same body on a surface that is not inclined.

SIMP.   Here I must think a little before I answer. Since there is no downward slope, there cannot be a natural tendency to move; since there is no upward slope, there cannot be a resistance to being moved; thus, the body would be indifferent to motion, and have neither a propensity nor a resistance to it; I think, therefore, that it should remain there naturally at rest. Sorry to have forgotten, for I now remember that not long ago Sagredo explained to me that this is what would happen.

SALV.   I think so, if one were to place it there motionless; but if it were given an impetus in some direction, what would happen?

SIMP.   It would move in that direction.

SALV.   But with what sort of motion? A continuously accelerated one, as on a downward slope, or a progressively retarded one, as on an upward slope?

SIMP.   I see no cause for acceleration or retardation since there is neither descent nor ascent.

SALV.   Yes. But if there is no cause for retardation, still less is there cause for rest. So, how long do you think the moving body would remain in motion?

SIMP.   As long as the extension of that surface which is sloping neither upward nor downward.

SALV.   Therefore, if such a surface were endless, the motion on it would likewise be endless, namely, perpetual?

SIMP.   I think so, as long as the moving body was made of durable material.

SALV.   This has already been supposed, for we have already said that all accidental and external impediments should be removed, and in this regard the body's fragility is one of the accidental impediments.[47] Now tell me, what do you think is the reason why that ball

---

47. The agreement here reached by Salviati and Simplicio embodies an important physical principle, which may be called the principle of the conservation of motion; it represents Galileo's approximation to two fundamental laws of classical physics—the law of inertia and the law of the conservation of momentum. Cf. Newton 1999, 416, and the principle of indifferent motion in §3.1.

moves spontaneously on the downward path and not without force on the upward one?

[174] SIMP.   Because the tendency of heavy bodies is to move toward the center of the earth, and only by force do they move upward away from it; and by moving down on an inclined surface one gets closer to the center, and by moving up one gets further away.

SALV.   Therefore, a surface sloping neither downward nor upward would have to be equidistant from the center at all of its points. But are there any such surfaces in the world?

SIMP.   There is no lack of them: one is the surface of our terrestrial globe, if it were smoothed out, and not rough and mountainous, as it is; another is the surface of the water when it is calm and tranquil.

SALV.   Therefore, a ship moving in a calm sea is a body going over a surface that slopes neither downward nor upward, and so it has the tendency to move endlessly and uniformly with the impulse once acquired if all accidental and external obstacles are removed.

SIMP.   It seems that it must be so.

SALV.   Now, when the rock at the top of the mast is being carried by the ship, does it not also move along the circumference of a circle around the center, and consequently with a motion indelibly inherent in it as long as external impediments are removed? And is this motion not as fast as that of the ship?

SIMP.   So far, so good; but what about the rest?

SALV.   You should be able to draw the last consequence yourself, if on your own you have discovered all the premises.

SIMP.   By the last conclusion you mean that, since the rock is moving with a motion indelibly impressed on it, it will not leave but follow the ship, and at the end it will fall at the same spot where it falls when the ship stands still; and I, too, say that this would follow if there were no external impediments to disturb the rock's motion after being released. However, there are two such impediments: one is that the moving body is incapable of parting the air merely by means of its impetus, once it loses that of the oars' power, which it shared when it was part of the ship while still at the top of the mast; the other is the newly acquired motion of falling down, which must be an impediment to its horizontal motion.

SALV.   Regarding the impediment of the air, I do not deny it; and if the falling body were made of a light material like a feather or a lock [175] of wool, the retardation would be very great; but for a heavy rock it is very little. A short while ago you said yourself that the force of the strongest wind does not suffice to displace a big rock;

now, think what will happen when the calm air meets the rock moving no faster than the ship as a whole. However, as I said, I grant you the small effect which may result from this impediment, just as I know you will grant me that if the air were moving at the same speed as the ship and the rock, the impediment would be absolutely nil.

Regarding the impediment of the newly acquired downward motion, first it is clear that these two motions (namely, the circular around the center and the straight toward the center) are neither contrary nor incompatible nor destructive of each other; for the moving body has no repugnance toward such motion; you yourself already granted that its repugnance is to motion which takes it farther from the center, and that its inclination is to motion which brings it closer to the center; so it follows necessarily that the moving body has neither repugnance nor propensity to motion that takes it neither farther from nor closer to the center, and consequently there is no reason for any decrease in the power impressed on it. Moreover, the cause of motion is not a single one, which might diminish on account of the new action; instead there are two distinct causes, of which gravity attends only to drawing the body toward the center, and the impressed power to leading it around the center; therefore, there is no reason for an impediment.

[§8.6 Day III: Heliocentrism and the Role of the Telescope][48]

[346] SALV.   We ought to leave this question and go back to our main subject; here the next point to consider is the annual motion, which is commonly attributed to the sun, but which was taken away from the sun and given to the earth first by Aristarchus of Samos and later by Copernicus. Against this position I see Simplicio comes well equipped, in particular with the sword and shield of the booklet of mathematical conclusions or disquisitions;[49] it would be good to begin by proposing its attacks.

SIMP.   If you do not mind, I would like to leave them to the end, as they are the last to have been discovered.

---

48. Galilei 1890–1909, 7: 346.25–368.31; translated by Finocchiaro (1997, 221–44).

49. Johannes Locher, *Disquisitiones mathematicae de controversiis et novitatibus astronomicis* (Ingolstadt, 1614). This book is severely criticized in other parts of the *Dialogue*.

SALV.   Then, in accordance with the procedure followed until now, you must [347] advance in a systematic manner the contrary reasons—those of Aristotle as well as those of the other ancients; I will also contribute to this, so that nothing is left out without being carefully considered and examined; likewise, Sagredo will bring forth the thoughts that his lively intellect will awaken in him.

SAGR.   I will do it with my usual frankness; you will be obliged to excuse it since you made this request.

SALV.   Our obligation will be to thank you for the favor, not to excuse you. However, let Simplicio begin to advance those difficulties that prevent him from being able to believe that the earth, like the other planets, can move in an orbit around a fixed center.

SIMP.   The first and greatest difficulty is the repugnance and incompatibility between being at the center and being away from it; for if the terrestrial globe should move in the course of a year along the circumference of a circle, namely, along the zodiac, it would be impossible for it to be simultaneously at the center of the zodiac; but Aristotle, Ptolemy, and others have proved in many ways that the earth is at this center.

SALV.   You speak very well; there is no doubt that whoever wants the earth to move along the circumference of a circle must first prove that it is not at the center of this circle. Therefore, it follows that we should determine whether or not the earth is at this center, around which I say it turns, and at which you say it is fixed; and before doing this, we must also see whether or not you and I have the same conception of this center. So tell me what and where you understand this center to be.

SIMP.   By this center I understand the center of the universe, of the world, of the stellar sphere, of the heavens.

SALV.   I could very reasonably dispute with you whether there is such a center in nature since neither you nor others have ever proved whether the world is finite and bounded or infinite and boundless; however, granting for now that it is finite and bounded by a spherical figure, and hence that it has a center, we must decide how credible it is that the earth, rather than some other body, is located at this center.

SIMP.   That the world is finite, bounded, and spherical is proved by Aristotle with many demonstrations.[50]

---

50. Cf. Aristotle, *On the Heavens,* I, 5–7.

SALV.   All these, however, reduce to one, and this single one to [348] nothing; for he proves that the universe is finite and bounded only if it is in motion, and so all his demonstrations fall to pieces if I deny his assumption that the universe is in motion. However, in order not to multiply the disputes, let us concede for now that the world is finite and spherical and has a center. Since such a shape and center have been proved on the basis of its mobility, it will be very reasonable to proceed to the particular investigation of the exact location of such a center on the basis of the same circular motions of the heavenly bodies; indeed Aristotle himself reasoned and proceeded in the same manner, making the center of the universe that point around which all the celestial spheres turn and at which he saw fit to place the terrestrial globe. Now, tell me, Simplicio: suppose Aristotle were forced by the clearest observations to change in part his arrangement and structure of the universe, and to admit he was wrong in regard to one of the two following propositions (that is, either in placing the earth at the center or in saying that the celestial spheres move around such a center); which of the two alternatives do you think he would choose?

SIMP.   I believe that in this case the Peripatetics . . .[51]

SALV.   I am not asking about the Peripatetics, but about Aristotle himself; for I know very well what they would answer. As the most submissive and slavish servants of Aristotle, they would deny all experience and all observation in the world and even refuse to use their senses, in order not to have to make the confession; they would say the world is as Aristotle said and not as nature wants; for if they lose the support of this authority, with what would you want them to appear in the field? So tell me what Aristotle himself would do.

SIMP.   Really, I could not decide which of the two inconveniences he would regard as the lesser one.

SALV.   Please do not use this term; do not call inconvenient what could turn out to be necessarily so. To want to place the earth at the center of the heavenly revolutions was indeed inconvenient. However, since you do not know which way he would be inclined to go, and since I regard him as a man of great intellect, let us examine which of the two choices is more reasonable, and let us take that one to be what Aristotle would choose. Let us resume our earlier discussion, then, [349] and let us assume (with Aristotle) that the universe

---

51. This ellipsis is in Galileo's original text, for he wants to portray an interruption in Simplicio's speech caused by Salviati's next interjection.

has a spherical shape and moves circularly, so that it necessarily has a center in regard to both its shape and its motion; although we have no observational information about the size of the universe other than that deriving from the fixed stars, we are certain that inside the stellar sphere there are many orbs, one inside the other, each with its own heavenly body, and that they also move circularly; we are inquiring about which is more reasonable to believe and say, either that these nested orbs move around the same center of the universe, or that they move around some other center very far from there. Now, Simplicio, tell us your opinion about this particular detail.

SIMP.   If we could limit ourselves only to this issue and be sure not to encounter any other difficulty, I would say it is much more reasonable to claim that the container and the contained parts all move around a common center than around several.

SALV.   Now, if it is true that the center of the universe is the same as that around which the orbs of the heavenly bodies (namely, of the planets) move, then it is most certain that the sun rather than the earth is found placed at the center of the universe; thus, as regards this first simple and general point, the place in the middle belongs to the sun, and the earth is as far away from the center as from the sun itself.

SIMP.   But what is the basis of your argument that the sun rather than the earth is at the center of the revolutions of the planets?

SALV.   I conclude this from observations that are very evident and hence necessarily binding. The most palpable of these observations that exclude the earth from this center and place the sun there is the fact that all planets are found to be sometimes closer to the earth and sometimes farther; these differences are so large that, for example, when Venus is farthest it is six times farther from us than when it is closest, and Mars recedes almost eight times more in one position than in the other. So you can see whether Aristotle was wrong by a small amount in thinking that they are always equally distant from us.

SIMP.   What, then, are the indications that their motions are around the sun?

SALV.   For the three superior planets (Mars, Jupiter, and Saturn) this is inferred from their being always found closest to the earth when they are in opposition to the sun and farthest when they are near conjunction; [350] this variation in distance is so significant that when Mars is closest it appears sixty times greater than when it is farthest. Then, in regard to Venus and Mercury, we are certain of their revolving around the sun from their never receding much from it and from our seeing them sometimes beyond it and sometimes in between; the latter is conclusively proved by the changes in the apparent shape of Venus. For the case of the moon, it is indeed true that it cannot be separated from the earth, for reasons which will be given more clearly as we proceed.

SAGR.   I expect to hear more marvelous things that depend on this annual motion of the earth than was the case for those that depend on the diurnal rotation.

SALV.   You are absolutely right. For, the action of the diurnal motion on the heavenly bodies was and could be nothing but to make the universe appear to us to be hastily running in the opposite direction; but this annual motion, by mixing with the particular motions of all the planets, produces very many oddities that so far have made all the greatest men in the world lose their bearings. Now, returning to the first general considerations, I repeat that it is the sun that is the center of the heavenly revolutions of the five planets (Saturn, Jupiter, Mars, Venus, and Mercury); and it will also be the center of the earth's motion if we can manage to place it in the heavens. Then, as regards the moon, it has a circular motion around the earth, from which (as I said) it cannot be separated in any way; but this does not mean that it fails to go around the sun together with the earth in the annual motion.

SIMP.   I still do not comprehend this arrangement too well; perhaps by drawing a diagram we will understand it better and be able to discuss it more easily.

SALV.   So be it. Indeed, for your greater satisfaction and amazement, I want you to draw it yourself and see that you understand it very well, even though you think you do not grasp it; by merely answering my questions, you will draw it to the last detail. So, take a sheet of paper and a compass, and let this white paper be the immense expanse of the universe where you have to locate and arrange its parts in accordance with the dictates of reason. First, without my teaching it to you, you firmly believe the earth to be located in this universe; so, take a point of your own choosing around which you understand it to be located, and mark it with some symbol.

[351] SIMP.   Let this, which is marked A, be the location of the terrestrial globe.

SALV.   Very well. Second, I know you know very well that the earth is neither located inside the solar body nor contiguous to it, but is separated from it by a certain distance; so, assign to the sun some other place of your choice, as far from the earth as you wish, and mark this too.

SIMP.   It is done; let the location of the solar body be this, marked O.

SALV.   Having fixed these two, I want us to think about accommodating the body of Venus in such a way that its state and motion can satisfy what sensory appearances show us about them. So, recall what, from previous discussions or your own observations, you understand to occur in regard to this star; then assign to it the position you deem appropriate.

SIMP.   Let us suppose the truth of the appearances which you related and which I also read in the booklet of conclusions: that is, that this star never recedes from the sun more than a determinate interval of little more than forty degrees, so that it not only never 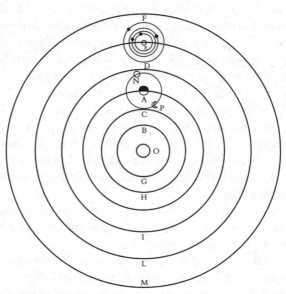 reaches opposition to the sun, but not even quadrature,[52] nor so much as the sextile configuration;[53] further, that it appears sometimes forty times larger than at other times, namely, largest when it is in retrograde motion and approaches evening conjunction with the sun, and smallest when it is in direct motion and approaches morning

---

52. *Quadrature* is a configuration of the apparent position of two heavenly bodies when they form a right angle with the earth, namely when they appear to be ninety degrees apart as seen from the earth; for example, a half moon is seen when the sun and moon are "in quadrature."
53. *Sextile configuration* is a configuration of the apparent position of two heavenly bodies when they are sixty degrees apart as seen from the earth.

conjunction; moreover, that it is true that when it appears largest it shows a horned shape, and when it appears smallest it is seen perfectly round. Given that all these appearances are true, I do not see how we can escape the conclusion that this star revolves in a circle around the sun; for this circle cannot in any way be said to enclose or to contain within it the earth, nor to be below the sun (namely, between it and the earth), nor to be above the sun. This circle cannot enclose the earth because then Venus would sometimes come into opposition to the sun; it cannot be below the sun because then Venus would appear sickle shaped at both conjunctions with the sun; and it cannot be above the sun because [352] then it would appear always round and never horned. So, for its position I will mark the circle *CH* around the sun, without making it enclose the earth.

SALV.   Having accommodated Venus, you should think about Mercury; as you know, the latter stays always near the sun and recedes from it much less than Venus does.

SIMP.   There is no doubt that, since it imitates Venus, a very appropriate place for it will be a smaller circle inside that of Venus and also around the sun; a very conclusive argument or reason for this, especially for its vicinity to the sun, is the vividness of its shining, which is greater than that of Venus and the other planets. So, on this basis we can draw its circle, marking it with the letters *BG*.

SALV.   Where, then, shall we place Mars?

SIMP.   Because Mars reaches opposition to the sun, it is necessary that its circle enclose the earth. But I see that it must necessarily enclose the sun as well; for when this planet reaches conjunction with the sun it would appear horned (like Venus and the moon) if it were not beyond the sun but rather in between; however, it always appears round. Therefore, its circle must enclose both the earth and the sun.

Moreover, I remember your having said that when it is in opposition to the sun it appears sixty times larger than when it is near conjunction; so, I think these appearances will agree very well with a circle around the center of the sun and enclosing the earth, which I am now drawing and marking *DI*. Here, at the point *D*, Mars is closest to the earth and in opposition to the sun; but, when it is at the point *I*, it is in conjunction with the sun and farthest from the earth.

Finally, the same appearances are observed in regard to Jupiter and Saturn, although with much less variation for Jupiter than for Mars, and still less with Saturn than with Jupiter; so, I think I understand that these two planets will also be very adequately accommodated by means of two circles also around the sun. The first one is for Jupiter and is marked *EL;* the other larger one is for Saturn and is labeled *FM.*

SALV.   So far you have conducted yourself splendidly. Now, as you can see, the variation in distance for the three superior planets is measured by an amount twice the distance between the earth and the sun; hence, [353] the variation is greater for Mars than for Jupiter since Mars's circle *DI* is smaller than Jupiter's circle *EL;* similarly, because *EL* is smaller than Saturn's circle *FM,* the variation is even less for Saturn than for Jupiter; this corresponds exactly to observation. What remains for you now is to think about the place to assign to the moon.

SIMP.   Let us use the same argument, which seems to me to be very conclusive. Because we see the moon reach both conjunction and opposition with the sun, it is necessary to say that its circle encloses the earth; but we must not say that it encloses the sun because then near conjunction it would not appear horned but always round and full of light; furthermore, it could never produce, as it often does, an eclipse of the sun by coming between it and us. Therefore, it is necessary to assign to it a circle around the earth, such as this marked *NP;* thus, when positioned at *P,* from the earth *A* it appears in conjunction with the sun and so can eclipse it sometimes; and when located at *N* it is seen in opposition to the sun, and in this configuration it can come into the earth's shadow and eclipse itself.

SALV.   What shall we do now with the fixed stars, Simplicio? Do we want to spread them in the immense space of the universe, at different distances from any determinate point? Or do we want to place them on a surface extending spherically around its center, such that each of them is equidistant from the same center?

SIMP.   I would rather follow an intermediate path. I would assign them an orb constructed around a determinate center and contained between two spherical surfaces, namely, a very high concave one and another convex one below it; and I would place the countless multitude of stars between them, but at different heights. This could be called the sphere of the universe, and it would contain inside it the orbs of the planets we have already drawn.

SALV.   So far, then, Simplicio, the heavenly bodies have been arranged just as in the Copernican system, and you have done this yourself. Moreover, you have assigned individual motions to all except the sun, the earth, and the stellar sphere; to Mercury and Venus you have attributed a circular motion around the sun, without enclosing the earth; you make the three superior planets (Mars, Jupiter, and

Saturn) move around the same sun, encompassing the earth inside their circles; then the moon can move in no other [354] way but around the earth, without enclosing the sun; and in regard to these motions you again agree with Copernicus.

Three things now remain to be assigned to the sun, earth, and stellar sphere: that is, rest, which appears to belong to the earth; the annual motion along the zodiac, which appears to belong to the sun; and the diurnal motion, which appears to belong to the stellar sphere and to be shared by all the rest of the universe except the earth. Since it is true that all the orbs of the planets (namely, Mercury, Venus, Mars, Jupiter, and Saturn) move around the sun as their center, it seems much more reasonable that rest belongs to the sun than to the earth, inasmuch as it is more reasonable that the center of moving spheres rather than any other point away from this center is motionless; therefore, leaving the state of rest for the sun, it is very appropriate to attribute the annual motion to the earth, which is located in the middle of moving parts; that is, between Venus and Mars, the first of which completes its revolution in nine months, and the second in two years. If this is so, then it follows as a necessary consequence that the diurnal motion also belongs to the earth; for if the sun were standing still and the earth did not rotate upon itself but only had the annual motion around the sun, then the cycle of night and day would be exactly one year long; that is, we would have six months of daylight and six months of night, as we have stated other times. So you see how appropriately the extremely rapid motion of twenty-four hours is taken away from the universe, and how the fixed stars (which are so many suns) enjoy perpetual rest like our sun. Notice also how elegant this first sketch is for the purpose of explaining why such significant phenomena appear in the heavenly bodies.

SAGR.   I see it very well. However, just as from this simplicity you infer a high probability for the truth of this system, others, on the other hand, might perhaps draw contrary conclusions; because such an arrangement is the very ancient one of the Pythagoreans and agrees so well with the observations, one might wonder (not without reason) how it could have had so few followers in the course of thousands of years, how it could have been rejected by Aristotle himself, and how even after Copernicus it could continue to suffer the same fate.

SALV.   Sagredo, if you had ever happened to hear (as I have very many times) what kinds of stupidities suffice to make the common people stubbornly unwilling [355] to listen to (let alone accept) these novelties, I think you would wonder much less about the fact that there have been so few followers of this view. However, in my opinion, we should pay little attention to such brains; to confirm the earth's immobility and to remain unmoved in this belief, they regard as a very conclusive proof the fact that they cannot eat in Constantinople in the morning and have supper in Japan in the evening; and they are certain that the earth, being very heavy, cannot go up above the sun only to come back crashing down. We need not take into account these people, whose number is infinite, nor keep track of their stupidities; we need not try to gain the support of men whose definition contains only the genus but lacks the difference, in order to have them as companions in very subtle and delicate discussions. Moreover, what gain would you think you could ever make with all the demonstrations in the world when dealing with brains so dull that they are incapable of recognizing their extreme follies?

My wonderment, Sagredo, is much different from yours. You are surprised that there are so few followers of the Pythagorean opinion, whereas I am amazed at how there could ever have been anyone who accepted and followed it; nor can I ever sufficiently admire the eminence of mind of those who have accepted and regarded it as true, and who with the liveliness of their intellect have done violence to their own senses, so much so that they have been able to prefer what their theorizing told them over what their sensory experiences showed them very clearly to the contrary. We have already seen that the reasons against the earth's diurnal rotation, which have been examined, appear to be very good; the fact that they have been regarded as most conclusive by the Ptolemaics, Aristotelians, and all their followers is a very good argument for their effectiveness. However, the observations that clearly contradict its annual motion appear to be even more powerful, so much so that (I repeat it) there is no end to my admiration of how in Aristarchus and Copernicus their reason could have done so much violence to their senses as to become, in opposition to the latter, mistress of their belief.

SAGR.   Are we, then, also going to hear other powerful objections against this annual motion?

SALV.   We are. These are so clearly based on our sense experience that, if a higher and better sense than the common and natural ones had not joined with [356] reason, I suspect that I too would have been much more recalcitrant against the Copernican system than I have been since a lamp clearer than usual has shed light on my path.

SAGR.   Now then, Salviati, let us join the fray, for any word uttered for any other purpose seems to me to be wasted.

SALV.   I am ready to serve you.[54] I have already explained to you
the structure of the Copernican system. [357] Against its truth the
first extremely fierce assault comes from Mars itself: if it were true
that its distance from the earth varies such that the farthest minus the
closest distance [358] equals twice the distance from the earth to the
sun, it would be necessary that when it is closest to us its disk should
appear more than sixty times larger than when it is farthest; [359]
however, this variation of apparent size is not perceived; instead, at
opposition to the sun, when it is close to the earth, it appears barely
four or five times larger than near [360] conjunction, when it is hidden behind the sun's rays. Another and greater difficulty is due to
Venus: if (as Copernicus claims) it should turn around the sun and be
sometimes beyond the sun and sometimes in between, and if it should
recede from us [361] and approach us by a difference equal to the diameter of the circle it describes, then when it is positioned between
us and the sun and is closest to us its disk would appear almost forty
times larger [362] than when it positioned beyond the sun and is near
its other conjunction; however, the difference is almost imperceptible.
To this we should add another difficulty: it seems reasonable that the
body of Venus is inherently dark and shines only because of the sun's
illumination, like the moon; if this is so, then when positioned between us and the sun it should appear sickle shaped, as the moon does
when it is likewise near the sun; but this phenomenon is not observed
in Venus. Thus, Copernicus declared that either it is inherently luminous, or its substance is such as to be capable of absorbing sunlight
and transmitting it through its interior, so that it appears to be always

---

54. In the original 1632 edition of the *Dialogue,* there is no indication of a
gap or an addendum at this point in the text. But in his own copy of the
book, at this point Galileo made a handwritten note stating that it would be
a good idea to insert some new text here, and at the end of the Day III he inserted several sheets of paper on which he wrote the text of the addendum.
Favaro (1890–1909, 7: 356–62) prints this addendum in a note to the main
text; Drake (1967, 328–33) inserts this additional text at this point, placing it
in square brackets. I have omitted the addendum from my translation because
the additional text has primarily rhetorical import but little scientific or
philosophical significance. Finally, note that in the rest of this paragraph, the
pagination of the critical edition shows a rapid succession of pages; this is because on each of these pages the addendum printed as a footnote takes up
most of the space and there are only a few lines of the main text.

shining; this is how Copernicus excused Venus for not changing its apparent shape;[55] as regards the small variation in its apparent size, he said nothing. About Mars he said much less than was necessary; I believe the reason is that he was unable to account to his own satisfaction for a phenomenon so incompatible with his position; and yet, persuaded by many other confirmations, he stuck to it and regarded it as true. Furthermore, there is a feature that alters the order in such a way as to render it unlikely and false: all planets together with the earth move around the sun, which is at the center of their revolutions; only the moon perturbs this order, by performing its proper motion around the earth; and then it, the earth, and the whole elemental sphere all together move around the sun in one year.

These are the difficulties that make me marvel at Aristarchus and Copernicus; they must have known about those difficulties but were unable to solve them; and yet, because of other wonderful confirmations, they trusted what reason told them so much that they confidently asserted that the [363] structure of the universe can have no other configuration but the one constructed by them. There are then other very serious and very beautiful difficulties which are not easily solved by mediocre intellects, but which were understood and explained by Copernicus; we will discuss them below, after answering other objections which seem to undermine this position. Now, coming to the clarifications and solutions of the three very serious objections advanced above, I say that the first two not only do not contradict the Copernican system, but favor it considerably and absolutely; for both Mars and Venus do vary in apparent size in accordance with the required proportions, and Venus does appear sickle shaped when between us and the sun and, in general, changes in apparent shape exactly like the moon.

SAGR.   But how could this be hidden from Copernicus and revealed to you?

SALV.   These things can be understood only with the sense of vision, which nature has not granted us in such a perfect state as to be able to discern such differences; indeed the very instrument for seeing contains impediments within itself. However, in our time God saw fit to allow the human mind to make a marvelous invention, which renders our vision more perfect by increasing its power by four,

---

55. Cf. Copernicus, *On the Revolutions,* I, 10 (1992, 18–22).

six, ten, twenty, thirty, and forty times; as a result, countless objects that were invisible to us because of their distance or extremely small size are now rendered highly visible by means of the telescope.

SAGR.   But Venus and Mars are not objects that are invisible because of their distance or small size; indeed we perceive them with our simple natural vision. So why do we not distinguish the variations in their size and shape?

SALV.   Here the major impediment stems from our eyes themselves, as I just mentioned. Objects that are shining and distant are not represented by our eyes as simple and sharp; instead, they are presented to us adorned with adventitious and extraneous rays, so long and thick that their bare little body appears to us enlarged ten, twenty, one hundred, and one thousand times more than it would be presented to us without the radiant head of hair which is not part of it.

SAGR.   I now remember reading something on this subject, perhaps in the *Sunspot Letters* or in *The Assayer* published by our common friend. You ought to explain more clearly how this matter stands, both to refresh my memory [364] and for the understanding of Simplicio, who may not have seen these writings; I think this information is essential in order to comprehend what we are dealing with.

SIMP.   Frankly, everything that Salviati is now advancing is new to me, for, to tell you the truth, I have not had the curiosity to read those books. Nor have I so far placed much trust in the newly introduced spyglass; on the contrary, following in the footsteps of my fellow Peripatetic philosophers, I have regarded as fallacies and deceptions of the lenses what others have admired as stupendous achievements. However, if I have been in error so far, I should like to be freed from it; enticed by the other novelties I heard from you, I will more carefully listen to the rest.

SALV.   The confidence these men have in their own cleverness is as unjustified as the little regard they have for the judgment of others; it is very revealing that they should consider themselves to be better qualified to judge this instrument, without having ever experimented with it, than those who have made thousands of experiments with it and continue to make them every day. However, please let us forget about such stubborn persons, who cannot even be criticized without doing them more honor than they deserve.

Returning to our purpose, I say that shining objects appear to our eyes surrounded by additional rays, either because their light is refracted by the fluids covering the pupils, or because it is reflected by the edges of the eyelids (thus scattering the reflected rays onto the same pupils), or for some other reason; hence, these objects appear much larger than if their bodies were represented without such irradiation. This enlargement becomes proportionately greater and greater as such brilliant objects are smaller and smaller; for example, if we assume that the increase due to the shining hair is four inches, and that this addition is made around a circle with a diameter of four inches, then its apparent size is increased nine times, but . . .[56]

SIMP.   I suspect you meant to say "three times"; for by adding four inches on one side and four on the other to a circle with a diameter of four inches, you are tripling its dimensions, not increasing them nine times.

SALV.   A little geometry is needed, Simplicio. It is true that the diameter [365] increases threefold, but the surface (which is what we are talking about) increases ninefold; for, Simplicio, the surfaces of circles are to each other as the squares of their diameters, and so a circle with a diameter of four inches is to another of twelve as the square of four is to the square of twelve, namely, as 16 is to 144; hence, the latter will be nine times larger, not three. So, please be careful, Simplicio.

Now, let us go forward. If we were to add the same head of hair four inches wide to a circle with a diameter of only two inches, the diameter of the whole wreath would be ten inches, and its whole surface compared to the area of the naked little body would be as one hundred to four (for these are the squares of ten and two); therefore, the enlargement would be twenty-five times. Finally, the four inches of hair added to a small circle with a diameter of one inch would enlarge it eighty-one times. Thus, the enlargements constantly take place in greater and greater proportions as the real objects being enlarged are smaller and smaller.

SAGR.   The difficulty that troubled Simplicio did not really trouble me; but there are some things which I want to understand better. In particular, I should like to know on what basis you claim that this enlargement is always equal for all visible objects.

SALV.   I already explained myself in part when I said that only brilliant objects are enlarged, not dark ones; now I shall add the rest. Brilliant objects that shine with a brighter light produce a greater and stronger reflection on our pupils, and so they appear to be enlarged

---

56. This ellipsis is in the original; Galileo wants to represent an interruption of Salviati's speech by Simplicio.

much more than those which are less bright. In order not to dwell on this particular any longer, let us see what our true mentor teaches us. Tonight, when it is very dark, let us look at the planet Jupiter; we will see it appear very bright and very large. Let us look at it through a tube, or through a small hole made with a fine needle in a piece of paper, or even through the small slit we can create by closing our hand and leaving some space between our palm and fingers; we will then see the disk of the same Jupiter stripped of its rays and so small that we will easily judge it smaller than one-sixtieth the size it appears when its great torch is observed with the naked eye. [366] Let us then look at the Dog Star, which is very beautiful and larger than any other fixed star, and which appears to the naked eye not much smaller than Jupiter; when we remove its head of hair in the manner indicated, its disk will be seen to be so small that it will be judged one-twentieth that of Jupiter; indeed, whoever lacks perfect vision will have great difficulty perceiving it; from this we may reasonably conclude that, insofar as the light of this star is much brighter than that of Jupiter, it produces a greater irradiation than Jupiter does. Furthermore, the irradiations of the sun and moon are almost nothing, due to the fact that their size by itself takes up so much space in our eye as to leave no room for the adventitious rays; thus, their disks are seen shaved and clear cut. We can ascertain the same truth by means of another experiment, which I have made several times; I am referring to ascertaining that bodies shining with a brighter light are surrounded by rays much more than those whose light is dimmer. I have observed Jupiter and Venus together several times when they were twenty-five or thirty degrees away from the sun and the sky was very dark; when I observed them with the naked eye, Venus appeared at least eight and perhaps even ten times larger than Jupiter; but when they were observed with a telescope, the disk of Jupiter was seen to be at least four times larger than that of Venus, and the brightness of Venus' shine was incomparably greater than the extremely dim light of Jupiter; this derived only from the fact that Jupiter was extremely far from the sun and from us, and Venus was close to us and the sun.

Having explained these things, it will not be hard to understand how it can happen that, when Mars is in opposition to the sun and hence more than seven times closer to the earth than when it is near conjunction, it appears to us four or five times larger in the former configuration than in the latter, although we should see it more than fifty times larger. The cause of this is simply the irradiation; for if we strip it of the adventitious rays, we will find it enlarged exactly by the required proportion. To strip it of its head of hair, the only excellent means is the telescope, which enlarges its disk by nine hundred or a thousand times; thus, we see it bare and clear cut like that of the moon, and different in size in the two positions exactly in accordance with the required proportion.

Then, as regards Venus, it should appear almost forty times larger at its evening conjunction below the sun than at its other morning conjunction; and yet it is seen as not even doubled. [367] Here, besides the irradiation effect, what is happening is that it is sickle shaped and its horns not only are very thin but also are receiving the sunlight obliquely; hence, this light is very dim in intensity and little in amount, and consequently its irradiation is less than when the planet's hemisphere appears entirely illuminated. On the other hand, the telescope clearly shows us its horns as clear cut and distinct as those of the moon; and they are seen as part of a very large circle, which is almost forty times larger than its same disk when it is beyond the sun at the end of its appearance as a morning star.

SAGR.   Oh, Nicolaus Copernicus, how pleased you would have been to see this part of your system confirmed by such clear observations!

SALV.   Indeed; but how much less would have been his reputation among the experts for preeminence of intellect! For, as I said before, he constantly continued to claim what was in accordance with arguments even though it was contrary to sensory experiences; and I cannot stop marveling at the fact that he should have persisted in saying that Venus turns around the sun and is sometimes more than six times farther from us than at other times, although it always appears equal to itself, even when it should appear forty times larger.

SAGR.   In regard to Jupiter, Saturn, and Mercury, I think we should also see differences in their apparent size corresponding exactly to their different distances.

SALV.   In the case of the two superior planets, I have exactly observed these differences almost every year for the past twenty-two years.

In the case of Mercury, no observation of any consequence is possible because it becomes visible only at its maximum elongations[57] from the sun (where its distances from the earth are insignificantly

---

57. *Elongation* is the angular distance (as seen from the earth) of one heavenly body from another.

different), and hence these differences are imperceptible. It is similar with its changes of shape, which must occur absolutely as in Venus; that is, when we see Mercury, it should appear in the shape of a semicircle, as Venus also does at its maximum elongation; but Mercury's disk is so small and its light so bright (due to its being so close to the sun) that the power of the telescope is not enough to shave its hair and make it appear completely shorn.

There remains what seemed to be a great difficulty with the earth's motion; that is, unlike all the other planets that revolve around the sun, [368] it alone does so (in one year) accompanied by the moon together with the whole elemental sphere, while the same moon moves every month around the earth. Here we must, once again, proclaim and exalt the admirable perspicacity of Copernicus and at the same time pity his misfortune; for he does not live in our time when, to remove the apparent absurdity of the shared motion of the earth and moon, we can see that Jupiter (being almost another earth) goes around the sun in twelve years accompanied not by one moon but by four moons, together with all that may be contained within the orbs of the four Medicean Stars.

SAGR.   For what reason do you call the four planets surrounding Jupiter moons?

SALV.   They would appear such to someone who looked at them while standing on Jupiter. For they are inherently dark and receive light from the sun, which is evident from their being eclipsed when they enter inside the cone of Jupiter's shadow; moreover, because the only part of them that is illuminated is the hemisphere facing the sun, they appear always entirely lit to us who are outside their orbits and closer to the sun; but to someone on Jupiter they would appear entirely lit when they were in the parts of their orbits away from the sun, whereas when in the inner parts (namely, between Jupiter and the sun), from Jupiter they would be seen as sickle shaped; in short, to Jupiter's inhabitants they would show the same changes of shape which the moon shows to us terrestrials.

Now you see how wonderfully in tune with the Copernican system are these first three strings that at first seemed so out of tune. Furthermore, from this Simplicio will be able to see the degree of probability with which one may conclude that the sun rather than the earth is the center of the revolutions of the planets. Finally, the earth is placed between heavenly bodies that undoubtedly move around the sun, namely, above Mercury and Venus and below Saturn, Jupiter, and Mars; therefore, likewise will it not be highly probable and per-haps necessary to grant that it too goes around the sun?

[§8.7 Day IV: The Cause of the Tides and the Inescapability of Error][58]

[445] SIMP.   Salviati, these phenomena[59] d·d not just start to happen; they are very old and have been observed by infinitely many persons. Many have striven to explain them by means of some reason or other. Just a few miles from here, a great Peripatetic has advanced a new cause fished out of a certain text of Aristotle not duly noticed by his interpreters; from this text he gathers that the true cause of these mo-tions derives from nothing but the different depths of the seas; for where the depth is greater, the water is greater in quantity and hence heavier, and so it displaces the more shallow water; once raised, this water wants to go down; the ebb and flow derives from this constant struggle. Then there are many who refer this to the moon, saying that it has special dominion over the water. Lately a certain clergyman[60] has published a small treatise in which he says that, as the moon moves through the sky, it attracts and raises toward itself a bulge of water which constantly follows it, so that there is always a high tide in the part which lies under the [446] moon; but since the high tide returns when it is under the horizon,[61] he claims that to explain this effect one must say that the moon not only keeps this faculty naturally within it-self, but also has the power of giving it to the opposite point of the zodiac. As I believe you know, others also say that the moon with its

---

58. Galilei 1890–1909, 7: 445.22–462.15; translated by Finocchiaro (1997, 282–303).
59. The tides have just been described briefly and presented as a fact to be explained; Salviati has proposed explaining them by the hypothesis that the earth moves.
60. Marcantonio de Dominis (1566–1624), archbishop of the Dalmatian city of Split, who had published a book on the subject (*Euripus, seu de fluxu et re-fluxu maris sententia,* Rome, 1624).
61. It was then well known that normally there are two high and two low tides a day, the high and low alternating at approximately six-hour intervals.

moderate heat has the power of rarefying the water, which rises as it expands.[62] We have also had someone who . . .[63]

SAGR.   Please, Simplicio, do not tell us any more, for I do not think it is worthwhile to take the time to recount them or waste words to confute them; if you give your assent to these or similar trifles, you do an injustice to your judgment, which we know to be very seasoned.

SALV.   I am calmer than you, Sagredo, and so I will expend fifty words for the sake of Simplicio, should he perhaps think that there is any probability in the things he related. This is what I say. It is true, Simplicio, that waters whose exterior surface is higher displace those which are below them and lower; but this does not happen with those which are higher by reason of depth; and, once the higher ones have displaced the lower ones, they quickly calm down and level out. This Peripatetic of yours must be thinking that all the lakes in the world (which stay calm) and all the seas where the ebb and flow is unnoticeable have a bottom whose depth does not vary in the least; whereas I was so simple minded as to believe that, even without any other sounding, the islands which emerge above the waters are a very clear indication of the variability of the bottom. To that clergyman you can say that the moon every day comes over the whole Mediterranean, but that the waters rise only at its eastern end and here for us in Venice. To those who say that the moderate heat is capable of making the water swell, tell them to start a fire under a boiler full of water and keep their right hand in it until the water rises by a single inch due to the heat, and then to take it out and write about the swelling of the sea; or at least ask them to teach you how the moon manages to rarefy a certain part of the water and not the rest, namely, the one here in Venice and not that at Ancona, Naples, or Genoa. One is forced to say that poetical minds are of two kinds: some adept and inclined to invent fables, others disposed and accustomed to believe them.

SIMP.   I do not think anyone believes in fables while [447] knowing them to be such. In regard to the opinions about the causes of the ebb and flow (which are many), I know that the primary and true cause of an effect is only one, and so I understand very well and am

---

62. This idea had been advanced by one of Galileo's teachers at the University of Pisa, Girolamo Borro (1512–92), in *Dialogo del flusso e reflusso del mare* (Lucca, 1561).
63. Ellipsis in Galileo's text, to convey the impression that Sagredo interrupts Simplicio's speech.

sure that at most one can be true, and I know that all the rest are fictitious and false; and perhaps the true one is not even among those which have been produced so far. Indeed, I truly believe this is the way it is, for it would be strange if the truth produced so little light that nothing would appear among the darkness of so many falsehoods. However, taking the liberty which we allow among ourselves, I will say that to introduce the earth's motion and make it the cause of the ebb and flow seems to me already to be an idea no less fictitious than the others I have heard; and if I were not offered reasons more in accordance with the nature of things, then without any reluctance I would go on to believe that this is a supernatural effect and hence miraculous and inscrutable to the human intellect; this would be like the infinitely many others which are dependent directly on the omnipotent hand of God.

SALV.   You speak very prudently and also in accordance with Aristotle's doctrine; as you know, at the beginning of his *Questions of Mechanics*[64] he attributes to a miracle things whose causes are unknowable. However, as to whether the true cause of the ebb and flow is one of the impenetrable ones, I think the strongest indication you have for this is your seeing that, of all the causes which have so far been advanced as true ones, there is none from which we can reproduce a similar effect, regardless of whatever artifice we employ; for by means of the light of the moon or sun or temperate heat or differences of depth, we will never make the water contained in a motionless vessel artificially run back and forth and go up and down at one place but not another. On the other hand, if by moving the vessel very simply and without any artifice I can represent to you exactly all those changes that are observed in seawater, why do you want to reject this cause and resort to a miracle?

SIMP.   I want to resort to a miracle if you do not convince me of natural causes other than the motion of the basins containing the waters of the sea, because I know that these basins do not move, the whole terrestrial globe being motionless by nature.

SALV.   But do you not believe the terrestrial globe could be made to move supernaturally, namely, by the absolute power of God?

SIMP.   Who could doubt that?

---

64. Pseudo-Aristotle, *Questions of Mechanics,* no. 1, 847a11.

[448] SALV.   Therefore, Simplicio, since we must introduce a miracle to produce the ebb and flow of the sea, let us make the earth move miraculously, and then this motion will naturally make the sea move. This operation will be all the simpler (and, I shall say, the more natural, among the miraculous ones), inasmuch as giving a turning motion to one globe (of which we see so many moving[65]) is less difficult than making an immense quantity of water go back and forth (in some places faster and in others slower) as well as rise and fall (more in some places, less in others, and not at all in still others), and having all these variations take place in the same containing vessel. Moreover, the latter involves many different miracles, the former only one. Finally, the miracle of making the water move implies another miracle as a consequence; that is, keeping the earth motionless against the impulses of the water, which are powerful enough to make it waver in this or in that direction unless it were miraculously restrained.

SAGR.   Please, Simplicio, let us suspend our judgment about declaring false the new view which Salviati wants to explain to us, and let us not be too quick to place it in a pigeonhole with the old ridiculous accounts. As regards the miracle, let us resort to it after we have listened to discussions confined within the limits of natural reason, although I am inclined to find miraculous all works of nature and of God.[66]

SALV.   My judgment is the same; to say that the natural cause of the tides is the earth's motion does not prevent this process from being miraculous.

Now, to resume our reasoning, I repeat and reaffirm that so far it is not known how it can happen that the waters contained in our Mediterranean basin undergo the motions they are seen to have as long as the containing basin or vessel remains itself motionless; what generates the difficulty and renders this subject inextricable are the things I will mention below which are observed every day. So, listen.

We are here in Venice, where there is a low tide and the sea is tranquil and the air calm. The water begins to rise, and within five or six hours, it rises ten palms or more. Such a rise does not derive from the expansion of the water that was there before, but rather from new water that has come here, water of the same kind as the old, of the

---

65. In this parenthetical clause, the translation in Finocchiaro 1997, 286, has been corrected slightly.
66. In this speech by Sagredo, the translation in Finocchiaro 1997, 286, has been corrected by changing "useless" to "false" and "miracles" to "the miracle."

same salinity, of the same density, and of the same weight; [449] boats float on it, Simplicio, just as they did on the old water, without subsiding a hair lower; a barrel of this new water does not weigh a single grain more or less than an equal volume of the old water; it is as cold as the other, without any change; in short, it is new water which has visibly entered the bay through the narrows and mouth of the Lido.[67] Now, you tell me whence and how it has come here.

Are there perhaps around here some openings and caves at the bottom of the sea through which the earth inhales and regurgitates the water, breathing as if it were an immense and enormous whale?[68] If this is so, how is it that in a period of six hours the water does not rise likewise in Ancona, Dubrovnik, and Corfu, where the rise is very small and perhaps unobservable? Who will find a means of injecting new water into a motionless vessel and ensuring that it will rise only in a definite part of it and not elsewhere?

Will you say perhaps that the new water is supplied by the ocean, coming through the Strait of Gibraltar? This does not remove the difficulties already mentioned and carries with it some more serious ones. First, tell me what must be the speed of the water which enters the strait and in six hours reaches the extreme shores of the Mediterranean (covering a distance of two or three thousand miles), and which then again covers the same distance in the same time when it returns? What will happen to the various ships at sea? What will happen to those which might be in the strait, where there would be such a constant and impetuous flow of an immense quantity of water that, by using a channel no more than eight miles wide, it would provide enough water to flood in six hours an area hundreds of miles wide and thousands of miles long? What tiger or falcon ever ran or flew at such a speed? I mean a speed of four hundred and more miles per hour. There are indeed currents along the strait (I do not deny it), but they are so slow that rowboats outrun them, although not without a delay in their course. Furthermore, if this water comes through the

---

67. The city of Venice, where this book's discussion occurs, is built on many small islands separated by canals and located in the middle of a shallow bay, the Lagoon of Venice; this bay is separated from the Adriatic Sea by a series of long and narrow islands, one of which is the Lido. The tides are especially noticeable there.

68. This explanation is distinct from the ones discussed above. According to Sosio (1970, lxxiv), it is found in several authors of classical antiquity, the medieval Arab world, and the Renaissance (including Leonardo da Vinci).

strait, the other difficulty still remains; that is, how it manages to rise so much here in a region so remote, without first rising by a similar or greater height in the nearer regions.

In short, I do not think that either stubbornness or intellectual subtlety can ever find solutions to these difficulties and consequently uphold the earth's stability against them, as long as we confine ourselves within natural limits.

SAGR.   I comprehend this very well already and am eagerly waiting to hear how these puzzling phenomena can without hindrance follow from the motions already attributed to the earth.

[450] SALV.   In regard to the manner in which these effects should follow as a consequence of the motions that naturally belong to the earth, not only must they find no repugnance or hindrance, but they must follow easily; indeed, not only must they follow with ease, but with necessity, so that it is impossible for them to happen otherwise; for such is the character or mark of true natural phenomena. We have established the impossibility of explaining the motions we see in the water while simultaneously maintaining the immobility of the containing vessel; so, let us go on to see whether the motion of the container can produce the effect and make it happen in the way it is observed to happen.

There are two kinds of motions which can be imparted to a vessel and from which the water contained in it can acquire the power to flow alternately toward one of its extremities and toward the other, and alternately to rise and fall there. The first would occur when either one of the extremities is lowered, for then the water (flowing toward the inclined point) would be alternately raised and lowered, now at this extremity and now at that one. However, this rising and falling are nothing but a motion away from and toward the center of the earth, and hence this kind of motion cannot be attributed to the basins in the earth itself which contain the water; regardless of any motion attributed to the terrestrial globe, the parts of these containing vessels can neither approach nor recede from its center.

The other kind of motion occurs when, without tilting in any way, the vessel moves with forward motion at a speed that is not uniform but changing, by sometimes accelerating and sometimes being retarded. The water contained in the vessel is not rigidly attached to it as its other solid parts are; instead, as a fluid, the water is almost separate, free, and not obliged to go along with all the changes of its container; it follows that, when the vessel is retarded, the water retains a part of the impetus already acquired and so flows toward the forward end, where it necessarily rises; on the contrary, if the vessel should acquire additional speed, the water would retain a part of its slowness and remain somewhat behind, and so (before getting used to the new impetus) it would flow toward the rear of the vessel, where it would rise by a certain amount. These effects can be more clearly explained and shown to the senses by means of the example of one of those boats that constantly come from Lizzafusina, full of the fresh water used by the city. [451] Let us then imagine such a boat moving at moderate speed across the lagoon and calmly carrying the water with which it is filled; suppose then that it is considerably retarded, either by running aground or due to some other obstacle in its way; the water contained in the boat will not thereby lose the already acquired impetus (as the boat itself will), but will conserve it and flow forward toward the bow, where it will noticeably rise while dropping astern; but if, on the contrary, while the same boat is on its quiet course it acquires additional speed by a noticeable amount, then before the contained water gets used to the new speed it will retain its slowness and remain behind, namely, toward the stern, where it will consequently rise while dropping at the bow.

This effect is indubitable and clear and can be experienced at any time. There are three particulars about it that I now want us to note. The first is that, in order to make the water rise at one end of the vessel, there is no need of any new water, nor need it flow there from the other end. The second is that the water in the middle does not noticeably rise or fall, unless the course of the boat is very fast and the collision or other restraining obstacle is sudden and very strong, in which case all the water could not only flow forward but even spill out of the boat for the most part; the same thing would also happen if, while going slowly, it should suddenly receive an extremely powerful impetus; but if its quiet motion undergoes a moderate retardation or acceleration, the water in the middle rises and falls imperceptibly (as I said), and for the rest, the closer it is to the middle the less it rises, and the farther it is the more it rises. The third is that, whereas the water near the middle undergoes little variation by rising and falling as compared with that at the end, on the contrary it flows a great deal forward and backward as compared with the same.

Now, gentlemen, what the boat does in relation to the water contained in it and what the contained water does in relation to the boat are exactly the same as what the Mediterranean basin does in relation

to the water contained in it and what the contained water does in relation to the Mediterranean basin. Next, we need to demonstrate how
and in what manner it happens that the Mediterranean and all the
other basins (in short, all parts of the earth) move with a significantly
nonuniform motion, although only motions that are regular and uniform are assigned to the whole globe.

[452] SIMP.   To me, who am neither a mathematician nor an astronomer, this seems at first sight like a great paradox; if it is true that
while the motion of the whole is regular, the motion of the parts
that remain always attached to the whole can be irregular, then the
paradox will destroy the axiom affirming that the reasoning applying
to the whole and to the parts is the same.

SALV.   I will demonstrate my paradox and will leave to you, Simplicio, the task of defending the axiom from it or making them consistent; my demonstration will be short and very easy and will depend
on the things discussed at length in our past arguments, when we did
not introduce so much as a word about the tides.

We said that there are two motions attributed to the terrestrial
globe: the first is the annual motion performed by its center along the
circumference of the annual orbit in the plane of the ecliptic and in
the order of the signs of the zodiac, namely, from west to east; the
other is performed by the same globe rotating around its own center
in twenty-four hours, likewise from west to east, but around an axis
somewhat inclined and not parallel to that of the annual revolution.
From the combination of these two motions, each of which is in itself uniform, there results, I say, a variable motion for the parts of the
earth; I will explain this by drawing a diagram, so that it can be more
easily understood.

First, around the center A, I
describe the circumference of the
annual orbit BC; on it let us take
any point whatever B, and using
B as a center let us describe this
smaller circle DEFG, representing the terrestrial globe; then let
us assume the center B to run
along the whole circumference
of the annual orbit from west to
east, namely, from B toward C;
and let us further assume the

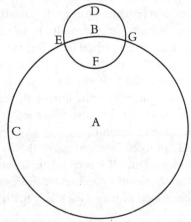

terrestrial globe to turn around its own center B in the period of twenty-four hours, also from west to east, namely, according to the order of the points D, E, F, and G. Here we must note carefully that as a circle turns around its own center, each part of it must move in opposite directions at different times; this is clear by considering that, while the parts of the circumference around the point D move toward the left (namely, toward E), those on the opposite side (which are around F) advance toward the [453] right (namely, toward G), so that when the parts D are at F their motion is contrary to what it was when they were at D; furthermore, at the same time that the parts E descend (so to speak) toward F, the parts G ascend toward D. Given such a contrariety in the motions of the parts of the terrestrial surface as it turns around its own center, it is necessary that in combining this diurnal motion with the other annual one there results an absolute motion of the parts of the terrestrial surface that is sometimes highly accelerated and sometimes retarded by the same amount. This is clear from the following considerations: the absolute motion of the part around D is very fast since it originates from two motions in the same direction, namely, toward the left; the first of these is the annual motion common to all parts of the globe, the other is the motion of point D carried also toward the left by the diurnal rotation; hence, in this case the diurnal motion increases and accelerates the annual motion; the opposite of this happens at the opposite side F, which is carried toward the right by the diurnal rotation while together with the whole globe it is carried toward the left by the common annual motion; thus, the diurnal motion takes away from the annual, and so the absolute motion resulting from the combination of the two turns out to be greatly retarded; finally, around the points E and G the absolute motion remains equal to the annual alone, for the diurnal motion adds or subtracts little or nothing, its direction being neither left nor right but down and up. Therefore, we conclude that, just as it is true that the motion of the whole globe and of each of its parts would be invariable and uniform if it were moving with a single motion (be it the simple annual or the diurnal alone), so it is necessary that the mixture of these two motions together gives the parts of the globe variable motions (sometimes accelerated and sometimes retarded) by means of additions or subtractions of the diurnal rotation and the annual revolution. Thus, if it is true (and it is most true, as experience shows) that the acceleration and retardation of a vessel's motion make the water contained in it run back and forth along its length and rise and fall at

its ends, who will want to raise difficulties about granting that such
an effect can (or rather, must necessarily) happen in seawater, which
is contained in various basins subject to similar variations, especially in
those whose length stretches out from west to east (which is the direction along which these basins move)?

[454] Now, let this be the primary and most important cause of
the tides, without which this effect would not happen at all. However, there are many different particular phenomena which can be
observed in different places and at different times, and which must depend on other different concomitant causes, although these must all
be connected with the primary cause; hence, it is proper to present
and examine the various factors that may be the causes of such various phenomena.

The first of these is that whenever water is made to flow toward
one or the other end of a containing vessel by a noticeable retardation or acceleration of that vessel, and it rises at one end and subsides
at the other, it does not thereby remain in such a state even if the primary cause should cease; instead, in virtue of its own weight and natural inclination to level and balance itself out, it spontaneously and
quickly goes back; and, being heavy and fluid, not only does it move
toward equilibrium, but carried by its own impetus, it goes beyond
and rises at the end where earlier it was lower; not resting here either,
it again goes back, and with more repeated oscillations, it indicates
that it does not want to change suddenly from the acquired speed to
the absence of motion and state of rest, but that it wants to do it gradually and slowly. This is similar to the way in which a pendulum, after
being displaced from its state of rest (namely, from the perpendicular), spontaneously returns to it and to rest, but not before having
gone beyond it many times with a back-and-forth motion.

The second factor to notice is that the reciprocal motions just
mentioned take place and are repeated with greater or lesser frequency, namely, in shorter or longer times, depending on the length
of the vessels containing the water; thus, the oscillations are more frequent for the shorter distances and rarer for the longer. And this is exactly what happens in the same example of pendulums, where we see
that the oscillations of those hanging from a longer string are less frequent than those of pendulums hanging from shorter strings.

And here is a third important point to know: it is not only the
greater or lesser length of the vessel that causes the water to make its
oscillations in different times, but the greater or lesser depth brings

about the same thing; what happens is that, for water contained [455] in vessels of equal length but of unequal depth, the one which is deeper makes its oscillations in shorter times, and the vibrations of less deep water are less frequent.[69]

Fourth, worthy of notice and of diligent observation are two effects produced by water in such vibrations. One is the alternating rising and falling at both ends; the other is the flowing back and forth, horizontally, so to speak. These two different motions affect different parts of the water differently. For its ends are the parts that rise and fall the most; those at the middle do not move up or down at all; and as for the rest, those that are nearer the ends rise and fall proportionately more than the farther parts. On the contrary, in regard to the lateral motion back and forth, the middle parts go forth and come back a great deal; the water at the ends does not flow at all except insofar as by rising it goes over the embankment and overflows its original bed, but where the embankment stands in the way and can hold it, it only rises and falls; finally, the water in the middle is not the only part that flows back and forth, for this is also done proportionately by its other parts, as they flow more or less depending on how far or near they are relative to the middle.

The fifth particular factor must be considered much more carefully, insofar as it is impossible for us to reproduce it experimentally and practically.[70] The point is this. In artificial vessels which, like the boats mentioned above, move now more and now less swiftly, the acceleration or retardation is shared to the same extent by the whole vessel and all its parts: thus, for example, as the boat slows down, the forward part is not retarded any more than the back, but they all share the same retardation equally; the same happens in acceleration; that is, as the boat acquires greater speed, both the bow and the stern are accelerated in the same way. However, in very large vessels like the

---

69. The last two paragraphs contain an approximation to an important law in hydrodynamics. Combining the two points, Galileo says that the period of oscillation of water in a vessel varies directly with the length of the vessel and inversely with its depth. The relationship is actually more complicated insofar as the dependence on the length involves its square root. Cf. Strauss 1891, 568 n. 9; Pagnini 1964, 3: 243 n. 1.

70. This remark seems to contradict Salviati's claim in the penultimate sentence of this speech, namely, that he has under construction such a machine. Perhaps Galileo meant not that it is impossible but that it is very difficult. For an attempt to resolve the apparent contradiction, see Drake 1970, 200–13.

very long basins of the seas, though they are nothing but certain hollows carved out of the solid terrestrial globe, nevertheless amazingly their extremities do not increase or diminish their motion together, equally, and simultaneously; [456] instead it happens that, when one extremity is greatly retarded in virtue of the combination of the diurnal and annual motions, the other extremity finds itself still experiencing very fast motion.

For easier comprehension, let us explain this by referring to the diagram drawn here. In it, let us consider, for example, a portion of water spanning a quarter of the globe, such as the arc *BC;* here, as we explained above, the parts at *B* are in very fast motion due to the combination of the diurnal and annual motions in the same direction, whereas the parts at *C* are retarded insofar as they lack the forward motion deriving from the diurnal rotation. If, then, we take a sea basin whose length equals the arc *BC,* we see how its extremities move simultaneously with great inequality. The differences would be greatest for the speeds of an ocean a hemisphere long and situated in the position of the arc *BCD,* for the end *B* would be in very fast motion, the other *D* would be in very slow motion, and the middle parts at

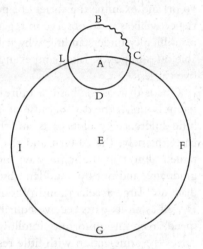

C would have an intermediate speed; further, the shorter a given sea is, the less will it experience this curious effect of having its parts moving at different speeds during certain hours of the day. Thus, if, as in the first case, we observe acceleration and retardation causing the contained water to flow back and forth despite the fact that they are shared equally by all parts of the vessel, what shall we think must happen in a vessel placed so curiously that its parts acquire retardation and acceleration very unequally? It seems certain we can say only that here we have a greater and more amazing cause of even stranger movements in the water. Though many will consider it impossible that we could experiment with the effects of such an arrangement by means of machines and artificial vessels, nevertheless it is not entirely impossible; I have under construction a machine in which one can observe in detail the effect of these amazing combinations of motions. However, regarding the present subject, let us be satisfied with what you may have been able to understand with your imagination so far.

[457] SAGR.   For my part, I understand very well how this marvelous phenomenon must necessarily take place in the sea basins, especially in those that extend for long distances from west to east, namely, along the course of the motions of the terrestrial globe; moreover, just as it is in a way inconceivable and unparalleled among the motions we can reproduce, so I have no difficulty believing that it may produce effects which cannot be duplicated with our artificial experiments.

SALV.   After these things have been clarified, it is time for us to go on and examine the variety of particular phenomena which experience enables us to observe in regard to the tides. First, there will be no difficulty understanding why it happens that there are no noticeable tides in ponds, lakes, and even small seas; this has two very effective causes.

One is that, as the basin acquires different degrees of speed at different hours of the day, because of its smallness they are acquired with little difference by all its parts, and the forward as well as the backward parts (namely, the eastern and the western) are accelerated and retarded almost in the same way; moreover, since this change occurs gradually, and not by a sudden obstacle and retardation or an immediate and large acceleration in the motion of the containing basin, it as well as all its parts receive equally and slowly the same degrees of speed; from this uniformity it follows that the contained water too receives the same action with little resistance, and consequently it gives very little sign of rising and falling and of flowing toward this or the other end. This effect is also clearly seen in small artificial containers, in which the water acquires the same degrees of speed whenever the acceleration or the retardation takes place in a relatively slow and uniform manner. However, in sea basins that extend for a great distance from east to west the acceleration or retardation is much more noticeable and unequal, for while one end is undergoing very retarded motion the other is still moving very rapidly.

The other cause is the reciprocal vibration of the water stemming from the impetus it also receives from the container, which vibration has very frequent oscillations in small vessels, as we have seen: for [458] the earth's motions can cause agitation in the waters only at twelve-hour intervals, since the motion of the containing basins is retarded and is accelerated the maximum amount only once a day, respectively; but the second cause depends on the weight of the water while in the process of reaching equilibrium, and it has its oscillations at intervals of one hour, or two, or three, etc., depending on the length of the basin; now, mixed with the former cause, which is very small in small vessels, the latter renders it completely imperceptible; for before the end of the operation of the primary cause with the twelve-hour period, the secondary one due to the weight of the water comes about, and with its period of one hour, two, three, or four, etc. (depending on the size and depth of the basin), it perturbs and removes the first, without allowing it to reach the maximum or the middle of its effect. From this contraposition, any sign of tides remains completely annihilated or much obscured.

I say nothing of the constant alterations due to air; disturbing the water, they would not allow us to ascertain a very small rise or fall of half an inch or less, which might actually be taking place in water basins that are no longer than a degree[71] or two.

Second, I come to resolving the difficulty of how tidal periods can commonly appear to be six hours, even though the primary cause embodies a principle for moving the water only at twelve-hour intervals, that is, once for the maximum speed of motion and once for maximum slowness. To this I answer that such a determination cannot in any way result from the primary cause alone; instead we must add the secondary ones, namely, the greater or lesser length of the vessels and the greater or lesser depth of the water contained in them. Although these causes do not act to bring about the motions of the water (since this action originates only from the primary cause), nevertheless they have a key role in determining the periods of the oscillations, and this role is so powerful that the primary cause remains subject to them. Thus, the six-hour interval is no more proper or natural than other time intervals, although it is perhaps the one most commonly observed since it occurs in our Mediterranean, which for many centuries was the only accessible sea; however, such a period is not [459] observed in all its regions, for in some of the more narrow areas such as the Hellespont and the Aegean, the periods are much shorter and also much different from each other. Some say that

---

71. By *degree,* here Galileo means 1 of 360 degrees in a circle; so, when the circle is the equator (which is about 24,000 miles), one degree is about sixty-seven miles.

Aristotle long observed these variations from some cliffs in Euboea and found their causes incomprehensible, and that because of this, (overcome with despair) he jumped into the sea and drowned himself.[72]

Third, we can quickly explain why it happens that although some seas are very long—for example, the Red Sea—nevertheless they are almost entirely lacking in tides. This occurs because its length does not extend from east to west, but from southeast to northwest. For, the earth's motions being from west to east, the impulses received by the water always cross the meridians and do not move from one parallel to another; so, in seas that extend transversely in the direction of the poles and that are narrow in the other direction, no cause of tides remains but the contribution of some other sea with which they are connected and which is subject to large motions.

Fourth, we can very easily understand the reason why, in regard to the rise and fall of the water, tides are greatest at the extremities of gulfs and smallest in the middle. This is shown by daily experience here in Venice, which is located at the end of the Adriatic and where this variation amounts to five or six feet; but in areas of the Mediterranean far from the extremities, such a variation is very small, as is the case in the islands of Corsica and Sardinia and on the shores of Rome and Leghorn, where it does not exceed half a foot. We can also understand how, on the contrary, in places where the rise and the fall are very small, the flow back and forth is large. I say it is easy to understand the cause of these phenomena because we can make clear tests in all sorts of vessels we can artificially build; here the same effects are seen to follow naturally from our making them move with a motion which is nonuniform, namely, sometimes accelerated and sometimes retarded.

Fifth, considering how the same quantity of water that moves slowly through a wide area must flow with great impetus when passing through a narrow place, we shall have no difficulty in understanding the cause of the immense currents which flow in the narrow channel that separates Calabria from [460] Sicily; for although all the water contained in the eastern Mediterranean and bound by the width of the island and the Ionian Gulf may slowly flow into it toward the west, nevertheless, when constricted into this strait between

---

72. This is not a true story, and later in Day IV Galileo himself treats it as a mere legend (Galilei 1890–1901, 7: 472; 1967, 447). In fact, Aristotle discusses the tides only briefly in *Meteorology* I, 1.

Scylla and Charybdis,[73] it flows rapidly and undergoes very great agitation. Similar to this and much greater we understand are the currents between Africa and the large island of Madagascar, as the waters of the North and South Indian Ocean, which surround it, flow and become constricted in the smaller channel between it and the South African coast. Very great must be the currents in the Strait of Magellan, which connects the extremely vast South Atlantic and South Pacific Oceans.

Sixth, to account for some more obscure and implausible phenomena observed in this subject, we now have to make another important consideration about the two principal causes of tides and then mix them together. The first and simpler of these is (as we have said several times) the definite acceleration and retardation of the earth's parts, from which the water would acquire a definite tendency to flow toward the east and to go back toward the west within a period of twenty-four hours. The other is the one that depends on the mere weight of water: once stirred by the primary cause, it then tries to reach equilibrium by repeated oscillations; these are not determined by a single period in advance, but they have as many temporal differences as the different lengths and depths of sea basins; and insofar as they depend on this second principle, some oscillations might flow back and forth in one hour, others in two, four, six, eight, ten, etc. Now, let us begin to join together the primary cause, whose fixed period is twelve hours, with one of the secondary causes whose period is, for example, five hours: sometimes it will happen that the primary and secondary causes agree by both producing impulses in the same direction, and with such a combination (a unanimous consent, so to speak) the tides are large; other times, the primary impulse being somehow opposite to that of the secondary cause, and thus one principle taking away what the other one gives, the watery motions will weaken and the sea will reduce to a very calm and almost motionless state; finally, [461] on still other occasions, when the same two causes neither oppose nor reinforce each other, there will be other variations in the increase or decrease of the tides. It may also happen that of two very large seas connected by a narrow channel, due to the mixture of the two causes of motion, one sea has tidal motions in one direction

---

73. This refers to the Strait of Messina separating the island of Sicily from Calabria on the Italian peninsula and joining the Ionian and the Tyrrhenian Seas.

while the other has them in the opposite; in this case, in the channel where the two seas meet there are extraordinary agitations with contrary motions, vortices, and very dangerous boilings, as it is in fact constantly observed and reported. These conflicting motions, dependent on the different positions and lengths of interconnected seas and on their different depths, give rise sometimes to those irregular disturbances of the water whose causes have worried and continue to worry sailors, who experience them without seeing winds or any other serious atmospheric disturbance that might produce them.

These atmospheric disturbances must be significantly taken into account in other cases, and we must regard them as a tertiary accidental cause, capable of significantly altering the occurrence of the effects produced by the primary and more important causes. For example, there is no doubt that very strong winds from the east can support the water and prevent it from ebbing; then, when at the appropriate time there is a second wave of flow (and a third), it will rise a great deal; thus, if sustained for a few days by the power of the wind, it will rise more than usual and produce extraordinary flooding.

Seventh, we must also note another cause of motion dependent on the great quantity of river water flowing into seas that are not very large. Here, in channels or straits connected with such seas, the water is seen flowing always in the same direction; for example, this happens at the Bosporus near Constantinople, where the water always flows from the Black Sea to the Sea of Marmara. For, in the Black Sea, because of its smallness, the principal causes of the tides are of little effect; on the contrary, very large rivers flow into it, and so with such a superabundance of water having to go through the strait, here the flow is very noticeable and always southward. Moreover, we must note that although this strait is very narrow, it is not [462] subject to perturbations like those in the strait of Scylla and Charybdis. For, the former has the Black Sea on the north and the Sea of Marmara, the Aegean, and the Mediterranean on the south; and, as we have already noted, insofar as a sea extends in a north-south direction it is not subject to tides; on the contrary, because the strait of Sicily is interposed between two parts of the Mediterranean that extend for long distances in an east-west direction, namely, in the direction of tidal currents, in the latter the disturbances are very large. Similarly, they would be larger between the Pillars of Hercules,[74] if the Strait of

---

74. This is the ancient mythological name for the Strait of Gibraltar, separating Europe from Africa, and connecting the Mediterranean Sea and the Atlantic Ocean.

Gibraltar were less wide; and they are reported to be very large in the Strait of Magellan.

For now, this is all I can think of telling you about the causes of this first (diurnal) period of the tides and related phenomena; if you want to advance any comments, you can do it now, so that we can then go on to discuss the two other (monthly and annual) periods.[75]

[§8.8 Day IV: Ending][76]

[485] SAGR.   I think you have done a great deal in opening up for us the first door to such a lofty speculation. Even if you had given us [486] only the first basic proposition, in my opinion that alone so greatly surpasses the inanities introduced by so many others that merely thinking of them nauseates me; I mean the proposition (which seems unobjectionable to me) declaring very convincingly that if the vessels containing the seawater stood still, it would be impossible by the common course of nature for it to exhibit the motions we see, and on the contrary, given the motions attributed for other reasons by Copernicus to the terrestrial globe, such changes in the seas must necessarily follow. I am very surprised that among men of sublime intellect (of whom there have been many) no one has seen the incompatibility between the reciprocal motion of the contained water and the immobility of the containing vessel; this incompatibility seems very evident to me now.

SALV.   What is more surprising is that, while some have thought of finding the cause of the tides in the earth's motion (thus showing greater perspicacity than is common), when they then came to the point, they grasped nothing; they did not understand that it is not enough to have a single uniform motion (such as, for example, the mere diurnal motion of the terrestrial globe), but that we need an unequal motion, sometimes accelerated and sometimes retarded; for when the motion of a vessel is uniform, the water contained therein will get used to it and will never undergo any change. Moreover, it is

---

75. The monthly period of the tides is the phenomenon that during certain times of the month the daily high tides are higher than usual and the daily low tides are lower than usual; similarly, the annual period is the phenomenon that during certain periods of the year the daily high tides are higher and the daily low tides lower than usual.

76. Galilei 1890–1909, 7: 485.36–489.20; translated by Finocchiaro (1997, 303–8).

totally useless to say (as an ancient mathematician[77] is reported to have said) that when the earth's motion encounters the motion of the lunar orb, such a contrast causes the tides; for it is neither explained nor self-evident how this is supposed to happen, but rather we can see its manifest falsity, given that the earth's rotation is not contrary to the moon's motion but in the same direction. Thus, what has been stated and thought so far by others is, in my opinion, completely invalid. However, of all great men who have philosophized on such a puzzling effect of nature, I am more surprised about Kepler than about anyone else; although he had a free and penetrating intellect and grasped the motions attributed to the earth, he lent his ear and gave his assent to the dominion of the moon over the water, to occult properties, and to similar childish ideas.

SAGR.   I am of the opinion that these better thinkers experienced what is now happening to me, too; that is, one cannot understand [487] how the three periods (annual, monthly, and daily) are entangled and how their causes appear to depend on the sun and moon without the sun and moon having anything to do with the water. For a full understanding of this business I need a longer and more focused application of my mind, which at the moment is very confused by its novelty and difficulty; but I do not despair of being able to grasp it if, in solitude and silence, I can return to chewing over what remains improperly digested in my mind.

Thus, the discussions of these four days provide strong indications in favor of the Copernican system. Among them, these three appear to be very convincing: first, the one taken from the stoppings and retrogressions of the planets and their approaching and receding from the earth; second, the one from the sun's rotation on itself and from what is observed about its spots; and third, the one from the ebb and flow of the sea.

SALV.   Soon we could perhaps add a fourth one and possibly even a fifth one. That is, the fourth one would be taken from the fixed stars, if the most exact observations were to reveal in them those minute changes which Copernicus assumes to be imperceptible.[78] There is now a fifth novelty from which one might be able to argue for the motion of the terrestrial globe. This refers to the extremely subtle

---

77. In a marginal note Galileo identifies this author as Seleucus.
78. That is, the annual parallax of fixed stars, which however was not detected until 1838, by Friedrich W. Bessel.

things being discovered by the most illustrious Mr. Cesare Marsili,[79] member of a very noble family of Bologna, and also a Lincean Academician; in a most learned essay he states that he has observed a constant though extremely slow motion of the meridian line. Having lately seen this essay with astonishment, I hope he sends copies of it to all students of the marvels of nature.

SAGR.   This is not the first time I have heard of this gentleman's refined learning and of his great concern to be a patron of all scholars. If this or some other work of his comes out, we can be sure that it will be a thing of distinction.

SALV.   Now, since it is time to put an end to our discussions, it remains for me to ask you to please excuse my faults if, when more calmly going over the things I have put forth, you should encounter difficulties and doubts not adequately resolved. You should excuse me because these ideas are novel, my mind is imperfect, and the subject is a great one; finally, I do not ask and have not asked from others an assent which I myself do not give to this fancy, and I could very easily [488] regard it as a most unreal chimera and a most solemn paradox. As for you, Sagredo, although in the discussions we have had you have shown many times by means of strong endorsements that you were satisfied with some of my thoughts, I feel that in part this derived more from their novelty than from their certainty, and even much more from your courtesy; for by means of your assent you have wanted to give me the satisfaction which one naturally feels from the approval and praise of one's own creations. Moreover, just as I am obliged to you for your politeness, so I appreciate the sincerity of Simplicio; indeed, I have become very fond of him for defending his master's doctrine so steadfastly, so forcefully, and so courageously. Finally, just as I express thanks to you, Sagredo, for your very courteous feelings, so I beg forgiveness of Simplicio if I have upset him sometimes with my excessively bold and resolute language; there should be no question that I have not done this out of any malicious motive, but only to give him a greater opportunity to advance better thoughts, so that I could learn more.

---

79. Cesare Marsili (1592–1633) was a patron and friend of Galileo's and an amateur scientist. Marsili's essay has been lost and so it is impossible to evaluate his alleged discovery. But it is likely that the reported deviation of the meridian was due to observational error, and in any case it is unclear how the deviation would have supported the earth's motion.

SIMP.   There is no need for you to give these excuses, which are superfluous, especially to me who am used to being in social discussions and public disputes; indeed, innumerable times I have heard the opponents not only get upset and angry at each other, but also burst out into insulting words, and sometimes come very close to physical violence. As for the discussions we have had, especially the last one about the explanation of the tides, I really do not understand it completely. However, from the superficial conception I have been able to grasp, I confess that your idea seems to me much more ingenious than any others I have heard, but that I do not thereby regard it as truthful and convincing. Indeed, I always keep before my mind's eye a very firm doctrine, which I once learned from a man of great knowledge and eminence, and before which one must give pause.[80] From it I know what you would answer if both of you are asked whether God with His infinite power and wisdom could give to the element water the back and forth motion we see in it by some means other than by moving the containing basin; I say you will answer that He would have the power and the knowledge to do this in many ways, some of them even inconceivable by our intellect. Thus, I immediately conclude that in view of this it would be excessively bold if someone should want to limit and compel divine power and wisdom to a particular fancy of his.

[489] SALV.   An admirable and truly angelic doctrine, to which there corresponds very harmoniously another one that is also divine. This is the doctrine which, while it allows us to argue about the constitution of the world, tells us that we are not about to discover how His hands built it (perhaps in order that the exercise of the human mind would not be stopped or destroyed).[81] Thus let this exercise,

---

80. This refers to Pope Urban VIII, who found the objection Simplicio proceeds to state a powerful and indeed unanswerable argument against Copernicanism; Galileo knew the pope's opinion from personal discussions during special audiences, first in 1624 after the pope's election, when Galileo went to Rome to pay him homage, and then again in 1630 after Galileo had finished his book and visited that city to get permission to publish it. The lengthy negotiations for this purpose included the stipulation that he would end the book with this argument.

81. Cf. Ecclesiastes, 3:10–11 (King James Version): "I have seen the travail, which God hath given to the sons of men to be exercised in it. He hath made every *thing* beautiful in his time: also he hath set the world in their heart, so that no man can find out the work that God maketh from the beginning to the end."

granted and commanded to us by God, suffice to acknowledge His greatness; the less we are able to fathom the profound depths of His infinite wisdom, the more we shall admire that greatness.

SAGR.   This can very well be the final ending of our arguments over the last four days. Hereafter, if Salviati wants to take some rest, it is proper that our curiosity grant it to him, but on one condition; that is, when he finds it least inconvenient, he should comply with the wish, especially mine, to discuss the problems which we have set aside and which I have recorded, by having one or two other sessions, as we agreed. Above all I shall be looking forward with great eagerness to hear the elements of our Academician's new science of motion (natural and violent). Finally, now we can, as usual, go for an hour to enjoy some fresh air in the gondola that is waiting for us.

CHAPTER 9[1]

From the Later Trial-Documents (1632–33)[2]

§9.1 Special Commission's Report on the *Dialogue* (September 1632)[3]

[§9.1.1] In accordance with the order of Your Holiness, we have laid out the whole series of events pertaining to the printing of Galilei's book, which printing then took place in Florence. In essence the affair developed this way.

In the year 1630 Galileo took his book manuscript to the Father Master of the Sacred Palace in Rome, in order to have it reviewed for printing. The Father Master gave it for review to Father Raffaello Visconti, a friend of his and a professor of mathematics, who after several emendations was ready to give his approval as usual, if the book were to be printed in Rome.

We have written the said Father to send the said certificate, and we are now waiting for it. We have also written to get the original manuscript, in order to see the corrections made.

The Master of the Sacred Palace wanted to review the book himself; but, in order to shorten the time and to facilitate negotiations with printers, he stipulated that it be shown him page by page, and gave it the imprimatur for Rome.

Then the author went back to Florence and petitioned the Father Master for permission to print it in that city, which permission was denied. But the latter forwarded the case to the Inquisitor of Florence, thus removing himself from the transaction. Moreover, the Father Master notified the Inquisitor of what was required for publication, leaving to him the task of having it printed or not.

---

1. Reprinted from: Maurice A. Finocchiaro, trans. and ed., *The Galileo Affair: A Documentary History*, © 1989 by the Regents of the University of California. Published by the University of California Press.
2. For the historical background, see the Introduction, especially §0.9.
3. Galilei 1890–1909, 19: 324–327; translated by Finocchiaro (1989, 218–22).

The Master of the Sacred Palace has shown a copy of the letter he wrote the Inquisitor about this business, as well as a copy of the Inquisitor's reply to the said |325| Master of the Sacred Palace. In it the Inquisitor says that he gave the manuscript for correction to Father Stefani, consultant to the Holy Office.

After this the Master of the Sacred Palace did not hear anything, except that he saw the book printed in Florence and published with the Inquisitor's imprimatur, and that there is also an imprimatur for Rome.

We think that Galileo may have overstepped his instructions by asserting absolutely the earth's motion and the sun's immobility and thus deviating from hypothesis; that he may have wrongly attributed the existing ebb and flow of the sea to the nonexistent immobility of the sun and motion of the earth, which are the main things; and that he may have been deceitfully silent about an injunction given him by the Holy Office in the year 1616, whose tenor is: "that he abandon completely the above-mentioned opinion that the sun is the center of the world and the earth moves, nor henceforth hold, teach, or defend it in any way whatever, orally or in writing; otherwise the Holy Office would start proceedings against him. He acquiesced in this injunction and promised to obey."

One must now consider how to proceed, both against the person and concerning the printed book.

[§9.1.2] In point of fact:

1. Galilei did come to Rome in the year 1630, and he brought and showed his original manuscript to be reviewed for printing. Though he had been ordered to discuss the Copernican system only as a pure mathematical hypothesis, one found immediately that the book was not like this, but that it spoke absolutely, presenting the reasons for and against though without deciding. Thus the Master of the Sacred Palace determined that the book be reviewed and be changed to the hypothetical mode: it should have a preface to which the body would conform, which would describe this manner of proceeding, and which would prescribe it to the whole dispute to follow, including the part against the Ptolemaic system, carried on merely ad hominem and to show that in reproving the Copernican system the Holy Congregation had heard all the arguments.

2. To follow this through, the book was given for review with these orders to Father Raffaello Visconti, a friend of the Master of the Sacred Palace, since he was a professor of mathematics. He reviewed

it and emended it in many places, informing the Master about others disputed with the author, which the Master took out without further discussion. Having approved it for the rest, Father Visconti was ready to give it his endorsement to be placed at the beginning of the book as usual, if the book were to be printed in Rome as it was then presumed.

We have written the Inquisitor to send this endorsement to us and are expecting to receive it momentarily, and we have also sent for the original so that we can see the corrections made.

3. The Master of the Sacred Palace wanted to review the book himself, but, since the author complained about the unusual practice of a second revision and about the delay, to facilitate the process it was decided that before sending it to press the Master would see it page by page. In the meantime, to enable the author to negotiate with printers, he [326] was given the imprimatur for Rome, the book's beginning was compiled, and printing was expected to begin soon.

4. The author then went back to Florence, and after a certain period he petitioned to print it in that city. The Master of the Sacred Palace absolutely denied the request, answering by saying that the original should be brought back to him to make the last revision agreed upon, and that without this he for his part would have never given permission to print it. The reply was that the original could not be sent because of the dangers of loss and the plague. Nevertheless, after the intervention of His Highness there, it was decided that the Master of the Sacred Palace would remove himself from the case and refer it to the Inquisitor of Florence: the Master would describe to him what was required for the correction of the book and would leave him the decision to print it or not, so that he would be using his authority, without any responsibility on the part of the Master's office. Accordingly, he wrote to the Inquisitor the letter whose copy is appended here, labeled A, dated 24 May 1631, received and acknowledged by the Inquisitor with the letter labeled B, where he says he entrusted the book to Father Stefani, consultant to the Holy Office there.

Then a brief composition of the book's preface was sent to the Inquisitor so that the author would incorporate it with the whole, would embellish it in his own way, and would make the ending of the *Dialogue* conform with it. A copy of the sketch that was sent is enclosed labeled C, and a copy of the accompanying letter is enclosed labeled D.

5. After this the Master of the Sacred Palace was no longer involved in the matter, except when, the book having been printed and published without his knowledge, he received the first few copies and held them in customs, seeing that the instructions had not been followed. Then, upon orders from Our Master, he had them all seized where it was not too late and diligence made it possible to do so.

6. Moreover, there are in the book the following things to consider, as specific items of indictment:

i.[4] That he used the imprimatur for Rome without permission and without sharing the fact of the book's being published with those who are said to have granted it.

ii. That he had the preface printed with a different type and rendered it useless by its separation from the body of the work; and that he put the "medicine of the end" in the mouth of a fool and in a place where it can only be found with difficulty, and then he had it approved coldly by the other speaker by merely mentioning but not elaborating the positive things he seems to utter against his will.

iii. That many times in the work there is a lack of and deviation from hypothesis, either by asserting absolutely the earth's motion and the sun's immobility, or by characterizing the supporting arguments as demonstrative and necessary, or by treating the negative side as impossible.

iv. He treats the issue as undecided and as if one should await rather than presuppose the resolution.

[327] v. The mistreatment of contrary authors and those most used by the Holy Church.

vi. That he wrongly asserts and declares a certain equality between the human and the divine intellect in the understanding of geometrical matters.

vii. That he gives as an argument for the truth the fact that Ptolemaics occasionally become Copernicans, but the reverse never happens.

viii. That he wrongly attributed the existing ebb and flow of the sea to the nonexistent immobility of the sun and motion of the earth.

All these things could be emended if the book were judged to have some utility which would warrant such a favor.

---

4. Here, to avoid confusion between the two sets of numbers, the arabic numerals of the original have been replaced by roman numerals.

7. In 1616 the author had from the Holy Office the injunction that "he abandon completely the above-mentioned opinion that the sun is the center of the world and the earth moves, nor henceforth hold, teach, or defend it in any way, orally or in writing; otherwise the Holy Office would start proceedings against him. He acquiesced in this injunction and promised to obey."

§9.2 Galileo's First Deposition (12 April 1633)[5]

Summoned, there appeared personally in Rome at the palace of the Holy Office, in the usual quarters of the Reverend Father Commissary, fully in the presence of the Reverend Father Fra Vincenzo Maculano of Firenzuola, [337] Commissary General, and of his assistant Reverend Father Carlo Sinceri, Prosecutor of the Holy Office, etc.

Galileo, son of the late Vincenzio Galilei, Florentine, seventy years old, who, having taken a formal oath to tell the truth, was asked by the Fathers the following:

Q:[6] By what means and how long ago did he come to Rome.

A: I arrived in Rome the first Sunday of Lent, and I came in a litter.

Q: Whether he came of his own accord, or was called, or was ordered by someone to come to Rome, and by whom.

A: In Florence the Father Inquisitor ordered me to come to Rome and present myself to the Holy Office, this being an injunction by the officials of the Holy Office.

Q: Whether he knows or can guess the reason why he was ordered to come to Rome.

A: I imagine that the reason why I have been ordered to present myself to the Holy Office in Rome is to account for my recently printed book. I imagine this because of the injunction to the printer and to myself, a few days before I was ordered to come to Rome, not to issue any more of these books, and similarly because the printer

---

5. Galilei 1890–1909, 19: 336–342; translated by Finocchiaro (1989, 256–62).

6. Here and in other depositions, the questions are recorded as *indirect* queries, so that the letter Q ought to be taken to mean "He was asked," rather than simply "Question."

was ordered by the Father Inquisitor to send the original manuscript of my book to the Holy Office in Rome.

Q: That he explain the character of the book on account of which he thinks he was ordered to come to Rome.

A: It is a book written in dialogue form, and it treats of the constitution of the world, that is, of the two chief systems, and of the arrangement of the heavens and the elements.

Q: Whether, if he were shown the said book, he is prepared to identify it as his.

A: I hope so; I hope that if the book is shown me I shall recognize it.

And having been shown one of the books printed in Florence in 1632, whose title is *Dialogue of Galileo Galilei Lincean* etc., which examines the two systems of the world, and having looked at it and inspected it carefully, he said: I know this book very well; it is one of those printed in Florence; and I acknowledge it as mine and written by me.

Q: Whether he likewise acknowledges each and every thing contained in the said book as his.

A: I know this book shown to me, for it is one of those printed in Florence; and I acknowledge all it contains as having been written by me.

Q: When and where he composed the said book, and how long it took him.

[338] A: In regard to the place, I composed it in Florence, beginning ten or twelve years ago; and it must have taken me seven or eight years, but not continuously.

Q: Whether he was in Rome other times, especially in the year 1616, and for what occasion.

A: I was in Rome in the year 1616; then I was here in the second year of His Holiness Urban VIII's pontificate; and lastly I was here three years ago, the occasion being that I wanted to have my book printed. The occasion for my being in Rome in the year 1616 was that, having heard objections to Nicolaus Copernicus' opinion on the earth's motion, the sun's stability, and the arrangement of the heavenly spheres, in order to be sure of holding only holy and Catholic opinions, I came to hear what was proper to hold in regard to this topic.

Q: Whether he came of his own accord or was summoned, what the reason was why he was summoned, and with which person or persons he discussed the above-mentioned topics.

A: In 1616 I came to Rome of my own accord, without being summoned, for the reason I mentioned. In Rome I discussed this matter with some cardinals who oversaw the Holy Office at that time, especially with Cardinals Bellarmine, Aracoeli, San Eusebio, Bonsi, and d'Ascoli.

Q: What specifically he discussed with the above-mentioned cardinals.

A: The occasion for discussing with the said cardinals was that they wanted to be informed about Copernicus' doctrine, his book being very difficult to understand for those who are not professional mathematicians and astronomers. In particular they wanted to understand the arrangement of the heavenly spheres according to Copernicus' hypothesis, how he places the sun at the center of the planets' orbits, how around the sun he places next the orbit of Mercury, around the latter that of Venus, then the moon around the earth, and around this Mars, Jupiter, and Saturn; and in regard to motion, how he makes the sun stationary at the center and the earth turn on itself and around the sun, that is, on itself with the diurnal motion and around the sun with the annual motion.

Q: Since, as he says, he came to Rome to be able to have the resolution and the truth regarding the above, what then was decided about this matter.

A: Regarding the controversy which centered on the above-mentioned opinion of the sun's stability and earth's motion, it was decided by the Holy Congregation of the Index that this opinion, taken absolutely, is repugnant to Holy Scripture, and that it is to be admitted only suppositionally, in the way that Copernicus takes it.

Q: Whether he was then notified of the said decision, and by whom.

A: I was indeed notified of the said decision of the Congregation of the Index, and I was notified by Lord Cardinal Bellarmine.

Q: What the Most Eminent Bellarmine told him about the said decision, whether he said anything else about the matter, and if so, what.

[339] A: Lord Cardinal Bellarmine told me that Copernicus' opinion could be held suppositionally, as Copernicus himself had held it. His Eminence knew that I held it suppositionally, namely in the way that Copernicus held it, as you can see from an answer by the same Lord Cardinal to a letter of Father Master Paolo Antonio Foscarini, Provincial of the Carmelites; I have a copy of this, and in it one finds these words: "I say that it seems to me that Your Paternity and Mr.

Galileo are proceeding prudently by limiting yourselves to speaking suppositionally and not absolutely." This letter by the said Lord Cardinal is dated 12 April 1615. Moreover, he told me that otherwise, namely, taken absolutely, the opinion could be neither held nor defended.

Q: What was decided and then made known to him precisely in the month of February 1616.

A: In the month of February 1616, Lord Cardinal Bellarmine told me that since Copernicus' opinion, taken absolutely, was contrary to Holy Scripture, it could be neither held nor defended, but that it could be taken and used suppositionally. In conformity with this I keep a certificate by Lord Cardinal Bellarmine himself, dated 26 May 1616, in which he says that Copernicus' opinion cannot be held or defended, being against Holy Scripture. I present a copy of this certificate, and here it is.

And he showed a sheet of paper with twelve lines of writing on one side only, beginning "We Robert Cardinal Bellarmine have" and ending "on this 26th day of May 1616," signed "The same mentioned above, Robert Cardinal Bellarmine." This evidence was accepted and marked with the letter B.

Then he added: I have the original of this certificate with me in Rome, and it is written all in the hand of the above-mentioned Lord Cardinal Bellarmine.

Q: Whether, when he was notified of the above-mentioned matters, there were others present, and who they were.

A: When Lord Cardinal Bellarmine notified me of what I mentioned regarding Copernicus' opinion, there were some Dominican Fathers present, but I did not know them nor have I seen them since.

Q: Whether at that time, in the presence of those Fathers, he was given any injunction either by them or by someone else concerning the same matter, and if so what.

A: As I remember it, the affair took place in the following manner. One morning Lord Cardinal Bellarmine sent for me, and he told me a certain detail that I should like to speak to the ear of His Holiness before telling others; but then at the end he told me that Copernicus' opinion could not be held [340] or defended, being contrary to Holy Scripture. I do not recall whether those Dominican Fathers were there at first or came afterwards; nor do I recall whether they were present when the Lord Cardinal told me that the said opinion could not be held. Finally, it may be that I was given an injunction not to hold or defend the said opinion, but I do not recall it since this is something of many years ago.

Q: Whether, if one were to read to him what he was then told and ordered with injunction, he would remember that.

A: I do not recall that I was told anything else, nor can I know whether I shall remember what was then told me, even if it is read to me. I am saying freely what I recall because I do not claim not [sic][7] to have in any way violated that injunction, that is, not to have held or defended at all the said opinion of the earth's motion and sun's stability.

And having been told that the said injunction, given to him then in the presence of witnesses, states that he cannot in any way hold, defend, or teach the said opinion, he was asked whether he remembers how and by whom he was so ordered.

A: I do not recall that this injunction was given me any other way than orally by Lord Cardinal Bellarmine. I do remember that the injunction was that I could not hold or defend, and maybe even that I could "not teach." I do not recall, further, that there was the phrase "in any way whatever," but maybe there was; in fact, I did not think about it or keep it in mind, having received a few months thereafter Lord Cardinal Bellarmine's certificate dated 26 May, which I have presented and in which is explained the order given to me not to hold or defend the said opinion. Regarding the other two phrases in the said injunction now mentioned, namely "not to teach" and "in any way whatever," I did not retain them in my memory, I think because they are not contained in the said certificate, which I relied upon and kept as a reminder.

Q: Whether, after the issuing of the said injunction, he obtained any permission to write the book identified by himself, which he later sent to the printer.

A: After the above-mentioned injunction I did not seek permission to write the above-mentioned book which I have identified, because I do not think that by writing this book I was contradicting at all the injunction given me not to hold, defend, or teach the said opinion, but rather that I was refuting it.

---

7. The original sentence does explicitly have this double negative, suggesting an admission of some wrongdoing on Galileo's part. This is puzzling, especially in view of the denial later on the same page. Thus, the double negative may have been a slip of the tongue.

Q: Whether he obtained permission for the printing of the same book, by whom, and whether for himself or for someone else.

A: To obtain permission to print the above-mentioned book, although I was receiving profitable offers from France, Germany, and Venice, I refused them and spontaneously came to Rome three years ago to place it into the hands of the chief censor, namely the Master of the Sacred Palace, [341] giving him absolute authority to add, delete, and change as he saw fit. After having it examined very diligently by his associate Father Visconti, the said Master of the Sacred Palace reviewed it again himself and licensed it; that is, having approved the book, he gave me permission but ordered to have the book printed in Rome. Since, in view of the approaching summer, I wanted to go back home to avoid the danger of getting sick, having been away all of May and June, we agreed that I was to return here the autumn immediately following. While I was in Florence, the plague broke out and commerce was stopped; so, seeing that I could not come to Rome, by correspondence I requested of the same Master of the Sacred Palace permission for the book to be printed in Florence. He communicated to me that he would want to review my original manuscript, and that therefore I should send it to him. Despite having used every possible care and having contacted even the highest secretaries of the Grand Duke and the directors of the postal service, to try to send the said original safely, I received no assurance that this could be done, and it certainly would have been damaged, washed out, or burned, such was the strictness at the borders. I related to the same Father Master this difficulty concerning the shipping of the book, and he ordered me to have the book again very scrupulously reviewed by a person acceptable to him; the person he was pleased to designate was Father Master Giacinto Stefani, a Dominican, professor of Sacred Scripture at the University of Florence, preacher for the Most Serene Highnesses, and consultant to the Holy Office. The book was handed over by me to the Father Inquisitor of Florence and by the Father Inquisitor to the above-mentioned Father Giacinto Stefani; the latter returned it to the Father Inquisitor, who sent it to Mr. Niccolò dell'Antella, reviewer of books to be printed for the Most Serene Highness of Florence; the printer, named Landini, received it from this Mr. Niccolò and, having negotiated with the Father Inquisitor, printed it, observing strictly every order given by the Father Master of the Sacred Palace.

Q: Whether, when he asked the above-mentioned Master of the Sacred Palace for permission to print the above-mentioned book, he revealed to the same Most Reverend Father Master the injunction previously given to him concerning the directive of the Holy Congregation, mentioned above.

A: When I asked him for permission to print the book, I did not say anything to the Father Master of the Sacred Palace about the above-mentioned injunction because I did not judge it necessary to tell it to him, having no scruples since with the said book I had neither held nor defended the opinion of the earth's motion and sun's stability; on the contrary, in the said book I show the contrary of Copernicus' opinion, and that Copernicus' reasons are invalid and inconclusive.

With this the deposition ended, and he was assigned a certain room in the dormitory of the officials, located in the palace of the Holy Office, in lieu of prison,[8] with [342] the injunction not to leave it without special permission, under penalty to be decided by the Holy Congregation; and he was ordered to sign below and was sworn to silence.

I, Galileo Galilei have testified as above.

§9.3 Galileo's Second Deposition (30 April 1633)[9]

Called personally to the hall of the Congregations, in the presence and with the assistance of those mentioned above and of myself, the above-mentioned Galileo Galilei, who has since then petitioned to be heard, having sworn an oath to tell the truth, was asked by the Fathers the following:

Q: That he state whatever he wished to say.

A: For several days I have been thinking continuously and directly about the interrogations I underwent on the sixteenth of this month,[10] and in particular about the question whether sixteen years ago I had been prohibited, by order of the Holy Office, from holding,

---

8. From 12 to 30 April 1633, Galileo was detained at the Inquisition palace but allowed to lodge in the prosecutor's apartment.
9. Galilei 1890–1909, 19: 342–44; translated by Finocchiaro (1989, 277–79).
10. The only previous deposition of which we have a record is the one dated 12 April (see §9.2).

defending, and teaching in any way whatever the opinion, then condemned, of the earth's motion and sun's stability. It dawned on me to
reread my printed *Dialogue,* [343] which over the last three years I had
not even looked at. I wanted to check very carefully whether, against
my purest intention, through my oversight, there might have fallen
from my pen not only something enabling readers or superiors to
infer a defect of disobedience on my part, but also other details
through which one might think of me as a transgressor of the orders
of the Holy Church. Being at liberty, through the generous approval
of superiors, to send one of my servants for errands, I managed to get
a copy of my book, and I started to read it with the greatest concen-
tration and to examine it in the most detailed manner. Not having
seen it for so long, I found it almost a new book by another author.
Now, I freely confess that it appeared to me in several places to be
written in such a way that a reader, not aware of my intention, would
have had reason to form the opinion that the arguments for the false
side, which I intended to confute, were so stated as to be capable of
convincing because of their strength, rather than being easy to answer. In particular, two arguments, one based on sunspots and the
other on the tides, are presented favorably to the reader as being
strong and powerful, more than would seem proper for someone who
deemed them to be inconclusive and wanted to confute them, as indeed I inwardly and truly did and do hold them to be inconclusive
and refutable. As an excuse for myself, within myself, for having fallen
into an error so foreign to my intention, I was not completely satisfied with saying that when one presents arguments for the opposite
side with the intention of confuting them, they must be explained in
the fairest way and not be made out of straw to the disadvantage of
the opponent, especially when one is writing in dialogue form. Being
dissatisfied with this excuse, as I said, I resorted to that of the natural
gratification everyone feels for his own subtleties and for showing
himself to be cleverer than the average man, by finding ingenious and
apparent considerations of probability even in favor of false propositions. Nevertheless—even though, to use Cicero's words, "I am more
desirous of glory than is suitable"—if I had to write out the same arguments now, there is no doubt that I would weaken them in such a
way that they could not appear to exhibit a force which they really
and essentially lack. My error then was, and I confess it, one of vain
ambition, pure ignorance, and inadvertence. This is as much as I need
to say on this occasion, and it occurred to me as I reread my book.

With this, having obtained his signature, and having sworn him to silence, the Fathers formally concluded the hearing.

I, Galileo Galilei have testified as above.

[344] And returning after a little, he said:

And for greater confirmation that I neither did hold nor do hold as true the condemned opinion of the earth's motion and sun's stability, if, as I desire, I am granted the possibility and the time to prove it more clearly, I am ready to do so. The occasion for it is readily available since in the book already published the speakers agree that after a certain time they should meet again to discuss various physical problems other than the subject already dealt with. Hence, with this pretext to add one or two other Days, I promise to reconsider the arguments already presented in favor of the said false and condemned opinion and to confute them in the most effective way that the blessed God will enable me. So I beg this Holy Tribunal to cooperate with me in this good resolution, by granting me the permission to put it into practice.

And again he signed.

I, Galileo Galilei, affirm the above.

§9.4 Galileo's Third Deposition (10 May 1633)[11]

[345] Summoned, there appeared personally at the hall of Congregations of the palace of the Holy Office in Rome, in the presence of the very Reverend Father Fra Vincenzo Maculano, O.P., Commissary General of the Holy Office, etc.

Galileo Galilei mentioned above; and, called before his Paternity, the same Father Commissary gave him a deadline of eight days to present his defense, if he wanted and intended to do it.

Having heard this, he said: I understand what Your Paternity has told me. In reply I say that I do want to present something in my defense, namely, in order to show the sincerity and purity of my intention, not at all to excuse my having transgressed in some ways, as I have already said. I present the following statement, together with a certificate by the late Most Eminent Lord Cardinal Bellarmine, written with his own hand by the Lord Cardinal himself, of which I

---

11. Galilei 1890–1909, 19: 345; translated by Finocchiaro (1989, 279).

earlier presented a copy by my hand. For the rest I rely in every way on the usual mercy and clemency of this tribunal.

After signing his name, he was sent back to the house of the above-mentioned ambassador of the Most Serene Grand Duke, under the conditions already communicated to him.

I, Galileo Galilei, with my own hand.

§9.5 Galileo's Defense (10 May 1633)[12]

In an earlier interrogation, I was asked whether I had informed the Most Reverend Father Master of the Sacred Palace about the private injunction issued to me sixteen years ago by order of the Holy Office—"not to hold, defend, or teach in any way" the opinion of the earth's motion and sun's stability—and I answered No. Since I was not asked the reason why I did not inform him, I did not have the opportunity to say anything else. Now it seems to me necessary to mention it, in order to reveal my very pure mind, always averse to using simulation and deceit in any of my actions.

[346] I say, then, that at that time some of my enemies were spreading the rumor that I had been called by the Lord Cardinal Bellarmine in order to abjure some opinions and doctrines of mine, that I had had to abjure, that I had also received punishments for them, etc., and so I was forced to resort to His Eminence and to beg him to give me a certificate explaining why I had been called. I received this certificate, written by his own hand, and it is what I attach to the present statement. In it one clearly sees that I was only told not to hold or defend Copernicus' doctrine of the earth's motion and sun's stability; but one cannot see any trace that, besides this general pronouncement applicable to all, I was given any other special order. Having the reminder of this authentic certificate, handwritten by the one who issued the order himself, I did not try to recall or give any other thought to the words used to give me orally the said injunction, to the effect that one cannot defend or hold, etc.; thus, the two phrases—besides "holding" and "defending," which I hear are contained in the injunction given to me and recorded—that is, "teaching" and "in any way whatever," struck me as very new and unheard.

---

12. Galilei 1890–1909, 19: 345–47; translated by Finocchiaro (1989, 279–81).

I do not think I should be mistrusted about the fact that in the course of fourteen or sixteen years I lost any memory of them, especially since I had no need to give the matter any thought, having such a valid reminder in writing. Now, when those two phrases are removed and we retain only the other two mentioned in the attached certificate, there is no reason to doubt that the order contained in it is the same as the injunction issued by the decree of the Holy Congregation of the Index. From this I feel very reasonably excused for not notifying the Father Master of the Sacred Palace of the injunction given to me in private, the latter being the same as the one of the Congregation of the Index.

Given that my book was not subject to more stringent censures than those required by the decree of the Index, I followed the surest and most effective way to protect it and to purge it of any trace of blemish. It seems to me that this is very obvious, since I handed it over to the supreme Inquisitor [347] at a time when many books on the same subjects were being prohibited solely on account of the above-mentioned decree.

From the things I am saying, I think I can firmly hope that the idea of my having knowingly and willingly disobeyed the orders given me will be kept out of the minds of the Most Eminent and Most Prudent Lord Judges. Thus, those flaws that can be seen scattered in my book were not introduced through the cunning of a disguised and insincere intention, but rather through the vain ambition and satisfaction of appearing clever above and beyond the average among popular writers; this was an inadvertent result of my writing, as I confessed in another deposition of mine. I am ready to make amends and to compensate for this flaw by every possible means, whenever I may be either ordered or allowed by their Most Eminent Lordships.

Finally, I am left with asking you to consider the pitiable state of ill health to which I am reduced, due to ten months of constant mental distress, and to the discomforts of a long and tiresome journey in the most awful season and at the age of seventy; I feel I have lost the greater part of the years which my previous state of health promised me. I am encouraged to do this by the faith I have in the clemency and kindness of heart of the Most Eminent Lordships, my judges; and I hope that, if their sense of justice perceives anything lacking among so many ailments as adequate punishment for my crimes, they will, begged by me, condone it out of regard for my declining old age, which I humbly also ask them to consider. Equally, I want them to consider my honor and reputation against the slanders of those who hate me, and I hope that when the latter insist on disparaging my reputation, the Most Eminent Lordships will take it as evidence why it became necessary for me to obtain from the Most Eminent Lord Cardinal Bellarmine the certificate attached herewith.

§9.6 Galileo's Fourth Deposition (21 June 1633)[13]

Called personally to the hall of Congregations in the palace of the Holy Office in Rome, fully in the presence of the Reverend Father Commissary General of the Holy Office, assisted by the Reverend Father Prosecutor, etc.

Galileo Galilei, Florentine, mentioned previously, having sworn an oath to tell the truth, was asked by the Fathers the following:

Q: Whether he had anything to say.

A: I have nothing to say.

Q: Whether he holds or has held, and for how long, that the sun is the center of the world and the earth is not the center of the world but moves also with diurnal motion.

A: A long time ago, that is, before the decision of the Holy Congregation of the Index, and before I was issued that injunction, I was undecided and regarded the two opinions, those of Ptolemy and Copernicus, as disputable, because either the one or the other could be true in nature. But after the above-mentioned decision, assured by the prudence of the authorities, all my uncertainty stopped, and I held, as I still hold, as very true and undoubted Ptolemy's opinion, namely the stability of the earth and the motion of the sun.

Having been told that he is presumed to have held the said opinion after that time, from the manner and procedure in which the said opinion is discussed and defended in the book he published after that time, indeed from the very fact that he wrote and published the said book, therefore he was asked to freely tell the truth whether he holds or has held that opinion.

A: In regard to my writing of the *Dialogue* already published, I did not do so because I held Copernicus' opinion to be true. Instead, deeming only to be doing a beneficial service, I explained the physical

---

13. Galilei 1890–1909, 19: 361–362; translated by Finocchiaro (1989, 286–87).

and astronomical reasons that can be advanced for one side and for the other; I tried to show that none of these, neither those in favor of this opinion or that, had the strength of a conclusive proof and that therefore to proceed with certainty one had to resort to the determination of more subtle doctrines, as one can see in many places in the *Dialogue*. So for my part I conclude [362] that I do not hold and, after the determination of the authorities, I have not held the condemned opinion.

Having been told that from the book itself and the reasons advanced for the affirmative side, namely, that the earth moves and the sun is motionless, he is presumed, as it was stated, that he holds Copernicus' opinion, or at least that he held it at the time, therefore he was told that unless he decided to proffer the truth, one would have recourse to the remedies of the law and to appropriate steps against him.

A: I do not hold this opinion of Copernicus, and I have not held it after being ordered by injunction to abandon it. For the rest, here I am in your hands; do as you please.

And he was told to tell the truth, otherwise one would have recourse to torture.

A: I am here to obey, but I have not held this opinion after the determination was made, as I said.

And since nothing else could be done for the execution of the decision,[14] after he signed he was sent to his place.

I, Galileo Galilei, have testified as above.

§9.7 Inquisition's Sentence (22 June 1633)[15]

We: Gaspare Borgia, with the title of the Holy Cross in Jerusalem; Fra Felice Centini, with the title of Santa Anastasia, called d'Ascoli; Guido Bentivoglio, with the title of Santa Maria del Popolo; Fra Desiderio Scaglia, with the title of San Carlo, called di Cremona; Fra Antonio Barberini, called di Sant'Onofrio; Laudivio Zacchia, with the title of San Pietro in Vincoli, called di San Sisto; [403] Berlinghiero Gessi, with the title of Sant'Agostino; Fabrizio Verospi, with the title of San

---

14. That is, the pope's decision at the Inquisition meeting of 16 June, that Galileo be interrogated about his intention, under the formal threat of torture. Cf. Galilei 1890–1909, 19: 282–83, 360–61; Finocchiaro 2005, 247.
15. Galilei 1890–1909, 19: 402–6; translated by Finocchiaro (1989, 287–91).

Lorenzo in Panisperna, of the order of priests; Francesco Barberini, with the title of San Lorenzo in Damaso; and Marzio Ginetti, with the title of Santa Maria Nuova, of the order of deacons;

By the grace of God, Cardinals of the Holy Roman Church, and especially commissioned by the Holy Apostolic See as Inquisitors-General against heretical depravity in all of Christendom.

Whereas you, Galileo, son of the late Vincenzio Galilei, Florentine, aged seventy years, were denounced to this Holy Office in 1615 for holding as true the false doctrine taught by some that the sun is the center of the world and motionless and the earth moves even with diurnal motion; for having disciples to whom you taught the same doctrine; for being in correspondence with some German mathematicians about it; for having published some letters entitled *On Sunspots,* in which you explained the same doctrine as true; for interpreting Holy Scripture according to your own meaning in response to objections based on Scripture which were sometimes made to you; and whereas later we received a copy of an essay in the form of a letter, which was said to have been written by you to a former disciple of yours and which in accordance with Copernicus' position contains various propositions against the authority and true meaning of the Holy Scripture;

And whereas this Holy Tribunal wanted to remedy the disorder and the harm which derived from it and which was growing to the detriment of the Holy Faith, by order of His Holiness and the Most Eminent and Most Reverend Lord Cardinals of this Supreme and Universal Inquisition, the Assessor Theologians assessed the two propositions of the sun's stability and the earth's motion, as follows:

That the sun is the center of the world and motionless is a proposition which is philosophically absurd and false, and formally heretical, for being explicitly contrary to Holy Scripture;

That the earth is neither the center of the world nor motionless but moves even with diurnal motion is philosophically equally absurd and false, and theologically at least erroneous in the Faith.

Whereas however we wanted to treat you with benignity at that time, it was decided at the Holy Congregation held in the presence of His Holiness on 25 February 1616 that the Most Eminent Lord Cardinal Bellarmine would order you to abandon this false opinion completely; that if you refused to do this, the Commissary of the Holy Office would give you an injunction to abandon this doctrine, not to teach it to others, not to defend it, and not to treat of it; and that if you did not acquiesce in this injunction, you should be imprisoned. To execute this decision, the following day at the palace of and in the presence of the above-mentioned Most Eminent Lord Cardinal Bellarmine, after being informed and warned in a friendly way by the same Lord Cardinal, you were given an injunction by the then Father Commissary of the Holy Office [404] in the presence of a notary and witnesses to the effect that you must completely abandon the said false opinion, and that in the future you could neither hold, nor defend, nor teach it in any way whatever, either orally or in writing; having promised to obey, you were dismissed.

Furthermore, in order to do away completely with such a pernicious doctrine, and not let it creep any longer to the great detriment of Catholic truth, the Holy Congregation of the Index issued a decree which prohibited books treating of such a doctrine, and which declared it false and wholly contrary to the divine and Holy Scripture.

And whereas a book has appeared here lately, printed in Florence last year, whose inscription showed that you were the author, the title being *Dialogue by Galileo Galilei on the Two Chief World Systems, Ptolemaic and Copernican;* and whereas the Holy Congregation was informed that with the printing of this book the false opinion of the earth's motion and sun's stability was being disseminated and taking hold more and more every day, the said book was diligently examined and was found to violate explicitly the above-mentioned injunction given to you; for in the same book you have defended the said opinion already condemned and so declared to your face, although in the said book you try by means of various subterfuges to give the impression of leaving it undecided and labeled as probable; this is still a very serious error, since there is no way an opinion declared and defined contrary to divine Scripture may be probable.

Therefore, by our order you were summoned to this Holy Office, where, examined under oath, you acknowledged the book as written and published by you. You confessed that about ten or twelve years ago, after having been given the injunction mentioned above, you began writing the said book, and that you asked for permission to print it without explaining to those who gave you such permission that you were under the injunction of not holding, defending, or teaching such a doctrine in any way whatever.

Likewise, you confessed that in several places the exposition of the said book is expressed in such a way that a reader could get the idea that the arguments given for the false side were effective enough to be capable of convincing, rather than being easy to refute. Your excuses for having committed an error, as you said, so foreign from your intention, were that you had written in dialogue form, and that everyone feels a natural satisfaction for one's own subtleties and for showing oneself sharper than the average man by finding ingenious and apparently probable arguments even in favor of false propositions.

Having been given suitable terms to present your defense, you produced a certificate in the handwriting of the Most Eminent Lord Cardinal Bellarmine, which you said you obtained to defend yourself from the calumnies of your enemies, who were claiming that you had abjured and had been punished by the Holy Office. This [405] certificate says that you had neither abjured nor been punished, but only that you had been notified of the declaration made by His Holiness and published by the Holy Congregation of the Index, whose content is that the doctrine of the earth's motion and sun's stability is contrary to Holy Scripture and so can be neither defended nor held. Because this certificate does not contain the two phrases of the injunction, namely "to teach" and "in any way whatever," one is supposed to believe that in the course of fourteen or sixteen years you had lost any recollection of them, and that for this same reason you had been silent about the injunction when you applied for the license to publish the book. Furthermore, one is supposed to believe that you point out all of this not to excuse the error, but in order to have it attributed to conceited ambition rather than to malice. However, the said certificate you produced in your defense aggravates your case further since, while it says that the said opinion is contrary to Holy Scripture, yet you dared to treat of it, defend it, and show it as probable; nor are you helped by the license you artfully and cunningly extorted since you did not mention the injunction you were under.

Because we did not think you had said the whole truth about your intention, we deemed it necessary to proceed against you by a rigorous examination. Here you answered in a Catholic manner, though without prejudice to the above-mentioned things confessed by you and deduced against you about your intention.

Therefore, having seen and seriously considered the merits of your case, together with the above-mentioned confessions and excuses and with any other reasonable matter worth seeing and considering, we have come to the final sentence against you given below.

Therefore, invoking the Most Holy name of Our Lord Jesus Christ and of his most glorious Mother, ever Virgin Mary; and sitting as a tribunal, with the advice and counsel of the Reverend Masters of Sacred Theology and the Doctors of both laws, our consultants; in this written opinion we pronounce final judgment on the case pending before us between the Magnificent Carlo Sinceri, Doctor of both laws, and Prosecuting Attorney of this Holy Office, on one side, and you the above-mentioned Galileo Galilei, the culprit here present, examined, tried, and confessed as above, on the other side:

We say, pronounce, sentence, and declare that you, the above-mentioned Galileo, because of the things deduced in the trial and confessed by you as above, have rendered yourself according to this Holy Office vehemently suspected of heresy,[16] namely of having held and believed a doctrine which is false and contrary to the divine and Holy Scripture: that the sun is the center of the world and does not move from east to west, and the earth moves and is not the center of the world, and that one may hold and defend as probable an opinion after it has been declared and defined contrary to Holy Scripture. Consequently you have incurred all the censures and penalties imposed and promulgated by the sacred canons and all particular and general laws against such delinquents. We are willing to absolve you from them provided that first, with a sincere heart and unfeigned faith, in front of us you abjure, curse, and detest the above-mentioned errors and [406] heresies, and every other error and heresy contrary to the Catholic and Apostolic Church, in the manner and form we will prescribe to you.

Furthermore, so that this serious and pernicious error and transgression of yours does not remain completely unpunished, and so that you will be more cautious in the future and an example for others to abstain from similar crimes, we order that the book *Dialogue* by Galileo Galilei be prohibited by public edict.

We condemn you to formal imprisonment in this Holy Office at our pleasure. As a salutary penance we impose on you to recite the seven penitential Psalms once a week for the next three years. And we reserve the authority to moderate, change, or condone wholly or in part the above-mentioned penalties and penances.

This we say, pronounce, sentence, declare, order, and reserve by this or any other better manner or form that we reasonably can or shall think of.

---

16. "Vehement suspicion of heresy" was a technical term meaning a specific category of religious crime, second in seriousness only to "formal heresy."

So we the undersigned[17] Cardinals pronounce: Felice Cardinal d'Ascoli; Guido Cardinal Bentivoglio; Fra Desiderio Cardinal di Cremona; Fra Antonio Cardinal di Sant'Onofrio; Berlinghiero Cardinal Gessi; Fabrizio Cardinal Verospi; Marzio Cardinal Ginetti.

§9.8 Galileo's Abjuration (22 June 1633)[18]

I, Galileo, son of the late Vincenzio Galilei of Florence, seventy years of age, arraigned personally for judgment, kneeling before you Most Eminent and Most Reverend Cardinals Inquisitors-General against heretical depravity in all of Christendom, having before my eyes and touching with my hands the Holy Gospels, swear that I have always believed, I believe now, and with God's help I will believe in the future all that the Holy Catholic and Apostolic Church holds, preaches, and teaches. However, whereas, after having been judicially instructed with injunction by the Holy Office to abandon completely the false opinion that the sun is the center of the world and does not move and the earth is not the center of the world and moves, and not to hold, defend, or teach this false doctrine in any way whatever, orally or in writing; and after having been notified that this doctrine is contrary to Holy Scripture; I wrote and published a book in which I treat of this already condemned doctrine and adduce very effective reasons in its favor, without refuting them in any way; therefore, I have been judged vehemently suspected of heresy, namely of having held and believed that the sun is the center of the world and motionless and the earth is not the center and moves.

Therefore, desiring to remove from the minds of Your Eminences and every faithful [407] Christian this vehement suspicion, rightly conceived against me, with a sincere heart and unfeigned faith I abjure, curse, and detest the above-mentioned errors and heresies, and in general each and every other error, heresy, and sect contrary to the Holy Church; and I swear that in the future I will never again say or assert, orally or in writing, anything which might cause a similar suspicion about me; on the contrary, if I should come to know any

---

17. Note that only seven out of the ten cardinals in the commission signed the sentence. This fact is worthy of further reflection. See, for example, Santillana 1955, 310–11; Langford 1966, 153; Redondi 1987, 260–61.
18. Galilei 1890–1909, 19: 406–7; translated by Finocchiaro (1989, 292–93).

heretic or anyone suspected of heresy, I will denounce him to this Holy Office, or to the Inquisitor or Ordinary of the place where I happen to be.

Furthermore, I swear and promise to comply with and observe completely all the penances which have been or will be imposed upon me by this Holy Office; and should I fail to keep any of these promises and oaths, which God forbid, I submit myself to all the penalties and punishments imposed and promulgated by the sacred canons and other particular and general laws against similar delinquents. So help me God and these Holy Gospels of His, which I touch with my hands.

I, the above mentioned Galileo Galilei, have abjured, sworn, promised, and obliged myself as above; and in witness of the truth I have signed with my own hand the present document of abjuration and have recited it word for word in Rome, at the convent of the Minerva, this twenty-second day of June 1633.

I, Galileo Galilei, have abjured as above, by my own hand.

CHAPTER 10

From *Two New Sciences* (1638)[1]

[§10.1 Day I: The Problem of Scaling][2]

[49] SALV. The constant activity which you Venetians display in your famous shipyard suggests to the studious mind a large field of philosophizing, especially the part that involves mechanics. For in this department all types of instruments and machines are constantly being constructed by many artisans, among whom there must be some who, partly by inherited experience and partly by their own observations, have acquired the highest expertise and the most refined reasoning ability.

SAGR. You are quite right. Indeed, I myself, being curious by nature, frequently visit this place for the mere pleasure of observing the work of those who, on account of their superiority over other artisans, we call "first-rank men." Meeting with them has often helped me in the investigation of the reason for certain effects, including not only those that are striking, but also those that are recondite and almost incredible. At times also I have been put to confusion and driven to despair of ever explaining something for which I could not account, but which my senses told me to be true. And notwithstanding the fact that what the old man told us a little while ago is proverbial and commonly accepted, yet it seemed to me altogether false, like many other sayings that are current among the ignorant; for I think they say these things [50] in order to give the appearance of knowing something about matters which they do not understand.

SALV. You refer, perhaps, to that last remark of his when we asked the reason why they employed supports, scaffolding, and bracings of larger dimensions for launching a big vessel than they do for a

---

1. For the historical background, see the Introduction, especially §0.2 and the end of §0.9.
2. Galilei 1890–1909, 8: 49–54; translated by Crew and De Salvio (1914, 1–6); revised by Finocchiaro for this volume.

small one. He answered that they did this in order to avoid the danger of the ship parting under the heavy weight of its great size, a danger to which small boats are not subject.

SAGR.   Yes, that is what I mean. I refer especially to his last assertion, which I have always regarded as a false, though popular, opinion. That is, that in dealing with these and other similar machines one cannot argue from the small to the large, because many devices that succeed on a small scale do not work on a large scale. Now, since all reasoning in mechanics has its foundation in geometry, I do not see that the properties of circles, triangles, cylinders, cones, and other solid figures will change with their size. If, therefore, a large machine be constructed in such a way that its parts bear to one another the same ratio as in a smaller one, and if the smaller is sufficiently strong for the purpose for which it was designed, I do not see why the larger also should not be able to withstand any severe and destructive tests to which it may be subjected.

SALV.   The common opinion is here absolutely wrong. Indeed, it is so far wrong that precisely the opposite is true, namely, that many machines can be constructed even more perfectly on a large scale than on a small; for instance, a clock that indicates and strikes the hour can be made more accurate on a large scale than on a small. There are some intelligent people who maintain this same opinion, but on more reasonable grounds, when they cut loose from geometry and argue that the better performance of the large machine is owing to the imperfections and variations of the material. [51] Here I trust you will not charge me with arrogance if I say that imperfections in the material, even those that are great enough to invalidate the clearest mathematical proof, are not sufficient to explain the deviations observed between machines in the concrete and in the abstract. Yet I shall say it and will affirm that, even if the imperfections did not exist and matter were absolutely perfect, unalterable, and free from all accidental variations, still the mere fact that it is matter makes the larger machine, built of the same material and in the same proportion as the smaller, correspond exactly to the smaller in every respect except that it will not be so strong or so resistant against violent treatment; the larger the machine, the greater its weakness. Since I assume matter to be unchangeable and always the same, it is clear that we are no less able to treat this constant and invariable property in a rigorous manner than if it belonged to simple and pure mathematics.

Therefore, Sagredo, you would do well to change the opinion which you, and perhaps also many other students of mechanics, have entertained concerning the ability of machines and structures to resist external disturbances; namely, that when they are built of the same material and maintain the same ratio between parts, they are able equally, or rather, proportionally, to resist or yield to such external disturbances and blows. For we can demonstrate by geometry that the large machine is not proportionately stronger than the small. Finally, we may say that, for every machine and structure, whether artificial or natural, there is set a necessary limit beyond which neither art nor nature can pass; it is here understood, of course, that the material is the same and the proportion is preserved.

SAGR.   My brain already reels. My mind, like a cloud momentarily illuminated by a lightning flash, is for an instant filled with an unusual light, which beckons to me and suddenly mingles and obscures strange and crude ideas. From what you have said it appears to me impossible to build [52] two similar structures of the same material but of different sizes, and have them proportionately strong; and if this were so, it would also not be possible to find even two poles made of the same wood that shall be alike in strength and resistance but unequal in size.

SALV.   So it is, Sagredo. But let us make sure we understand each other. I say that if we take a wooden rod of a certain length and breadth, fitted into a wall at right angles, i.e., parallel to the horizon, and we reduce it to such a length that it will just support itself (so that if a hair's breadth be added to its length it will break under its own weight), then it will be the only rod of the kind in the world. Thus if, for instance, its length be a hundred times its breadth, you will not be able to find another rod whose length is also a hundred times its breadth and which, like the former, is just able to sustain its own weight and no more. Rather, all the larger ones will break, while all the smaller ones will be strong enough to support something more than their own weight. And what I have said about the ability to support itself must be understood to apply also to other cases; so that if a scantling will carry the weight of ten equal to itself, a beam having the same proportions will not be able to support ten equal beams.

Please observe, gentlemen, how facts that at first seem improbable will, even on scant explanation, drop the cloak that has hidden them and stand forth in naked and simple beauty. Who does not know that a horse falling from a height of three or four cubits will break his bones, while a dog falling from the same height or a cat from a height of eight or ten cubits will suffer no injury? Equally harmless would be the fall of a grasshopper from a tower or the fall of an ant from the distance of the moon. Do not children fall with impunity from heights that would cost their elders a broken leg or perhaps a fractured skull? And just as smaller animals are proportionately stronger and more robust than the larger, so also smaller plants are able to stand up better than larger. I am certain you both know that an oak two hundred cubits high would not be able to sustain its own branches if they were distributed as in a tree of ordinary size; and that [53] nature cannot produce a horse as large as twenty ordinary horses or a giant ten times taller than an ordinary man, unless by miracle or by greatly altering the proportions of the limbs and especially of the bones, which would have to be thickened way beyond their ordinary symmetry. Likewise the current belief that, in the case of artificial machines, the very large and the very small are equally feasible and lasting is a manifest error. Thus, for example, small spires, columns, and other solid figures can certainly be handled, laid down, and set up without danger of breaking, while the large ones will go to pieces under the slightest provocation, and that purely on account of their own weight.

And here I must relate a story that is worthy of your attention, as indeed are all events that happen contrary to expectation, especially when a precautionary measure turns out to be a cause of disaster. A very large marble column was laid out so that its two ends rested each upon a piece of beam. A little later it occurred to a mechanic that, in order to be doubly sure of its not breaking in the middle by its own weight, it would be wise to lay a third support midway. This seemed to all an excellent idea. But the sequel showed that it was quite the opposite, for not many months passed before the column was found cracked and broken exactly above the new middle support.

SIMP.   A very remarkable and thoroughly unexpected accident, especially if caused by placing that new support in the middle.

SALV.   Surely this is the explanation, and the moment the cause is known our surprise vanishes. For when the two pieces of the column were placed on level ground it was observed that one of the end beams had, after a long while, become decayed and sunken, but that the middle one remained hard and strong, thus causing one half of the column to project in the air without any support; thus, its own weight made it behave differently from what it would have done if supported only upon the first two beams, because no matter how much they might have sunk the column would have gone with them. There is no doubt that this accident would not have happened to a small column, even though made of the same stone and having a length [54] relative to its thickness preserving the ratio between length and thickness found in the large pillar.

SAGR.   I am quite convinced of the facts of the case, but I do not understand the reason why the strength and resistance are not multiplied in the same proportion as the size of the material. And I am the more puzzled because, on the contrary, I have noticed in other cases that the strength and resistance against breaking increase in a larger ratio than the size[3] of material. For instance, if two nails be driven into a wall, the one that is twice as big as the other will support not only twice as much weight as the other, but three or four times as much.

SALV.   Indeed you will not be far wrong if you say eight times as much; nor does this phenomenon contradict the other even though in appearance they seem so different.

SAGR.   Will you not then, Salviati, remove these difficulties and clear away these obscurities if possible? For I imagine that this problem of resistance opens up a field of beautiful and useful ideas. And if you are willing to make this the subject of today's reasoning, you will place Simplicio and me under many obligations.

SALV.   I am at your service if only I can call to mind what I learned from our Academician, who has thought much upon this subject; and according to his custom, he has demonstrated everything by geometrical methods, so that one might fairly call this a new science. For, although some of his conclusions had been reached by others, first of all by Aristotle, these are not the most beautiful, and what is more important, they had not been proven by necessary demonstrations from fundamental and indubitable principles. Now, since I wish to assure you by means of demonstrations rather than to persuade you by mere probable reasoning, I shall suppose that you are familiar with present-day mechanics so far as it is needed in our discussion.

---

3. Here I follow Drake (1974, 15) in translating *ingrossamento della materia* as increase of the *size* of material, rather than increase of the *amount* of material, as Crew and De Salvio (1914, 6) have it.

[§10.2 Day I: Critique of Aristotle's Law of Fall][4]

[105] SAGR.   I quite agree with the Peripatetic philosophers in denying the penetrability of matter. As to the vacuum, I should like to
hear a thorough discussion of Aristotle's demonstration in which he
opposes it and what you, Salviati, have to say in reply. I beg of you,
Simplicio, that you give us the precise proof of the Philosopher and
that you, Salviati, give us the reply.

SIMP.   So far as I remember, Aristotle[5] inveighs against the ancient view that a vacuum is a necessary prerequisite for motion and
that the latter could not occur without the former. In opposition to
this view Aristotle shows that it is precisely the phenomenon of motion, as we shall see, which renders untenable the idea of a vacuum.
His procedure is the following. He begins with two assumptions. The
first concerns bodies of different weights moving in the same
medium; the second, one and the same body [106] moving in different media. In the first case he supposes bodies of different weights to
move in one and the same medium with different speeds that stand to
one another in the same ratio as the weights; so that, for example, a
body that is ten times as heavy as another will move ten times as rapidly as the other. In the second case he assumes that the speeds of one
and the same body moving in different media are in inverse ratio to
the densities of these media; thus, for instance, if the density of water
were ten times that of air, the speed in air would be ten times greater
than in water. From this second supposition, he gives the following
demonstration: since the thinness of a vacuum differs infinitely from
that of any medium filled with matter however rare, any body that
moves in a plenum through a certain space in a certain time ought to
move through a vacuum instantaneously; but instantaneous motion is
an impossibility; it is therefore impossible that the existence of a vacuum should result from the existence of motion.

SALV.   The argument is, as you see, ad hominem; that is, it is directed against those who thought the vacuum a prerequisite for motion. Now if I admit the argument to be conclusive and concede also
that motion cannot take place in a vacuum, the assumption of a

4. Galilei 1890–1909, 8: 105–13; translated by Crew and De Salvio (1914,
61–68); revised by Finocchiaro for this volume.
5. Aristotle, *Physics*, IV, 6–9, 213a11–216b21.

vacuum considered absolutely and not with reference to motion is not thereby invalidated. But to tell you what the ancients might possibly have replied and in order to better understand just how conclusive Aristotle's demonstration is, we may, in my opinion, deny both of his assumptions. And as to the first, I greatly doubt that Aristotle ever tested by experiment whether it be true that two stones, one weighing ten times as much as the other, if allowed to fall at the same instant from a height of, say, one hundred cubits, would so differ in speed that when the heavier had reached the ground, the other would not have fallen more than ten cubits.

SIMP.   His language would seem to indicate that he had tried the experiment, because he says, "we see the heavier"; now the word *see* shows that he had made the experiment.

SAGR.   But I, Simplicio, who have made the test can assure you [107] that a cannon ball weighing one or two hundred pounds, or even more, will not reach the ground by as much as a span ahead of a musket ball weighing only half a pound, provided both are dropped from a height of two hundred cubits.

SALV.   But, even without further experiment, it is possible to prove clearly, by means of a short and conclusive argument, that a heavier body does not move more rapidly than a lighter one, provided both bodies are of the same material—in short, such as those mentioned by Aristotle. But tell me, Simplicio, whether you admit that each falling body acquires a definite speed fixed by nature, a velocity that cannot be increased or diminished except by the use of force or resistance.

SIMP.   There can be no doubt but that one and the same body moving in a single medium has a fixed velocity that is determined by nature and that cannot be increased except by the addition of some impetus or diminished except by some resistance that retards it.

SALV.   If then we take two bodies whose natural speeds are different, it is clear that on uniting the two, the more rapid one will be partly retarded by the slower, and the slower will be somewhat hastened by the swifter. Do you not agree with me in this opinion?

SIMP.   You are unquestionably right.

SALV.   But if this is true, and if a large stone moves with a speed of, say, eight units while a smaller moves with a speed of four, then when they are united, the system will move with a speed less than eight units. But the two stones when tied together make a stone larger than that which before moved with a speed of eight units. Hence the heavier body moves with less speed than the lighter—an effect that is contrary to [108] your supposition. Thus you see how, from your assumption that the heavier body moves more rapidly than the lighter one, I infer that the heavier body moves more slowly.

SIMP. I am all at sea because it appears to me that the smaller stone when added to the larger increases its weight, and by adding weight I do not see how it can fail to increase its speed or, at least, not to diminish it.

SALV. Here again you are in error, Simplicio, because it is not true that the smaller stone adds weight to the larger.

SIMP. This is, indeed, quite beyond my comprehension.

SALV. It will not be beyond you once I have shown you the equivocation under which you are laboring. Note that it is necessary to distinguish between heavy bodies in motion and the same bodies at rest. A large stone placed in a balance not only acquires additional weight by having another stone placed upon it, but even by the addition of a handful of hemp its weight is augmented six to ten ounces according to the quantity of hemp. But if you tie the hemp to the stone and allow them to fall freely from some height, do you believe that the hemp will press down upon the stone and thus accelerate its motion, or do you think the motion will be retarded by a partial upward pressure? One always feels the pressure upon his shoulders when he prevents the motion of a load resting upon him; but if one descends just as rapidly as the load would fall, how can it gravitate or press upon him? Do you not see that this would be the same as trying to strike a man with a lance when he is running away from you with a speed that is equal to, or even greater, than that with which you are following him? You must therefore conclude that, during free and natural fall, the small stone does not press upon the larger and consequently does not increase its weight as it does when at rest.

SIMP. But what if we should place the larger stone upon the smaller?

[109] SALV. Its weight would be increased if the larger stone moved more rapidly; but we have already concluded that when the small stone moves more slowly it retards to some extent the speed of the larger, so that the combination of the two, which is a heavier body than the larger of the two stones, would move less rapidly—a conclusion that is contrary to your hypothesis. We infer therefore that large and small bodies move with the same speed provided they are of the same specific gravity.

SIMP.   Your discussion is really admirable; yet I do not find it easy to believe that a bird-shot falls as swiftly as a cannon ball.

SALV.   Why not say a grain of sand as rapidly as a grindstone? But, Simplicio, I trust you will not follow the example of many others who divert the discussion from its main intent and fasten upon some statement of mine that lacks a hairsbreadth of the truth and, under this hair, hide the fault of someone else that is as big as a ship's cable. Aristotle says that "an iron ball of one hundred pounds falling from a height of one hundred cubits reaches the ground before a one-pound ball has fallen a single cubit." I say that they arrive at the same time. You find, on making the experiment, that the larger outstrips the smaller by two inches; that is, when the larger has reached the ground, the other is short of it by two inches. Now you would not hide behind these two inches the ninety-nine cubits of Aristotle, nor would you mention my small error and at the same time pass over in silence his very large one. Aristotle declares that bodies of different weights, in the same medium, travel (in so far as their motion depends upon gravity) with speeds that are proportional to their weights; this he illustrates by means of bodies in which it is possible to perceive the pure and unadulterated effect of gravity, disregarding other considerations such as shape and certain extremely small disturbances; these influences are greatly dependent upon the medium, which modifies the simple effect of gravity alone. Thus we observe that gold, the densest of all substances, when beaten out into a very thin leaf, goes floating through the air; the same thing happens with stone when ground into a very fine powder. But if you wish to maintain the general proposition, you will have to show that the [110] same ratio of speeds is preserved in the case of all heavy bodies, and that a stone of twenty pounds moves ten times as rapidly as one of two; and I claim that this is false and that, if they fall from a height of fifty or a hundred cubits, they will reach the ground at the same moment.

SIMP.   Perhaps the result would be different if the fall took place not from a few cubits but from some thousands of cubits.

SALV.   If this were what Aristotle meant, you would burden him with another error, which would amount to a lie. For there is no such sheer height available on earth, and so it is clear that Aristotle could not have made the experiment; yet he wishes to give us the impression of his having performed it when he speaks of such an effect as one which we see.

SIMP.   In fact, Aristotle does not employ this principle but uses the other one, which is not, I believe, subject to these same difficulties.

SALV.   But the other is as false as this one. And I am surprised that you yourself do not see the fallacy and do not perceive this. For if it were true that, in media of different densities and different resistances, such as water and air, one and the same body moved in air more rapidly than in water in proportion as the density of water is greater than that of air, then it would follow that any body that falls through air ought also to fall through water. But this conclusion is false inasmuch as many bodies that descend in air not only do not descend in water, but actually rise.

SIMP.   I do not understand the necessity of your inference; and in addition I will say that Aristotle discusses only those bodies that fall in both media, not those that fall in air but rise in water.

SALV.   The defense which you advance for the Philosopher is such that he himself would have certainly avoided it, so as not to aggravate his first mistake. But [111] tell me now whether the density of the water, or whatever it may be that retards the motion, bears a definite ratio to the density of air, which retards it less; and if so fix a value for it at your pleasure.

SIMP.   Such a ratio does exist. Let us assume it to be ten. Then, for a body that falls in both these media, the speed in water will be ten times slower than in air.

SALV.   I shall now take one of those bodies that fall in air but not in water, say a wooden ball, and I shall ask you to assign to it any speed you please for its descent through air.

SIMP.   Let us suppose it moves with a speed of twenty units.

SALV.   Very well. Then it is clear that this speed bears to some smaller speed the same ratio as the density of water bears to that of air; and the value of this smaller speed is two units. Thus really if we follow exactly the assumption of Aristotle, we ought to infer that the wooden ball that falls in air (a substance ten times less resisting than water) with a speed of twenty units would fall in water with a speed of two, instead of coming to the surface from the bottom as it does; unless perhaps you wish to reply, which I do not believe you will, that the rising of the wood through the water is the same as its falling with a speed of two units. But since the wooden ball does not go to the bottom, I think you will agree with me that we can find a ball of another material, not wood, which does fall in water with a speed of two.

SIMP.   Undoubtedly we can; but it must be of a substance considerably heavier than wood.

SALV.   That is it exactly. But if this second ball falls in water with
a speed of two units, what will be its speed of descent in air? If you
hold to the rule of Aristotle you must reply that it will move at the
rate of twenty units; but twenty is the speed which you yourself have
already assigned to the wooden ball; hence this and the other heavier
ball will each move through air with the same speed. But now how
does the Philosopher harmonize this result with his other, namely,
that bodies of different weight move through the same medium with
different speeds—speeds that are proportional to their weights? But
without going into the matter more deeply, how [112] have these
common and obvious properties escaped your notice? Have you not
observed that two bodies that fall in water, one with a speed a hundred times as great as that of the other, will fall in air with speeds so
nearly equal that one will not surpass the other by as much as one-
hundredth part? Thus, for example, an egg made of marble will descend in water one hundred times more rapidly than a hen's egg,
while in air falling from a height of twenty cubits the one will fall
short of the other by less than four inches. A heavy body that sinks
through ten cubits of water in three hours will traverse ten cubits of
air in one or two pulse beats. And if the heavy body be a ball of lead
it will easily traverse the ten cubits of water in less than double the
time required for ten cubits of air.

And here, Simplicio, I am sure you understand that there is no
room for hairsplitting or reply. We conclude, therefore, that the argument does not show anything against the existence of a vacuum. If
it did, it would only do away with vacuums of considerable size,
which neither I nor, in my opinion, the ancients ever believed to exist
in nature; but they might possibly be produced by force, as may be
gathered from various experiments whose description would here occupy too much time.

SAGR.   Seeing that Simplicio is silent, I will take the opportunity
of saying something. You have clearly demonstrated that bodies of
different weights do not move in one and the same medium with velocities proportional to their weights but that they all move with the
same speed; and here we understand of course that they are of the
same substance or at least of the same specific gravity, certainly not of
different specific gravities, for I hardly think you would have us believe a [113] ball of cork moves with the same speed as one of lead.

And you have clearly demonstrated that one and the same body moving through differently resisting media does not acquire speeds that are inversely proportional to the resistances. As a result, I am curious to learn what are the ratios actually observed in these two cases.

[§10.3 Day I: The Pendulum][6]

[127] SIMP.   I had thought the previous experiments left something to be desired; but now I am fully satisfied.

SALV.   The things set forth by me up to this point are new—in particular, my saying that differences of weight, even when very great, are without effect in changing the speed of falling bodies, so that as far as weight is concerned they all fall with equal speed. This idea is, I say, so new, and at first glance so remote from fact, that if we do not have the means of making it just as clear as sunlight, it had better not be mentioned; but having once allowed it to pass my lips, I must neglect no experiment or argument to corroborate it.

SAGR.   Not only this, but also many other of your views are so far removed from the commonly accepted opinions and doctrines that if you were to publish them, you would stir up a large number of antagonists; for human nature is such that men do not look with favor upon discoveries—either of truth or falsity—in their own field, when made by someone other than themselves. They call him an innovator of doctrine, an unpleasant title, by which they hope to cut those knots which they cannot untie, and by subterranean mines they seek to destroy structures which patient artisans have built with customary tools. [128] But as for ourselves who have no such thoughts, the experiments and arguments which you have thus far adduced are fully satisfactory; however, if you have any experiments that are more direct or any arguments that are more convincing, we will hear them with pleasure.

SALV.   The experiment made to ascertain whether two bodies differing greatly in weight will fall from a given height with the same speed offers some difficulty. For if the height is considerable, the retarding effect of the medium, which must be penetrated and thrust

---

6. Galilei 1890–1909, 8: 127–41; translated by Crew and De Salvio (1914, 83–98); revised by Finocchiaro for this volume.

aside by the falling body, will be greater in the case of the small momentum of the very light body than in the case of the great force of the very heavy body. Thus, in a long distance, the light body will be left behind; and if the height be small, one may well doubt whether there is any difference, and whether it will be observable even if there is.

It occurred to me, therefore, to repeat many times the fall through a small height in such a way that I might accumulate all those small intervals of time that elapse between the arrival of the heavy and light bodies respectively at their common terminus, so that this sum makes an interval of time that is not only observable, but easily observable. In order to employ the slowest speeds possible and thus reduce the change which the resisting medium produces upon the simple effect of gravity, it occurred to me to allow the bodies to fall along a plane slightly inclined to the horizontal; for in such a plane, just as well as in a vertical plane, one may discover how bodies of different weight behave. Besides this, I also wished to rid myself of the resistance that might arise from contact of the moving body with the aforesaid inclined plane.

Accordingly, I took two balls, one of lead and one of cork, the former more than a hundred times heavier than the latter, and suspended them by means of two equal fine threads, each four or five cubits long. Pulling each ball aside from the perpendicular, I let them go at the same instant, and they, falling along the circumferences of circles having these equal strings for radii, passed beyond the perpendicular and returned along the same path. This free oscillation repeated a hundred times showed clearly [129] that the heavy ball maintains so nearly the period of the light ball that neither in a hundred swings nor even in a thousand will the former anticipate the latter by as much as a single moment, so perfectly do they keep step. We can also observe the effect of the medium which, by the resistance which it offers to motion diminishes the oscillation of the cork more than that of the lead, but without altering the frequency of either; even when the arc traversed by the cork did not exceed five or six degrees and that of the lead fifty or sixty, the swings were performed in equal times.

SIMP.   If this be so, why is not the speed of the lead greater than that of the cork, seeing that the former traverses sixty degrees in the same interval in which the latter covers scarcely six?

SALV.   But what would you say, Simplicio, if both covered their paths in the same time when the cork, drawn aside through thirty degrees, traverses an arc of sixty, while the lead pulled aside only two degrees traverses an arc of four? Would not then the cork be proportionately swifter? And yet experiment shows that this is what happens. For note this.

Having pulled aside the pendulum of lead, say through an arc of fifty degrees, and set it free, it swings beyond the perpendicular almost fifty degrees, thus describing an arc of nearly one hundred degrees. On the return swing it describes a little smaller arc. And after a large number of such oscillations it finally comes to rest. Each oscillation, whether of ninety, fifty, twenty, ten, or four degrees, takes the same time. Accordingly, the speed of the moving body keeps on diminishing, since in equal intervals of time it traverses arcs that grow smaller and smaller.

Precisely the same things happen with the pendulum of cork suspended by a string of equal length, except that a smaller number of oscillations is required to bring it to rest, since on account of its lightness it is less able to overcome the resistance of the air. Nevertheless, the oscillations, whether large or small, are all performed in time intervals that are not only equal among themselves, but also equal to the period of the lead pendulum. Hence, if while the lead is traversing an arc of fifty degrees the cork covers one of only ten, it is true that the cork moves [130] more slowly than the lead; but on the other hand, it is also true that the cork covers an arc of fifty while the lead passes over one of only ten or six; thus, at different times, we have now the cork, now the lead, moving more rapidly. But if these same bodies traverse equal arcs in equal times, we may rest assured that their speeds are equal.

SIMP.   I hesitate to admit the conclusiveness of this argument because of the confusion that arises from your making both bodies move now rapidly, now slowly and now very slowly, which leaves me in doubt as to whether their velocities are always equal.

SAGR.   Allow me, if you please, Salviati, to say just a few words. Now tell me, Simplicio, whether you admit that one can say with certainty that the speeds of the cork and the lead are equal whenever both, starting from rest at the same moment and descending the same slopes, always traverse equal spaces in equal times?

SIMP.   This can neither be doubted nor gainsaid.

SAGR.   Now it happens, in the case of the pendulums, that each of them traverses now an arc of sixty degrees, now one of fifty, or thirty or ten or eight or four or two, etc.; and when they both swing through an arc of sixty degrees they do so in equal intervals of time; the same thing happens when the arc is fifty degrees or thirty or ten or any other number; and therefore we conclude that the speed of the lead in an arc of sixty degrees is equal to the speed of the cork when the latter also swings through an arc of sixty degrees; in the case of a fifty-degree arc these speeds are also equal to each other; so also in the case of other arcs. But this is not saying that the speed which occurs in an arc of sixty is the same as that which occurs in an arc of fifty; nor is the speed in an arc of fifty equal to that in one of thirty, etc.; but the smaller the arcs, the smaller the speeds; this is inferred from our sensibly seeing that one and the same moving body requires the same time for traversing a large arc of sixty degrees as for a small arc of fifty or even a very small arc of ten; all these arcs, indeed, are covered in the same interval of time. It is true therefore that [131] the lead and the cork each diminish their speed in proportion as their arcs diminish; but this does not contradict the fact that they maintain equal speeds in equal arcs.

My reason for saying these things has been rather because I wanted to learn whether I had correctly understood Salviati, than because I thought Simplicio had any need of a clearer explanation than that given by Salviati; like everything else of his, this is extremely lucid, and indeed such that when he solves questions that are difficult not merely in appearance, but in reality and in fact, he does so with reasons, observations, and experiments that are common and familiar to everyone. In this manner he has, as I have learned from various sources, given occasion to some highly esteemed professors for undervaluing his discoveries on the ground that they are commonplace and established upon a lowly and vulgar basis; as if it were not a most admirable and praiseworthy feature of the demonstrative sciences that they spring from and grow out of principles well known, understood, and conceded by all.

But let us continue with this light diet. If Simplicio is satisfied to understand and admit that the weight inherent in various falling bodies has nothing to do with the difference of speed observed among them, and that all bodies, insofar as their speeds depend upon it, would move with the same velocity, pray tell us, Salviati, how you explain the appreciable and evident inequality of motion. Please reply also to the objection urged by Simplicio—an objection in which I concur—namely, that a cannon ball falls more rapidly than a birdshot. Actually, this difference of speed is small as compared to the one

I have in mind: that is, bodies of the same substance moving through a single medium, such that the larger ones will descend, during a single pulse beat, a distance which the smaller ones will not traverse in an hour, or in four, or even in twenty hours; as for instance in the case of stones and fine sand, and especially that very fine sand that produces muddy water and that in many hours will not fall through as much as two cubits, a distance which stones not very large will traverse in a single pulse beat.

SALV.   The action of the medium in producing a greater retardation upon those bodies that have a smaller specific gravity has already been explained by showing that this results from a diminution of weight. But to explain how one and the same medium produces such different retardations in bodies [132] that are made of the same material and have the same shape, but differ only in size, requires a discussion more subtle than that by which one explains how a more expanded shape or an opposing motion of the medium retards the speed of the moving body. The solution of the present problem lies, I think, in the roughness and porosity that are generally and almost necessarily found in the surfaces of solid bodies. When the body is in motion these rough places strike the air or other ambient medium. The evidence for this is found in the humming that accompanies the rapid motion of a body through air, even when that body is as round as possible. One hears not only humming, but also hissing and whistling, whenever there is any appreciable cavity or elevation upon the body. We observe also that a round solid body rotating in a lathe produces a current of air. But what more do we need? When a top spins on the ground at its greatest speed, do we not hear a distinct buzzing of high pitch? This sibilant note diminishes in pitch as the speed of rotation slackens, which is evidence that these small wrinkles on the surface meet resistance in the air. There can be no doubt, therefore, that in the motion of falling bodies these irregularities strike the surrounding fluid and retard the speed; and this they do so much the more in proportion as the surface is larger, which is the case of small bodies as compared with larger.

SIMP.   Stop a moment please, as I am getting confused. For although I understand and admit that friction of the medium upon the surface of the body retards its motion and that, other things being equal, the larger surface suffers greater retardation, I do not see on what ground you say that the surface of the smaller body is larger. Besides, if, as you say, the larger surface suffers greater retardation, the larger solid should move more slowly, which is not the case. But this objection can be easily met by saying that, although the larger body has a larger surface, it has also a greater weight, in comparison with which the resistance of the larger surface is no more than the resistance of the small surface in comparison with its smaller weight; so the speed of the larger solid does not become less. I therefore see no reason for expecting any difference [133] of speed so long as the driving weight diminishes in the same proportion as the retarding power of the surface.

SALV.   I shall answer all your objections at once. You will admit, of course, Simplicio, that if we take two equal bodies of the same material and same shape (bodies that would therefore fall with equal speeds), and if we diminish the weight of one of them in the same proportion as its surface (maintaining the similarity of shape), we would not thereby diminish the speed of this body.

SIMP.   This inference seems to be in harmony with your theory, which states that the weight of a body has no effect in either accelerating or retarding its motion.

SALV.   I quite agree with you in this opinion, from which it appears to follow that if the weight of a body is diminished in greater proportion than its surface, the motion is retarded to a certain extent; and this retardation is greater and greater in proportion as the diminution of weight exceeds that of the surface.

SIMP.   This I admit without hesitation.

SALV.   Now you must know, Simplicio, that it is not possible to diminish the surface of a solid body in the same ratio as the weight, and at the same time maintain similarity of shape. For since it is clear that in the case of a diminishing solid the weight grows less in proportion to the volume, if the volume diminishes more rapidly than the surface (and the same shape is maintained) then the weight must diminish more rapidly than the surface. But geometry teaches us that, in the case of similar solids, the ratio of the volumes is greater than the ratio of their surfaces; which, for the sake of better understanding, I shall illustrate by a particular case.

Take, for example, a cube two inches on a side, so that each face has an area of four square inches and the total area, i.e., the sum of the six faces, amounts to twenty-four square inches. Now imagine this cube to be sawed through three times so as to divide it into eight smaller cubes: each is one inch on the side; each face is one square inch; and the total [134] surface of each cube is six square inches, instead of twenty-four as in the case of the larger cube. It is evident that the surface of the little cube is only one-fourth that of the larger, namely, the ratio of six to twenty-four; but the volume of the smaller cube is only one-eighth that of the large one; the volume, and hence also the weight, diminishes therefore much more rapidly than the surface. If we now divide the little cube into eight others, we shall have, for the total surface of one of these, one and one-half square inches, which is one-sixteenth of the surface of the original cube; but its volume is only one-sixty-fourth. Thus, by two divisions, you see that the volume is diminished four times as much as the surface. And if the subdivision be continued until the original solid be reduced to a fine powder, we shall find that the weight of one of these smallest particles has diminished hundreds and hundreds of times as much as its surface. And this, which I have illustrated in the case of cubes, holds also in the case of all similar solids, where the volumes are to each other as the three-halves power of their surfaces.

Thus you see how much greater is the resistance, arising from contact of the surface of the moving body with the medium, in the case of small bodies than in the case of large. And when one considers that the irregularities on the very small surfaces of fine dust particles are perhaps no smaller than those on the surfaces of larger solids that have been carefully polished, one will see how important it is that the medium should be very fluid and offer no resistance to being thrust aside, easily yielding to a small force. You see, therefore, Simplicio, that I was not mistaken when, not long ago, I said that the surface of a small solid is comparatively greater than that of a large one.

SIMP.   I am quite convinced. And believe me, if I were again beginning my studies, I should follow the advice of Plato and start with the mathematical sciences, which proceed very cautiously and admit nothing as established until it has been rigorously demonstrated.

SAGR.   This discussion has afforded me great pleasure. But before proceeding further, I should like to hear the explanation . . .[7]

[139] SALV.   Let us see whether we cannot derive from the pendulum a satisfactory solution of all these difficulties. And first, as to the question whether one and the same pendulum really performs its oscillations, large, medium, and small, all in exactly the same time, I

---

7. Here I am omitting the passage in Galilei 1890–1909, 8: 134.33–139.7; Crew and De Salvio 1914, 91–95.

shall rely upon what I have already heard from our Academician. He has clearly shown that the time of descent is the same along all chords, whatever the arcs that subtend them, whether the arc is 180 degrees (corresponding to the whole diameter), 100 degrees, 60 degrees, 10 degrees, 2 degrees, 1/2 degree, or 4 minutes; it is understood, of course, that these chords all terminate at the lowest point of the circle, where it touches the horizontal plane.

Now, if we consider descent along arcs instead of their chords, then (provided they do not exceed ninety degrees) experiment shows that they are all traversed in equal times; but these times are shorter for the arcs than for the chords, an effect that is all the more remarkable because at first glance one would think just the opposite to be true. For since the terminal points of the two motions are the same and since the straight line included between these two points is the shortest distance between them, it would seem reasonable that motion along this line should be executed in the shortest time; but this is not the case, for the shortest time—and therefore the most rapid motion—is that employed along the arc of which this straight line is the chord.

As to the times of oscillation of bodies suspended by threads of different lengths, they bear to each other the same proportion as the square roots of the lengths of the thread; or one might say the lengths are to each other as the squares of the times. For example, if one wishes to make the oscillation time of one pendulum twice that of another, one must make its suspension thread four times [140] as long; in like manner, if one pendulum has a thread nine times as long as another, this second pendulum will execute three oscillations during each one of the first. From this it follows that the lengths of the suspending cords bear to each other the [inverse] ratio of the squares of the number of oscillations performed in the same time.

SAGR.   Then, if I understand you correctly, I can easily measure the length of a string whose upper end is attached at any height whatever even if this end were invisible and I could see only the lower extremity. For if I attach to the lower end of this string a rather heavy weight and give it a to-and-fro motion, and if I ask a friend to count the number of its oscillations while I, during the same time interval, count the number of oscillations of a pendulum which is exactly one cubit in length, then knowing the number of oscillations which each pendulum makes in the given interval of time one can determine the length of the string. Suppose, for example, that my friend counts 20 oscillations of the long cord during the same time in which I count

240 of my string, which is one cubit in length; taking the squares of the two numbers, 20 and 240, namely, 400 and 57,600, then, I say, the long string contains 57,600 units of length as compared to the 400 contained in my string; and since the length of my string is one cubit, I shall divide 57,600 by 400 and thus obtain 144. Accordingly, I shall call the length of the other string 144 cubits.

SALV.   Nor will you miss it by as much as a palm's breadth, especially if you observe a large number of oscillations.

SAGR.   You give me frequent occasion to admire the wealth and profusion of nature when, from such common and even trivial phenomena, you derive facts that are not only striking and new but that are often far removed from what we would have imagined. Thousands of times I have observed, especially in churches, oscillations of lamps suspended by long cords and inadvertently set into motion. But the most I could infer from these observations was the improbability of the view of those who think that such oscillations are maintained by the medium, namely, the air; for, in that case, the air must needs have considerable judgment and little else to do but kill [141] time by pushing back and forth a hanging weight with perfect regularity. But I never dreamed of learning that one and the same body, when suspended from a string a hundred cubits long and pulled aside first through an arc of ninety degrees and then through one degree or half a degree, would employ the same time in passing through the least as through the largest of these arcs; indeed, it still strikes me as almost impossible. Now I am waiting to hear how these same simple phenomena can furnish solutions for those acoustical problems—solutions that will be at least partly satisfactory.

SALV.   First of all one must observe that each pendulum has its own time of oscillation so definite and determinate that it is not possible to make it move with any other period than that which nature has given it. For let anyone take in his hand a cord to which a weight is attached and try, as much as he pleases, to increase or diminish the frequency of its oscillations; it will be time wasted. On the other hand, one can confer motion upon even a heavy pendulum that is at rest by simply blowing against it; by repeating these blasts with a frequency which is the same as that of the pendulum, one can impart considerable motion. Suppose that by the first puff we have displaced the pendulum from the vertical by, say, half an inch; then if we add a second puff after the pendulum has returned and is about to begin the second oscillation, we shall impart additional motion; and so on with other blasts provided they are applied at the right instant, and not when the pendulum is coming toward us, since in this case the blast would impede rather than aid the motion. Continuing thus with many impulses, we impart to the pendulum such impetus that a much greater force than that of a single blast will be needed to stop it.

[§10.4 Day II: The Mathematics of Strength, Size, and Weight][8]

[151] SAGR.   While Simplicio and I were awaiting your arrival, we were trying to recall that last consideration which you advanced as a principle and basis for the results you intended to obtain. This consideration dealt with the resistance which all solids offer to fracture, and which depends upon a certain cement that holds the parts glued together so that they yield and separate only under considerable pull. Later we tried to find the explanation for this coherence, seeking it mainly in the vacuum. This was the occasion of our many digressions, which occupied the entire day and led us far afield from the original subject. As I have already stated, that was the investigation of the resistance which solids offer to fracture.

SALV.   I remember it all very well. Resuming the thread of our discussion, whatever the nature of this resistance which solids offer to powerful pulling, there can at least be no doubt of its existence. And although this resistance is very great in the case of a direct pull, it is found, as a rule, to be less in the case of bending forces. Thus, for example, a rod of steel or of glass will sustain a longitudinal pull of a thousand pounds, whereas a weight of fifty pounds would be quite sufficient to break it if the rod were fastened at right angles into a vertical wall. It is this second type of resistance which we must consider, seeking to discover in [152] what proportion it is found in prisms and cylinders of the same material, whether alike or unlike in shape, length, and thickness. In this discussion I shall take for granted the well-known mechanical principle that has been shown to govern the behavior of a lever, namely, that the force bears to the resistance the inverse ratio of the distances that separate the fulcrum from the force and resistance respectively.

---

8. Galilei 1890–1909, 8: 151–71; translated by Crew and De Salvio (1914, 109–33); revised by Finocchiaro for this volume.

SIMP.   This was demonstrated first of all by Aristotle, in his *Questions of Mechanics.*[9]

SALV.   Yes, I am willing to concede him priority in point of time. But as regards rigor of demonstration, the first place must be given to Archimedes, since upon a single proposition proved in his book *On the Equilibrium of Planes* depends not only the explanation of the lever, but also those of most other mechanical devices.[10]

SAGR.   Now, since this principle is fundamental to all the demonstrations which you propose to set forth, would it not be advisable to give us a complete and thorough proof of this proposition, unless possibly it would take too much time?

SALV.   Yes, that would be quite proper. But it is better, I think, to approach our subject in a manner somewhat different from that employed by Archimedes. That is, I shall assume merely that equal weights placed in a balance of equal arms will produce equilibrium— a principle also assumed by Archimedes—and then prove two things: that it is no less true that unequal weights produce equilibrium when the arms of the steelyard have lengths inversely proportional to the weights suspended from them; and that it amounts to the same thing whether one places equal weights at equal distances or unequal weights at distances that bear to each other the inverse ratio of the weights.

In order to make this matter clear, imagine a prism or solid cylinder, *AB*, suspended at each end to the rod *HI*, and supported by two threads *HA* and *IB*; it is evident that if I attach a thread, *C*, at the middle point of the balance beam *HI*, the entire prism *AB* will, according to the principle assumed, hang in equilibrium since one-half its weight lies on one side, and the other half on the other side, of the point of suspension *C*. Now suppose [153] the prism to be divided into unequal parts by a plane through the line *D*, and let the part *DA* be the larger and *DB* the smaller; this division having been made, imagine a thread *ED*, attached at the point *E* and supporting the parts *AD* and *DB*, in order that these parts may remain in the same position relative to line *HI*; and since the relative position of the prism and the beam *HI* remains unchanged, there can be no doubt but that the prism will maintain its former state of equilibrium. But circumstances would remain the same if that part of the prism which is now held

---

9. Pseudo-Aristotle, *Questions of Mechanics*, no. 3.
10. Archimedes, *On the Equilibrium of Planes*, book 1, propositions 6–7.

up at the ends by the
threads *AH* and *DE* were
supported at the middle by
a single thread *GL*; and
likewise the other part *DB*
would not change position

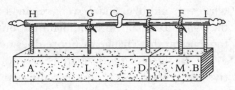

if held by a thread *FM* placed at its middle point. Suppose now the
threads *HA*, *ED*, and *IB* to be removed, leaving only the two *GL* and
FM; then the same equilibrium will be maintained so long as the suspension is at *C*. Now let us consider that we have here two heavy
bodies *AD* and *DB* hung at the ends *G* and *F* of a balance beam *GF*
in equilibrium about the point *C*, so that the line *CG* is the distance
from *C* to the point of suspension of the heavy body *AD*, while *CF*
is the distance at which the other heavy body, *DB*, is supported. It remains now only to show that these distances bear to each other the
inverse ratio of the weights themselves; that is, the distance *GC* is to
the distance *CF* as the prism *DB* is to the prism *DA*—a proposition
which we shall prove as follows. Since the line *GE* is half of *EH*, and
EF is half of *EI*, the whole length *GF* will be half of the entire line
HI, and therefore equal to *CI*; if now we subtract the common part
CF, the remainder *GC* will be equal to the remainder *FI*, that is, to
FE; and if to each of these we add *CE*, we shall have *GE* equal to
CF; hence *GE* is to *EF* as *FC* is to *CG*. But *GE* and *EF* bear the same
ratio to each other as do their doubles *HE* and *EI*, that is, the same
ratio as the prism *AD* to *DB*. Therefore, by equidistance of ratios[11]
and by inversion, we have that the distance *GC* is to the distance *CF*
as the weight *BD* is to the weight *DA*. This is what I desired to prove.

[154] If what precedes is clear, you will not hesitate, I think, to
admit that the two prisms *AD* and *DB* are in equilibrium about the
point *C* since one-half of the whole body *AB* lies on the right of the
suspension *C* and the other half on the left; in other words, this
arrangement is equivalent to two equal weights disposed at equal
distances. I do not see how anyone can doubt, if the two prisms *AD*
and *DB* were transformed into cubes, spheres, or any other figure

---

11. Here and in the rest of this chapter, *equidistance of ratios* translates Galileo's
phrase *egual proporzione*. With this rendition, I am adopting Drake's (1974,
xxxii, 111) translation, thus revising Crew and De Salvio's *equating ratios,* as
well as the traditional *ratio ex aequali*. This notion comes from Euclid, *Elements*, book 5, definition 17 and proposition 22. For the meaning, see the
Glossary.

whatever, and if G and F were retained as points of suspension, that they would remain in equilibrium about the point $C;$ for it is only too evident that change of figure does not produce change of weight so long as the quantity of matter does not vary. From this we may derive the general conclusion that any two heavy bodies are in equilibrium at distances that are inversely proportional to their weights.

This principle established, I desire, before going further, to call your attention to the fact that these forces, resistances, moments, figures, etc., may be considered either in the abstract, dissociated from matter, or in the concrete, associated with matter. Hence the properties which belong to figures that are merely geometrical and nonmaterial must be modified when we fill these figures with matter and so give them weight. Take, for example, the lever BA, which, resting upon the support E, is used to lift a heavy stone D. The principle just

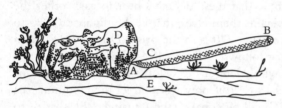

demonstrated makes it clear that a force applied at the extremity B will just suffice to balance the resistance offered by the heavy body D provided this force bears to the force at D the same ratio as the distance AC bears to the distance $CB;$ and this is true so long as we consider only the moments of the single force at B and of the resistance at D, treating the lever as an immaterial body devoid of weight. But if we take into account the weight of the lever itself—an instrument that may be made either of wood or of iron—it is manifest that, when this weight has been added to the force at B, [155] the ratio will be changed and must therefore be expressed in different terms. Hence before going further let us agree to distinguish between these two points of view: when we consider an instrument in the abstract, i.e., apart from the weight of its own matter, we shall speak of *taking it in an absolute sense;* but if we fill one of these simple and absolute figures with matter and thus give it weight, we shall refer to such a material figure as a *moment, or compound force.*

SAGR.   I must break my resolution about not leading you off into a digression, for I cannot concentrate my attention upon what is to follow until a certain doubt is removed from my mind. That is, you seem to compare the force at B with the total weight of the stone D, a part of which—possibly the greater part—rests upon the horizontal plane, so that . . .[12]

SALV.   I understand perfectly; you need go no further. However, please observe that I have not mentioned the total weight of the stone. I spoke only of its force at the point A, the extremity of the lever BA; this force is always less than the total weight of the stone and varies with its shape and elevation.

SAGR.   Good; but there occurs to me another question about which I am curious. For a complete understanding of this matter, I should like you to show me, if possible, how one can determine what part of the total weight is supported by the underlying plane and what part by the end A of the lever.

SALV.   The explanation will not delay us long, and I shall therefore be glad to grant your request. In the following figure, let us understand that the weight having its center of gravity at A rests with the end B upon the horizontal plane and with the other end upon the lever CG. Let N be the fulcrum of the lever to which a force is applied at G. Drop the perpendiculars, AO and CF, from the center A and the end C. Then, I say, the moment of the entire weight bears to the moment of the force at G a ratio compounded of the ratio between the two distances GN and NC

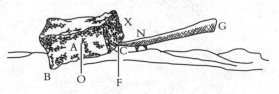

and the ratio between FB and BO.

Lay off a distance X such that the ratio of FB to BO is the same as that of NC to X. But since the total weight A is supported by the two forces at B and at C, [156] it follows that the force at B is to that at C as the distance FO is to the distance BO. Hence, by addition, the sum of the forces at B and C, that is, the total weight A, is to the force at C as the line FB is to the line BO, that is, as NC is to X. But the force applied at C is to the force applied at G as the distance GN is to the distance NC. Hence it follows, by perturbed equidistance of ratios,[13]

---

12. Ellipsis in the original, to indicate Salviati's interruption of Sagredo's speech.

13. Here and in the rest of this chapter, *perturbed equidistance of ratios* translates Galileo's phrase *proporzione perturbata*. With this rendition, I am adopting

that the entire weight A is to the force applied at G as the distance GN is to X. But the ratio of GN to X is compounded of the ratio of GN to NC and of NC to X, that is, of FB to BO. Hence the weight A bears to the supporting force at G a ratio compounded of that of GN to NC and of FB to BO. This is what had to be demonstrated.

Let us now return to our original subject. If what has hitherto been said is clear, it will be easily understood why the following (*Proposition 1*) is true: *A prism or solid cylinder of glass, steel, wood, or other breakable material, which is capable of sustaining a very heavy weight when applied longitudinally, is (as previously remarked) easily broken by the transverse application of a weight that may be much smaller in proportion as the length of the cylinder exceeds its thickness.*

Let us imagine a solid prism $ABCD$ fastened into a wall at the end AB, and supporting a weight E at the other end; understand also that the wall is vertical and that the prism or cylinder is fastened at right angles to the wall. It is

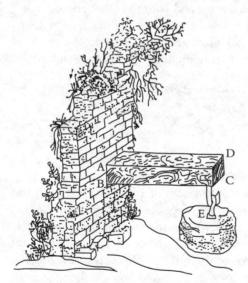

clear that if the prism breaks, fracture will occur at the point B where the edge of the slot in the wall acts as a fulcrum. The length BC acts as the part of the lever to which the force is applied. The thickness BA of the solid is the other arm of the lever in which is located the resistance. This resistance opposes the separation of the part of the solid BD lying outside the wall from the portion lying inside. From the preceding, it follows that the moment of the force applied at C bears to the moment of the

---

Drake's (1974, xxxiii, 114) translation, thus revising Crew and De Salvio's translation (which mostly uses the Latin phrase *ex aequali in proportione perturbata*), as well as the traditional *equality in perturbed proportion*. This notion again comes from Euclid, *Elements,* definition 18 and proposition 23. For the meaning, see the Glossary.

resistance found in the thickness of the prism (i.e., in the attachment of the base *BA* to its contiguous parts) the same ratio which the length *CB* bears to half of *BA*. [157] Now if we call absolute resistance to fracture that offered to a longitudinal pull (in which case the stretching force moves by the same amount as the stretched body), then we can say that the absolute resistance of the prism *BD* is to the breaking load placed at the end of the lever *BC* in the same ratio as the length *BC* is to the half of *AB* in the case of a prism, or the radius in the case of a cylinder. This is our first proposition.

Note that in what has here been said the weight of the solid *BD* itself has been left out of consideration, or rather, the prism has been assumed to be devoid of weight. But if the weight of the prism is to be taken into account in conjunction with the weight *E*, we must add to the weight *E* one half that of the prism *BD*. Thus, for example, if the latter weighs two pounds and the weight *E* is ten pounds, we must treat the weight *E* as if it were eleven pounds.

SIMP.   Why not twelve?

SALV.   The weight *E*, my dear Simplicio, hanging at the extreme end *C* acts upon the lever *BC* with its full moment of ten pounds. If suspended at the same point, the solid *BD* would also exert its full moment of two pounds. But as you know, this solid is uniformly distributed throughout its entire length, *BC*, so that the parts which lie near the end *B* are less effective than those more remote. Accordingly, if we strike a balance between the two, the weight of the entire prism may be considered as concentrated at its center of gravity, which lies at the midpoint of the lever *BC*. But a weight hung at the extremity *C* exerts a moment twice as great as it would if suspended from the middle. Therefore, [158] if we consider the moments of both as located at the end *C*, we must add to the weight *E* one-half that of the prism.

SIMP.   I understand perfectly. Moreover, if I am not mistaken, the force of the two weights *BD* and *E*, thus disposed, would exert the same moment as would the entire weight *BD* together with twice the weight *E* suspended at the middle of the lever *BC*.

SALV.   Precisely so, and a fact worth remembering. Now we can readily understand *Proposition 2: How and in what proportion a rod, or rather a prism, whose width is greater than its thickness offers more resistance to fracture when the force is applied in the direction of its width than in the direction of its thickness.*

For the sake of clarity, take a ruler *ad* whose width is *ac* and whose thickness, *cb*, is much less than its width. The question now is why

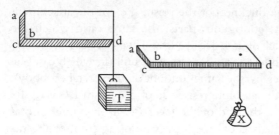

will the ruler, if stood on edge, as in the first figure, withstand a great weight *T*, while, when laid flat, as in the second figure, it will not support the weight *X*, which is less than *T*. The answer is evident when we remember that in the one case the fulcrum is at the line *bc*, and in the other case at *ca*, while the distance at which the force is applied is the same in both cases, namely, the length *bd*. But in the first case the distance of the resistance from the fulcrum—half the line *ca*—is greater than in the other case where it is only half of *bc*. Therefore, the weight *T* is greater than *X* in the same ratio as half the width *ca* is greater than half the thickness *bc*, since the former acts as a lever arm for *ca*, and the latter for *cb*, against the same resistance, namely, the strength of all the fibers in the cross section *ab*. We conclude, therefore, that any given ruler, or prism, whose width exceeds its thickness, will offer greater resistance to fracture when standing on edge than when lying flat, and this in the ratio of the width to the thickness.

Proposition 3: Consider now the case of a prism or cylinder lying horizontal and growing longer in a horizontal direction. We must find out in what ratio the moment of its own weight increases in comparison [159] with its resistance to fracture. This moment I find increases in proportion to the square of the length.

In order to prove this, let *AD* be a prism or cylinder lying horizontal with its end *A* firmly fixed in a wall. Let the length of the prism be increased by the addition of the portion *BE*. It is clear that merely changing the length of the lever from *AB* to *AC* will, if we disregard its weight, increase the moment of the force tending to produce fracture at A in the ratio of CA to BA. But, besides this, the weight of the solid portion BE, added to the weight of the solid AB, increases the moment of the total weight in the ratio of the weight of the prism AE to that of the prism AB, which is the same as the ratio of the length AC to AB. It follows, therefore, that, when the length and weight are simultaneously increased in any given proportion, the moment, which is the product of these two, is increased in a ratio that is the square of the preceding proportion. The conclusion is then that the bending moments due to the weight of prisms and cylinders that have the same thickness but different lengths bear to each other a ratio that is the square of the ratio of their lengths, or, what is the same thing, the ratio of the squares of their lengths.

We shall next show in what ratio the resistance to fracture in prisms and cylinders increases with increasing thickness while [160] the length remains unchanged. Here I say that (*Proposition 4*): *In prisms and cylinders of equal length but of unequal thicknesses, the resistance to fracture increases in the same ratio as the cube of the diameter of the thickness, i.e., of the base.*

Let A and B be two cylinders of equal lengths DG, FH; let their bases be unequal, namely, the circles with the diameters CD, EF. Then I say that the resistance to fracture offered by the cylinder B is to that offered by A as the cube of the diameter EF is to the cube of the diameter CD. For if we consider the resistance to fracture by longitudinal pull as dependent upon the bases, i.e., upon the circles EF and CD, no one can doubt that the resistance of the cylinder B is greater than that of A in the same proportion in which the area of the circle EF exceeds that of

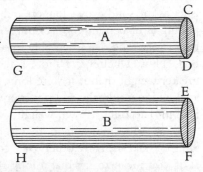

CD; this is so because it is precisely in this ratio that the number of fibers binding the parts of the solid together in the one cylinder exceeds that in the other cylinder. But in the case of a force acting transversely, it must be remembered that we are employing two levers in which the forces are applied at distances DG and FH, and the fulcrums are located at the points D and F; and the resistances act at distances that are equal to the radii of the circles CD and EF, since the fibers distributed over these entire cross sections act as if concentrated at the centers. Remembering this and remembering also that the arms, *DG* and *FH,* through which the forces *G* and *H* act are equal, we can understand that the resistance located at the center of the base *EF* and acting against the force H is greater than the resistance at the center of the base *CD* opposing the force *G* in the ratio of the radius *EF* to the radius *CD.* Accordingly, the resistance to fracture offered by the cylinder *B* is greater than that of the cylinder *A* in a ratio which is compounded of that of the area of the circles *EF* and *CD* and that of their radii, or of their diameters. But the areas of circles are as the squares of their diameters. Therefore, the ratio of the resistances, being the product of the two preceding ratios, is the same as that of the cubes [161] of the diameters. This is what I set out to prove.

Moreover, since the volume of a cube varies as the third power of its edge, we may say that the resistance of a cylinder whose length remains constant varies as the third power of its diameter. So from the preceding we are also able to derive a *Corollary: The resistance of a prism or cylinder of constant length varies as the three-halves power of its volume or weight.* This is evident as follows. The volume of a prism or cylinder of constant altitude varies directly as the area of its base, i.e., as the square of a side or diameter of this base. But as just demonstrated, the resistance varies as the cube of this same side or diameter. Hence, the resistance varies as the three-halves power of the volume—and consequently also of the weight—of the solid itself.

SIMP.   Before proceeding further I should like to have one of my difficulties removed. Up to this point you have not taken into consideration a certain other kind of resistance that, it appears to me, diminishes as the solid grows longer, and this is quite as true in the case of pulling as of bending. For example, in the case of a rope we observe that a very long one is less able to support a large weight than a short one. Thus, I believe, a short rod of wood or iron will support a greater weight than if it were long, provided that the force be always applied longitudinally and not transversely, and provided also that we take into account its own weight, which increases with its length.

SALV.   I fear, Simplicio, that in this particular you are making the same mistake as many others, if I correctly catch your meaning; that is, if you mean to say that a long rope, one of perhaps forty cubits, cannot hold up so great a weight as a shorter length, say one or two cubits, of the same rope.

SIMP.   That is what I meant, and as far as I see the proposition is highly probable.

SALV.   On the contrary, I consider it not merely improbable but false; and I think I can easily convince you of your error. Let *AB* represent the rope, fastened at the upper end *A*. At the lower end, attach a weight *C* whose force is just sufficient to break the rope. Now, Simplicio, point out the exact place where you think the break ought to occur.

[162] SIMP.   Let us say *D*.

SALV.   And why at *D*?

SIMP.   Because at this point the rope is not strong enough to support, say, one hundred pounds, made up of the portion of the rope *DB* and the stone *C*.

SALV.   Accordingly, whenever the rope is stretched with the weight of one hundred pounds at *D*, it will break there.

SIMP.   I think so.

SALV.   But tell me, if instead of attaching the weight at the end of the rope, *B*, one fastens it at a point nearer *D*, say, at *E*; or if instead of fixing the upper end of the rope at *A*, one fastens it at some point *F*, just above *D*; will not the rope, at the point *D*, be subject to the same pull of one hundred pounds?

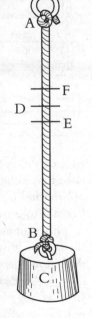

SIMP.   It would, provided you include with the stone *C* the portion of rope *EB*.

SALV.   Let us therefore suppose that the rope is stretched at the point *D* with a weight of one hundred pounds. Then, according to your own admission, it will break. But *FE* is only a small portion of *AB*. How can you therefore maintain that the long rope is weaker than the short one? Give up then this erroneous view which you share with many very intelligent people, and let us proceed.

We have already demonstrated that in the case of prisms and cylinders of constant thickness, the moment of force tending to produce fracture varies as the square of the length; and likewise we have shown that when the length is constant and the thickness varies, the resistance to fracture varies as the cube of the side or diameter of the base; so let us go on to the investigation of the case of solids that simultaneously vary in both length and thickness. Here I formulate *Proposition 5: Prisms and cylinders that differ in both length and thickness offer resistances to fracture that are directly proportional* [163] *to the cubes of the diameters of their bases and inversely proportional to their lengths.*

Let *ABC* and *DEF* be two such cylinders; then the resistance of the cylinder *AC* bears to the resistance of the cylinder *DF* a ratio that is the product of the cube of the diameter *AB* divided by the cube of the diameter *DE,* and the length *EF* divided by the length *BC.* Make *EG* equal to *BC;* let *H* be the third proportional to the lines *AB* and *DE;* let *I* be the fourth proportional; and let *I* be to *S* as *EF* is to *BC.*

Now, since the resistance of the cylinder *AC* is to that of the cylinder *DG* as the cube of *AB* is to the cube of *DE,* that is, as the length *AB* is to the length *I;* and since the resistance of the cylinder *DG* is to that of the cylinder *DF* as the length *FE* is to *EG,* that is, as *I* is to *S;* it follows, by equidistance of ratios, that the resistance of the cylinder *AC* is to that of the cylinder *DF* as the length *AB* is to *S.* But the line *AB* bears to *S* a ratio that is the product of *AB/I* and *I/S.* Hence the resistance of the cylinder *AC* bears to the resistance of the cylinder *DF* a ratio that is the product of *AB/I* (that is, the cube of *AB* to the cube of *DE*) and *I/S* (that is, the length *EF* to the length *BC*). This is what I meant to prove.

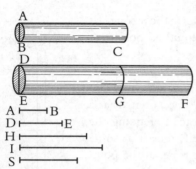

This proposition having been demonstrated, let us next consider the case of prisms and cylinders that are similar. Concerning these we shall show *Proposition 6: In the case of similar cylinders and prisms, the compound moments, namely, those produced by their own weight and length (which latter acts as a lever arm), bear to each other a ratio that is the three-halves power of the ratio between the resistances of their bases.*

In order to prove this, let us consider the two similar cylinders *AB* and *CD.* Then I say that the moment of the cylinder *AB,* opposing the resistance of its base *B,* bears to the moment of *CD,* opposing the resistance of its base *D,* a [164] ratio that is the three-halves power of the ratio between the resistance of the base *B* and the resistance of the base *D.* For, the solids *AB* and *CD* are effective in opposing the resistances of their bases *B* and *D* in proportion to both their weights and the mechanical advantages of their lever arms; and the advantage of the lever arm *AB* is equal to the advantage of the lever arm *CD*

(this is true because, in virtue of
the similarity of the cylinders, A
the length AB is to the radius of
the base B as the length CD is to   C
the radius of the base D); so it

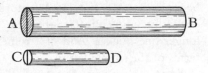

follows that the total moment of the cylinder AB is to the total moment of the cylinder CD as the weight alone of the cylinder AB is to
the weight alone of the cylinder CD, that is, as the volume of the
cylinder AB is to the volume CD; but these are as the cubes of the
diameters of their bases B and D; and the resistances of the bases,
being to each other as their areas, are to each other consequently as
the squares of their diameters; therefore, the moments of the cylinders are to each other as the three-halves power of the resistances of
their bases.

SIMP.   This proposition strikes me as both new and surprising. At
first glance it is very different from anything which I myself should
have guessed. For since these figures are similar in all other respects, I
should have certainly thought that the moments and the resistances of
these cylinders would have borne to each other the same ratio.

SAGR.   This is the proof of the proposition to which I referred,
at the very beginning of our discussion, as one imperfectly understood by me.

SALV.   For a while, Simplicio, I used to think, as you do, that the
resistances of similar solids were similar. But a certain casual observation showed me that similar solids do not exhibit a strength that is
proportional to their size, the larger ones being less fitted to undergo
rough usage just as tall men are more apt than small children to be in-
jured by a fall. [165] And as we remarked at the outset, a large beam
or column falling from a given height will go to pieces when under
the same circumstances a small scantling or small marble cylinder will
not break. It was this observation that led me to the investigation of
the fact which I am about to demonstrate to you: it is a very remarkable thing that, among the infinite variety of solids that are similar one
to another, there are no two whose moments are related in the same
ratio to their own resistances.

SIMP.   You remind me now of a passage in Aristotle's *Questions of
Mechanics*[14] in which he tries to explain why it is that a wooden beam

---

14. Pseudo-Aristotle, *Questions of Mechanics*, no. 27.

becomes weaker and can be more easily bent as it grows longer, notwithstanding the fact that the shorter beam is thinner and the longer one thicker. And, if I remember correctly, he explains it in terms of the simple lever.

SALV.   Very true. But, since this solution seemed to leave room for doubt, Monsignor di Guevara,[15] whose truly learned commentaries have greatly enriched and illuminated this work, indulges in additional clever speculations with the hope of thus overcoming all difficulties. Nevertheless, even he is confused as regards this particular point, namely, whether, when the length and thickness of these solid figures increase in the same ratio, their strength and resistance to fracture, as well as to bending, remain constant. After much thought upon this subject, I have reached the following results. First I shall show that (*Proposition 7*): *Among prisms or cylinders that are similar and have weight, there is one and only one which, under the stress of its own weight, lies just on the limit between breaking and not breaking, such that every larger one is unable to carry the load of its own weight and breaks, while every smaller one is able to withstand some additional force tending to break it.*

Let *AB* be a prism, the longest possible that will just sustain its own weight, so that if it be lengthened the least bit it will break. Then, I say, this prism is unique among all similar prisms—infinite in number—in occupying [166] that boundary line between breaking and not breaking; so that every larger one will break under its own weight, and every smaller one will not break but will be able to withstand some force in addition to its own weight. Let the prism *CE* be

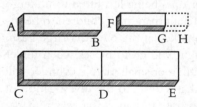

similar to, but larger than, *AB;* then, I say, it will not remain intact but will break under its own weight. Lay off the portion *CD,* equal in length to *AB.* Since the resistance of *CD* is to that of *AB* as the cube of the thickness of *CD* is to the cube of the thickness of *AB,* that is, as the prism *CE* is to the similar prism *AB,* it follows that the weight of *CE* is the utmost load which a prism of the length *CD* can sustain; but the length of *CE* is greater; therefore the prism *CE* will break. Now take

15. Giovanni di Guevara (1561–1641), Bishop of Teano, author of a commentary on the pseudo-Aristotelian *Questions of Mechanics* entitled *In Aristotelis mechanicas commentarii* (Rome, 1627).

another prism *FG* smaller than *AB,* and let *FH* equal *AB.* Then it can
be shown in a similar manner that the resistance of *FG* is to that of
AB as the prism *FG* is to the prism *AB,* provided the distance *AB*
(that is, *FH*) is equal to the distance *FG;* but *AB* is greater than *FG;*
therefore the moment of the prism *FG* applied at *G* is not sufficient
to break the prism *FG.*

SAGR.   The demonstration is short and clear; while the proposition which, at first glance, appeared improbable is now seen to be both
true and inevitable. In order therefore to bring this prism into that
limiting condition that separates breaking from not breaking, it would
be necessary to change the ratio between thickness and length either
by increasing the thickness or by diminishing the length. An investigation of this limiting state will, I believe, demand equal ingenuity.

SALV.   Nay, even more; for the question is more difficult. This I
know because I spent no small amount of time in its discovery which
I now wish to share with you. *Proposition 8: Given a cylinder or prism of*
the greatest length consistent with its not breaking under its own weight, and
given a greater length, to find the thickness of another cylinder or prism of this
greater length that shall be the only and largest one capable of withstanding its
own weight.

Let *BC* be the largest cylinder capable of sustaining its own weight;
and let *DE* be a length greater than *AC.* The problem is to find the
thickness of the [167] cylinder which, having the length *DE,* shall be
the largest one just able to with-
stand its own weight. Let *I* be the
third proportional to the lengths
DE and *AC;* let the diameter *FD*
be to the diameter *BA* as *DE* is to
I; draw the cylinder *FE;* then, I
say, among all cylinders having
the same proportions, this is the
largest and only one just capable
of sustaining its own weight. Let *M* be the third proportional to *DE*
and *I;* also let *O* be the fourth proportional to *DE, I,* and *M;* lay off
FG equal to *AC.* Now since the diameter *FD* is to the diameter *AB*
as the length *DE* is to *I,* and since *O* is the fourth proportional to *DE,*
I, and *M,* it follows that the cube of *FD* is to the cube of *BA* as *DE*
is to *O;* but the resistance of the cylinder *DG* is to the resistance of
the cylinder *BC* as the cube of *FD* is to the cube of *BA;* hence the
resistance of the cylinder *DG* is to that of cylinder *BC* as the length

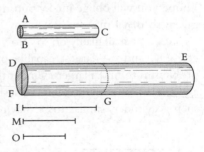

DE is to *O*. And since the moment of the cylinder *BC* is held in equilibrium by its resistance, we shall accomplish our end (which is to prove that the moment of the cylinder *FE* is equal to the resistance located at *FD*), if we show that the moment of the cylinder *FE* is to the moment of the cylinder *BC* as the resistance *DF* is to the resistance *BA*, that is, as the cube of *FD* is to the cube of *BA*, or as the length *DE* is to *O*. But the moment of the cylinder *FE* is to the moment of the cylinder *DG* as the square of *DE* is to the square of *AC*, that is, as the length *DE* is to *I*; and the moment of the cylinder *DG* is to the moment of the cylinder *BC* as the square of *DF* is to the square of *BA*, that is, as the square of *DE* is to the square of *I*, or as the square of *I* is to the square of *M*, or as *I* is to *O*. Therefore, by equidistance of ratios, it results that the moment of the cylinder *FE* is to the moment of the cylinder *BC* as the length *DE* is to *O*, that is, as the cube of *DF* is to the cube of *BA*, or as the resistance of the base *DF* is to the resistance of the base *BA*. This is what was being sought.

SAGR.   This demonstration, Salviati, is rather long and difficult to keep in mind from a single hearing. Will you not, therefore, be good enough to repeat it?

SALV.   As you like. But I would suggest instead a more direct and a shorter proof. This will, however, necessitate a different figure.

[168] SAGR.   The favor will be that much greater. Nevertheless, I hope you will oblige me by putting into written form the proof just given, so that I may study it at my leisure.

SALV.   I shall gladly do so. Now, let *A* denote a cylinder of diameter *DC* and the largest capable of sustaining its own weight; the problem is to find a larger cylinder that shall be at once the maximum and the unique one capable of sustaining its own weight. Let E be such a cylinder, similar to *A*, having an assigned length, and having the diameter *KL*; let *MN* be the third proportional to the two lengths *DC* and *KL*; let *MN* also be the diameter of another cylinder, *X*, having the same length as *E*; then, I say, *X* is the cylinder sought. For the resistance of the base *DC* is to the resistance of the base *KL* as the square of *DC* is to the square of *KL*, that is, as

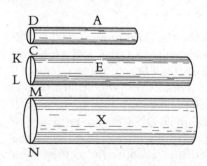

the square of *KL* is to the square of *MN*, or, as the cylinder *E* is to
the cylinder *X*, that is, as the moment of *E* is to the moment of *X*;
but the resistance of the base *KL* is to the resistance of the base *MN*
as the cube of *KL* is to the cube of *MN*, that is, as the cube of *DC* is
to the cube of *KL*, or, as the cylinder *A* is to the cylinder *E*, that is,
as the moment of *A* is to the moment of *E*; hence it follows, by perturbed equidistance of ratios, that the moment of *A* is to the moment
of *X* as the resistance of the base *DC* is to the resistance of the base
MN; therefore, moment and resistance are related to each other in
prism *X* precisely as they are in prism *A*.

Let us now generalize the problem. Then the proposition will read
as follows: *Given a cylinder* AC *in which moment and resistance are related
in any manner whatsoever, and given that* DE *is the length of another cylinder,
then determine what its thickness must be in order that the relation between its
moment and resistance shall be identical with that of the cylinder* AC.

Using again the penultimate figure and almost in the same manner,
we may say the following. Since the moment of the cylinder *FE* is to
the moment of the portion *DG* as the square of *ED* is to the square
of *FG*, that is, as the length *DE* is to *I*; and since the moment of the
cylinder *FG* is to the moment of the cylinder *AC* as the square of *FD*
is to the square of *AB*, or, as the square of *ED* is to the square of *I*,
or, as the square of *I* is to the square of *M*, [169] that is, as the length
I is to *O*; it follows, by equidistance of ratios, that the moment of the
cylinder *FE* is to the moment of the cylinder *AC* as the length *DE* is
to *O*, that is, as the cube of *DE* is to the cube of *I*, or, as the cube of
FD is to the cube of *AB*, that is, as the resistance of the base *FD* is to
the resistance of the base *AB*. This is what was to be proven.

From what has been demonstrated so far, you can plainly see the
impossibility of increasing the size of structures to vast dimensions either in art or in nature. Thus, it would be impossible to build ships,
palaces, or temples of enormous size in such a way that their oars,
masts, beams, iron bolts, and, in short, all their other parts will hold
together. Nor could nature produce trees of extraordinary size, because the branches would break down under their own weight. Likewise it would be impossible to build up the bony structures of men,
horses, or other animals so as to hold together and perform their nor-
mal functions; for these animals would have to be increased enormously in height and this increase could be accomplished only by
employing a material that is harder and stronger than usual, or by en-
larging the size of the bones, thus changing their shape until the form

and appearance of the animals would be monstrous. This is perhaps what our wise poet had in mind, when he said, in describing a huge giant: "Impossible it is to reckon his height / So beyond measure is his size."[16]

To illustrate briefly, I have sketched a bone whose natural length has been increased three times and whose thickness has been multiplied until, for a correspondingly large animal, it would perform the same function which the small bone performs for its small animal. From the figures here shown you can see how out of proportion the enlarged bone appears. Clearly then if one wishes to maintain in a

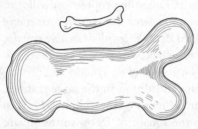

great giant the same proportion of limb as that found in an ordinary man, one must either find [170] a harder and stronger material for making the bones, or one must admit a diminution of strength in comparison with men of medium stature; for if his height be increased inordinately, he will fall and be crushed under his own weight. On the other hand, if the size of a body be diminished, the strength of that body is not diminished in the same proportion; indeed the smaller the body the greater its relative strength. Thus a small dog could probably carry on his back two or three dogs of his own size; but I believe that a horse could not carry even one of his own size.

SIMP.   This may be so. But I am led to doubt it on account of the enormous size reached by certain fish, such as the whale which, I understand, is ten times as large as an elephant; yet they all support themselves.

SALV.   Your question, Simplicio, suggests another principle, one that had hitherto escaped my attention and that enables giants and other animals of vast size to support themselves and to move about as well as smaller animals do. This result may be secured by increasing the strength of the bones and other parts intended to carry not only their weight but also the superincumbent load. But there is another way: keeping the proportions of the bony structure constant, the skeleton will hold together in the same manner or even more easily provided one diminishes, in the proper proportion, the weight of the

---

16. Ludovico Ariosto (1474–1533), *Orlando Furioso,* XVII, 30.

bony material, of the flesh, and of anything else which the skeleton has to carry. It is this second principle that is employed by nature in the structure of fish, making their bones and muscles not merely light but entirely devoid of weight.

SIMP.   The trend of your argument, Salviati, is evident. Since fish live in water, which on account of its density or (as others would say) heaviness diminishes the weight of bodies immersed in it, you mean to say that, for this reason, the bodies of fish will be devoid of weight and will be supported without injury to their bones. But this is not all; for although the remainder of the body of the fish may be without weight, there can be no question but that their bones have weight. Take the case of a whale's rib, having the dimensions of a beam; who can deny its great weight or [171] its tendency to go to the bottom when placed in water? One would, therefore, hardly expect these great masses to sustain themselves.

SALV.   A very shrewd objection! And now, in reply, tell me whether you have ever seen fish stand motionless at will under water, neither descending to the bottom nor rising to the top, without the exertion of force by swimming?

SIMP.   This is a well-known phenomenon.

SALV.   The fact then that fish are able to remain motionless under water is a conclusive reason for thinking that the material of their bodies has the same specific gravity as that of water; accordingly, if in their make-up there are certain parts that are heavier than water, there must be others that are lighter, for otherwise they would not produce equilibrium. Hence, if the bones are heavier, it is necessary that the muscles or other constituents of the body should be lighter, in order that their buoyancy may counterbalance the weight of the bones. In aquatic animals, therefore, circumstances are just reversed from what they are with land animals, inasmuch as in the latter the bones sustain not only their own weight but also that of the flesh, while in the former it is the flesh that supports not only its own weight but also that of the bones. We must therefore cease to wonder why these enormously large animals inhabit the water rather than the land, that is to say the air.

SIMP.   I am convinced. I only wish to add that what we call land animals ought really to be called air animals, seeing that they live in the air, are surrounded by air, and breathe air.

SAGR.   I have enjoyed Simplicio's discussion, including both the question raised and its answer. Moreover, I can easily understand that one of these giant fishes, if pulled ashore, would perhaps not sustain itself for any great length of time, but would be crushed under its own mass as soon as the connections between the bones gave way.

[§10.5 Day III: A New Science of Motion][17]

[190] My purpose is to set forth a very new science dealing with a very ancient subject. There is, in nature, perhaps nothing older than motion, concerning which the books written by philosophers are neither few nor small. Nevertheless, I have discovered[18] some properties of it that are worth knowing and that have not hitherto been either observed or demonstrated. Some superficial properties have indeed been noted, such as, for instance, that the natural motion of a heavy falling body is continuously accelerated. But in just what proportion this acceleration occurs has not yet been shown. For, as far as I know, no one has yet demonstrated that the distances traversed during equal intervals of time by a body falling from rest stand to one another in the same ratio as the odd numbers beginning with unity. It has been observed that missiles and projectiles describe a curved path of some sort. However, no one has pointed out the fact that this path is a parabola. But this and other facts, not few in number or less worth knowing, I have succeeded in demonstrating. And, what I consider more important, this will open the doors to a vast and most excellent science, of which my work is merely the beginning; then other minds more acute than mine will explore its remote corners.

This discussion is divided into three parts. The first part deals with motion that is steady or uniform. The second treats of motion as we find it accelerated in nature. The third deals with violent motions, or projectiles.

---

17. Galilei 1890–1909, 8: 190; translated by Crew and De Salvio (1914, 153–54); revised by Finocchiaro for this volume.
18. Here the original Latin reads simply *comperio,* and so I have dropped the phrase *by experiment,* which Crew and De Salvio (1914, 153) add immediately after the word *discovered.* As Koyré (1943, 209–10) pointed out, this unjustified addition is a sign of Crew and De Salvio's empiricist leanings.

[§10.6 Day III: Definition of Uniform Acceleration][19]

[196] SALV.   The preceding is what our Author has written concerning uniform motion. We turn now to a newer and more discriminating discussion, dealing with naturally accelerated motion, such as that generally experienced by heavy falling bodies. The title is "On Naturally Accelerated Motion," and here is the introduction:

[197] The properties belonging to uniform motion have been discussed in the preceding section; but accelerated motion remains to be considered.

And first of all, it seems desirable to investigate and explain the definition that best corresponds to the accelerated motion which nature uses. For anyone may invent an arbitrary type of motion and discuss its properties; thus, for instance, some have imagined helices and conchoids as described by certain motions that are not met with in nature, and they have very commendably established the properties which these curves possess in virtue of their definitions. But we have decided to consider the properties of bodies falling with an acceleration such as actually occurs in nature and to make our definition of accelerated motion exhibit the essential features of observed accelerated motions. And this, at last, after repeated efforts we trust we have succeeded in doing. In this belief we are confirmed mainly by the consideration that experimental results are seen to agree with and exactly correspond with those properties that have been, one after another, demonstrated by us. Finally, in the investigation of naturally accelerated motion we were led, by hand as it were, in following the habit and custom of nature herself in all her various other processes, to employ only those means that are most common, simple, and easy. For I think no one believes that swimming or flying can be accomplished in a manner simpler or easier than that instinctively employed by fishes and birds.

When, therefore, I observe a stone initially at rest falling from an elevated position and continually acquiring new increments of speed, why should I not believe that such increases take place in a manner that is exceedingly simple and rather obvious to everybody? If now we examine the matter carefully, we find no addition or increment

---

19. Galilei 1890–1909, 8: 196.23–205.6; translated by Crew and De Salvio (1914, 160–69); revised by Finocchiaro for this volume.

simpler than that which repeats itself always in the same manner. This we readily understand when we consider the intimate relationship between time and motion: first, uniformity of motion is defined by and conceived through equal times and equal spaces, and so we call a motion uniform when equal distances are traversed during equal time intervals; then in a similar manner, we may, through equal time intervals, conceive additions of speed as taking place with equal simplicity, [198] and so we may picture to our mind a motion as uniformly and continuously accelerated when, during any equal intervals of time whatever, equal increments of speed are given to it. Thus, if any number of equal intervals of time are considered, counting from the time at which the moving body left its position of rest and began to descend, the amount of speed acquired during the first two time intervals will be double that acquired during the first time interval alone; the amount added during three of these time intervals will be triple; and during four, quadruple that of the first time interval. To put the matter more clearly, if a body were to continue its motion with the same degree of speed which it had acquired during the first time interval and were to retain this same speed uniformly, then its motion would be twice as slow as that which it would have if its velocity had been acquired during two time intervals.

And thus, it seems, we shall not be far wrong if we put the degree of speed as proportional to the time elapsed. Hence the definition of motion which we are about to discuss may be stated as follows: *A motion is said to be uniformly accelerated when, starting from rest, it acquires equal increments of speed during equal time intervals.*

SAGR.   Although I can offer no rational objection to this or indeed to any other definition devised by any author whomsoever, since all definitions are arbitrary, I may nevertheless without offense be allowed to doubt whether such a definition as the above, established in an abstract manner, corresponds to and describes that kind of accelerated motion which we meet in nature in the case of freely falling bodies. And since the Author apparently maintains that the motion described in his definition is that of freely falling bodies, I would like to clear my mind of certain difficulties in order that I may later apply myself more earnestly to the propositions and their demonstrations.

SALV.   It is well that you and Simplicio raise these difficulties. They are, I imagine, the same which occurred to me when I first saw this treatise, and which were removed either by discussion with the Author himself, or by turning the matter over in my own mind.

SAGR.   When I think of a heavy body falling from rest, that is, starting with zero speed and [199] gaining speed in proportion to the time from the beginning of the motion, such a motion would, for instance, in eight beats of the pulse acquire eight degrees of speed, having acquired four degrees at the end of the fourth beat, two at the end of the second, and one at the end of the first. Now since time is divisible without limit, it follows from all these considerations that if the earlier speed of a body is less than its present speed in a constant ratio, then there is no degree of speed however small (or, one may say, no degree of slowness however great) with which we may not find this body traveling after starting from infinite slowness, i.e., from rest. So if the speed which the body had at the end of the fourth beat was such that, if kept uniform, it would traverse two miles in an hour, and if keeping the speed which it had at the end of the second beat, it would traverse one mile an hour, we must infer that, as the instant of starting is more and more nearly approached, the body moves so slowly that, if it kept on moving at this rate, it would not traverse a mile in an hour, or in a day, or in a year, or in a thousand years; indeed, it would not traverse a palm in an even greater time. This is a phenomenon that baffles the imagination, while our senses show us that a heavy falling body suddenly acquires great speed.

SALV.   This is one of the difficulties which I also experienced at the beginning, but which I shortly afterwards removed; and the removal was effected by the very experiment that creates the difficulty for you. You say the experiment appears to show that immediately after a heavy body starts from rest it acquires a very considerable speed; and I say that the same experiment makes clear the fact that the initial motions of a falling body, no matter how heavy, are very slow and gentle. Place a heavy body upon a yielding material, and leave it there without any pressure except that owing to its own weight. It is clear that if one lifts this body a cubit or two and allows it to fall upon the same material, it will, with this impulse, exert a new and greater pressure than that caused by its mere weight; and this effect is brought about by the weight of the falling body together with the velocity acquired during the fall, an effect that will be greater and greater according to the height of the fall, that is, according as the velocity of the falling body becomes greater. From the quality and intensity of the blow we are thus enabled to accurately estimate the speed of a falling body. But tell me, gentlemen, is it not true that if a sledgehammer be allowed to fall upon a stake from a height of [200] four cubits and drives it into the earth, say, four inches, then coming from a height of two cubits it will drive the stake a much smaller distance, and from the height of one cubit still less, and from a height of one palm even less? Finally, if the block be lifted only one inch, how much more will it accomplish than if merely laid on top of the stake without percussion? Certainly very little. If it be lifted only the thickness of a leaf, the effect will be altogether imperceptible. And since the effect of the blow depends upon the velocity of the striking body, can anyone doubt that the motion is very slow and the speed extremely small whenever the effect is imperceptible? See now the power of truth: the same experiment that at first glance seemed to show one thing, when more carefully examined assures us of the contrary.

But without depending upon the above experiment, which is doubtless very conclusive, it seems to me that it ought not to be difficult to establish such a fact by reasoning alone. Imagine a heavy stone held in the air at rest; the support is removed and the stone set free; then since it is heavier than the air, it begins to fall, and not with uniform motion but slowly at the beginning and with a continuously accelerated motion. Now since velocity can be increased and diminished without limit, what reason is there to believe that such a moving body starting with infinite slowness, that is, from rest, immediately acquires a speed of ten degrees rather than a speed of four, or of two, or of one, or of a half, or of a hundredth; or, indeed, of any of the infinite number of smaller values? Pray listen. I hardly think you will refuse to grant that the gain of speed of the stone falling from rest follows the same sequence as the diminution and loss of this same speed when, by some impelling force, the stone is thrown to its former elevation; but if this is so, I do not see how you can doubt that the ascending stone, diminishing in speed, must before coming to rest pass through every possible degree of slowness.

SIMP.   But if the number of degrees of greater and greater slowness is limitless, they will never be all exhausted; therefore, such an ascending heavy body will never reach rest, but will continue to move without limit always at a slower rate. But this is not the observed fact.

SALV.   This would happen, Simplicio, if the moving body were to maintain its speed for any length of time at each degree of velocity. But it merely passes each point without delaying more than an instant; and since [201] each time interval (however small) may be divided into an infinite number of instants, these will always be sufficient to correspond to the infinite degrees of diminished velocity.

That such a heavy rising body does not remain for any length of time at any given degree of velocity is evident from the following: some time interval having been assigned, if the body moves with the same speed in the last as in the first instant of that time interval, it could from this second degree of elevation be in like manner raised through an equal height, just as it was transferred from the first elevation to the second, and for the same reason it would pass from the second to the third and would finally continue in uniform motion forever.

SAGR. From these considerations it appears to me that we may obtain a proper solution of the problem discussed by philosophers, namely, what causes the acceleration in the natural motion of heavy bodies. Since, as it seems to me, the force impressed by the agent projecting the body upwards diminishes continuously, this force, so long as it was greater than the contrary force of gravity, impelled the body upwards; when the two are in equilibrium the body ceases to rise and passes through the state of rest in which the impressed impetus is not destroyed, but only its excess over the weight of the body has been consumed—the excess that caused the body to rise. Then as the diminution of the external impetus continues, and gravity gains the upper hand, the fall begins, but slowly at first on account of the opposition of the impressed force, a large portion of which still remains in the body; but as this continues to diminish, it also continues to be more and more overcome by gravity, and hence the continuous acceleration of motion results.

SIMP. The idea is clever, yet more subtle than sound. For even if the argument were conclusive, it would explain only the case where a natural motion is preceded by a violent motion in which there still remains active a portion of the external force; but where there is no such remaining portion and the body starts from an antecedent state of rest, the cogency of the whole argument fails.

SAGR. I believe that you are mistaken and that this distinction between cases which you make is superfluous or, rather, nonexistent. But, tell me, cannot a projectile receive from the projector either a large or a small force, and thus be thrown to a height of a hundred cubits, as well as twenty or four or one?

[202] SIMP. Undoubtedly, yes.

SAGR. So this impressed force may exceed the resistance of gravity so slightly as to raise it only an inch; and finally the force of the projector may be just large enough to exactly balance the resistance of gravity, so that the body is not lifted at all but merely sustained. When you hold a stone in your hand, do you do anything but give it a force impelling it upwards equal to the power of gravity drawing it downwards? And do you not continuously impress this force upon the stone as long as you hold it in the hand? Does it perhaps diminish with the time during which you hold the stone? And what does it matter whether this support that prevents the stone from falling is furnished by one's hand, or by a table, or by a rope from which it hangs? Certainly nothing at all. You must conclude, therefore, Simplicio, that it makes no difference whatever whether the fall of the stone is preceded by a period of rest that is long, short, or instantaneous, provided only that the fall does not begin as long as the stone is acted upon by a force opposed to its weight and sufficient to hold it at rest.

SALV.   The present does not seem to be the proper time to investigate the cause of the acceleration of natural motion, concerning which various opinions have been expressed by various philosophers. That is, some explain it by attraction to the center; others reduce it to the gradual decrease of the amount of medium to be overcome; still others attribute it to a certain pressure of the surrounding medium, which closes in behind the falling body and drives it from one position to another. Now, all these fantasies, and others too, ought to be examined; but it is not really worth while. At present it is the purpose of our Author merely to investigate and to demonstrate some of the properties of an accelerated motion such that (whatever the cause of this acceleration may be) the moments of its velocity go on increasing after departure from rest in simple proportionality to the time, which is the same as saying that in equal time intervals the body receives equal increments of velocity; and if we find that the properties to be demonstrated later are realized in freely falling and accelerated bodies, we may conclude that the assumed definition includes such a motion of falling bodies, and that it is true [203] that their speed goes on increasing as the time and the duration of the motion.

SAGR.   So far as I see at present, the definition might have been put a little more clearly perhaps without changing the fundamental idea. That is, uniformly accelerated motion is motion such that its speed increases in proportion to the space traversed; so that, for example, the speed acquired by a body in falling four cubits would be double that acquired in falling two cubits, and this latter speed would be double that acquired in the first cubit. For there is no doubt but that a heavy body falling from the height of six cubits has, and strikes with, an impetus double that which it had at the end of three cubits, triple that which it had at the end of two, and six times that which it had at the end of one.

SALV.   It is very comforting to me to have had such a companion in error. Moreover, let me tell you that your reasoning seems so highly likely and probable that our Author himself admitted, when I put it forward to him, that he had for some time shared the same fallacy. But what most surprised me was to see two propositions proven in a few simple words to be not only false but also impossible, even though they are so inherently likely that they have commanded the assent of everyone to whom I have presented them.

SIMP.   I am one of those who accept them. I believe that a falling body acquires force in its descent, its velocity increasing in proportion to the space, and that the moment of the same striking body is double when it falls from a double height. These propositions, it appears to me, ought to be conceded without hesitation or controversy.

SALV.   And yet they are as false and impossible as that motion should be completed instantaneously. Here is a very clear demonstration of it. When the velocities are in proportion to the spaces traversed or to be traversed, these spaces are traversed in equal intervals of time; if, therefore, the velocities[20] with which the falling body traverses a space of four cubits were double the velocities with which it covered the first two cubits (since the one distance is double the other), then the time intervals required for these passages would be equal; but for one and the same body to move four cubits and two cubits in the same time is possible only in the case of [204] instantaneous motion; but observation shows us that the motion of a falling body takes time, and less of it in covering a distance of two cubits than of four cubits; therefore, it is false that its velocity increases in proportion to the space.

The falsity of the other proposition may be shown with equal clearness. For if we consider a single striking body, the difference in the moment of its percussions can depend only upon a difference of velocity; thus, if the striking body falling from a double height were to deliver a percussion of double moment, it would be necessary for this

---

20. In this clause I am changing Crew and De Salvio's (1914, 168) *velocity* in the singular to the plural. This is in accordance with the literal meaning of Galileo's original Italian *le velocità* and with suggestions made by Drake (1970, 231; 1974, 160). For the significance of this difference, see Drake (1970, 229–37; 1973); Finocchiaro (1972; 1973).

body to strike with a double velocity; with this double speed it would traverse a double space in the same time interval; but observation shows that the time required for fall from the greater height is longer.

SAGR.   You present these recondite matters with too much evidence and ease. This great facility makes them less appreciated than they would be had they been presented in a more abstruse manner. For, in my opinion, people esteem more lightly that knowledge which they acquire with so little labor than that acquired through long and obscure discussion.

SALV.   If those who demonstrate with brevity and clearness the fallacy of many popular beliefs were treated with contempt instead of gratitude, the injury would be quite bearable. But on the other hand, it is very unpleasant and annoying to see men who claim to be peers of anyone in a certain field of study take for granted conclusions that later are quickly and easily shown by another to be false. I do not call such a feeling envy, which usually degenerates into hatred and anger against those who discover such fallacies; I would call it a strong desire to maintain old errors, rather than accept newly discovered truths. This desire at times induces them to unite against these truths, although at heart believing in them, merely for the purpose of lowering the esteem in which certain others are held by the unthinking crowd. Indeed, I have heard our Academician talk about many such false propositions, held as true but easily refutable; and I have even made a list of some of them.

SAGR.   You must not withhold them from us, but must tell us about them at the proper time, even though an extra session be necessary. [205] For now, continuing the thread of our discussion, it would seem that so far we have formulated the definition of the uniformly accelerated motion to be treated in what follows. It is this: *A motion is said to be equally or uniformly accelerated when, starting from rest, its velocity receives equal increments in equal times.*

[§10.7 Day III: Laws of Falling Bodies][21]

SALV.   This definition established, the Author assumes the truth of a single principle, namely: *The speeds acquired by one and the same*

---

21. Galilei 1890–1909, 8: 205.7–219.33; translated by Crew and De Salvio (1914, 169–85); revised by Finocchiaro for this volume.

body moving down planes of different inclinations are equal when the heights of these planes are equal.

By the height of an inclined plane he means the perpendicular let fall from the upper end of the plane upon the horizontal line drawn through the lower end of the same plane. Thus, to illustrate, let the line *AB* be horizontal, and let the planes *CA* and *CD* be inclined to it; then the Author calls the perpendicular *CB* the "height" of the planes *CA* and *CD*. He supposes that the speeds acquired by one and the same body descending along the planes *CA* and *CD* to the terminal points *A* and *D* are equal since the heights of these planes are the same, *CB*; and also it must be understood that this speed is that which would be acquired by the same body falling from *C* to *B*.

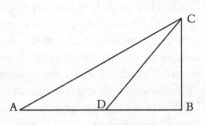

SAGR.   Your assumption appears to me so probable that it ought to be conceded without question, provided of course that there are no accidental or external resistances, and that the planes are hard and smooth and the shape of the moving body is perfectly round, so that neither plane nor moving body is rough. All resistance and opposition having been removed, my natural instinct tells me at once that a heavy and perfectly round ball descending along the lines *CA, CD, CB* would reach the terminal points *A, D, B* with the same impetus.

SALV.   What you say is very plausible. But, going beyond likelihood, I hope by experiment to increase its probability to such an extent that it shall be little short of a necessary demonstration. [206] Imagine this page to represent a vertical wall, with a nail driven into it; and from the nail let there be suspended a lead ball of one or two ounces by means of a fine vertical thread, *AB*, say two or three cubits long; on this wall draw a horizontal line *DC*, at right angles to the vertical thread *AB*, which hangs about two inches in front of the wall. Now bring the thread *AB* with the attached ball into the position *AC* and set it free; first it will be observed to

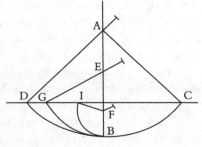

descend along the arc *CBD*, to pass the point *B*, and to travel along the arc *BD*, till it almost reaches the horizontal *CD*, a slight shortage being caused by the resistance of the air and of the string; from this we may rightly infer that the ball in its descent through the arc *CB* acquired an impetus on reaching *B* that was just sufficient to carry it through a similar arc *BD* to the same height. Having repeated this experiment many times, let us now drive a nail into the wall close to the perpendicular *AB*, say at *E* or *F*, so that it projects out some five or six inches in order that the thread, again carrying the ball through the arc *CB*, may strike upon the nail *E* when the ball reaches *B*, and thus compel it to traverse the arc *BG*, described about *E* as center; from this we can see what can be done by the same impetus that, previously starting at the same point *B*, carried the same body through the arc *BD* to the horizontal *CD*. Now, gentlemen, you will observe with pleasure that the ball swings to the point *G* in the horizontal, and you would see the same thing happen if the obstacle were placed at some lower point, say at *F*, about which the ball would describe the arc *BI*, the rise of the ball always terminating exactly on the line *CD*. But when the nail is placed so low that the remainder of the thread below it will not reach to the height *CD* (which would happen [207] if the nail were placed nearer to *B* than to the intersection of *AB* with the horizontal *CD*), then the thread leaps over the nail and twists itself about it.

This experiment leaves no room for doubt as to the truth of our supposition. For since the two arcs *CB* and *DB* are equal and similarly placed, the momentum acquired by the fall through the arc CB is the same as that gained by fall through the arc *DB;* but the momentum acquired at *B* owing to fall through *CB* is able to lift the same body through the arc *BD;* therefore, the momentum acquired in the fall *DB* is equal to that which lifts the same body through the same arc from *B* to *D;* so, in general, every momentum acquired by fall through an arc is equal to that which can lift the same body through the same arc. But all these momenta that cause a rise through the arcs *BD*, *BG*, and *BI* are equal, since they are produced by the same momentum, gained by fall through *CB*, as experiment shows. Therefore, all the momenta gained by fall through the arcs *DB*, *GB*, and *IB* are equal.

SAGR.   The argument seems to me so conclusive and the experiment so well adapted to establish the postulate that we may, indeed, accept it as if it were demonstrated.

SALV.   I do not wish, Sagredo, that we trouble ourselves too much about this matter, especially since we are going to apply this principle mainly to motions that occur on plane surfaces, and not upon curved ones, along which acceleration varies in a manner greatly different from that which we have assumed for planes. Thus, although the above experiment shows us that the descent of the moving body through the arc *CB* confers upon it enough momentum to carry it to the same height through any of the arcs *BD*, *BG*, or *BI*, we are not able to show with similar evidence that the same would happen in the case of a perfectly round ball descending along planes whose inclinations are respectively the same as the chords of these arcs. Instead, since these planes form angles at the point *B*, it seems likely that they will present an obstacle to the ball that has descended along the chord *CB* and starts to rise along the chords *BD*, *BG*, or *BI*; in striking these planes, it will lose some of its impetus and will not be able to rise to the height of the line *CD*. But if one removes this obstacle, which is prejudicial to the experiment, it is clear to the intellect that the impetus (which gains [208] strength by the amount of descent) will be able to carry the body to the same height. Let us then, for the present, take this as a postulate, the absolute truth of which will be established when we find that the conclusions based on this hypothesis correspond to and agree perfectly with experiment. The Author having assumed this single principle, he passes next to the propositions which he conclusively demonstrates. The first of these is as follows.

Theorem 1, Proposition 1: The time in which any space is traversed by a body starting from rest and uniformly accelerated is equal to the time in which that same space would be traversed by the same body moving at a uniform speed whose value is one-half the highest and final speed reached during the previous uniformly accelerated motion.

Let us represent by the line *AB* the time in which the space *CD* is traversed by a body that starts from rest at *C* and is uniformly accelerated; let the final and highest value of the speed gained during the interval *AB* be represented by the line *EB*, drawn at right angles to *AB*; draw also the line *AE*; then all lines drawn from equidistant points on *AB* and parallel to *BE* will represent the increasing values of the speed, beginning with the instant *A*. Let the point *F* bisect the line

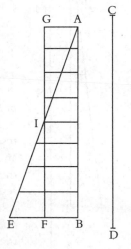

EB; draw *FG* parallel to *BA,* and *GA* parallel to *FB,* thus forming a parallelogram *AGFB,* whose area will be equal to that of the triangle *AEB,* and whose side *GF* bisects the side *AE* at the point *I.*

Now, if the parallel lines in the triangle *AEB* are extended to *GI,* then the aggregate of all the parallels contained in the quadrilateral is equal to the aggregate of those contained in the triangle *AEB;* for those in the triangle *IEF* are equal to those contained in the triangle *GIA,* while those included in the trapezium *AIFB* are common. Furthermore, each and every instant of time in the time interval *AB* has its corresponding point on the line *AB,* from which points the parallels drawn in and limited by the triangle *AEB* represent the increasing values of the growing velocity; and the parallels contained within the rectangle represent the values of a speed that is not increasing but constant. [209] Hence it appears that the moments of speed acquired by the moving body may be represented, in the case of the accelerated motion, by the increasing parallels of the triangle *AEB,* and in the case of the uniform motion, by the parallels of the rectangle *GB;* for, what the moments of speed may lack in the first part of the accelerated motion (the deficiency of the moments being represented by the parallels of the triangle *AGI*) is made up by the moments represented by the parallels of the triangle *IEF.* Therefore, it is clear that equal spaces will be traversed in equal times by two bodies, one of which starts from rest and moves with uniform acceleration, while the other moves with a uniform speed whose moment is one-half the maximum moment of speed under the accelerated motion. QED.

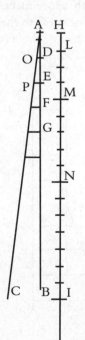

Theorem 2, Proposition 2: If a body falls from rest with a uniformly accelerated motion, then the spaces traversed are to each other as the squares of the time intervals employed in traversing them.

Let the time beginning with any instant *A* be represented by the straight line *AB,* in which are taken any two time intervals *AD* and *AE.* Let *HI* represent the distance through which the body, starting from rest at *H,* falls with uniform acceleration. If *HL* represents the space traversed during the time interval *AD,* and *HM* that covered during the interval *AE,* then the space *HM* stands to the space *HL* in a ratio that is the square of the ratio of the time AE to the time AD; or we may say simply that the distances HM and HL are related as the squares of AE and AD.

Draw the line AC making any angle whatever with the line AB; and from the points D and E, draw the parallel lines DO and EP; of these two lines, DO represents the greatest velocity attained during the time interval AD, while EP represents the maximum velocity acquired during the time AE. But it has just been proved that so far as distances traversed are concerned, it is precisely the same whether a body falls from rest with a uniform acceleration or whether it falls during an equal time interval with a constant speed that is one-half the maximum speed attained during the accelerated motion. It follows therefore that the distances HM and HL are the same as would be traversed during the time intervals AE and AD by uniform velocities equal to one-half those represented by EP and DO respectively. If, therefore, one can show that the distances HM and HL are in [210] the same ratio as the squares of the time intervals AE and AD, our proposition will be proven. But in the fourth proposition of the first section above,[22] it has been shown that the spaces traversed by two bodies in uniform motion bear to one another a ratio that is equal to the product of the ratio of the velocities by the ratio of the times; and in the present case the ratio of the velocities is the same as the ratio of the time intervals, for the ratio of one-half EP to one-half DO, or of EP to DO, is the same as that of AE to AD; hence the ratio of the spaces traversed is the same as the squared ratio of the time intervals. QED.

It also clearly follows that the ratio of the distances is the square of the ratio of the final velocities, that is, of the lines EP and DO, since these are to each other as AE to AD.

Corollary 1: Hence it is clear that if we take any number of consecutive equal intervals of time, counting from the beginning of the motion, such as AD, DE, EF, FG, *in which the spaces* HL, LM, MN, NI *are traversed, these spaces will bear to one another the same ratio as the series of odd numbers, 1, 3, 5, 7.*

For this is the ratio of the differences of the squares of the lines which exceed one another by equal amounts and whose excess is equal to the smallest of these same lines; or we may say that this is the ratio of the differences of the squares of the natural numbers

---

22. That is, the first section, on uniform motion, of the treatise *On Local Motion*, presented at the beginning of Day III of *Two New Sciences* and omitted here. See Galilei 1890–1909, 8: 194; Crew and De Salvio 1914, 157.

beginning with unity. Therefore, whereas after equal time intervals the velocities increase as the natural numbers, the increments in the distances traversed during these equal time intervals are to one another as the odd numbers beginning with unity.

SAGR.   Please suspend the reading for a moment, since there just occurs to me an idea which I want to illustrate by means of a diagram in order that it may be clearer both to you and to me. Let the line *AI* represent the lapse of time measured from the initial instant *A;* through *A* draw the straight line *AF* making any angle whatever; join the terminal points *I* and *F;* divide the time *AI* in half at *C;* draw *CB* parallel to *IF.* Let us consider *CB* as the maximum value of the velocity that increases from zero at the beginning in simple proportionality to the segments (inside the triangle *ABC*) of lines drawn parallel to *BC;* or what is the same thing, let us suppose the velocity to increase in proportion to the time; then I admit without question, in view of the preceding argument, that the space traversed by a body falling in the aforesaid manner will be equal to the space traversed by the [211] same body during the same length of time traveling with a uniform speed equal to *EC,* or half of *BC.* Further let us imagine that

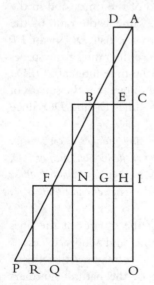

the body has fallen with accelerated motion so that at the instant *C* it has the velocity *BC.* It is clear that if the body continued to descend with the same speed *BC,* without acceleration, it would in the next time interval *CI* traverse double the distance covered during the interval *AC* with the uniform speed *EC,* which is half of *BC.* But since the falling body acquires equal increments of speed during equal increments of time, it follows that the velocity *BC,* during the next time interval *CI,* will be increased by an amount represented by the parallels of the triangle *BFG,* which is equal to the triangle *ABC.* Thus, if one adds to the velocity *GI* half of the velocity *FG,* the maximum increment of speed acquired by the accelerated motion and determined by the parallels of the triangle *BFG,* one will have the uniform velocity *IN* with which the same space would have been traversed in the time *CI.* And since this speed *IN* is three times as great as *EC,* it follows that the space traversed during the interval *CI* is three times as great as that traversed during the interval *AC.* Now, let us imagine the motion extended over another equal time interval *IO,* and the triangle extended to *APO;* it is then evident that if the motion continues during the *interval IO,* at the constant rate *IF* acquired by acceleration during the time *AI,* the space traversed during the interval *IO* will be four times that traversed during the first interval *AC,* because the speed *IF* is four times the speed *EC.* But if we enlarge our triangle so as to include *FPQ,* which is equal to *ABC,* still assuming the acceleration to be constant, we shall add to the uniform speed an increment *RQ,* equal to *EC;* then the value of the equivalent uniform speed during the time interval *IO* will be five times that during the first time interval *AC;* therefore, the space traversed will be quintuple that during the first interval *AC.* It is thus evident by this simple computation that a moving body starting from rest and acquiring velocity at a rate proportional to the time, will, during equal intervals of time, traverse distances that [212] are related to each other as the odd numbers beginning with unity, 1, 3, 5; or considering the total space traversed, that covered in double time will be quadruple that covered during unit time; in triple time, the space is nine times as great as in unit time. And in general the spaces traversed are in the squared ratio of the times, i.e., in the ratio of the squares of the times.

SIMP.   In truth, I find more pleasure in this simple and clear argument of Sagredo than in the Author's demonstration, which to me appears rather obscure; thus, I am convinced that matters are as described, once having accepted the definition of uniformly accelerated motion. But as to whether this acceleration is that which nature employs in the case of falling bodies, I am still doubtful. So it seems to me, not only for my own sake but also for all those who think as I do, that this would be the proper moment to introduce one of those experiments—and there are many of them, I understand—which correspond in several ways to the conclusions demonstrated.

SALV.   The request which you make, like a true scientist,[23] is a very reasonable one. For this is the custom—and properly so—in those sciences where mathematical demonstrations are applied to natural phenomena; this is seen in the case of perspective, astronomy, mechanics, music, and others, which by sense experience confirm the

---

23. Here the Italian text does indeed read *scienziato.*

principles that become the foundations of the entire superstructure. I hope therefore it will not appear to be a waste of time if we discuss at considerable length this first and most fundamental question upon which hinge numerous consequences; of these we have in this book only a small number, placed there by the Author, who has done so much to open a pathway hitherto closed to minds of a speculative turn. As far as experiments go, they have not been neglected by the Author; and often, in his company, I have myself performed the tests to ascertain that the acceleration of naturally falling bodies is that above described.

We took a piece of wooden molding or scantling, about twelve cubits long, half a cubit wide, and three inches thick; on its edge we cut a channel a little more than one inch in breadth; having made this groove very straight, smooth, and polished, and having lined it with parchment, also as smooth and polished as possible, we rolled along it a hard, smooth, and very round bronze ball. [213] Having placed this board in a sloping position, by lifting one end some one or two cubits above the other, we rolled the ball, as I was just saying, along the channel, noting, in a manner presently to be described, the time required to make the entire descent. We repeated this experiment many times in order to measure the time with an accuracy such that the deviation between two measurements never exceeded one-tenth of a pulse beat. Having performed this operation and having assured ourselves of its reliability, we now rolled the ball only one-quarter the length of the channel; and having measured the time of its descent, we found it precisely one-half of the former. Next we tried other distances, comparing the time for the whole length with that for half, or with that for two-thirds, or three-fourths, or indeed for any fraction; in such experiments, repeated a full hundred times, we always found that the spaces traversed were to each other as the squares of the times, and this was true for all inclinations of the plane, i.e., of the channel along which we rolled the ball. We also observed that the times of descent, for various inclinations of the plane, bore to one another precisely that ratio that, as we shall see later, the Author had predicted and demonstrated for them.

For the measurement of time, we employed a large vessel of water placed in an elevated position. To the bottom of this vessel was soldered a pipe of small diameter giving a thin jet of water, which we collected in a small glass during the time of each descent, whether for the whole length of the channel or for a part of its length. The water thus collected after each descent was weighed on a very accurate balance. The differences and ratios of these weights gave us the differences and ratios of the times, and this with such accuracy that although the operation was repeated many, many times, there was no appreciable discrepancy in the results.

SIMP.   I would like to have been present at these experiments. But feeling confidence in the care with which you performed them, and in the fidelity with which you relate them, I am satisfied and accept them as true and most certain.

SALV.   Then we can resume our reading and proceed.

[214] *Corollary 2: Secondly, it follows that, starting from any initial point, if we take any two distances, traversed in any time intervals whatsoever, these time intervals bear to one another the same ratio as one of the distances to the mean proportional of the two distances.*

That is, if from the initial point *S* we take two distances *ST* and *SV* and their mean proportional is *SX,* the time of fall through *ST* is to the time of fall through *SV* as *ST* is to *SX;* and the time of fall through *SV* is to the time of fall through *ST* as *SV* is to *SX.* For since it has been shown that the spaces traversed are in the same ratio as the squares of the times; and since, moreover, the ratio of the space *SV* to the space *ST* is the square of the ratio *SV* to *SX;* it follows that the ratio of the times of fall through *SV* and *ST* is the ratio of the distances *SV* and *SX.*

Scholium: The above corollary has been proven for the case of vertical fall. But it holds also for planes inclined at any angle; for it is to be assumed that along these planes the velocity increases in the same ratio, that is, in proportion to the time, or, if you prefer, as the series of natural numbers.[24]

Here, Sagredo, I should like, if it be not too tedious to Simplicio, to interrupt for a moment the present reading in order to make some additions on the basis of what has already been proved and of what mechanical principles we have already learned from our Academician. This addition I make for the greater confirmation of the truth of the

---

24. The dialogue that follows did not appear in the original 1638 edition of *Two New Sciences.* It was composed in 1639 jointly by Galileo and his pupil Vincenzio Viviani, and it was intended to be added to future editions. In including it, I am following Crew and De Salvio (1914, 180–85), as well as Drake (1974, 171–75).

principle which we have considered above by means of probable arguments and experiments; and what is more important, for the purpose of deriving it geometrically, after first demonstrating a single lemma that is fundamental in the study of impetus.

SAGR.   If the advance which you propose to make is such as will confirm and fully establish these sciences of motion, I will gladly devote to it any length of time. Indeed, I shall not only be glad [215] to have you proceed, but I beg of you at once to satisfy the curiosity which you have awakened in me concerning this particular point. And I think that Simplicio is of the same mind.

SIMP.   Quite right.

SALV.   Since then I have your permission, let us first of all consider this notable fact—that the momenta or speeds of one and the same moving body vary with the inclination of the plane. The speed reaches a maximum along a vertical direction, and for other directions it diminishes as the plane diverges from the vertical. Therefore the impetus, strength, energy, or, one might say, the momentum of descent of the moving body is diminished by the plane upon which it is supported and along which it rolls.

For the sake of greater clearness, erect the line *AB* perpendicular to the horizontal *AC;* next draw *AD, AE, AF,* etc., at different inclinations to the horizontal. Then I say that all the impetus of the falling body is along the vertical and is a maximum when it falls in that direction; the momentum is less along *DA* and still less along *EA,* and even less yet along the more inclined *FA.* Finally, on the horizontal *CA* the impetus vanishes altogether; the body finds itself in a condition of indifference as to motion or rest; it has no inherent tendency to move in any direction and offers no resistance to being set in motion. For just as a heavy body or system of bodies cannot of itself move upwards, or recede from the common center toward which all heavy things tend, so it is impossible for any body of its own accord to assume any motion other than one that carries it nearer to the aforesaid common center. Hence, along the horizontal, by which we understand a surface every point of which is

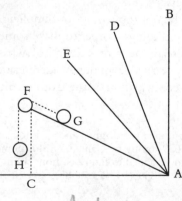

Actual experiment; compare to Bacon

equidistant from this same common center, the body will have no impetus or momentum whatever.

[216] This change of impetus being clear, it is here necessary for me to explain something which our Academician wrote when in Padua, embodying it in a treatise on mechanics prepared solely for the use of his students, and proving it at length and conclusively when considering the origin and nature of that marvelous instrument, the screw. What he proved is the manner in which the impetus varies with the inclination of the plane, as for instance that of the plane FA, one end of which is elevated through a vertical distance FC. This direction FC is that along which the impetus of a heavy body and the momentum of descent become maximum; let us try to determine what ratio this momentum bears to that of the same body moving along the incline FA. This ratio, I say, is the inverse of that of the aforesaid lengths. This is the lemma preceding the theorem which I hope to demonstrate later.

It is clear that the impetus of a falling body is equal to the least resistance or force sufficient to hinder it and stop it. In order to measure this force or resistance, I propose to use the weight of another body. Let us place upon the plane FA a body G connected to the weight H by means of a string passing over the point F; then the body H will ascend or descend, along the perpendicular, the same distance which the body G moves along the incline FA; but this distance will not be equal to the rise or fall of G along the vertical, in which direction alone G, like other bodies, exerts its resistance. This is clear. For consider that the motion of the body G from A to F in the triangle AFC is made up of a horizontal component AC and a vertical component CF; and remember that this body experiences no resistance [217] to motion along the horizontal (because by such a motion the body neither gains nor loses distance from the common center of heavy things, which distance is constant along the horizontal); then it follows that resistance is met only in consequence of the body rising through the vertical distance CF. Since then the body G in moving from A to F offers resistance only in so far as it rises through the vertical distance CF, while the other body H must fall vertically an amount equivalent to the entire distance FA; and since this ratio is maintained whether the motion be large or small, the two bodies being tied together; hence, we are able to assert positively that in case of equilibrium (namely, when the two bodies are at rest) the momenta, the velocities, or their propensities to motion, i.e., the spaces that would be traversed by them in equal times, must be in the inverse ratio to their weights.[25] This is what has been demonstrated in every case of mechanical motion. Thus, in order to hold the weight G at rest, one must give H a weight smaller in the same ratio as the distance CF is smaller than FA.

If we do this, namely, we let the ratio of the weight G to the weight H be the same as FA to FC, then equilibrium will occur, that is, the weights H and G will have equal moments and the two bodies will come to rest. And since we are agreed that the impetus, energy, momentum, or propensity to motion of a moving body is as great as the least force or resistance sufficient to stop it; and since we have found that the weight H is capable of preventing motion in the weight G; it follows that the lesser weight H, whose entire moment is along the perpendicular FC, will be an exact measure of the partial moment which the larger weight G exerts along the inclined plane FA. But the measure of the total moment of the body G is its own weight, since to prevent its fall it is only necessary to balance it with an equal weight, provided this second weight be free to move vertically. Therefore, the partial impetus or moment of G along the incline FA will bear to the maximum and total impetus of this same body G along the perpendicular FC the same ratio as the weight H to the weight G; this ratio is, by construction, the same which the height FC of the incline bears to the length FA. We have here the lemma which I proposed to demonstrate and which, as you will see, has been assumed by our Author in the second part of the sixth proposition of the present treatise.

SAGR.   From what you have shown thus far, it appears to me that one might infer, arguing by perturbed equidistance of ratios, that the moments of one and the same body moving along planes differently inclined but having the same vertical height, such as FA and FI,[26] are to each other inversely as the lengths of the planes.

[218] SALV.   Perfectly right. This point established, I pass to the demonstration of the following theorem: *If a body falls freely along smooth planes inclined at any angle whatsoever but of the same height, the*

---

25. As Crew and De Salvio (1914, 183) note, this is an approximation to the principle of virtual work elaborated by Jean Bernoulli in 1717.
26. Galileo did not draw FI in the previous diagram, but he must have been thinking of a line from F to a point somewhere along the line AC.

speeds which it has when reaching the bottom are equal, provided that all impediments are removed.

First we must recall the fact that on a plane of any inclination whatever a body starting from rest gains speed, or quantity of impetus, in direct proportion to the time, in agreement with the definition of naturally accelerated motion given by the Author. Hence, as he has shown in the preceding proposition, the distances traversed are proportional to the squares of the times and therefore to the squares of the speeds. Whatever impetus is gained at the first instant, the increments of speed during the same time will be respectively the same, since in each case the gain of speed is proportional to the time.

Let *AB* be an inclined plane whose height above the horizontal *BC* is the vertical *AC*. As we have seen above, the impetus of a body falling along the vertical *AC* is to the impetus of the same body along the incline *AB* as *AB* is to *AC*. On the incline *AB*, lay off *AD*, the third proportional to *AB* and *AC;* then the impetus

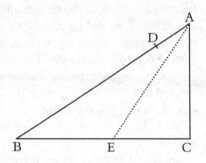

along *AC* is to that along *AB* (i.e., along *AD*) as the length *AC* is to the length *AD*. Therefore, the body will traverse the space *AD*, along the incline *AB*, in the same time which it would take in falling the vertical distance *AC* (since the moments are in the same ratio as the distances); and the speed at *C* is to the speed at *D* as the distance *AC* is to the distance *AD*. But according to the definition of accelerated motion, the speed at *B* is to the speed of the same body at *D* as the time required to traverse *AB* is to the time required for *AD;* and according to the last corollary of the second proposition, the time for passing through the distance *AB* bears to the time for passing through *AD* the same ratio as the distance *AC* (the mean proportional between *AB* and *AD*) to *AD*. Accordingly the two speeds at *B* and *C* each bear to the speed at *D* the same ratio, namely, that of the distance *AC* to *AD;* hence they are equal. This is the theorem which I set out to prove.

From the above we are better able to demonstrate the following third proposition of the Author, in which proposition he employs the preceding principle: *The time required to traverse an incline is to that required to fall through the vertical height of the incline in the same ratio as the length of the incline to* [219] *its height.*

For, according to the second corollary of the second proposition, if *AB* represents the time required to pass over the distance *AB*, the time required to pass the distance *AD* will be the mean proportional between these two distances and will be represented by the line *AC;* but if *AC* represents the time needed to traverse *AD,* it will also represent the time required to fall through the distance *AC,* since the distances *AC* and *AD* are traversed in equal times; consequently, if AB represents the time required for *AB,* then *AC* will represent the time required for AC. Hence, the times required to traverse *AB* and *AC* are to each other as the distances *AB* and *AC.*

By the same reasoning it can be shown that the time required to fall through *AC* is to the time required for any other incline *AE* as the length *AC* is to the length *AE;* therefore, by equidistance of ratios, the time of fall along the incline *AB* is to that along *AE* as the distance *AB* is to the distance *AE,* etc.[27]

One might, by applying this same theorem, as Sagredo will readily see, immediately demonstrate the sixth proposition of the Author. But let us end this digression here, which Sagredo has perhaps found rather tedious, though I consider it quite important for the theory of motion.

SAGR.   On the contrary it has given me great satisfaction, and indeed I find it necessary for a complete grasp of that principle.

SALV.   I will now resume the reading of the text.

[§10.8 Day IV: The Parabolic Path of Projectiles][28]

[268] SALV.   Once more, Simplicio is here on time. So let us, without rest, take up the question of motion. Here is the text of our Author "On the Motion of Projectiles":

In the preceding pages we have discussed the properties of uniform motion and of motion naturally accelerated along planes of all inclinations. I now propose to set forth those properties that belong to a body whose motion is compounded of two other motions, namely,

---

27. Crew and De Salvio (1914, 185) note that in modern notation this argument would read as follows: $AC = \frac{1}{2}gt_c^2$; $AD = \frac{1}{2}(AC/AB)gt_d^2$; since $AC^2 = AB \star AD$, it follows that $t_d = t_c$.
28. Galilei 1890–1909, 8: 268–79; translated by Crew and De Salvio (1914, 244–57); revised by Finocchiaro for this volume.

one uniform and one naturally accelerated; these properties, well worth knowing, I propose to demonstrate in a rigorous manner. This is the kind of motion seen in a moving projectile; its origin I conceive to be as follows.

Imagine any particle projected along a horizontal plane without friction. Then we know, from what has been more fully explained in the preceding pages, that this particle will move along this same plane with a motion that is uniform and perpetual, provided the plane has no limits. But if the plane is limited and elevated, then the moving particle, which we imagine to be a heavy body, will on passing over the edge of the plane acquire, in addition to its previous uniform and enduring motion, a downward propensity due to its own weight; and so the resulting motion, which I call projection, is compounded of one that is uniform and horizontal and another that is downward and naturally accelerated. We now proceed to demonstrate some of its properties, the first of which is as follows.

[269] *Theorem 1, Proposition 1: A projectile that is carried by a uniform horizontal motion compounded with a naturally accelerated downward motion describes a path that is a semiparabola.*

SAGR.   Here, Salviati, it will be necessary to stop a little while for my sake and, I believe, also for the benefit of Simplicio; for it so happens that I have not gone very far in my study of Apollonius[29] and am merely aware of the fact that he treats of the parabola and other conic sections, without an understanding of which I hardly think one will be able to follow the proof of other propositions depending upon them. Since even in this first beautiful theorem the author finds it necessary to prove that the path of a projectile is a parabola, I imagine we shall have to deal with this kind of curve, and so it will be absolutely necessary to have a thorough understanding, if not of all the properties which Apollonius has demonstrated for these figures, at least of those that are needed for the present treatment.

SALV.   You are quite too modest, pretending ignorance of facts which not long ago you acknowledged as well known—I mean at the time when we were discussing the strength of materials and needed to use a certain theorem of Apollonius that gave you no trouble.

SAGR.   I may have chanced to know it; or I may possibly have assumed it since it was needed only once in that discussion. But now

---

29. Apollonius of Perga (c. 262–c. 200 B.C.), Greek mathematician, author of the classical treatise on conic sections (parabola, hyperbola, and ellipse).

when we have to follow all these demonstrations about such curves, we ought not, as they say, to swallow it whole, and thus waste time and energy.

SIMP.   And then, even if Sagredo were, as I believe, well equipped for all his needs, I do not understand even the elementary terms; for although our philosophers have treated the motion of projectiles, I do not recall their having described the path of a projectile except to state in a general way that it is always a curved line, unless the projection be vertically upwards. Thus, if [270] the little geometry I have learned from Euclid since our previous discussion does not enable me to understand the demonstrations that are to follow, then I shall be obliged to accept the theorems on faith, without fully comprehending them.

SALV.   On the contrary, I desire that you should understand them from the Author himself, who, when he allowed me to see this work of his, was good enough to prove for me two of the principal properties of the parabola because I did not happen to have at hand the books of Apollonius. These properties, which are the only ones we shall need in the present discussion, he proved in such a way that no prerequisite knowledge was required. These theorems are, indeed, proved by Apollonius, but after many preceding ones, which would take a long time to follow. I wish to shorten our task by deriving the first property purely and simply from the mode of generation of the parabola and proving the second immediately from the first.

Beginning now with the first, imagine a right cone, erected upon the circular base *ibkc* with apex at *l*. The section *bac* of this cone made by a plane drawn parallel to the side *lk* is the curve that is called a parabola. The base of this parabola *bc* cuts at right angles the diameter *ik* of the circle *ibkc,* and the axis *ad* is parallel to the side *lk.* Now having taken any point *f* in the curve *bfa,* draw the straight line *fe* parallel to *bd.*

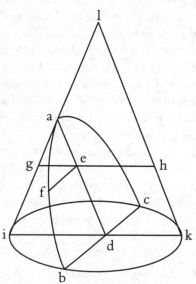

Then, I say, the square of *bd* is to the square of *fe* in the same ratio as the axis *ad* is to the portion *ae*.

Now, through the point *e* pass a plane parallel to the circle *ibkc*, producing in the cone a circular section whose diameter is the line *geh*. Since *bd* is at right angles to *ik* in the circle *ibk*, the square of *bd* is equal to the rectangle formed by *id* and *dk*; so also in the upper circle that passes through the points *gfh*, the square of *fe* is equal to the rectangle formed by *ge* and *eh*; hence the square of *bd* is to the square of *fe* as the rectangle *id-dk* is to the rectangle *ge-eh*. And since the line *ed* is parallel to *hk*, the line *eh*, being parallel to *dk*, is equal to it; therefore the rectangle *id-dk* is to the rectangle *ge-eh* as [271] *id* is to *ge*, that is, as *da* is to *ae*; hence also the rectangle *id-dk* is to the rectangle *ge-eh*, that is, the square of *bd* is to the square of *fe*, as the axis *da* is to the portion *ae*. QED.

The other proposition necessary for this discussion we demonstrate as follows. Let us draw a parabola whose axis *ca* is prolonged upwards to a point *d*; from any point *b* draw the line *bc* parallel to the base of the parabola; if now the point *d* is chosen so that *da* equals *ca*, then, I say, the straight line drawn through the points *b* and *d* will be tangent to the parabola at *b*.

For imagine it were possible that this line cuts the parabola above or that its prolongation cuts it below; then through any point *g* on this line draw the straight line *fge*. Since the square of *fe* is greater than the square of *ge*, the square of *fe* will bear a greater ratio to the square of *bc* than the square of *ge* to that of *bc*; and since, by the preceding proposition, the square of *fe* is to that of *bc* as the line *ea* is to *ca*; it follows that the line *ea* will bear to the line *ca* a greater ratio than the square of *ge* to that of *bc*, or, than the square of *ed* to that of *cd*

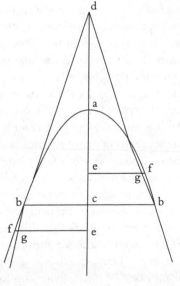

(the sides of the triangles *deg* and *dcb* being proportional). But the line *ea* is to *ca*, or *da*, in the same ratio as four times the rectangle *ea-ad* is to four times the square of *ad*, or, what is the same, to the square of *cd* (since this is four times the square of *ad*). Hence four times the rectangle *ea-ad* bears to the square of *cd* a greater ratio than the square of *ed* to the square of *cd*. But that would make four times the rectangle *ea-ad* greater than the square of *ed*. This is false, the fact being just the opposite, because the two portions *ea* and *ad* of the line *ed* are not equal. Therefore the line *db* touches the parabola without cutting it. QED.

SIMP.   Your demonstration proceeds too rapidly and, it seems to me, you keep on assuming that all [272] of Euclid's theorems are as familiar and available to me as his first axioms, which is far from true. For example, you just sprang upon us that four times the rectangle *ea-ad* is less than the square of *ed* because the two portions *ea* and *ad* of the line *ed* are not equal; and this brings me little composure of mind, but rather leaves me in suspense.

SALV.   Indeed, all real mathematicians assume on the part of the reader perfect familiarity with at least the *Elements* of Euclid. Here it is necessary in your case only to recall the proposition of Book II[30] in which he proves that when a line is cut at two points into equal and unequal parts respectively, the rectangle formed on the unequal parts is less than that formed on the equal (i.e., less than the square on half the line), by an amount that is the square of the segment between the two cut points; from this it is clear that the square of the whole line, which is equal to four times the square of the half, is greater than four times the rectangle of the unequal parts. In order to understand the following portions of this treatise it will be necessary to keep in mind the two elementary theorems from conic sections which we have just demonstrated; these two theorems are indeed the only ones which the Author uses. We can now resume the reading of the text and see how he demonstrates his first proposition, in which he shows that a projectile undergoing motion compounded of uniform horizontal motion and naturally accelerated fall describes a semiparabola.

Let us imagine an elevated horizontal line or plane *ab* along which a body moves with uniform speed from *a* to *b*. Suppose this plane to end abruptly at *b;* then at this point the body will, on account of its weight, acquire also a natural motion downwards along the perpendicular *bn*. Draw the line *be* along the plane *ab* to represent the flow, or measure, of time; divide this line into a number of segments, *bc, cd,*

---

30. Euclid, *Elements*, book 2, proposition 5.

de, representing equal
intervals of time; and
from the points *c, d, e,*
let fall lines that are
parallel to the perpen-
dicular *bn.* On the first
of these lay off any dis-
tance *ci;* [273] on the
second a distance four
times as long, *df;* on

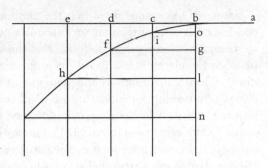

the third, one nine times as long, *eh;* and so on, in proportion to the
squares of *ch, db, eb,* or, we may say, in the squared ratio of these same
lines. Accordingly we see that while the body moves from *b* to *c* with
uniform speed, it also falls perpendicularly through the distance *ci,*
and at the end of the time interval *bc* it finds itself at the point *i.* In
like manner at the end of the time interval *bd,* which is the double of
bc, the vertical fall will be four times the first distance *ci;* for it has been
shown in a previous discussion that the distance traversed by a freely
falling body varies as the square of the time. In like manner the space
eh traversed during the time *be* will be nine times *ci.* Thus it is evident
that the distances *eh, df, ci* will be to one another as the squares of the
lines *be, bd, bc.* Now, from the points *i, f, h* draw the straight lines *io,*
fg, hl parallel to *be;* these lines *hl, fg, io* are equal to *eb, db,* and *cb,* respectively; so also are the lines *bo, bg, bl* respectively equal to *ci, df,* and
eh; furthermore, the square of *hl* is to that of *fg* as the line *lb* is to *gb,*
and the square of *fg* is to that of *io* as *gb* is to *ob;* therefore the points
i, f, h lie on one and the same parabola. In like manner it may be
shown that if we take equal time intervals of any size whatever, and
if we imagine the body to be carried by a similar compound motion,
its positions at the end of these time intervals will lie on one and the
same parabola. QED.

This conclusion follows from the converse of the first of the two
propositions given above. For, having drawn a parabola through the
points *b* and *h,* any other two points, *f* and *i,* not falling on the
parabola must lie either within or without; consequently the line *fg* is
either longer or shorter than the line that terminates on the parabola.
Therefore the square of *hl* will not bear to the square of *fg* the same
ratio as the line *lb* to *gb,* but a greater or smaller. The fact is, however,
that the square of *hl* does bear this same ratio to the square of *fg.*
Hence the point *f* does lie on the parabola, and so do all the others.

SAGR.   One cannot deny that the argument is new, subtle, and conclusive. It also rests upon various assumptions, namely, that the horizontal motion remains uniform, that the vertical motion continues to be accelerated downwards in proportion to the square of the time, and that such motions and velocities as these combine without altering, disturbing, or hindering each other, so that as the motion proceeds the path of the projectile does not change into a different curve. But this, in my opinion, [274] is impossible. For the axis of the parabola along which we suppose the natural motion of a falling body to take place stands perpendicular to a horizontal surface and ends at the center of the earth; and since the parabola deviates more and more from its axis, no projectile can ever reach the center of the earth or, if it does, as seems necessary, then the path of the projectile must transform itself into some other curve very different from the parabola.

SIMP.   To these difficulties, I may add others. One of these is that we suppose the horizontal plane, which slopes neither up nor down, to be represented by a straight line as if each point on this line were equally distant from the center. This is not the case, for as one starts from the middle of the line and goes toward either end, one departs farther and farther from the center of the earth and so is constantly going uphill; whence it follows that the motion cannot remain uniform through any distance whatever, but must continually diminish. Besides, I do not see how it is possible to avoid the resistance of the medium, which must destroy the uniformity of the horizontal motion and change the law of acceleration of falling bodies. These various difficulties render it highly improbable that a result derived from such unreliable assumptions should hold true in practical experience.

SALV.   All these difficulties and objections which you urge are so well founded that it is impossible to remove them; and as for me, I am ready to admit them all, which indeed I think our Author would also do. I grant that these conclusions proved in the abstract will be different when applied in the concrete and will be false to this extent, that neither will the horizontal motion be uniform, nor will the natural acceleration be in the ratio assumed, nor will the path of the projectile be a parabola, etc. But, on the other hand, I ask you not to begrudge our Author that which other eminent men have assumed, even if not strictly true.

The authority of Archimedes alone will satisfy everybody. In his works on mechanics and on the quadrature of the parabola, he takes for granted that the beam of a balance or steelyard is a straight line, every point of which is equidistant from the common center of all heavy bodies, and that the strings by which heavy bodies are suspended are parallel to each other. Some consider this assumption permissible because, in practice, our instruments and the distances [275] involved are so small in comparison with the enormous distance from the center of the earth that we may consider a minute of arc on a great circle as a straight line, and may regard the perpendiculars let fall from its two extremities as parallel. For if in actual practice one had to consider such small quantities, it would be necessary first of all to criticize the architects who presume, by the use of a plumb line, to erect high towers with parallel sides. I may add that, in all their discussions, Archimedes and the others considered themselves as located at an infinite distance from the center of the earth, in which case their assumptions were not false, and therefore their conclusions were absolutely correct. When we wish to apply our proven conclusions to distances which, though finite, are very large, it is necessary for us to infer, on the basis of demonstrated truth, what correction is to be made for the fact that our distance from the center of the earth is not really infinite, but merely very great in comparison with the small dimensions of our apparatus. The largest of these will be the range of our projectiles—and here we need consider only the artillery— which, however great, will never exceed four of those miles of which as many thousand separate us from the center of the earth; and since these paths terminate upon the surface of the earth, only very slight changes can take place in their parabolic shape, which, it is conceded, would be greatly altered if they terminated at the center of the earth.

As to the perturbation arising from the resistance of the medium, this is more considerable and does not, on account of its manifold forms, submit to fixed laws and exact description. Thus, if we consider only the resistance which the air offers to the motions studied by us, we shall see that it disturbs them all and disturbs them in an infinite variety of ways corresponding to the infinite variety in the form, weight, and velocity of the projectiles. As to velocity, the greater this is, the greater will be the resistance offered by the air; also resistance will be greater as the moving bodies become less dense. Thus, although the falling body ought to be accelerated in accordance with the rule of distance being proportional to the square of the duration of its motion, yet no matter how heavy the body is, if it falls from a very considerable height, the resistance of the air will be such as to eventually prevent any increase in [276] speed and render the motion uniform; and in proportion as the moving body is less dense, this uniformity will be attained more quickly and from smaller heights. Even horizontal motion, which would be uniform and constant if no impediment were offered, is altered by the resistance of the air and finally ceases; and here again, the less dense the body, the quicker the process.

Of such effects of weight, velocity, and also shape, which are infinite in number, it is not possible to give any exact description. Hence, in order to handle this matter in a scientific way, it is necessary to cut loose from these difficulties, to discover and demonstrate the theorems in the case of no impediments, and to use them and apply them with such limitations as experience will teach. The advantage of this method will not be small, for the material and shape of the projectile may be chosen as dense and round as possible, so that it will encounter the least resistance in the medium; and the spaces and velocities will be small enough for the most part that we shall be easily able to correct them with precision. Indeed, in the case of those projectiles we use, thrown from a sling or crossbow, and made of dense material and round in shape or of lighter material and cylindrical in shape (such as arrows), the deviation from an exact parabolic path is quite imperceptible. Furthermore, if you will allow me a little greater liberty, I can show you, by two experiments, that the dimensions of our apparatus are so small that these external and incidental resistances, among which that of the medium is the most considerable, are scarcely observable.

I proceed to the consideration of motions through the air, since it is with these that we are now especially concerned. The resistance of the air exhibits itself in two ways: first by offering greater impedance to less dense than to very dense bodies, and second by offering greater resistance to a body in rapid motion than to the same body in slow motion.

Regarding the first of these, consider the case of two balls having the same dimensions, but one weighing ten or twelve times as much as the other; one, say, of lead, the other of oak, both allowed to fall from an elevation of 150 or 200 cubits. Experiment shows that they will reach the ground with a slight difference in speed, showing us that in both cases the retardation caused by the air is small. For if both balls start at the same moment and at the same elevation, and if the leaden one be slightly retarded and the wooden one greatly retarded, then [277] the former ought to reach the earth a considerable distance in advance of the latter, since it is ten times as heavy; but this does not happen; instead, the gain in distance of one over the other does not amount to the hundredth part of the entire fall. And in the case of a ball of stone weighing only a third or half as much as one of lead, the difference in their times of reaching the ground will be scarcely noticeable. Now, the impetus acquired by a leaden ball in falling from a height of 200 cubits (which is such that if its motion became uniform the ball would traverse 400 cubits in a time interval equal to that of the fall) is very considerable in comparison with the speeds which we are able to give to our projectiles by the use of bows or other machines (except firearms); so it follows that we may, without noticeable error, regard as absolutely true those propositions which we are about to prove without considering the resistance of the medium.

Passing now to the second case, where we have to show that the resistance of the air for a rapidly moving body is not very much greater than for one moving slowly, ample proof is given by the following experiment. Attach to two threads of equal length—say four or five cubits—two equal leaden balls and suspend them from the ceiling; now pull them aside from the perpendicular, one through 80 or more degrees, the other through not more than 4 or 5 degrees; so that when set free, the first falls, passes through the perpendicular, and describes large but slowly decreasing arcs of 160, 150, 140 degrees, etc., and the other swings through small but also diminishing arcs of ten, eight, six degrees, etc. Here it must be remarked first of all that the first passes through its arcs of 180, 160 degrees, etc., in the same time that the other swings through its ten, eight degrees, etc.; from this it follows that the speed of the first ball is sixteen and eighteen times greater than that of the second; accordingly, if the air offers more resistance to the high speed than to the low, the frequency of oscillation in the large arcs of 180 or 160 degrees, etc., ought to be less than in the very small arcs of ten, eight, four, two degrees, or even one. But this prediction conflicts with experiment. For if two persons start to count the oscillations, one the large and the other the small, they will discover that after counting tens and even hundreds they will not differ by a single oscillation, not even by a fraction of one. This observation justifies the two following propositions, [278] namely, that oscillations of very large and very small amplitude all take the same time, and that the resistance of the air does not affect motions of high speed more than those of low speed, contrary to the opinion which we ourselves entertained earlier.

SAGR.   On the other hand, we cannot deny that the air hinders both of these motions since both become slower and finally vanish; so we have to admit that the retardation occurs in the same proportion in each case. But why? Because insofar as the greater resistance offered to one body than to the other originates from the greater impetus and speed of one body as compared to the other, then the speed with which a body moves is at once a cause and a measure of the resistance it meets; therefore, all motions, fast or slow, are hindered and diminished in the same proportion. And this is a result, it seems to me, of no small importance.

SALV.   Thus, in this second case too, we can say that the errors in the conclusions that will be demonstrated by neglecting external accidents are of little concern in our operations; these involve great speeds for the most part and distances that are negligible in comparison with the radius of the earth or one of its great circles.

SIMP.   I would like to hear your reason for separating the projectiles from firearms, i.e., those from the force of gunpowder, and the other projectiles from bows, slings, and crossbows, insofar as they are not equally subject to change and resistance from the air.

SALV.   I am led to this view by the excessive and, so to speak, supernatural violence with which the former projectiles are launched; indeed, it appears to me that without exaggeration one might say that the speed of a ball fired either from a musket or from a piece of artillery is supernatural. For if such a ball be allowed to fall from some great height, its speed will not go on increasing indefinitely, owing to the resistance of the air; what happens to bodies of small density in falling through short distances—I mean the reduction of their motion to uniformity—will also happen to a ball of iron or lead after [279] it has fallen a few thousand cubits; this terminal or final speed is the maximum which such a heavy body can naturally acquire in falling through the air. This speed I estimate to be much smaller than that impressed upon the ball by the burning gunpowder.

An appropriate experiment will serve to demonstrate this fact. From a height of one hundred or more cubits fire a rifle loaded with a lead bullet, vertically downwards upon a stone pavement; then with the same rifle shoot against a similar stone from a distance of one or two cubits; and observe which of the two balls is the more flattened. Now, if the ball that has come from the great height is found to be the less flattened of the two, this will show that the air has hindered and diminished the speed initially imparted to the bullet by the powder, and that the air will not permit a bullet to acquire too great a speed, no matter from what height it falls; but if the speed impressed upon the ball by the fire does not exceed that acquired by it in falling freely, then its downward blow ought to be greater rather than less. I have not performed this experiment, but I am of the opinion that a musket ball or cannon shot, falling from a height as great as you please, will not deliver so strong a blow as it would if fired into a wall only a few cubits away, i.e., at such a short range that the splitting or cutting of the air will not be sufficient to rob the shot of that excess of supernatural violence given it by the powder.

The enormous impetus of these violent shots may cause some deformation of the trajectory, making the beginning of the parabola flatter and less curved than the end. But, as far as our Author is concerned, this is a matter of small consequence in practical operations. The main one of these is the preparation of a table of ranges for shots of high elevation, giving the distance attained by the ball as a function of the angle of elevation. And since shots of this kind are fired from mortars using small charges and imparting no supernatural impetus, they follow their prescribed paths very exactly.

But now let us proceed with the reading of the treatise, at the point where the Author invites us to the study and investigation of the impetus of a body that moves with a motion compounded of two others. Next is the case in which the two components are uniform, one horizontal and the other vertical.

Index

A More Accurate Inquiry on Sunspots, 7
aberration of starlight, 24
abjuration, 2, 15, 23, 24, 293–94
Academician, 16, 26, 271, 299, 313,
    342, 351, 353. *See also* Author
Actaeon, 197
ad hominem, 26, 159, 273, 300
Adriatic Sea, 254n67, 264
advantage, mechanical, 326
Aegean, 263, 266
aether, 58, 84, 193n7, 208n29
Africa, 265, 266n74
air: and earth's motion, 209, 221,
    225–27; as an element, 28, 29,
    32, 193n7; vs. empty space, 132;
    fish vs. land animals, 333; in float-
    ing, 92–96; resistance to motion,
    230–33, 300, 303, 304, 305, 308,
    310, 314, 344, 363–67; and
    sounds, 187; and tides, 263
Ajalon, 8
alchemy, 197nn14–15
Aleppo, 204
Alexander of Aphrodisias, 199n17
Alps, the, 217
Altair, 181
America, 205
Amorites, 8
anatomical dissection, 194–95
Ancona, 251, 254
angelic doctrine, 270
annual motion, 26, 107, 202n21,
    203n22, 222, 233–50, 257, 258,
    261, 278
annual orbit, 28, 31, 257
ant falling from moon, 298
Antella, Niccolò dell', 281
anti-Copernican decree. *See* decree
    of the Index
Anti-Tycho, 183
Apelles, 7. *See also* Scheiner,
    Christoph
apogee, 26, 84, 184

Apollonius of Perga, 357, 358
approximation, methodological
    problem of, 362–67
Aquarius, 36
Aquila, 181
Aquinas, Saint Thomas, 132,
    143n35, 169
Aracoeli, Cardinal, 170, 278
Arcetri, 15, 16, 23, 24
Archimedes, ix, 3, 6, 85, 121, 124,
    316, 362, 363
arguments against earth's motion,
    4–5; annual stellar parallax, 4, 5,
    25, 203n22, 268n78; Bel-
    larmine's, 146–48; biblical, 8–9,
    103–45, 147–48, 160–63,
    164–66, 168–71; birds' flight,
    221; Church Fathers, 128–35,
    147, 162–63; deception of the
    senses, 148, 166–67; divine
    omnipotence, 270; east-west
    cannon shots, 215–16; extruding
    power of whirling, 221–22; lunar
    orbit, 83–84, 244, 249; Mars' ap-
    parent diameter, 184, 243; natu-
    ral motion, 213–14; north-south
    cannon shots, 216; point-blank
    cannon shots, 216; ship analogy,
    98–99n3, 215, 226–32; two mo-
    tions, 213; Venus' phases,
    243–44; vertical cannon shots,
    215; vertical fall, 214, 215,
    222–33; violent motion, 213;
    wind, 221
arguments for earth's motion:
    Copernicus' argument, 4; helio-
    centrism of planetary motions,
    157, 236–41; indifferent motion,
    209; law of revolution, 206–7;
    simplicity of terrestrial rotation,
    201–13; tides, 250–67
Aries, 36
Ariosto, Ludovico, 183n9, 332n16

Aristarchus of Samos, 26, 35, 121, 149, 233, 242, 244

Aristotle, ix, 2, 13, 30, 33, 34, 35, 86, 90, 92, 95, 100, 108, 111, 121, 149, 150n12, 169, 193, 195, 196, 198, 199, 200, 201, 202, 203, 204, 206, 209n32, 210, 212n34, 213, 214, 216, 217, 218, 219n40, 220, 223, 224, 225, 234, 235, 236, 250, 252, 264, 299, 300, 301, 303, 304, 305, 316, 327; abuse of his authority, 194–200; on center of universe, 234–36; on earth's motion, 213–14; on falling bodies, 300–5; on floating bodies, 85–96; on role of observation, 99–101

Arrighetti, Niccolò, 103, 104

arrows, 189, 364

artificial instruments, methodological problem of, 48–51, 244–50

artillery, 363, 366

Ascoli, Cardinal d', 278, 288, 293

Aselli, 67

astrology, 197nn14–15

Astronomical and Philosophical Balance, 12, 21, 179n3, 180n4

astronomical discoveries, 5; earth-heaven similarity, 8, 60–63, 99–101, 241; Jupiter's satellites, 67–84; lunar mountains, 51–63; Mars' variation in apparent diameter, 127, 157, 184, 236–37, 244, 247–48; Milky Way's composition, 66; nebular composition, 66–67; new fixed stars, 63–66; solar rotation, 97–99, 109, 142; sunspots, 97, 100; Venus' phases, 157, 159–60, 236–39, 243–45

Astronomical Disputation on the Three Comets of the Year 1618, 12, 179n3

Atlantic Ocean, 265, 266n74

atomism, 13, 22, 185–89

Attavanti, Giannozzo, 172, 174, 175

Augustine, Saint, 110, 118, 120, 126, 129, 134, 135, 136, 141, 166

Augustus, 30

Author, 335, 336, 340, 341, 342, 343, 345, 349, 350, 354, 355, 356, 358, 360, 362, 367. *See also* Academician

authority: Aristotle, 86, 90, 99–101, 193–201, 234–36; vs. individual freedom, 2, 15, 193–201; Scripture, 6, 9, 10, 15, 103–45, 147–48, 160–63, 164–66, 168–71; Tycho, 179–85

Avila, Bishop of, 135

Badovere, Jacques, 50

Barberini, Antonio, 288

Barberini, Francesco, 289

Barberini, Maffeo, 6, 12, 13, 21. *See also* Urban VIII, Pope

Baronio, Cesare, 119n18; Baronio's principle, 119

Bartolo da Sassoferrato, 183

Battistini, Andrea, 37, 40, 48n3, 49n4

begging the question, 161, 224

Bellarmine, Robert, viii, 10, 11, 14, 15, 20, 21, 26, 146, 148, 175, 178, 218n18, 220n41, 278, 279, 280, 284, 285, 287, 289, 290, 291; arguments against earth's motion, 146–48; certificate to Galileo, 14–15, 21, 178, 279–80, 284–87, 291; Galileo's criticism of his arguments, 148–67; warning to Galileo, 11, 14, 20

bending, 315, 323, 324, 328

Benedict XV, Pope, 30

Bentivoglio, Guido, 288, 293

Bernoulli, Jean, 354n25

Bessel, Friedrich, 25, 268n78

Biagioli, Mario, ix, 6n4, 7n6, 11n7, 37

Bible. *See* Scripture

biblical argument against Copernicanism, 8–9, 103–45, 147–48, 160–63, 164–66, 168–71

birds' flight, 221

Black Sea, 266

boat carrying water, 255–56

Boethius, 124

Bologna, 269

bones, 128, 298, 331, 332, 333, 334

Bonsi, Cardinal, 278

book of nature, 179, 183

Borgia, Gaspare, 288

Borro, Girolamo, 251n62

Bosporus, 266

Bradley, James, 24

Brahe, Tycho. See Tycho Brahe

breakage, 90, 206, 297, 298, 299, 315, 320, 321, 325, 327, 328, 329, 331. See also fracture

broken column, 298–99

Bruno, Giordano, 17

buoyancy, 29, 85–96, 333

Caccini, Tommaso, 10, 19, 20, 27, 170–75

Caesar, Julius, 30

Calabria, 29, 146, 264, 265n73

calendar reform, 112–13

Camerota, Michele, ix, 6nn4–5, 7n6, 11n7, 37

Cancer, 36

cannon balls, 215–16, 223, 226, 301, 303, 309, 367

Capiferreus, Franciscus Magdalenus, 178

Capricorn, 36

Capua, Cardinal of, 113, 153

Carlos, Edward Stafford. See Stafford Carlos, Edward

Carugo, Adriano, ix, 40

Castelli, Benedetto: 7, 27; Galileo's letter to Castelli, 9, 10, 19, 20, 103–9, 168n5, 169n6, 172

catapult, 189

Catholic Church, vii, 1, 11, 17, 22, 24, 30, 113, 114, 115, 119, 134, 136, 137, 139, 144, 147, 161, 163, 165, 197n13, 275, 283, 289, 292, 293

Catholic Counter-Reformation, 17

Catholic University of Milan, 25

causal investigations: floating, 85–96; fracture, 315–34; moon's secondary light, 60–63; tides, 250–67; uniform acceleration, 340

Cecilia, Cardinal of Santa, 172, 178

celestial sphere, 27, 28, 31, 32, 33, 34, 36, 107, 145, 154, 182, 203, 207, 207nn26–27, 210, 218, 234, 236, 240, 241

Centini, Felice, 288

centrifugal force, 4

Cesarini, Virginio, 12, 179n3

Cesi, Federico, 22, 31

Charybdis, Scylla and, 265, 266

Chiaramonti, Scipione, 183

China, 205

Christina of Lorraine, vii, 9, 109n7

Church Fathers, 23, 113, 118, 123, 124, 125, 136, 138, 140, 164, 166, 169, 171, 172, 174; Church Fathers argument, 128–35, 147, 162–63

Cicero, Marcus Tullius, 121, 283

Clavius, Christoph, 127

Colombe, Lodovico delle, 7

comets, 6, 11, 12–13, 21, 27, 46, 100, 121, 149, 179–85

Comparison of the Weights of the Assayer and the Balance, 12, 22

composition of motions, 4, 232–33, 356–57, 360–62, 367

cone, 33, 90, 296; conic sections, 357n29, 358–59; shadows of heavenly bodies, 28, 33, 249

confession of guilt, Galileo's, 15, 282–87

conjunction, 27, 60, 62, 63, 83, 157, 184, 236, 238, 239, 240, 243, 247, 248

conservation of motion, 31, 222, 231n47

Constantinople, 242, 266

Conversation with the Sidereal Messenger, 18

Copernicus, Nicolaus, ix, 1, 4, 9, 11, 17, 19, 20, 21, 24, 25, 36, 37, 41, 109, 112, 113, 114n14, 121, 126, 127, 132, 140, 146, 149, 150, 151, 152, 153, 154, 155, 156, 158, 159, 160, 162n23, 163, 167, 168, 170, 171, 177, 178, 179, 180, 183, 184, 202, 203n22, 207n27, 217, 218, 222, 223, 241, 242, 243, 244, 248, 249, 267, 268, 277, 278, 279, 282, 285, 287, 288, 289

Corfu, 204, 254

Corsica, 264

Cosimo II de' Medici, 6, 18, 21, 31, 45, 47, 109n7

Cremona, Cardinal di, 288, 293

Crete, 204

Crew, Henry, viii, 37, 39, 40, 295n2, 299n3, 300n4, 306n6, 312n7, 315n8, 317n11, 319–20n13, 334nn17–18, 335n19, 341n20, 342n21, 347n22, 351n24, 354n25, 356nn27–28

critical reasoning, role of, 165, 213, 218–20, 220n41

cubit, 27, 215, 226, 298, 301, 303, 305, 307, 310, 313, 314, 324, 337, 338, 339, 340, 341, 343, 350, 364, 365, 366, 367

cylinders, 91, 296, 315–31

Cyprus, 176, 204

Damascus steel, 89

Dangerous Adulation, 21

De Salvio, Alfonso, viii, 37, 39, 40, 295n2, 299n3, 300n4, 306n6, 312n7, 315n8, 317n11, 319–20n13, 334nn17–18, 335n19, 341n20, 342n21, 347n22, 351n24, 354n25, 356nn27–28

deception of the senses, 148, 166–67

declination, 27, 155, 181

decree of the Index, 11, 14, 20, 21, 23, 29, 36, 176–78, 178n23, 190, 286, 290

deferent, 28

definition containing genus but lacking difference, 242

Delphic Oracle, 200n18

depositions, 2, 10, 15, 20, 169; Caccini's, 170–75; Galileo's first, 276–82; Galileo's second, 282–84; Galileo's third, 284–85; Galileo's fourth, 287–88

Descartes, René, 1

Dialogue on the Two Chief World Systems, viii, 6, 13, 14, 15, 16, 19, 20, 22, 23, 24, 25, 34, 35, 37, 38, 39, 40, 42, 98–99n3, 183n7, 190–271, 272, 274, 277, 283, 287, 288, 290, 292; key thesis, 13–14; complaints about it, 14, 272–76

DiCanzio, Albert, ix

Diodati, Elia, 23

Dionysius the Areopagite, 135, 141, 142

direct motion, 27–28, 34, 68, 238

Discourse on Bodies in Water, viii, 6, 7, 19, 38, 40, 85–96

Discourse on the Comets, 12, 21, 179n3

"Discourse on the Tides," 20, 39

diurnal motion, 28, 34, 107, 109, 172, 201–22, 225, 226, 237, 241, 258, 267, 278, 287, 289

divine omnipotence, 191, 270, 275

Dog Star, 65, 247

Dominis, Marcantonio de, 250n60

Dorn, Matthias, ix

double-distance rule, 348

Drake, Stillman, viii, ix, 6n4, 7n6, 11n7, 37, 38, 40, 49n5, 85n3, 98n3, 181n5, 189n12, 243n54, 260n70, 299n3, 317n11, 319–20n13, 341n20, 351n24

Dubrovnik, 254

earth-heaven dichotomy, 8, 13, 60–63, 99–101, 241

ebony, 6, 86–96

eccentrics, 28, 146, 155, 156, 157, 163
Ecclesiastes, 121, 147, 171, 270n81
eclipses, 28, 61, 62, 63, 137, 240, 249
ecliptic, 28, 68, 70, 76, 79, 80, 81, 82, 140, 155, 257
economy, principle of, 205n24, 211–13, 241, 336
Ecphantus, 149
Egypt, 205
Einstein, Albert, 1, 41
elements, 28, 29, 32, 84, 101, 137, 165, 186, 187, 193, 209, 225, 244, 249, 270, 277
ellipse, 18, 27, 52, 84, 357n29
elongation, 248, 249
Endymion, 197
epicycles, 28, 34, 146, 156, 157, 158, 159, 163
epistemology, vii, 2, 3, 4, 10, 13. See also methodological or epistemological discussions
equal speeds from equal heights, postulate of, 342–44
equator, 31, 33; celestial, 27, 155, 208; terrestrial, 30, 263n71
equidistance of ratios, 28, 317, 326, 330, 331, 356
equinoxes: 132; precession of, 34, 207n27, 208n28
essences, vs. properties, 101–2
Euboea, 264
Eucharist, 22
Euclid, ix, 124, 317n11, 319–20n13, 358, 360
Europe, 266n74
Eusebio, Cardinal San, 278
experimentation, role of, 85–96, 222–33, 306–7, 349–51
extruding power of whirling, 221–22

faith, 9, 10, 30, 31, 103–48, 160–74, 289, 292, 293; matters of faith because of topic vs. matters of faith

because of the speaker, 157, 164–65
fallacy, 26, 88, 106, 111, 124, 125, 126, 138, 139, 149, 151, 161, 162, 219, 220, 222, 224, 245, 304, 341, 342
falling bodies, laws of, 1, 18, 342–56
Father of Modern Science, 1
Ferdinando I de' Medici, 18, 109n7
Ferdinando II de' Medici, 21
fifth essence, 193
Fifth Lateran Council, 112n9, 199n17
Findlen, Paula, ix
fire, 33, 101, 251; corpuscles, 188–89; element, 28, 29, 32, 193n7, 209; firearms, 366–67
firmament, 119, 132, 145
fish, 196, 335; bone structure and strength, 332, 333, 334
fixed stars, 18, 25, 26, 27, 28, 29, 34, 36, 46, 48, 50, 63–67, 68, 70, 81–83, 84, 118n17, 181, 202, 203n22, 205, 207, 208n29, 209, 210, 213, 219, 236, 240–41, 247, 268
floating, 6, 85–96, 254, 303
Florence, 5, 6, 8, 10, 12, 13, 15, 17, 18, 19, 21, 22, 23, 24, 27, 31, 34, 109, 150, 170, 171, 172, 173, 175, 192, 272, 273, 274, 276, 277, 281, 290, 293
Foscarini, Paolo A., 9, 10, 11, 19, 20, 23, 24, 25, 29, 146–48, 177, 278
Fossombrone, Bishop of, 112
Foucault, Léon, 25
founders of modern science, 1
fourth proportional, 29, 326, 329
fracture, 298, 315, 320, 321, 322, 323, 324, 325, 326, 328. See also breakage
friction, 32, 189, 310, 357

Gaeta, Bishop of, 143
galaxies, 31, 49, 66, 67

Galen, 124, 194–95n10
Galilei, Livia, 17
Galilei, Vincenzio (father of Galileo), 3, 276, 289, 293
Galilei, Vincenzio (son of Galileo), 16, 18
Galilei, Virginia, 17
Galileo affair: abjuration, 293–94; aftermath, 24–25; Bellarmine's certificate, 14–15, 21, 178, 279–80, 284–87, 291; Bellarmine's warning, 11, 14, 20; charges and complaints against Galileo, 168–75, 272–76; his confession of guilt, 15, 282–87; cultural significance, 1–2; decree of the Index, 11, 14, 20, 21, 23, 29, 36, 176–78, 178n23, 190, 286, 290; first deposition, 276–82; fourth deposition, 287–88; Galileo's defense, 285–87; Inquisition consultants' reports, 10, 20, 289; prison sentence commuted, 15, 23; rehabilitations of Galileo, 1, 25; second deposition, 282–84; sentence, 288–93; special injunction, 14, 15, 175–76, 178n23, 273, 276, 278–80, 285–87, 290; summary, 8–11, 13–15; terminological definition, 1; third deposition, 285–87; torture threatened, 15, 288, 288n14
Gamba, Marina, 17, 18
Gemini, 36
Genoa, 251
geokinetic theory, 4, 9, 13–14, 14, 20, 29, 35, 205n24
Gessi, Berlinghiero, 288, 293
Geymonat, Ludovico, ix, 40
giants, 298, 332, 334
Gibeon, 8
Gibraltar, Strait of, 254, 266n74, 267
Giese, Tiedemann, 113n13, 153n15
Gilbert, William, 150
Ginetti, Marzio, 288, 293
Gingerich, Owen, ix, 2n2, 41

Giordano, Paolo, 103
Giudice, Franco, ix
Goddu, André, ix
gold, 90, 94, 95, 96, 197, 303
Gonzaga, Ferdinando, 6
Grassi, Orazio, 12–13, 21, 22, 179n3, 180, 183
gravity: center of, 319, 321; force of, 29–30, 227, 233, 307, 339, 340; specific gravity, 35, 85–96, 300–6, 310, 333
great circle, 30, 59, 207, 208, 363, 366
greatest scandal in Christendom, 1
Greece, 205
Gregory XV, Pope, 21
Guevara, Giovanni di, 328
Guglielmini, Giambattista, 24–25
Guiducci, Mario, 12, 21, 179n3, 180, 184
gunshots, 189, 215–16, 366–67

Hagecius, Thaddeus, 181
Hawking, Stephen, 1, 40–41
heat, 101, 251, 252; caused by motion, 185–89
heliocentrism of planetary motions, 157, 236–41
Hellespont, 263
Heraclides of Pontus, 30, 121, 149
Hercules, 46, 198, 200, 266
heresy: formal, 20, 289, 292n16; vehement suspicion of, 15, 23, 292n16, 293
Hezekiah miracle, 135
Hicetas of Syracuse, 30, 121, 149
hide, compared to heaven, 129
History and Demonstrations Concerning Sunspots, viii, 7, 19, 20, 42, 97–102, 289
Holland, 25, 35
Holy Office, Congregation of, 168, 170, 172, 174, 175, 176, 273, 274, 276, 277, 278, 281, 282, 284, 285, 287, 289, 290, 291, 292, 293, 294. See also Inquisition

Holy Scripture. *See* Scripture
Holy Writ. *See* Scripture
horizontal motion, 32, 98, 223–24,
    232, 260, 353, 357, 360, 362, 364
house arrest, 15, 23
humming, 310
Huygens, Christiaan, 1
hydrodynamics, 260n69
hypothesis, 2, 11, 13, 14, 146–67,
    179, 180, 183, 184, 191, 194n8,
    212, 250n59, 273, 275, 278, 302,
    354; role of, 146–60, 163–68;
    250–71. *See also* supposition

igneous particles, 188–89
Iliad, 183
impetus, 30, 94, 98, 221, 230, 231,
    232, 256, 259, 262, 264, 301,
    315, 339, 340, 343, 344, 345,
    352, 353, 354, 355, 365, 366, 367
imprimatur, 12, 22, 272, 273, 274,
    275
inclined planes, 229, 230, 353, 354,
    355, 356
independent-mindedness, role of,
    193–201
Index, 10, 11, 14, 19, 20, 21, 23,
    24, 25, 30, 36, 162, 168n4, 176,
    178, 190n4, 278, 286, 287, 290,
    291
Indian Ocean, 265
indifferent motion, principle of, 32,
    85, 86, 97–99, 209, 231, 231n47
inertia, law of, 1, 4, 98n3, 231n47
infinity: infinite power, 211–12, 270;
    infinite slowness, 337–38; infinite
    universe, 234; infinite wisdom,
    270
Inquisition, 1, 2, 10, 11, 14, 17, 19,
    20, 22, 24, 27, 30, 168n4, 170,
    171n10, 172n12, 173n14, 282n8,
    288, 289. *See also* Holy Office,
    Congregation of
instantaneous motion: of light, 189;
    and space-proportionality, 341; in
    vacuum, 300

instrumentalism, 2, 11, 14, 35. *See
    also* hypothesis; save the appear-
    ances; supposition
Ionian Sea, 264, 265n73
ipse dixit, 195
irradiation effect, 245–48
Isaiah, 129nn26–27, 135n32, 171
Israel, 8
Italy, 33, 190

Japan, 242
Jasher, Book of, 9
Jeremiah, 132
Jerome, Saint, 123, 132
Joachim of Floris, 197n13
Job, 36, 132, 133, 177
John Paul II, Pope, 1, 25
Josephus, Flavius, 135
Joshua miracle, 8–9, 104, 107–9,
    135, 140–44, 147, 169, 170, 171
Jupiter (planet): 5, 34, 47, 157, 193,
    202, 236, 237, 239, 240, 241,
    247, 248, 249, 278; satellites, 1,
    18, 31, 46, 67–84, 207. *See also*
    Medicean planets or stars
Jupiter (Roman God), 46, 197,
    198

Kepler, Johannes, 1, 5, 18, 35, 41,
    150, 158n18, 206n25, 268
Kulm, Bishop of, 113, 153

Lactantius, 114
Laird, W. Roy, ix
Landini, printer of *Dialogue,* 281
Leghorn, 264
Leiden, 4, 24
Leo (constellation), 36
Leo X, Pope, 112, 171
Leo XIII, Pope, 25
Leonardo da Vinci, 258n68
Letter to Castelli, 10, 19, 20, 39,
    103–9
Letter to the Grand Duchess Christina,
    vii, 20, 23, 25, 39, 109–45,
    117n16

lever, 315–28
Libra, 36
Lido, 254
Lincean Academy, 7, 12, 16, 19, 21, 22, 26, 31, 34, 174, 179, 269, 277
literary and aesthetic significance of Galileo, 3n3
Livy, 183
Lizzafusina, 256
Locher, Johannes, 19, 233n49
logic, 219
Lombard, Peter, 118
Lorini, Niccolò, ix, 10, 19, 168, 169n6, 172, 174
Ludovisi, Alessandro, 21
luminaries, 84
lunar orbit argument, 83–84, 244, 249
Lydia, 200

machines, 260n70, 261, 295, 296, 297, 298, 365
Maculano, Vincenzo, 276, 284
Madagascar, 265
Maelcote, Odo van, 19
Magalhaens, Cosme, 143
Magellan, Strait of, 265, 267
magnitude: apparent size of heavenly body, 64–80 passim, 127n25; size or quantity in general, 28, 31, 33, 51, 208
Marmara, Sea of, 266
Mars, 34, 46, 127, 157, 158n18, 179, 183, 184, 207, 210, 236, 237, 239, 240, 241, 243, 244, 245, 247, 250, 278
Marsili, Cesare, 269
Master of the Sacred Palace, 162n23, 190n3, 272, 273, 274, 275, 181, 282, 285, 286
mathematics: and accounting and surveying, 124; book of nature, 179–83; mathematical blunders, 158–59, 180–82, 246; vs. mechanics, 295–99, 315–34; and natural phenomena, 349–51

matter (material substance), 22, 87, 88, 188, 300, 318
Matthew, 132
McMullin, Ernan, ix, 41, 117n16
mean proportional, 31, 351, 355, 356
mean-speed theorem, 345–46
Mechanics, 17, 23
mechanics, 354, 352; anti-Copernican objections, 5; vs. mathematics, 295–99, 315–34; mechanical advantage, 326; Mechanics, 17, 23; practical mechanics, 17, 23, 295–99, 316, 326, 349, 353; principles, 4, 315, 351; Questions of Mechanics, 34, 252, 316, 327, 328
Medicean planets or stars, 31, 47, 48, 83, 84, 122, 157, 207, 249. See also Jupiter
Medici, House of, 17
medicine of the end, 275
medicine, 3, 17, 124, 194n10, 275
Mediterranean Sea, 251, 253, 254, 256, 257, 263, 264, 266
medium, motion through, 29, 86, 92, 227, 300, 301, 303, 306, 306, 307, 310, 312, 314, 340, 362, 363, 364, 365
Mercury (planet), 34, 36, 49, 69, 157, 159, 236, 237, 239, 240, 241, 248, 249, 278
Mercury (Roman god), 46, 197–98
meridian, 30, 31, 143, 144, 155, 205, 216, 264, 269
Mersenne, Marin, 23, 24
Messina, Strait of, 29, 265n73
metaphysics, 2, 219, 222
methodological or epistemological discussions: approximation, 362–67; artificial instruments, 48–51, 244–50; causal investigation, 85–96, 315–34, 60–63, 250–67, 340; critical reasoning, 165, 218–20; experimentation, 85–96, 222–33, 306–7, 349–51; hypothesis, 146–60, 163–68;

250–71; independent-mindedness, 193–201; mathematical demonstration vs. natural phenomena, 349–51; mathematics language of book of nature, 183; mechanics vs. mathematics, 295–99, 315–34; open-mindedness, 150–52, 217–18, 218n39, 275; philosophical significance of Galileo's legacy, 2; primary vs. secondary qualities, 185–89; properties vs. essences, 101–2; Scripture not scientific authority, 103–45, 146–48, 160–63; simplicity and probability, 201–13; theology not queen of sciences, 123–28

Michelangelo, 24
Milky Way, 5, 18, 31, 48, 49, 66
Miller, David, ix
miracles, 107–9, 135, 140–44, 170, 172, 173, 174, 252–53
mixed motion, 209–11, 222–33, 360–62
moment, 29, 31, 318–31, 340, 341, 346, 352, 354, 355. *See also* momentum
momentum, 31, 231n47, 307, 344, 345, 352, 353, 354. *See also* moment
moon, 8, 9, 30, 32, 36, 64, 67, 101, 102, 108, 118, 141, 142, 143, 144, 148, 155, 167, 181, 202, 205, 247, 248, 298; and eclipses, 28, 137, 240; mountains of, 1, 5, 18, 48, 50, 51–60, 193; orbit of, 34, 83–84, 207, 210, 237, 240–41, 244, 249, 278; phases of, 27, 32, 33, 36, 239, 243; Roman goddess, 197; secondary light of, 60–63; and tides, 250–51, 252, 268
Morning Star, 118, 248
music, 3, 124, 349

Naples, 19, 150, 173, 177, 251
natural motion, 29, 31–32, 36, 108, 209, 210, 213, 215, 225, 226, 227, 334, 339, 350, 360, 362; anti-Copernican argument, 213–14. *See also* violent motion
natural philosophy, 10, 12, 24, 31, 34, 36
naturally accelerated motion, 335, 349–50
Naylor, Ron, ix
nebulas, 5, 18, 48, 49, 67
Neptune, 34
nerves, origin of, 194–95
neutral motion. *See* indifferent motion
New Astronomy, 18
Newton, Isaac, 1, 24, 29, 30, 31, 41, 98n3
novas, 100

odd numbers, law of, 18, 334, 347–49
odors, 185, 186, 187
omnipotence, of God, 191, 270, 275
On Motion, 17
On the Revolutions of the Heavenly Spheres, 11, 17, 21, 37, 177
Onofrio, Cardinal di Sant', 288, 293
open-mindedness, role of, 150–52, 217–18, 218n39, 275
Operations of the Geometric and Military Compass, 18, 24
opposition (in astronomy), 32, 56, 157, 236, 238, 239, 240, 243, 247
orb, 32, 207, 208, 209n30, 225, 240, 268. *See also* orbit
orbit, 26, 28, 31, 32, 33, 34, 36, 83, 84, 146n4, 157, 159, 206, 207, 234, 257, 278. *See also* orb
Orion, 65, 66, 67
Orlando Furioso, 183, 332n16
Orsini, Alessandro, 20
Osiander, Andreas, 158n18
Osler, Margaret, ix
out-of-court settlement, 15
Ovid, 196

Pacific Ocean, 265

Padua, 3, 5, 17, 18, 24, 27, 34, 48, 150, 173n15, 175, 353
Palazzo Firenze, 23
palm, 32, 90, 93, 253, 314, 337, 338
Palmieri, Paolo, ix
Pantin, Isabelle, viii, 40, 42, 48n3, 49nn4–5
parabola, 32, 334, 357–62, 367. *See also* parabolic trajectory
parabolic trajectory, 4, 27, 223–24n44, 356–67. *See also* parabola
parallax, annual stellar,' 4, 5, 25, 203n22, 268n78
parallel (on a spherical surface), 33, 221, 264
paralogism, 106, 139, 219, 220, 224
Paris, 13, 22, 23, 24, 25, 50
Parma, 150
Paul III, Pope, 30, 113, 152
Paul V, Pope, 20, 21, 176
Paul of Burgos, 135
Paul of Middelburg, 112n11
pendulum, 1, 25, 32, 259; isochronism, 307, 312–13, 314, 365; period, 313–14
penetrability of matter, 300
Pererius, Benedictus, 120
perigee, 33, 84, 184
Peripatetic, 33, 191, 192, 195, 204, 216, 217, 222, 235, 250, 251, 300
perpetual motion, 98, 231, 357
Persia, 205
perturbed equidistance of ratio, 33, 319, 331, 354
Perugia, 12, 183n7
Philolaus of Croton, 33, 121, 149
Philosopher and Chief Mathematician, 5, 18
physical laws, statements and proofs: conservation of motion, 231; composition of motions, 4, 232–33, 356–57, 360–62, 367; double-distance rule, 348; inertia, 98; equal speeds from equal heights, 342–44; lever, 315–18;

mean-speed theorem, 345–46; odd-numbers law, 347–49; parabolic trajectory, 357, 360–61; pendulum period, 313–14; periods of revolution, 206–7; relativity of motion, 202n20; times-squared fall, 346–47, 348–49; strength of materials, 318–34; uniform acceleration, 336, 342; virtual work, 353–54; water oscillation, 259–60
physics, vii, 1, 3, 4, 5, 6, 14, 16, 22, 29, 30, 31, 202n20, 209n32, 219, 231n47
Pisa, 3, 9, 17, 27, 126, 150, 172, 175, 183n7, 251n62
Pisces, 36
plague, 274, 281
Plato, ix, 121, 149, 312
plea bargaining, 15
Pleiades, 66
Plutarch, 121
Pluto (planet), 34
Pluto (Roman god), 197–98
Pontifical Academy of Sciences, 25
Pontifical Lateran University, 25
porosity of bodies, 310
Praesepe, 67
Prague, 181
precession of the equinoxes, 34, 207n27, 208n28
primary vs. secondary qualities, 13, 185–89
Prime Mobile, 34, 107, 108, 135, 140, 141, 155, 169, 207n26, 209n30n32, 210, 211, 213
prison sentence, 15, 23
probability, 12, 14, 19, 47, 88, 97, 100, 109, 117, 128, 143, 151, 191, 193, 201–13, 229, 241, 249, 250, 251, 283, 190, 291, 292, 297, 299, 314, 324, 325, 329, 332, 341, 343, 352, 262
Progymnasmata, 181
projectile motion, 1, 356–67
properties vs. essences, 101–2

Propertius, Sextus, 45n2
prosthaphaeresis, 133
Protestant Reformation, 17
Psalm, 129nn26–27, 147, 171, 292
Pseudo-Aristotle, 31, 252n64,
    316n9, 327n14
Ptolemy, Claudius, ix, 108, 111,
    124, 152, 154, 156, 179, 180,
    183, 184, 202, 203, 214, 217,
    218, 221, 223, 224, 234, 287
Pythagoras, 9, 19, 33, 54, 121, 149,
    177, 190, 241, 242

quadrature (on the celestial sphere),
    238
quadrature of the parabola, 362
qualities, primary vs. secondary, 13,
    40, 185–89
Questions of Mechanics, 34, 252, 316,
    327, 328n15
quintessence, 193n7

rarefaction, 189, 225, 251
rectilinear motion, 362–63
Red Sea, 264
reductio ad absurdum, 301–2, 341,
    359–60
Reeves, Eileen, viii, 7n6, 42
relativity of motion, principle of,
    202n20
resistance, mechanical, 6, 86–95, 99,
    221, 230, 231, 262, 296–331,
    339, 343, 344, 352, 353, 354,
    362, 363, 364, 365, 367
retrograde motion, 27–28, 34, 83,
    156, 238
revolution, law of periods of, 206–7
rhetoric, 219
Riccardi, Niccolò, 190n3
Roman College, 12, 19, 121, 180
Rome, 7, 10, 11, 12, 14, 15, 17, 19,
    20, 21, 22, 23, 25, 27, 112, 150,
    162n23, 168n4, 169, 173, 174,
    176, 178, 190, 264, 270n80, 272,
    273, 274, 275, 276, 277, 278,
    279, 281, 284, 287, 294

Rostock, 217

Sagittarius, 36
Sagredo, Giovanfrancesco, 16, 34,
    192
Salusbury, Thomas, viii, 40, 42,
    85nn2–3, 93n4
Salviati, Filippo, 6, 16, 34, 192
Santucci, Antonio, 126n23
Sardinia, 264
Sarpi, Paolo, 173n15
Sarsi Lotario, 12, 179n3, 180, 182,
    183, 184
Saturn, 18, 34, 206, 207, 236, 237,
    239, 240, 241, 248, 249, 278
save the appearances, 35, 147, 157,
    166. *See also* hypothesis; instru-
    mentalism; supposition
Scaglia, Desiderio, 288, 293
Scheiner, Christoph, 7, 8, 19, 22
Schoenberg, Nicolaus von, 113n12,
    153n14
science and religion, vii, 2, 25. *See
    also* Catholic Church; faith; Scrip-
    ture;
science of motion, 3–4, 334. *See also*
    physics
scientist, 446
Scorpio, 36
screw, 353
Scripture: authority in natural sci-
    ence, 103–45, 146–48, 160–63;
    biblical argument against Coperni-
    canism, 8–9, 103–45, 147–48,
    160–63, 164–66, 168–71. *See also*
    Baronio's principle; Church Fa-
    thers; theology
Scylla and Charybdis, 265, 266
Segizzi, Michelangelo, 170, 175
Segre, Michael, ix
Seleucus, 35, 121, 149, 268n77
Seneca, Lucius Annaeus, 121, 149,
    179, 184
sentence, in Galileo's trial, 2, 15, 23,
    24, 288–93
Serarius, Nicolaus, 171

sextile configuration, 238
Sfondrati, Paolo, 19, 168n4, 172n11, 178n21
Shank, Michael, ix
ship analogy argument, 98–99n3, 215, 226–32
shipyard, Venetian, 295
Sicily, 264, 265n73, 266
Siena, 23
simple motion, 210
simpleton, 35, 192n5, 275
Simplicio, 16, 35, 192n5, 270n80
simplicity: earth's annual revolution, 241; earth's diurnal rotation, 201–13; principle of, 205n24, 211–13; uniform acceleration, 336; tides, 252–53
Simplicius, 35, 192
Sinceri, Carlo, 276, 292
Sisto, Cardinal di San, 288
Socrates, 2: Socratic method, 229–32, 237–41
solstice, 143
sophism, 106, 125, 219, 220
Sophocles, 183
sounds, 13, 187
Spain, 36, 135nn31–32, 205
special commission, 22, 23, 272–76
special injunction, 14, 15, 175–76, 178n23, 273, 276, 278–80, 285–87, 290
Spina, Bartolomeo, 162n23
spyglass, 35, 48, 49, 50, 51, 60, 61, 64, 65, 66, 68, 69, 245. See also telescope
squares, law of, 4, 18, 346–47, 349
Stafford Carlos, Edward, viii, 39, 43, 45n1, 48n3, 49nn4–5
steelyard, 316, 363
Stefani, Giacinto, 273, 274, 281
stellar sphere. See celestial sphere
Strasbourg, 23
strength of materials, 295–99, 315–34
sun: annual motion, 241; center of planetary motions, 236–41; solar

rotation, 97–99, 109, 142; source of planetary motions, 109, 142–43; stopped in Joshua miracle, 8–9. See also sunspots
sunspots, 1, 5, 6, 7–8, 19, 20, 22, 97–102, 173, 174, 283, 289
supernatural speed, 366–67
supposition, 146–67, 203, 229, 278, 279, 300, 302, 344. See also hypothesis
syllogism, 195, 224
Syria, 204
Systema cosmicum, 23

tastes, 185, 186, 187
Taurus, 36, 66
telescope, 1, 2, 5, 7, 18, 35, 36, 48–51, 49n4, 127n24, 160, 179, 182, 184, 196, 198, 203n22, 233, 244–50. See also spyglass
Tertullian, Quintus, 116, 117n15
The Assayer, viii, ix, 11, 12, 13, 21, 22, 38, 40, 179–89, 245
The Sidereal Messenger, vii, viii, 5, 18, 19, 38, 39, 40, 43, 45–84, 127n35
theology, 4–5, 5, 10, 13, 20, 23, 25, 26–27, 27, 29, 114, 116, 120, 123, 130, 133, 134, 135, 139, 143, 144, 146, 163, 164, 168, 169, 170, 171, 172, 177, 289, 292; queen of sciences, 123–28
third proportional, 35, 326, 329, 330, 355
Thomas Aquinas, Saint, 132, 143n35, 169
Three Letters on Sunspots, 7
three-halves power, 207n25, 312, 324, 326, 327
tickling, 186–87
tides, 4, 14, 20, 191, 250–67, 267–71, 283
time measurement, 350–51
times-squared fall, law of. See squares, law of
Tolosani, Giovanni M., 162n23
Torricelli, Evangelista, 16, 24

torture, 15, 288, 288n14
Tost, David, 150
Tostado, Alfonso, 135n31
touch, as a secondary quality,
    185–89
Treatise on Fortifications, 17
Treatise on the Sphere, or Cosmography,
    17
Trent, Council of, 17, 30, 134,
    147n5, 163n24, 171, 176
Tuscany, 5, 6, 15, 17, 18, 21, 23,
    31, 45
Two New Sciences, viii, ix, 4, 6, 16,
    24, 34, 35, 37, 38, 39, 40,
    223–24n44, 295–367, 347n22,
    351n24
two-motions argument, 213
Tycho Brahe, 13, 17, 35, 36,
    179–87, 214; Tychonic system,
    13
Tyrrhenian Sea, 265n73

uniform acceleration, 335–565
universe, center of, 234–37
Uraniborg, 181
Uranus, 34
Urban VIII, Pope, 6, 12, 13, 21,
    270n80, 277. *See also* Barberini,
    Maffeo

vacuum, 315; impossible for Aris-
    totle, 300–6
Van Helden, Albert, viii, 40, 42, 43,
    48n3, 49nn4–5
Vatican Radio, 25
vehement suspicion of heresy, 15,
    23, 292, 293
Venice, 5, 17, 18, 150, 173, 183n7,
    192, 194, 204, 251, 253, 254n67,
    264, 281, 295
Venus, 36, 49, 61, 62, 64, 69, 118,
    127, 158–59, 184, 193, 202, 240,
    241, 247, 248, 249, 278; phases
    of, 1, 4, 5, 18, 33, 157, 159–60,
    236–39, 243–45

Verospi, Fabrizio, 288, 293
vertical fall, 4, 222–33, 351–56
Villa Medici, 15, 23
Vio, Thomas de, 143n35
violent motion, 29, 31–32, 36, 334,
    339; anti-Copernican argument,
    213. *See also* natural motion
Virgil, 196, 230n46
Virgo, 36
virtual work, principle of, 353–54
Visconti, Raffaello, 272, 273, 274,
    281
viscosity, 87
Viviani, Vincenzio, 24, 351n24

Wallace, William A., 43
wandering star, 33–34, 36, 49,
    118n17, 144
water, viii, 6, 7, 19, 54, 101, 102,
    166, 188, 189, 232; vs. air, 300,
    304, 305; bodies in water, 85–96,
    310, 333; element, 28, 29, 32,
    116, 193n7; oscillation laws,
    259–60; tides, 250–71; and time
    measurement, 350
wax, behavior in water, 35, 86–94
Welser, Marc, 7
Westman, Robert, ix, 43, 162n23
whales, 254, 331–33
wind: objection to earth's motion,
    221; tides, 263
Wray, K. Brad, ix
Wursteisen, Christian, 217

Ximenes, Emanuele, 173
Ximenes, Ferdinando, 171, 172, 174
Ximenes, Sebastiano, 173n14,
    174n16

Zacchia, Laudivio, 288
zenith, 181
zodiac, 27, 36, 69, 73, 76, 77, 79,
    81, 132, 140, 155, 156, 210, 234,
    241, 250, 257
Zúñiga, Diego de, 36, 133, 177